Spanish in Miami

Spanish in Miami reveals the multifaceted ways in which the language is ideologically rescaled and sociolinguistically reconfigured in this global city.

This book approaches Miami's sociolinguistic situation from language ideological and cultural perspectives, combining extensive survey data with two decades of observations, interviews, and conversations with Spanish speakers from all sectors of the city. Tracing the advent of postmodernity in sociolinguistic terms, separate chapters analyze the changing ideological representation of Spanish in mass media during the late twentieth century, its paradoxical (dis)continuity in the city's social life, the political and economic dimensions of the Miami/Havana divide, the boundaries of language through the perceptual lens of Anglicisms, and the potential of South Florida—as part of the Caribbean—to inform our understanding of the highly complex present and future of Spanish in the United States.

Spanish in Miami will be of interest to advanced students and researchers of Spanish, Sociolinguistics, and Latino Studies.

Andrew Lynch is Associate Professor of Spanish and Latin American Studies at the University of Miami, USA.

Routledge Studies in Hispanic and Lusophone Linguistics
Series Editor: Dale Koike, *University of Texas at Austin*

The Routledge Studies in Hispanic and Lusophone Linguistics series provides a showcase for the latest research on Spanish and Portuguese Linguistics. It publishes select research monographs on various topics in the field, reflecting strands of current interest.

Titles in the series:

Language Patterns in Spanish and Beyond
Structure, Context and Development
Edited by Juan J. Colomina-Almiñana and Sandro Sessarego

The Evolution of Spanish Past Forms
Gibran Delgado-Díaz

Sociolinguistic Approaches to Sibilant Variation in Spanish
Edited by Eva Núñez

Heritage Speakers of Spanish and Study Abroad
Edited by Rebecca Pozzi, Tracy Quan and Chelsea Escalante

Topics in Spanish Linguistic Perceptions
Edited by Luis Alfredo Ortiz López and Eva-María Suárez Büdenbender

Comunicación especializada y divulgación en la red
Aproximaciones basadas en corpus
Gianluca Pontrandolfo y Sara Piccioni

Spanish in Miami
Sociolinguistic Dimensions of Postmodernity
Andrew Lynch

For more information about this series please visit: www.routledge.com/ Routledge-Studies-in-Hispanic-and-Lusophone-Linguistics/book-series/ RSHLL

Spanish in Miami
Sociolinguistic Dimensions of Postmodernity

Andrew Lynch

Series Editor: Dale A. Koike
Spanish List Advisor: Javier Muñoz-Basols

LONDON AND NEW YORK

First published 2022
by Routledge
4 Park Square, Milton Park, Abingdon, Oxon OX14 4RN

and by Routledge
605 Third Avenue, New York, NY 10158

Routledge is an imprint of the Taylor & Francis Group, an informa business

© 2022 Andrew Lynch

The right of Andrew Lynch to be identified as author of this work has been asserted in accordance with sections 77 and 78 of the Copyright, Designs and Patents Act 1988.

All rights reserved. No part of this book may be reprinted or reproduced or utilised in any form or by any electronic, mechanical, or other means, now known or hereafter invented, including photocopying and recording, or in any information storage or retrieval system, without permission in writing from the publishers.

Trademark notice: Product or corporate names may be trademarks or registered trademarks, and are used only for identification and explanation without intent to infringe.

British Library Cataloguing-in-Publication Data
A catalogue record for this book is available from the British Library

Library of Congress Cataloging-in-Publication Data
A catalog record has been requested for this book

ISBN: 978-1-138-34452-5 (hbk)
ISBN: 978-1-032-25233-9 (pbk)
ISBN: 978-0-429-43836-3 (ebk)

DOI: 10.4324/9780429438363

Typeset in Times New Roman
by Newgen Publishing UK

Dedicated to the memory of
Mercedes Rubí Mursulí
(Camagüey, 1959 – Miami, 2019)

Contents

	Acknowledgments	viii
	Preface	xi
1	The linguistic order of (post)modernity	1
2	Imagining Spanish in Miami	66
3	The postmodern paradox of Spanish in Miami	118
4	Power and solidarity across the Miami/Havana divide	163
5	The boundaries of Anglicisms	208
6	Beyond Miami	262
	References	274
	Index	296

Acknowledgments

The voice in these pages is a polyphony of many scholars who have inspired my thinking and motivated my musings. I wish to thank the following publishers for granting me permission to reproduce the words of some of them as chapter epigraphs in this book: University of Minnesota Press for Arjun Appadurai's *Modernity at Large* (1996); University of Florida Press for T. D. Allman's *Miami: City of the Future* (1987); Taylor & Francis for Linda Hutcheon's *The Politics of Postmodernism* (2002); The MIT Press for Roger Brown and Albert Gilman's "The Pronouns of Power and Solidarity" (1960); University of Michigan Press for Édouard Glissant's *Poetics of Relation* (1997); and Duke University Press for Antonio Benítez-Rojo's *The Repeating Island* (1996).

Among my personal interlocutors, Francisca Aguiló Mora is owed sincere thanks for years of sustained dialogue with me about theoretical proposals and for her insightful comments throughout the various stages of this book's development. I am equally grateful to my friend and colleague Elena Grau-Lleveria, who enthusiastically encouraged me to pursue this sort of endeavor—at the crossroads of sociolinguistics and cultural theory—over a decade ago. Armando Rubí III has kept me constantly up to date on Miami popular urban culture and local language practices throughout the years; as my sounding board for various aspects of the studies presented in this book, his insights and experiences brought needed nuance to my thought. For also generously entertaining my constant curiosity about Spanish in Miami, I extend sincere thanks to Marelys Valencia, Phillip Carter, Lillian Manzor, and Annie Mendoza.

I would be remiss not to acknowledge the interest and assistance of so many undergraduate and graduate students in my research process, especially Antoni Fernández Parera, Zach Goodman, Erica Parrett-Cerione, and Melanie Gladding, as well as the time and enthusiasm of the hundreds of Spanish speakers in Miami who completed surveys, granted me interviews, and engaged me in metalinguistic conversations.

Throughout the writing process, the emphatic and unlimited words of support that Angel Martínez offered me were truly invaluable; I am indebted to him for caring so much about this book, and for repeatedly reminding me about the proverbial bigger picture. For their careful readings of individual chapters, I thank Vicente Lledó-Guillem, Rachel Varra, Mary Avalos, Carolina Gutiérrez-Rivas, and Dainerys Machado Vento; to Vicente and Rachel in particular, my gratitude for reaffirming the path I chose to take in this inquiry.

Mercedes Rubí Mursulí's uses of Spanish and English were of infinite marvel to me. I owe heartfelt thanks to her for always taking such pride in my work. Though it saddens me that the dedication of this book to her ended up being posthumous, I find some joy in the certainty that her bilingual brilliance now illuminates our afterlife.

Preface

Writing about Miami

Of the many possible ways in which one could portray Spanish in Miami, I chose the angle of postmodernity for this book. My hope was to capture the highly complex and, in some ways, paradoxical, contradictory, and enigmatic—not to say illusory—nature of the city's sociolinguistic reality, as best I could. This is not a sociolinguistic study in the traditional fashion, nor is it a sociological treatise, nor a cultural studies monograph. It contains elements of all those things at once, to different degrees at different moments. It is principally an account of ideas about Spanish, of representations of the language and of the ways in which people perceive it. The eclectic register of the book may discomfit some sociolinguists who could possibly regard it as not 'linguistic' enough, while some cultural studies scholars might find it too social scientific for their taste. Sociologists could perhaps consider it too personal, while ethnographers may find its macro-level focus insufficiently intimate.

In truth, while observing and studying Spanish in Miami, I have many times felt like the ethnographer in Borges' celebrated short story, who ultimately chose not to write anything because he realized the unrelatability of what he had learned in the field. How does one explain that Spanish is 'lost' yet at the same time spoken among successive generations in Miami? How to affirm that the language is marginalized in a city where the majority of people across all socioeconomic strata are actively speaking it—at home, on the street, at work, in commerce and retail, in major cultural and entertainment venues, and even in institutional settings? Spanish is heard practically everywhere, constantly present in the human, media, cultural, and economic flows that traverse all dimensions of the city, and yet it is fleeting. Spanish in Miami is both local and transnational without being national. It is accorded great prestige, and yet it is stigmatized. It is the immigrant in-group cultural code of wealth and also of poverty. It is now spoken by more people than ever before in the city's history, and yet its use evokes nostalgia. It can be characterized as a heritage language, yet it represents the city's future arguably just as much as English.

xii *Preface*

Struggling to explain this reality—even if only to myself—I took some solace in critical cultural theory, which uniformly asserts that irony, paradox, contradiction, and enigma are part and parcel of the postmodern condition. The premier postmodern city of the Americas, as Jan Nijman (2011) convincingly argued, Miami should be expected to present all of these troubling traits—troubling at least from an objective, social scientific perspective. And so, what began in the late 1990s as my modest effort to document the situation of Miami Cuban Spanish, drawing inspiration from Alejandro Portes and Alex Stepick's (1993) sociological portrait of immigration in Miami and Carmen Silva-Corvalán's (1994) variationist account of three generations of Mexican Spanish speakers in Los Angeles, morphed into something motivated more by cultural theory and the emergent field of language ideology. As I began to 'see' Miami more through those lenses, I gradually gave up on describing the situation of Spanish from a canonical variationist or language sociological perspective. I gave up not because I considered either of those possible perspectives inadequate or undue, but because I realized that, for me, the narrative voice most suited to relating the sociolinguistic marvel of Spanish-speaking Miami was probably of a different timbre.

I could begin this book with the affirmation that 'Miami,' by singular definition, is indefinable—a generally amorphous city possessing multiple personalities and lacking in social collectivities, home to many, culturally diverse, transient or transplanted peoples who lead highly divergent yet closely parallel lives within the same small geographic space, bounded by sea and wetlands. Within that unequivocally postmodern space much closer to Havana than to Tallahassee, which some have characterized as a time warp or an identity thief, language at times appears as a pawn or some sort of collateral in a bullish market. As numerous critics, scholars, and writers have previously stated, Miami seems constantly struggling to better its lot or at least become something different, and many people appear either to be arriving or leaving—at times reluctantly and at others hurriedly. The upside of this struggle is the sense of perpetual newness and boundless energy that pervade the city and make for a famously vibrant social and cultural scene, as well as a dynamic yet volatile economy. The downside is an infamously enigmatic and discontinuous civic life too often motivated by immediate self-interest and materialism; a city where everyone just wants to 'get ahead,' speaking in any language.

In retrospect, I recognize that my imagination regarding Miami was rather muddled before I first encountered the city in real life. As an adolescent in rural North Carolina in the 1980s, I was transported every Friday night, along with millions of other gullible Americans, to the glamorous and exotic locations of *Miami Vice*, where skyscrapers towered over tropical beaches and fast cars relayed drugs and firearms between ghettos and opulent mansions. On the radio I heard Gloria Estefan sing to a "bad, bad, bad, bad boy" who made her "feel so good," also warning that "the rhythm is gonna get you." Miami was glitzy, seductive, wild, and dangerous. Or was it? After all, the Golden

Preface xiii

Girls lived there, probably not too far from Tony Montana's mother and the members of the Miami Sound Machine. Nothing appeared more mundane than the quiet, secure, jovial, civic-minded, middle-class life of Rose, Dorothy, Blanche, and Sophia. Their occupations were far from glamorous or illicit. Their lives could have unfolded in any quintessential American city where everyone spoke only English.

After their house at 6151 Richmond Street was sold in the early 1990s, Miami changed substantially, again. Rosie O'Donnell became Gloria Estefan's neighbor—just across the water from Al Capone's old residence, which still stands as was. Madonna took up residence along Biscayne Bay and Gianni Versace moved to the decaying Art Deco District of South Beach, later fully restored to its pre-Depression status as a stylish tourist haven where Enrique Iglesias filmed the video for his global hit song "Bailamos." Shakira, Thalía, and Ricky Martin—among many others—recorded hit songs in Spanish just a few miles away, at Crescent Moon Studios. By then, music and television producers, real estate mavens, and global megabanks had replaced the drug cartels and shady money laundering fronts documented in *Cocaine Cowboys*. Certainly, crime and corruption still found their place in Miami, as in any other major city of the world, but the ubiquitous gun battles produced by the trade of uncontrolled substances in the 1920s and again in the 1980s fell silent to the debates of politics and culture approaching the new millennium. Miami assumed the moniker of "Capital of Latin America."

Culturally speaking, I believe that Joan Didion (1987), David Rieff (1993), and Hernán Iglesias Illa (2010) got it right about Miami, in that each affirmed, in their own way, that no one could get it right about Miami. Perhaps in this respect Miami is characteristically Caribbean, recalling the great lesson that Antonio Benítez-Rojo (1996) claimed to have learned: all intellectual ventures into Caribbeanness inevitably generate unending searches. The most persistent challenge I have faced while researching this book is reconciling the city's exceptionalism with its perceivable normality within the US sociolinguistic landscape, discerning between what is particular about the phenomenon of Spanish in South Florida and what is readily observable in other settings across the country. I suppose I could make six undebatable statements based on what I have so far learned: 1) Spanish is neither politically dominant nor socially predominant within the broader context of South Florida; 2) it is sometimes the scapegoat of ethnically and ideologically charged observations made by non-Hispanics about the majority Hispanic presence in Miami; 3) English is by far the preferred language of interaction among the Miami-born children of Spanish-speaking immigrants, despite the societal ubiquity of Spanish and the great value and prestige accorded it locally; 4) communicative abilities in Spanish are generally stronger and more widespread among US-born second-, third- and fourth-generation bilinguals in Miami than in other urban areas of the country; 5) oral repertoires in Spanish nonetheless reflect the same structural processes of linguistic attrition, incomplete acquisition, code-switching, and English-language lexical influence that have been

xiv *Preface*

attested among Latinx bilinguals in other parts of the US; and 6) Spanish is an essential element of many political, economic, and cultural imaginaries of Miami that project beyond South Florida and the US, to Latin America, Europe, and other far reaches of the globe through television, film, music, and other mass media.

What readers will encounter in the following pages is based upon more than twenty years of thoughtful observation and relentless questioning on the ground in the so-called Magic City, hundreds of structured surveys and interviews, and countless conversations—formal and informal—all funneled through the lens of theories about postmodernity and channeled with self-critical rationality, i.e. "the outcome of acknowledging the irreducible nature of complexity" (Cilliers 2016, 268).

I never intended—nor dare I purport—to write *the* book about Spanish in Miami, but rather *a* book about Spanish in Miami. Although it is surprisingly the first, I hope that many others will follow, written from other perspectives, by people whose insights and experiences far surpass my own. In light of all its complexity, Miami is surely deserving of the attention.

1 The linguistic order of (post)modernity

> ...the world in which we now live—in which modernity is decisively at large, irregularly self-conscious, and unevenly experienced—surely does involve a general break with all sorts of pasts.
>
> —Arjun Appadurai, *Modernity at Large* (1996)

In the summer of 2013, exactly 500 years after Spanish explorer Juan Ponce de León first charted the coastline of the land he would call *La Florida*, one could glimpse a Wells Fargo billboard advertisement driving south along Interstate 95, just inside the Miami city limits, which read: "When people talk, great things happen." The youthful faces pictured on the billboard were those of Lucille Ball and Desi Arnaz. As part of the megabank's national "Iconic Conversations" ad campaign, Lucy and Ricky urged potential customers to "start a conversation" with a banker, reminding them that "amazing outcomes often have simple beginnings." The image of twentieth-century Hollywood's favorite couple, whom Wells Fargo credited with having revolutionized television, lent itself to an additional, more local layer of meaning in Miami, one that perhaps escaped the bank's ad executives focused more broadly on the US context: "together we'll go far" when Spanish-speaking Cubans start a conversation with English-speaking Americans. It also tapped into a brand of nostalgia that is unique to exile Cubans, who have iconized Lucy and Ricky's marriage in the history of US-Cuba relations. The billboard seemed to pose an invitation, however unintended, for locals to reflect upon Miami's contemporary evolution as a bilingual city, the role of Spanish in the region's astounding economic growth since the time of *I Love Lucy*, and the identity of the city's Spanish-speaking majority. In the semiotic landscape, it reflected various phenomena that have been key to Miami's emergence as a global city in recent decades: banking, migration, television, and language. Indeed, South Florida is a microcosm of the ways in which the situation of the Spanish language throughout the world, particularly in its relationship to English, is gradually being reconfigured on local, national, and global scales.

From a relatively small and almost exclusively Anglophone urban area with no major industrial base in the 1950s, Miami morphed into one of the

DOI: 10.4324/9780429438363-1

2 *The linguistic order of (post)modernity*

most economically vital and culturally iconic bilingual cities of the Americas by the new millennium, true to the prediction of the city's founder Julia Tuttle upon its incorporation in 1896 (Campbell 2013). At that time, recognizing the city's intimate social, political, and geographic relationship to Cuba and other nations of the Caribbean and Latin America, Tuttle foresaw its inevitable economic ties to those countries in the coming century. However, she surely did not imagine the ways in which Miami's proximity to the Spanish-speaking world would ultimately manifest itself, within the spaces of online financial networks, mass media, and other information and communication technologies. Nor would Tuttle have likely imagined the massive scale of migratory flows between South Florida, the rest of the Caribbean, and all of Latin America approaching the new millennium. These phenomena have made the expansion of Miami concomitant with the expansion of Spanish, ultimately attributable to a broader process popularly dubbed globalization.

Migratory and media flows, cyberspace, the transnational neoliberal economic order, corporate consumerism, and the rise of NGOs and tertiary economies are commonly cited causes for the reworking of nation-state and center-periphery ideologies within the framework of globalization (Appadurai 1996; Heller 2011; Duchêne and Heller 2012; Pietikäinen et al. 2016). With the fall of the Communist Bloc, heralding the triumph of capitalism and the advent of global consumerism, modernity began to cede to rather different sorts of cultural and social phenomena often referred to as postmodern (Jameson 1991). This evolution has entailed a shift from entities and economies centered at either local or national levels to entities and economies whose activities take place on an international or transnational scale. Toward the end of the twentieth century, markets were devised on increasingly macro-level scales, creating a more interdependent and culturally complex relationship of the local to the global (Robertson 1992). In this incipient shift from modernity to postmodernity, which some characterize as postnational (Heller 2011), boundaries of all sorts are contested: national, ethnic, cultural, public/private, financial, commercial, and linguistic.

In *Modernity at Large*, Arjun Appadurai (1996) portrayed globalization as a series of 'scapes': ethnoscapes, mediascapes, technoscapes, financescapes, and ideoscapes. These scapes are the basis of imagined worlds that transcend nations and national identities which, during the modern era, were defined by and confined within particular geopolitical spaces, as reflected on a modern world map. As transnational flows traverse increasingly diverse local communities and intersect with national discourses, various social actors intervene: nation-states, diasporic communities, multinational corporations, cultural or political movements, and more intimate neighborhood constructs and face-to-face social networks (Appadurai 1996, 33). Within these scapes, the one nation–one language ideological imperative of modernity is contested by the fluid transnational paradigm of postmodernity (Heller 2007; Duchêne and Heller 2012).

The linguistic order of (post)modernity 3

As privatization of major industries and foreign investment in the 1990s fueled market-based crises in Latin America (Green 2003), the massive influx of Spanish-speaking immigrants in the US garnered not only the cultural concern of the Real Academia Española (Royal Spanish Academy) but also the pecuniary interest of companies in search of novel marketplace sectors (Del Valle 2007; Santamarina 2016). Wells Fargo's "Hispanic marketing journey" in the US began with Spanish-language advertisements in 1986 and bilingual advertisements by 2013, the year in which their "Iconic Conversations" campaign was launched with Lucy and Ricky. What had been in the 1960s a local northern California bank of historical stagecoach fame became the nation's seventh largest bank by the 1990s (Wells Fargo 2020), and subsequently the world's sixth largest bank by 2015 (Chen 2015). In tenth place on the Forbes list of the world's largest banks that same year was Spain's Banco Santander, having followed a similar trajectory as Wells Fargo in terms of globalization. Largely a regional financial institution in Spain in the 1960s, the bank undertook European expansion in the 1980s, then "a second period of intense expansion in Latin America" in the 1990s, finally arriving in the US retail and commercial sector by 2010 (Santander 2020).

The substantiation of a vital and profitable 'Hispanic market'—in which the use of Spanish was expected or even prescribed—in the US economy was concomitant with an incipient ideological shift of language-nation paradigm. Following suit with the consumerist commodification of language occurring in various other parts of the world (Heller 2007; Duchêne and Heller 2012), Spanish in the US was in some ways discursively divested of its value as ethnic identity marker as it became enmeshed in the discourse of the global economy. If 'nationness' was the spiritual driving force of post-Enlightenment political projects in the Americas and Europe, the inherently limited and sovereign political communities forged by those projects would inevitably evolve into culturally and economically interdependent, transnational communities in the era of late capitalism. One could affirm that capitalist ideology gave rise to the modern post-Enlightenment concept of the nation-state via markets of print capitalism and the structures of language that those markets devised (Anderson 1983). Perhaps ironically, that same ideology now poses a series of challenges to language-based constructs of nationness in the postmodern era. As we will see later, this ideological phenomenon reflects in some ways a tendency to revert to pre-Renaissance orders of language and collective identity, or what Trainor (1998) termed 'modern medievalism.'

Let us merely suggest that the discourse of late capitalism has created a particular brand of legitimacy for Spanish in the US, notwithstanding its subordination to English and sustained anti-immigrant sentiment across the country, framed within the 'Latino threat' narrative (Chavez 2013). English is not only the nation's common language but also enjoys a global hegemonic status, although Spanish is also a global language and has been increasingly legitimated in US public life in recent decades. Spanish 'belongs' not just to

4 *The linguistic order of (post)modernity*

local communities defined by ethnic identities, e.g. the Borderlands (Anzaldúa 1987) or the Barrio (Zentella 1997), but also increasingly to national and global marketplaces in which it is construed by corporate entities as a commodity, an asset, or a vehicle for sales. It is exploited to consumerist ends. In light of the vast historical, political, socioeconomic, ethnic, racial, and religious differences among them, Hispanics or Latinxs could arguably be a fiction of the late capitalist marketplace and the postmodern mass media enterprise—a niche category for consumerism or political device (Dávila 2001; Mora 2014). The 'demand' for Spanish in the economy or the political marketplace is now largely perceived as an empirical fact, i.e. people who speak Spanish have the power of a dollar and the power of a vote (Korzenny, Chapa, and Korzenny 2017). Through this neoliberal economic lens (Brown 2015), Spanish in some ways appears divested of national character (Del Valle 2007) or personal identity, as Da Silva, McLaughlin, and Richards (2007) noted about French in the tertiarization of the Canadian economy: "Language, as a commodity, is no longer an inherent quality of certain individuals or something that individuals own, but something that is external to their personhood" (185).

The neoliberal economic discourse of globalization has neither replaced nor displaced nationalist or ethnic identity discourses: one discursive frame does not deny the other. Rather, the global is introduced alongside the national, in complex and oftentimes contradictory ways (Appadurai 1996; Blommaert 2010; Heller and Duchêne 2012); nationalist movements have indeed found renewed strength in the past few years. In *Deciphering the Global*, Saskia Sassen (2007) affirmed that although transnational processes of globalization evade nation-state frameworks, they are at the same time constituted within them (1). Agreeing with Sassen that the national is not a closed system, and that the global, the national, and the local are not mutually exclusive phenomena, I consider that the contemporary situation of Spanish in the US simultaneously reflects all of these dimensions. The present inquiry is motivated in part by Sassen's observation that "conceiving globalization as partly inhabiting and even getting constituted inside the national opens up a vast research agenda that remains largely unaddressed" (2007, 2). Miami provides an ideal setting for the analysis of these phenomena in relation to the Spanish language.

Irrespective of whether one views language more as a question of 'pride' or 'profit' (Heller and Duchêne 2012), and whatever one's political posture or cultural concerns, the ideological transformation of Spanish in the US over the past four decades is undeniable. Of course, the traditional nineteenth- and twentieth-century anti-immigrant, English-only discourses of modernity remain vibrant in many sectors, but nationalist tendencies are now confronted with global flows. In this postmodern confrontation, and perhaps by virtue of it, Spanish has garnered a degree of legitimacy in public life never before seen in US history. But Spanish was, in Derridian terms, always already there. Its 'appearance,' in terms of public legitimacy, was owed not just to mass migration, the proliferation of media and cyberspace, or economic neoliberalist

The linguistic order of (post)modernity 5

trends. The postmodern phenomenon of Spanish in the US is also the result of a break with the past—a rupture of the linguistic order of modernity, which is where this book will begin. In what follows, I place the situation of Spanish in Miami in a broad macro-level historical context. In the first two sections of this chapter, I trace the evolution of ideologies of Spanish in the US according to the 'linguistic order' from modernity to postmodernity. In the third section, I describe the postmodern sociolinguistic circumstance of Spanish in Miami.

Language in modernity

Modernity, in a general sense, spans the Age of Reason and the Enlightenment of the eighteenth century through the period of intense nation-building and industrialization during the nineteenth century, waning in the latter twentieth century. The beginning of modernity depends upon disciplinary perspective, though most consider that the empiricism of Bacon, the rationalist thought of Descartes, and the political proposals of Hobbes and Locke all mark an important break with medievalism and hence the dawn of an early modern period. The philosophies of Descartes, Hobbes, Newton, and Galileo serve to abstract or 'unhinge' human reason from the medieval cosmic order of things through a discourse of scientific method and human progress in opposition to nature (Trainor 1998). Finding the early modern conceptualization of individual rights and self-determination at odds with medieval feudalism, societies began to evolve into nation-state collectivities by the sixteenth century. This evolution would eventually culminate in the Age of Revolution (Hobsbawm 1996), beginning with the American Revolution of 1776 and the French Revolution of 1789 and then throughout Europe and the Americas in the first half of the nineteenth century, in tandem with nationalism, industrialization, the spread of capitalism, and the rise of the bourgeoisie—all phenomena that characterize modernity proper. In the year 1500, bounded states with central governments occupied less than 20% of the world's land area; by the end of the twentieth century, Antarctica remained the only such politically unbounded space (Diamond 1999, 255). Clearly, the delineation of nation-state boundaries was a key characteristic of modernity. We now turn to the important implications of the modern boundary for the ways in which we think about language.

The emergence of language boundaries

In his classic work *Imagined Communities* (1983), Benedict Anderson argued that the independence movements of the Americas and the spread of nationalist sentiment in Europe served to entrench the ontological boundaries of language already being forged by the practices of print capitalism leading up to the Enlightenment. A particular 'fatality' of languages gradually emerged as those practices mapped a series of languages onto the vast landscape of

6   The linguistic order of (post)modernity

vernacular linguistic diversity existent in Western Europe: "Nothing served to 'assemble' related vernaculars more than capitalism, which, within the limits imposed by grammars and syntaxes, created mechanically reproduced print-languages capable of dissemination through the market" (Anderson 1983, 44). Reproducible print languages thus paved the way to national conscious-ness, and hence modernity, in the following ways: (1) by constructing formal, written codes of communication that united spoken vernaculars within par-ticular geopolitical spaces; (2) by giving 'fixity' to those codes and hence altering a perhaps more 'natural' course of language evolution by slowing the rate of change; and (3) by forging new languages of power and authority in the sense that particular varieties resembled the printed form more than others that had been subsumed by it. In this way, the economic practices of print capitalism lent themselves to the political endeavors of drawing national boundaries during the modern era. For Anderson, nations are *imagined com-munities* "because the members of even the smallest nation will never know most of their fellow-members, meet them, or even hear of them, yet in the minds of each lives the image of their communion" (6). He thus concluded that nationness and nationalism are discursive cultural artifacts, and that the collective imagination empowered the idea of the nation as a bounded and sovereign political community "conceived as a deep, horizontal comradeship" in which the bond of a common language was essential (7).

Gutenberg's printing press was not the only protagonist. As serial newspapers and mass produced novels served to establish collectivities by bringing the common reading public closer together in an imagined place in the age of modernity, watches and clocks served the same function on a tem-poral plane: "The cosmic clocking which had made intelligible our synchronic transoceanic pairings was increasingly felt to entail a wholly intramundane, *serial* view of social causality; and this sense of the world was now speedily deepening its grip on Western imaginations" (Anderson 1983, 194). The importance of universalizing time cannot be understated, as it coordinated human action on a global scale and created a sense of commitment to countering irrationality or chaos (Nowotny 1994). Ideologies of mechaniza-tion proliferated in society, e.g. the body as natural machine and mechanism as the basis of scientific understanding during the sixteenth and seventeenth cen-turies (Dijksterhuis 1961). For Michel Foucault, the effect entailed a change in the way that language, and concomitantly knowledge, was conceptualized. As written modes gained autonomy from the Renaissance into modernity, writing ceased to be a phenomenon of resemblance and similitude in nature—"a mark imprinted across the world which is a part of its most ineffaceable forms" (Foucault 1994, 42)—as it evolved into a matter of representation by the sixteenth century and, ultimately, signification:

> This new arrangement brought about the appearance of a new problem, unknown until then: in the sixteenth century, one asked oneself how it was possible to know that a sign did in fact designate what it signified; from

The linguistic order of (post)modernity 7

the seventeenth century, one began to ask how a sign could be linked to what it signified.... The primacy of the written word went into abeyance. And that uniform layer, in which the *seen* and the *read*, the visible and the expressible, were endlessly interwoven, vanished too. Things and words were to be separated from one another.

(Foucault 1994, 42–43)

Anderson (1983) reasoned that nationalism in nineteenth-century Europe was an aftereffect of the independence movements that swept the Americas. The spatial, temporal, and spiritual connotations of counterpart toponyms in the 'New' and 'Old' Worlds (e.g. New England, Nouvelle Orleans, Nueva España, etc.) led people "to think of themselves as living *lives parallel to* those of other substantial groups of people—if never meeting, yet certainly proceeding along the same trajectory" (188, emphasis in the original). This sense of parallelism was conditioned by technological advances in mapmaking, navigation, and shipbuilding, and was fomented by the collective imagination constructed through print capitalism: "It became conceivable to dwell on the Peruvian altiplano, on the pampas of Argentina, or by the harbours of 'New' England, and yet feel connected to certain regions or communities, thousands of miles away, in England or the Iberian peninsula" (188). That feeling confronted the great divide of the Atlantic Ocean, however, and it was precisely this vast placeholder that would condition a sense of parallelism and ultimately inspire the independence movements of the Americas, thus imbuing 'New' with the meaning of 'separate' in the given toponyms (cf. Benítez-Rojo 1996 on the particular situation of the Caribbean). Where aquatic space served to establish boundaries and engender a 'separate but equal' sense of parallel lives in the aspiring new American republics, language did not need to play an ideological role.

On the heels of the second generation of nationalist movements that would subsequently manifest in the 'Old' World, however, the spirit of time and place evolved in a fundamental way. Newness now fully realized, a genealogical criterion of continuity would emerge from the yearning for a historical grounding, the "return to an aboriginal essence" (Anderson 1983, 195). Language was the key: "'uncivilized' vernaculars began to function politically in the same way as the Atlantic Ocean had earlier done.... Once one starts thinking about nationality in terms of continuity, few things seem as historically deep-rooted as languages" (196). This marked a new way of thinking about language ontologically: the storehouse of one's roots, the essence of the nation, that which distinguishes or serves to separate one nation from another, an abstract entity charged with political meaning, bounded, limited, sovereign. As the viceroyalties of Nueva España and Nueva Granada, along with those of Perú and Río de la Plata, morphed into independent nations in the wake of Napoleon's invasion of Spain (1808–1814), the former center of the empire entered into crisis. With Spain's ties to the newly formed nations uncertain and its own future as a modern nation at stake, the continued role of Spain

8 *The linguistic order of (post)modernity*

in the Americas was much debated among intellectuals during the nineteenth century (Del Valle and Stheeman 2002).The matter of language represented two vital facets of the debate: the place of Spain's legacy in the national identity projects of the Americas, and the question of legitimate cultural referents in the construction of the newly bounded nation-states (Jiménez Ángel 2018, 41). As Rama affirmed in his influential argument *La ciudad letrada* (1998 [1984]) regarding the autonomy of modern Latin American nation-states, "la letra apareció como la palanca del ascenso social, de la respetabilidad pública y de la incorporación a los centros de poder" (63).

The linguistic legacy of Spain in the Americas

In the decade following Venezuela's independence, prominent statesman Andrés Bello argued that the 'unity' of Spanish language must be preserved in relation to Spain and in adherence to the dictates of the Real Academia Española (RAE). Bello saw the independence movements as an opportunity to implant Spanish culture in the Americas, something that Spain itself had been unable to do: "It is the Iberian element that has allowed us to prevail against the Mother country. Spanish culture has clashed against itself…. The veteran captains of the legions of transatlantic Iberia were defeated and humiliated by the caudillos and armies improvised by young Iberia" (cited in Criscenti 1993, 67). Bello's position was countered by Domingo Faustino Sarmiento, seventh president of Argentina (1868–1874) and author of the highly influential *Facundo: civilización y barbarie*. Sarmiento urged that in order for the newly formed nations to progress toward modernity, they had to break with Spain—a nation that in his mind was incapable of expressing modern ideas (Criscenti 1993, 65). That break would imply a deviation from the linguistic norms emanating from the RAE. Sarmiento affirmed: "Instead of concerning us with forms, with the purity of language,… with what Cervantes or Friar Luis de León wrote, acquire ideas… and when your mind awakens, observe your country,… and then write with love,… and that will be good even though the form may be incorrect" (cited in Criscenti 1993, 65). Bello replied that if the path advocated by Sarmiento were followed, "America will reproduce the confusion of dialects and gibberish, Babylonian chaos of the Middle Ages; and then people will lose one of their most powerful links, one of their most precious instruments of understanding" (cited in Criscenti 1993, 65).

By the late nineteenth century, the debate regarding language variation and change would be taken up by famed Colombian philologist Rufino José Cuervo and Spanish author and diplomat Juan Valera. By that time, the field of linguistics oriented increasingly toward a scientific paradigm, whose early notable theoretical exponents during the first half of the century were Friedrich Schlegel, Wilhelm von Humboldt, and Jacob Grimm. This emergent paradigm, to which Cuervo fervently adhered later in his career, not only brought greater attention to synchronic dimensions of language but also challenged prevalent precepts of language purity and the nature of origins

The linguistic order of (post)modernity   9

and change. Cuervo's studies demonstrated through an 'irrefutable' empirical method that many of the supposedly corrupt variants of Spanish in the Americas in fact had their origins in Spain and were evident in the writings of Cervantes, Santa Teresa, and Tirso de Molina. The ideological impact of this scientific turn in linguistics was far-reaching. Reinterpreted through a philological and linguistic lens as the embodiment of the laws of historical language evolution, the language of the common masses came to occupy a central place as a historical variant of Castilian in the Americas that was just as legitimate as Castilian in Spain (Jiménez Ángel 2018).

Carried out in close collaboration with longtime friend Miguel Antonio Caro, Cuervo's philological vindication of Latin American Spanish posed an important ideological challenge to the foundation of the RAE as the purveyor of 'pure' Spanish. The scientific philological approach not only undermined the legitimacy of traditional Spanish grammar—which found its voice in Valera—but it also transformed American variants of the language into necessary referents in the study of the history of Castilian (Jiménez Ángel 2018). The establishment of the first corresponding Spanish language *academias* in Latin America during the 1870s and 1880s, linked to Spain's RAE, resulted in part from intellectual concerns about the integrity of Spanish, as Rama (1998) noted: "Su aparición fue la respuesta de la *ciudad letrada* a la subversión que se estaba produciendo en la lengua por la democratización en curso, agravada en ciertos puntos por la inmigración extranjera, complicada en todas partes por la avasallante influencia francesa y amenazada por la fragmentación en nacionalidades" (68). Exalting the importance of Spanish in the Americas and asserting its cultural autonomy, Caro and Cuervo's position may nonetheless be characterized as 'Hispanocentric.' Their reinterpretation of linguistic unity through diversity, framed scientifically within natural laws of language, reflected their concern with the potential fragmentation of Spanish—a concern that aligned with the struggle of intellectual and political conservatives against the growing threat of radical liberalism: "La convicción en la existencia de determinadas leyes que regían la evolución de las lenguas, así como la concepción organicista del lenguaje en la que tal evolución se enmarcaba servirían de herramientas para reafirmar las pretensiones de control sobre la lengua de los intelectuales gramáticos" (Jiménez Ángel 2018, 49).

Concurrent with the emergent scientific paradigm in linguistics approaching the end of the nineteenth century, the political crisis of Spain deepened. Debates about linguistic differentiation or fragmentation versus homogeneity or unity were symbolic not only of the political relationship between Spain and its former colonies, but also between Spain and the growing intervention of the US in Latin America and, concomitantly, the influence of English on Spanish. Economic and political interests in the Caribbean culminated in military conflict between Spain and the US in 1898. Sugar trade, investment, and commercial interests in Cuba largely motivated the US to support the Cuban independence movement that had been ongoing since 1868. Throughout the nineteenth century, industry and trade had created vital links with the US,

10 *The linguistic order of (post)modernity*

and Cubans had become increasingly 'Americanized' not only through the penetration of US consumer products, institutions, and cultural forms in Cuba, but also through the cyclical migrations of Cubans to the north:

> Daily life and ordinary social relations in Cuba were influenced by ways and things North American, often with Cuban acknowledgment and acquiescence, for these forms had become one of the primary means by which Cubans arrived at self-definition. Long before the US intervention in 1898, many Cubans had already developed a familiarity with and an affinity for North American ways.
>
> (Pérez 1999, 8)

English language was an important dimension of that affinity, and Anglicisms began to proliferate in Cuban Spanish, particularly in relation to sports, technology, and consumerism (Sánchez Fajardo 2017). For growing numbers of Cubans, especially of the middle and upper classes, "English usage signified an alternative that went beyond Spanish to reach out to an opposing cultural system" (Pérez 1999, 53). That opposing cultural system to the north was viewed as the most viable model for Cuba's entry into nationhood and into modernity. Indeed, José Martí, iconic figure of the third and final war of Cuban liberation (1895–1898), commended his compatriot Nestor Ponce de León's 1883 publication of a bilingual terminological dictionary in response to the vitality of Anglicisms in Cuban Spanish: "Hace bien en injerir con discreción y propiedad la lengua corriente y necesaria de la industria y el comercio en el idioma español, para expresar los estados del alma" (cited in Sánchez Fajardo 2017, 190). Martí himself spent substantial time in the US, living and working as a journalist in New York, and organizing the Cuban War of Independence from his office there. He lobbied against US annexation of the island and, in 1892, founded the Cuban Revolutionary Party in dialogue with the exile communities of Key West and Tampa, who funded Martí's venture.

With the signing of the Treaty of Paris in 1898, Spain ceded Cuba, Puerto Rico, Guam, and the Philippines—its last remaining colonies—to US control. Some four months before the treaty's signing, the *New York Times* published an editorial insinuating that Spanish speakers in New Mexico, which had been annexed from Mexico as a US territory in 1848, had been sympathetic to Spain during the conflict over Cuba. The article clearly reflected modern one nation–one language ideology:

> The trouble with these disaffected, semi-traitorous citizens is that they have been allowed to attend schools in which only the Spanish language was spoken.... As long as this is permitted, of course a considerable majority of the inhabitants will remain 'Mexican' and will retain a pseudo-allegiance to the land which, if the matter were one of reason instead of instinct, they would detest much more vehemently than the

real American does. All through the territory there are to be found today thousands of children, as well as thousands of adults, to whom English is almost unknown, and therefore a more or less detested, tongue. Such a state of affairs is disgraceful as well as dangerous.... In the present attitude of these 'Mexicans,' who do not know that they are Americans, there is to be found a strong hint as to the course which should be pursued in Puerto Rico. Absolutely no official recognition should be given hereafter to the Spanish language in that island....

(*New York Times* 1898, E3)

Debate over the language question in Puerto Rico—which still today remains under political jurisdiction of the US—would continue well into the twentieth century (Negrón-Muntaner 1997).

Puerto Ricans countered the US government's efforts to annex the population linguistically and politically by reasserting their cultural ties to Spain. In 1934 Emilio Belaval proclaimed: "Somos españoles hasta la médula, y en nuestro contenido nacional hay una cantidad respetable de españolismo vital.... A la afirmación que más miedo le tenemos es a admitir que somos españoles, y por eso, es que hemos resistido sin que hasta ahora se nos rompa el espinazo"; and in 1940 Manuel Rivera Matos wrote: "Sabemos que el espíritu y la expresión de un pueblo son consustanciales con el idioma en el cual está contenido toda nuestra herencia cultural" (both cited in Vélez 2000, 12–13). During the US occupation of the Dominican Republic (1916–1924), celebrated Dominican philologist Pedro Henríquez Ureña asserted the use of Spanish as the nation's defense: "The feeling of ferocious preservation [of Spanish language] persists in our time in light of the illegal and unprovoked invasion ordered by the United States government. Santo Domingo defends itself... resisting foreign linguistic influence and using the Spanish language as its only weapon and shield at home and abroad" (cited in Valdez 2013, 194). In this regard, Hispanism constituted a bulwark against potential Americanization. Just prior to Puerto Rican Governor Luis Muñoz Marín's declaration in 1949 that Spanish would be the language of instruction in public schools, Salvador Tió published a jocose, tongue-in-cheek commentary on the Anglicization of Puerto Rico in which he ironically expressed concern about the harm that Puerto Ricans could inflict upon the English language: "No debemos cargar con la responsabilidad histórica de acabar con un gran idioma." Published in *Diario de Puerto Rico* in 1948, Tió's (1948) article would lead to today's widespread popular usage of the term appearing in its title: "Teoría del espanglish." He clarified: "El espanglismo pretende que usemos una lengua como si fuesen dos."

The question of language was inherent in the ideologically fraught debate over New Mexico's entry into the Union as well. New Mexico would not be accepted into statehood until 1912, more than a decade after the Spanish-American War and more than six decades after the signing of the Treaty of Guadalupe Hidalgo, by which Mexico ceded roughly half of its lands and

12 *The linguistic order of (post)modernity*

20% of its population to the US in 1848. *Nuevomexicanos*—many of whom traced their ancestry to Spain—and Anglo Republicans both opposed English-only provisions as a criterion for statehood: the former principally for reasons of cultural heritage (similar to the vast German-speaking communities of the Midwest), and the latter on the grounds that Anglicization would happen 'naturally' as a result of the influx of European and Anglo-American immigrants and thus need not be officially imposed (Nieto-Phillips 2004, 76–77). Despite the special status accorded to Spanish in New Mexico's 1912 Constitution, cross-generational shift to English dominance was indeed the ultimate outcome only a few decades later. The policy had proven to be essentially symbolic, with only two articles of the state's constitution pertaining to Spanish: 1) all laws must be published in Spanish—a requirement that was not enforced after the 1940s; and 2) teachers must be trained in Spanish—a mandate that was applied only to teachers of monolingual Spanish-speaking children (Bills 1997, 170).

Among those New Mexicans who took great pride in their Spanish ancestry was Aurelio Espinosa, a Stanford University professor regarded as the pioneer of Spanish language and folklore studies in the US at the turn of the century. Born in southern Colorado in 1880 to a *nuevomexicano* family, Espinosa traced his lineage to the original Spanish settlers accompanying Juan de Oñate at the end of the sixteenth century (Nieto-Phillips 2004, 178–79). Like his contemporaries Rufino José Cuervo in Colombia and Pedro Henríquez Ureña in the Dominican Republic (Valdez 2013), Espinosa viewed Spanish in the Americas as a historical continuation of the 'pure' varieties brought from Spain. In his classic three-tome *Studies in New Mexican Spanish*, he traced about 1,000 of the 1,400 local dialect features to Spain; he attributed another 300 to English, 75 to Nahuatl, and only 10 to autochthonous local origin (Nieto-Phillips 2004, 180–81). The tendency to ignore indigenous influences on Spanish in his work has been attributed to his concern with the purity of New Mexican Spanish linguistic and cultural forms in relation to Spain (Limón 2014). In the inaugural issue of the journal *Hispania*, of which he was the first editor-in-chief, Espinosa declared: "Aside from giving to problems of pure pedagogical interest the great attention which they deserve, [*Hispania*] will also attempt to interpret sympathetically to our pupils and teachers of Spanish the history and culture of the great Spain of the past and present" (1917, 19).

The academic tradition of folklore studies, of which Espinosa was one of North America's leading exponents, had its origins in nineteenth-century Romanticist thought concerning the evolution of racial, cultural, and linguistic forms. Matters of racial purity and superiority were prevalent in the academic and intellectual inquiry of the time. Clifford Kirkpatrick, Ivy League–educated, award-winning sociologist and one-time chair of the Department of Sociology at Indiana University, wrote in his 1926 volume *Intelligence and Immigration* that among the mass of newly arrived immigrants of southern and eastern European origin, "definite limits are set by heredity, and immigrants

The linguistic order of (post)modernity   13

of low innate ability cannot by any amount of Americanization be made into intelligent American citizens capable of appropriating and advancing a complex culture" (cited in Portes and Rumbaut 2014, 50). This line of inquiry would ultimately serve the interests of Nazism and related fascist movements in Europe. Devoutly Catholic, Espinosa was explicit regarding his support of Franco's nationalist regime in Spain, an ideological stance that links to his extensive work as a folklorist: "He sought to preserve Catholic traditions against the encroachment of threatening modern [left-wing] political forms.... In this way, folklore came to play a key role in shaping a political ideology that made Fascism and political conservativism synonymous with the preservation of tradition and a return to the idyllic past" (Limón 2014, 463). One must bear in mind that religious practice had become bound up with linguistic practice in the contact situation of the late nineteenth and early twentieth centuries in the Southwest: Spanish was the language of Catholicism and English was the ideological vehicle for Protestantism and, concomitantly, progress and modernity (DuBord 2013).

Another facet of this polemic finds its roots in the rivalry of the Spanish and British empires during colonial times. As explained by Powell (1971), "The basic premise of the Black Legend is that Spaniards have shown themselves, historically, to be uniquely cruel, bigoted, tyrannical, obscurantist, lazy, fanatical, greedy, and treacherous" (11). Many attribute this 'Hispanophobic' bias in historical documentation to propaganda of the British Crown and the Protestant Reformation beginning in the early sixteenth century; others argue that it predates the sixteenth century. According to Weber (2000), the English prejudice toward the Spanish was transplanted to North American soil, tainting contemporary US-Latin American relations and fomenting anti-Hispanic and racist sentiment within the context of the US. Along those lines, González Pino and Pino (2007) argued that the *leyenda negra* still influenced attitudes toward Spanish in the US Southwest. Their survey study revealed a mostly negative perception of Spain's legacy in the Americas among Spanish heritage language students in the region: some 50% claimed they were not proud of the Spanish heritage, and 63% characterized it negatively (235).

Approaching the end of the nineteenth century, the Romanticist longing for an idyllic past was in part related to the spoils of industrialization in the urban centers of Europe and the US. Difficult living conditions in overcrowded, polluted manufacturing centers such as Chicago and Pittsburgh prompted easterners to look westward, to New Mexico in particular. There, as Weber (2000) suggested, the Spanish settlers' so-called backwardness or inability to attain modernity came to be viewed by some as a virtue rather than a fault, and a romanticized cultural imaginary of days gone by emerged.

One of the most highly influential and widely popularized works of the time was journalist Charles Lummis' book *Some Strange Corners of Our Country*, first published in 1892, in which the natural marvels of the region and the social customs of its indigenous peoples were described—and at times exoticized—in depth of detail. With the same propagandistic sort of awe

14   *The linguistic order of (post)modernity*

with which he recalled having photographed the flagellation and crucifixion practices of the *penitentes* during Lent in 1888 (Lummis 1911 [1892], 90–93), he shared with the reader photographs of the "stone autograph-album" at El Morro, a wall-like sandstone promontory where numerous Spanish explorers, among them Juan de Oñate, carved their names as they passed through the area in the sixteenth and early seventeenth centuries. He observed: "All the old inscriptions are in Spanish—and many in very quaint old Spanish, of the days when spelling was a very elastic thing…. All around these brave old names… are Saxon names of the last few decades. Alas! Some of these late-comers have been vandals, and have even erased the names of ancient heroes to make a smooth place for their 'John Jones' and 'George Smith'" (168–69). In these lines, Lummis captured the early twentieth-century zeitgeist within which the contemporary US cultural phenomenon of 'Spanish heritage' first became manifest. Within that cultural imaginary, Anglo modernity—at times cast in a negative light—was ideologically confronted with a glorified Spanish colonial past. This narrative strategically served the broader political purpose of inserting the Southwest in the national imaginary of the US (DuBord 2013, 277). The trend has been termed 'Hispanophilia.'

US Hispanophilia[1]

Cultural interest in things Spanish around the turn of the century in the US was reflective of the ideology of *hispanismo* that had prevailed in Latin America throughout the 1800s: "The idea that Spanish American culture is nothing but Spanish culture transplanted to the New World; and the notion that Hispanic culture has an internal hierarchy in which Spain occupies a hegemonic position" (Del Valle and Gabriel-Stheeman 2002, 6). During the same years in which Puerto Rican and Dominican intellectuals resisted US intervention and Espinosa asserted the purity of New Mexican Spanish, the Panama-California Exposition was held in San Diego to commemorate the opening of the Panama Canal. The venue for the 1915–1917 exposition was given the name Balboa Park, in honor of the first Spanish explorer to reach the Pacific Ocean from the New World. For the construction of the site, Spanish Colonial Revival architecture was chosen, recalling Mission and Pueblo Revival styles of the Southwest and taking principal inspiration from the Spanish or Mediterranean Revival styles of the late 1800s. The San Diego exposition brought international acclaim to architect Bertram Goodhue's work in Balboa Park and established the vogue of Spanish Colonial Revival style across the US during the 1920s, the best examples of which are found in the cities of San Diego, Santa Barbara, and Coral Gables.

In the late 1800s, before making his way to Miami, Henry Flagler had already demonstrated that things Spanish loomed large in his vision of Florida. John D. Rockefeller's partner in Standard Oil, turned railroad and hotel magnate, Flagler was responsible for extending the Florida East Coast Railway to the shore of the Miami River at the behest of Julia Tuttle

The linguistic order of (post)modernity   15

in 1896. In the preceding years, Flagler had made St. Augustine a popular tourist destination by capitalizing on its Spanish legacy. There, wealthy northern vacationers lodged in the Ponce de León Hotel (now Flagler College) and the Alcázar Hotel (now Lightner Museum), posh Spanish Renaissance–style hotels that Flagler had erected and which his friend Thomas Edison had equipped with electricity. In 1897, Flagler opened the Royal Palm Hotel in Miami, extending his imagination of Florida's Spanish legacy to Biscayne Bay and establishing the location as an exclusive retreat for northern millionaires. International Harvester tycoon James Deering would follow suit with the construction of his Venetian-style Villa Vizcaya in 1916. It was rather predictable, then, that Mediterranean Revival–style architecture—particularly Andalusian—would lend the motif for one of the largest and most expensive development projects of Florida's 'great land boom' in the early 1920s: Coral Gables. Conceived by George Merrick in 1921 and incorporated in 1925, the city would be home to the University of Miami and the legendary Biltmore Hotel, as well as hundreds of grandiose Mediterranean-style residences on more than sixty-five miles of streets bearing Spanish names: Ponce de León, Alhambra, Granada, Sevilla, Giralda, Alcázar, etc. Also in 1925, the Spanish-themed Pueblo Feliz entertainment center was built in Miami Shores. Pérez (1999) affirmed that, during the 1920s, "the vogue of Havana insinuated itself into the vision of Miami: foreign, tropical, exotic, as ambience and circumstance through Spanish-language usage and Royal Palms landscaping" (432).

As in South Florida, the Spanish Colonial Revival style that came to be iconic of the Southern California architectural landscape by the end of the 1920s was a turn-of-the-century reimagination of the area's history—"almost totally a myth created by newcomers" during the late nineteenth century (Gebhard 1967, 131). The lead architect of the flimsily constructed San Diego exposition that gave impetus to the building fad affirmed that it was meant to be temporary, like stage scenery or "the fabric of a dream" (Goodhue 1916, 7). Goodhue was explicit regarding the relationship of the Spanish cultural imaginary to Southern California's 'rightful' heritage: "It is perhaps strange to say quite flatly that so many buildings that have given pleasure to so many should be destroyed; but, after all, this was the paramount idea in the minds of the Fair's designers, and only by thus razing all of the Temporary Buildings will San Diego enter upon the heritage that is rightfully hers" (9). Ultimately, several of the buildings were either retained or reconstructed, and remain to the present day, constituting the 'Spanish' image of Balboa Park. Along with Balboa Park, Coral Gables' Biltmore Hotel and Miami's Freedom Tower are among the more notable examples of Spanish Colonial Revival architecture in the US.

In keeping with the popular cultural imaginary of the early twentieth century, some of Hollywood's most famous film stars were identified as 'Spanish.' The official studio biography of Ramón Novarro, born José Ramón Samaniego in Durango, Mexico in 1899, stated that he was a Spaniard when, in fact, his family background was assuredly Mexican (Rodríguez 2004,

16   *The linguistic order of (post)modernity*

48–49). Novarro's cousin Dolores del Río was also described as a "Spanish actress" when she first rose to stardom. Pedro de Córdoba, who began his 116-film career starring in Cecil B. DeMille's *Carmen* in 1915, was born in New York City to a Parisian mother and a Cuban father. Because his father's grandparents had immigrated to Cuba from Spain, the press highlighted his ancestry: "Instinctively when one sees him, in one's mind rises visions of brave toreadors…, graciously fascinating women in waving mantillas and eyes dancing" (cited in Rodríguez 2004, 41). Actress Anita Page, star of the first sound film to win the Academy Award for Best Picture, was born Anita Pomares, the granddaughter of Salvadoran immigrants. In 1929, when *The Broadway Melody* won the Oscar, she was described in *Photoplay* magazine as "a blond, blue-eyed Latin" with "a dash of Spanish ancestry" (cited in Rodríguez 2004, 14). Numerous other Hollywood actors of the 1910s and 1920s changed their names to capitalize on the 'Latin' vogue of the time: New Mexican Joe Page rose to stardom as Don Alvarado; Viennese immigrant Jacob Krantz became Ricardo Cortez; and Mexican-born Paula Marie Osterman allegedly tried out three different names before Hollywood executives decided that Raquel Torres "sounded Spanish enough" (Rodríguez 2004, 16).

Hollywood's first famed 'Latin Lover,' Rudolph Valentino rose to stardom dancing tango in the nation's top-grossing film of 1921, *The Four Horsemen of the Apocalypse*. Most attribute the 'tango craze' that spread throughout Paris, London, and ultimately New York in the 1910s to the success of the musical comedy *The Sunshine Girl*, which premiered at London's Gaiety Theatre in February of 1912. Groppa (2004) observed that, in this production, the British performers "appeared on stage dressed like Spaniards," including Andalusian hat and Manila shawl, thus giving "a poor example to a nascent Hollywood film industry that never shook off this stereotype" (11). One year later, the show opened in New York's Knickerbocker Theatre, marking the entry of this style of music and dance born in the bordellos of Buenos Aires into the US cultural imaginary. By January of 1914, the *New York Times* ran a seven-column headline declaring "All New York Now Madly Whirling in the Tango"; there were some 700 dance halls across the city open from noon until dawn of the next day (Groppa 2004, 21). The fact that it came entirely into vogue among the city's aristocrats and the local social scene of the upper echelon secured its success.

Perhaps because the principal protagonists of the tango craze in New York were not Argentine (or even Argentine American), the linguistic dimension of the music was never fully conveyed. Groppa speculated that the reason so many prominent Argentine tango professionals did not prosper in New York at the time was the language barrier. This was still true in the 1930s for the world's best-known tango artist, Carlos Gardel, whose acting career with Paramount Pictures was curtailed by his reported inability to master English. Tucci (1969) recounted that at the New York premier of his 1934 film *Cuesta abajo* at the Teatro Campoamor in Spanish Harlem, crowds filled the street to catch a glimpse of the star. Undoubtedly, the throngs of fans who awaited

The linguistic order of (post)modernity 17

him were mostly Caribbean-origin Spanish speakers. New York's Hispanic population increased from 22,000 in 1916 to 134,000 in 1940; according to the 1930 Census, 41% of that population was Puerto Rican, and another 18% were Cuban or Dominican (Haslip-Viera 2010, 36). Puerto Rican (im)migration was driven by the economic prosperity of the so-called Roaring Twenties and the Jones Act of 1917, which granted Puerto Ricans US citizenship.

In sum, during the 1910s and 1920s—a time of economic prosperity across the US—things 'Spanish,' and to lesser extent 'Latin,' entered the nation's cultural imaginary for the first time, through seemingly localized phenomena: economic development and tourism in New Mexico; architectural styles in specific urban settings of Florida, California, and the Southwest; tango halls in New York City; and the spaces of Hollywood movies and the identities of actors who appeared in them. Because the film of that era was silent, language was a non-issue. With the advent of talkies in the late 1920s and early 1930s—coinciding with the nation's most catastrophic economic downturn and the resonance of political unrest in Europe—Latino actors, and particularly those who spoke Hispanic-accented English, began to be typecast. It was with good reason that US Spanish heritage speaker Margarita Carmen Cansino changed her name to Rita Hayworth shortly after entering the Hollywood film industry in the mid-1930s. During that time, Hispanophilia quickly waned as the consequences of the Wall Street Crash were felt, and political tensions between populist, nationalist, socialist, and communist ideologies grew across Europe and Latin America. Immigration quickly curtailed and deportations began.

It is noteworthy, for our purposes, that Hispanophilia was a proverbial double-edged sword in terms of the social status of Spanish in the US. There were significant increases in Spanish language study during the early twentieth century; in the midst of WWI, enrollments increased by more than 400% between 1916 and 1918 as US political and economic interests turned toward Latin America (Dulfano and Rubio 2014, 142). In various regions of the Southwest, the language was promoted to specific ends such as religion (DuBord 2013) and public health (Martínez 2013), yet at the same time it was socially maligned and politically constricted by modern Anglophone expansion. The present-day website of the American Association of Teachers of Spanish and Portuguese (AATSP), founded in 1917, explains a rise of Spanish language study at the time in rather skeptical terms: "American isolationism gave Spanish a boost when German was dropped from many schools during the First World War. Spanish became the language of choice, not through any love of the language, but for simple expediency…. So Spanish developed a constituency and a foothold in American education, but for unattractive and unsatisfactory reasons" (American Association of Teachers of Spanish and Portuguese, n.d.).

The cases of German and Spanish are highly illustrative of the linguistic order that emerged at the turn of the century. Within this order, non-English languages were at best viewed as a potential source of political distrust, and at

18 *The linguistic order of (post)modernity*

worst as a subversive element of American society. In his December of 1915 State of the Union address, with WWI already underway in Europe and the US about to invade the Dominican Republic purportedly to thwart a potential German incursion, President Woodrow Wilson emphasized the danger posed by German Americans who appeared sympathetic to Pan-Germanism:

> The gravest threats against our national peace and safety have been uttered within our own borders. There are citizens of the United States, I blush to admit, born under other flags but welcomed under our generous naturalization laws to the full freedom and opportunity of America, who have poured the poison of disloyalty into the very arteries of our national life; who have sought to bring the authority and good name of our Government into contempt, to destroy our industries wherever they thought it effective for their vindictive purposes to strike at them, and to debase our politics to the uses of foreign intrigue.... America never witnessed anything like this before. It never dreamed it possible that men sworn into its own citizenship... would ever turn in malign reaction against the Government and people who had welcomed and nurtured them and seek to make this proud country once more a hotbed of European passion.... Such creatures of passion, disloyalty, and anarchy must be crushed out. They are not many, but they are infinitely malignant, and the hand of our power should close over them at once.
>
> (Wilson 1915)

In the ensuing linguistic mistrust, use of German was banned in several midwestern states. In Iowa, the 1918 Babel Proclamation prohibited all non-English languages in public life—even in religious services and in telephone conversations. German newspapers disappeared, textbooks were burned, and language teachers were dismissed from their jobs as many German families chose to Anglicize the spellings of their surnames (Portes and Rumbaut 2014, 310–11). Simultaneously present in the popular political discourse and media of the time was the "pathologizing of Mexican culture" and the "problem" of large numbers of Mexican immigrants (Molina, 2006), principally in the Southwest, who fled the turmoil of the Mexican Revolution (1910–1920) and filled US labor demands in agriculture and manufacturing. Disease, delinquency, illiteracy, lack of discipline, disorganization, and retardation linked to child bilingualism were commonly attributed to them (McWilliams 1990, 163). The perceived threat of non-English-speaking immigrants would serve to entrench the linguistic order of the twentieth century.

The linguistic order

Leading up to WWI, mass migrations and the democratization of politics, which brought to the citizenry greater participation in and knowledge of dominant power structures by the turn of the century, meant that language use

The linguistic order of (post)modernity 19

would become a key consideration in debates around nationalism (Hobsbawm 1996). The focus on bounded monolingualism in a national standardized variety was a mechanism for assimilation of immigrants and top-down state control in general. US President Theodore Roosevelt's now-famous words in the wake of WWI in 1919 made this ideology patently clear: "We have room for but one language here, and that is the English language; for we intend to see that the crucible turns our people out as Americans, and not as dwellers in a polyglot boarding house; and we have room for but one sole loyalty, and that is the loyalty to the American people." In the previous decade, Roosevelt had signed into law the Naturalization Act of 1906, which required that immigrants demonstrate ability in English in order to be granted citizenship. Still to the present day, this requirement stands in the absence of any official federal language policy. This congressional language legislation was motivated by rapidly growing numbers of European immigrants by the end of the nineteenth century. As a result of this first great immigration, the overall percentage of the foreign-born population reached its highest rate in US history, exceeding the rates observed in the present-day context of the second great immigration (Portes and Rumbaut 2014). As we will see in the following section, the perception of non-English language use was of a somewhat different nature in the second great immigration than in the first—a phenomenon that I will attribute to a change in the political-economic order of things.

Between 1880 and 1920, more than 23 million immigrants arrived in the US, mostly of European origin. In 1910, nearly 15% of the US population was foreign-born; in urban areas, 22% (Portes and Rumbaut 2014, 42–43). During that time, the origins of those immigrants gradually shifted from the north of Europe in the 1880s to the south and east of Europe by the 1900s. These origins reflected the advance of industrialization throughout Europe and thus the uprooting of the peasant masses who, left in precarity by the economic transformation of their homelands, were forced to migrate: "This migration may thus be viewed as an adjustment of population to resources, that in its magnitude and the extent to which it adapted itself to purely economic needs has few parallels in history" (Kuznets cited in Portes and Rumbaut 2014, 43). Those immigrants crossed the Atlantic in a 'pull' effect, where they met the need of an ascendant class of industrial capitalists who sought cheap labor for their growing manufacturing enterprises. In this regard, economic development preceded migration, the result of industrialists' aim to break with the synergy of small-scale craftsmen-owners and independent farmers.

The massive arrival of those immigrants—especially Italians, Poles, Russians and Hungarians—radically transformed the concept and composition of the American working class, who evolved from skilled craftsmen and independent owners to unskilled wage laborers dependent upon trade and labor unions for a voice in political processes and their own working conditions (Portes and Rumbaut 2014, 42–47). Increased automation technology in manufacturing served to perpetuate the sociological trend. By 1910, nearly half of the nation's laborers (excluding farming and mining) were

20 *The linguistic order of (post)modernity*

foreign-born, as were four of every ten service workers (48). In the discourse of nativists, in their majority the descendants of British, Irish, German, and Scandinavian immigrants of the prior generations, those workers became a threat to the socioeconomic, religious, and racial order of things. Once the industrialization process began to slow, the former increasingly viewed the latter as a source of competition rather than a means to make profit. But more importantly, the latter came to be perceived as a threat to the US political order.

Countering capitalist exploitation, labor union movements emerged along with the rise of left-wing politics and were met with violence by police forces. Like language, the police and military, which would increase significantly in the leadup to WWII, were crucial to maintaining the economic and political order. Workers' movements depended upon the leadership of educated first-generation immigrants who brought political experience with them from Europe, along with the US-born second generation. In mining and industrial towns, Finns were key organizers for the Socialist Party; Russian Jews and Slavs comprised a majority of the communist Workers' Party; and the membership of garment and clothing unions was largely constituted by Italians and eastern Europeans (Portes and Rumbaut 2014). Russian immigrants were prominent in the American socialist movement—in fact Leon Trotsky was in New York when Tsar Nicholas II abdicated; following the Russian Revolution, Russian affiliations to the American Socialist and Communist Parties grew stronger. Simultaneously, leading up to WWI, a growing Pan-German movement in Berlin forged ties with the German American Central Alliance in the US (Portes and Rumbaut 2014, 254). As we saw in the previous section, this relationship would cast the German language in gravely suspicious light as the political environment in Europe deteriorated. In terms of the immigrant population overall, the politically involved left-wing element was a minority, and many were generally apolitical. By 1916, in the face of growing organized resistance among the immigrant work force, manufacturers would begin to recruit impoverished southern US African Americans. Automobile makers such as Ford in Detroit would be among the industries that, through active recruitment, prompted the 'Great Migration' of poor southerners to the urban industrial centers of the North (1916–1970). Like manufacturers in the East, agricultural industrialists in the West looked southward for cheap labor, following the purposeful displacement of the Chinese and Japanese workforce. The 'pull' flow of Mexicans by agricultural capitalist demand in California and the Southwest was further accelerated by the decade-long Mexican Revolution that began in 1910. In the 1890s, the US Immigration and Naturalization Service documented about 1,000 Mexican immigrants; by the 1910s the number increased to 219,000; and then nearly half a million by the decade of the 1920s (Portes and Rumbaut 2014, 55–57).

Within this political context, amid anti-immigrant fervor in the US and intense clashes between left-wing movements and growing right-wing nationalism in Europe, Ferdinand de Saussure's *Cours de Linguistique Générale*

The linguistic order of (post)modernity 21

appeared. In this work posthumously published in 1916 with the collaboration of Saussure's students, based on lectures he gave at the University of Geneva from 1907 to 1911, it was argued that language is an autonomous structural system that exists in the minds of speakers; social collectivities or 'speech communities' provide the blueprint for the system. Within it, formal oppositions give meaning to the linguistic sign (e.g. the meaning of /b/ is determined in its opposition to other phonemes such as /p/ or /k/). As a bounded and self-contained system of structural oppositions of a purely mental nature, language could thus be analyzed in isolation from social context because linguistic signs "are realities that have their seat in the brain" (Saussure 2000b [1916], 24). Saussure referred to the system of signs as *langue*, which underlies *parole* as individual social practice—a dichotomy taken up by Noam Chomsky in his formulation of *competence* vs. *performance* some fifty years later. Just as Chomsky would affirm that only the universal biological phenomenon of *competence* is consequential to a scientific understanding of language, Saussure argued that the sole concern of linguistics should be the mental construct of *langue*, since it "alone seems to lend itself to independent definition and provide a fulcrum that satisfies the mind" (22). The psychological thought-sound connection of signifier and signified that comprised the sign could thus be interpreted as arbitrary in nature: "Language is a form and not a substance" (Saussure 2000a [1916], 112).

Crucially, Saussure's argument bestowed boundedness to language constructs and imposed a mental order on language—as the essential system for social organization—through the arbitrariness of the sign. Saussure's contemporaries in Russia viewed this position as a denial of the materiality of language—in Marxist terms, a bourgeois attempt to subvert the consciousness of the proletariat by stripping language of its inherently social, economic, and historical basis (Voloshinov 1973 [1929]). For the scholars of the Bakhtin Circle in Moscow, Saussure's *langue* was a subjectivist preemption of the social essence of what they considered 'unitary' language—"language not as a system of abstract grammatical categories, but rather language conceived as ideologically saturated" and as the product of "forces working toward concrete verbal and ideological unification and centralization, which develop in vital connection with the processes of sociopolitical and cultural centralization" (Bakhtin 2000 [1934], 271). From the Bakhtinian perspective, there was nothing arbitrary, abstract or exclusively mental about the nature of language. They likened Saussure's proposal to study language as form and not substance to the possibility of contemplating a biological organism with no life:

> Discourse lives... in a living impulse toward the object; if we detach ourselves completely from this impulse all we have left is the naked corpse of the word, from which we can learn nothing at all about the social situation or the fate of a given word in life. *To study the word as such, ignoring the impulse that reaches out beyond it, is just as senseless as to*

22　*The linguistic order of (post)modernity*

> *study psychological experience outside the context of that real life toward*
> *which it was directed and by which it is determined.*
>
> (Bakhtin 2000 [1934], 277, emphasis in the original)

In their philosophical difference of opinion regarding the nature of language, Saussure and Bakhtin posed three points of interest to us. First, they posited quite contradictory understandings of the notion of 'order' in language, and hence order in society. Saussure considered that speech, or *parole*, is variable and fragmentary, but language, or *langue*, is uniform and homogeneous: "Taken as a whole, speech is many-sided and heterogeneous… we cannot put it into any category of human facts, for we cannot discover its unity. Language, on the contrary, is a self-contained whole and a principle of classification. As soon as we give language first place among the facts of speech, we introduce a natural order into a mass that lends itself to no other classification" (Saussure 2000b [1916], 22). As such, language brings uniform order to the heterogeneous mass to create a bounded and autonomous "self-contained whole." Bakhtin, on the other hand, posited that both centrifugal (i.e. stratifying, pluralizing) and centripetal (i.e. normative, centralizing) forces comprise language: "Every concrete utterance of a speaking subject serves as a point where centrifugal as well as centripetal forces are brought to bear. The processes… intersect in the utterance…. It is possible to give a concrete and detailed analysis of any utterance, once having exposed it as a contradiction-ridden, tension-filled unity of two embattled tendencies in the life of language" (Bakhtin 2000 [1934], 271).

These essential differences bring us to the second point of interest, which is that Saussure's proposals aligned well not only with the rationalist logico-philosophical tradition of language studies that reemerged in the mid-nineteenth century in response to Romanticism, but also with the prevailing nation-language political ideology of the Western Europe of his day, especially with regard to the necessary link between science and the modern concept of progress. The notion of the sign was of general intellectual interest and widespread debate throughout the Western world during Saussure's time; in this respect, he echoed proposals that many of his contemporaries had been discussing for over three decades, including the sign's arbitrary nature (Seuren 2016). Evidently, the inspiration for Saussure's mentalist account of language was Hippolyte Taine, one of the most celebrated historians and positivist cultural critics of nineteenth-century France (Aarsleff 1982; Seuren 2016). During the early years of the Third French Republic, Taine's historical account of the Paris Commune uprising in 1871 had a profound influence on the emergent science of crowd psychology or 'mass behavior,' which aimed at allaying the fears of the middle class regarding the violent upheavals of the lower class (Barrows 1981); the events of the Commune itself influenced the ideas of Karl Marx. The importance Taine placed on the rise of science as key to democratic modern nation-states was linked to what he saw as the necessary repurposing of the role of the upper classes. In 1877 Taine wrote in

The linguistic order of (post)modernity   23

personal correspondence the following: "I see only one function for the upper class in modern democracy: excluded from political command, it can become a secular clergy, a scientific adviser of a higher and independent kind; I see no other future for a man of good family and wealth, than the cultivation of a science, especially a moral science" (cited in Jones 1999, 92).

One might thus conclude, as did Jones (1999), that Taine "was interested in using the spiritual power of science to shore up the social importance of inherited wealth, now that it had been driven out of politics.... His chief hope lay not in a counter-revolutionary political project... but in an alliance of brains and birth" (92). In this regard, Taine's views on countering the 'excesses of democracy,' i.e. rule by the common masses, through an alliance of traditional social institutions and scientific intellect driven by the elite were especially appealing to right-wing conservatives (Jones 1999). One can venture that Saussure, from an aristocratic family of scientific intellectuals in Geneva, would have most likely identified with this view: his great-grandfather was a renowned geologist and botanist; his grandfather was a notable chemist; his father was an entomologist; and his younger brother was a mathematician (Seuren 2016).

Thus, one could suppose that Saussure's ideological approach to language and linguistics was tied to Taine's regard for the scientific intellectual paradigm within the political environment of their time. By privileging *langue* and in turn defining it from a mechanistic perspective on the human mind—language as form rather than substance, a self-contained whole that is uniform and homogeneous—Saussure also, albeit perhaps unintentionally, projected the imperative of bounded nation-state forms within which *langue* resides. Indeed, in his argument regarding 'legitimate language' decades later, Bourdieu (1991) would interpret Saussure's mental construct precisely as the sort of political privileging of social class that Taine had espoused. Bourdieu wrote:

> Saussure's *langue*... has in fact all the properties commonly attributed to official language. As opposed to dialect, it has benefited from the institutional conditions necessary for its generalized codification and imposition. Thus known and recognized (more or less completely) throughout the whole jurisdiction of a certain political authority, it helps in turn to reinforce the authority which is the source of its dominance.... To speak of *the* language, as linguists do, is tacitly to accept the *official* definition of the *official* language of a political unit.
>
> (1991, 44–45)

One must not think for too long to encounter compelling evidence to support Bourdieu's argument. The notions of phoneme and allophone (corresponding to *langue* and *parole*, respectively) reveal the official character—and written mode—of the overarching phoneme, e.g. in Spanish /s/ serves as phoneme while [h] serves as dialectal allophone. One could suppose that had [h] come to be regarded as the standard or 'legitimate' realization of the grapheme *s*

24   *The linguistic order of (post)modernity*

in syllable- and word-final position in the evolution of Spanish, /h/ would have been designated as phoneme in the Saussurean order of things, and [s] a dialectal allophone. Of course, in such case, the grapheme would have likely evolved into *h* as well.

On the other hand, the notions of tension and struggle inherent in Bakhtin's proposals—suppressed in Russia during his lifetime and unknown in the West until later in the century—resonated with Russian populism, aimed at blocking the advance of capitalism and eradicating classism (Brandist 2000, 72). Bakhtin explicitly recognized the essential nature of the 'unitary language' in what he calls the verbal-ideological life of the nation, but he emphasized that "actual social life and historical becoming create within an abstractly unitary national language a multitude of concrete worlds, a multitude of bounded verbal-ideological and social belief systems" (2000 [1934], 274). His views on intertextuality, heteroglossia, and polyglossia reflect the circumstances of his life trajectory. He acquired both Russian and German as a child, and as an adolescent he lived in Vilnius where Lithuanian, Polish, Yiddish, and Hebrew were widely spoken, in addition to official Russian. He also lived in Odessa, a multicultural and multilingual port city on the Black Sea that was a vital enclave for eastern European Jews (Holquist 2002, 1). In the tumult that ensued after the October Revolution in 1917, Bakthin moved to the countryside, where he became involved with a small group of young intellectuals who debated the cultural and political issues of the moment and discussed Kant's philosophy—hence his effort to synthesize or reconcile the 'inside' and 'outside' worlds through dialogism. The discussions of this so-called Bakhtin Circle took place both privately and publicly, organized by the local committee of the Communist Party (Holquist 2002, 3–4). Bakhtin's most definitive influences were the neo-Kantian philosophers Hermann Cohen and Matvaei Isaevich Kagan, his close friend, who was a mathematician by training. Bakhtin took great interest in mathematics, physiology, and physics, including the proposals of his contemporary Albert Einstein. This interest likely explains his concerted attempt to relate matter to mind, or body to spirit (Holquist 2002, 6). In 1924, he returned to Leningrad, where over the next five years he authored several of the works that would garner him recognition during the years just before his death in 1975.

Bakhtin's 1920s works, including *Marxism and the Philosophy of Language* (1973 [1929], published under Valentin Voloshinov), dealt more specifically with how traditional disciplines—linguistics among them—would relate to communist practice. His stance regarding the necessity to account for plurality and otherness in *Problems of Dostoevsky's Poetics* (Bakhtin 1984 [1929]) can be interpreted as an admonishment of growing authoritarianism and cultural homogeneity under Stalin. These works led to his arrest and subsequent exile in Kazakhstan in 1929, in Stalin's coming purge of Russian intellectuals (Holquist 2002, 8–9). Clearly, then, Bakhtin's arguments were developed in relation to Marxist theory and the intellectual debates of the

The linguistic order of (post)modernity 25

communist revolution under Lenin. The Bakhtin Circle engaged explicitly with Saussure's *Cours*.

By highlighting these matters of political environment, I am in no way suggesting that Saussure and Bakhtin's views on language somehow influenced intellectual or political life at the time, much less the ideological conflicts that led to WWII. Nor am I insinuating that either sought to advance a contemporary political agenda in his respective context. Indeed, neither one's work was much known or discussed until later in the century. Rather, I pose their ideas as intellectual orientations that reflect the stark contrast of prevailing ideological currents of the early twentieth century with respect to political order, language, and nation. This brings us to the third point of necessary interest to us. Despite having been relatively unknown and little published during their lifetimes (though Bakhtin did begin to acquire some degree of fame in the last decade of his life), both men would go on to become two of the most influential figures of cultural, linguistic, and literary studies later in the century. Bakhtin's concepts of dialogism, voicing, chronotopes, heteroglossia, genres, and the carnivalesque are among the most influential and widely cited in literary and cultural studies, influencing the work of Julia Kristeva and Tzvetan Todorov. Saussure never achieved academic notoriety in his lifetime, but his *Cours* would become what many regard as the twentieth century's most influential treatise on linguistics, providing the theoretical basis of structuralism. His proposals constitute the starting point for the work of some of the later twentieth century's most illustrious intellectuals: Roman Jakobson, Roland Barthes, Michel Foucault, Jacques Derrida, Claude Levi-Strauss, Jacques Lacan, and Judith Butler, among others. Importantly, Saussure's view provided an ordered account of language, and hence societal order, that must have had great ideological appeal for those who were opposed to—or were even merely apprehensive of—the growing radical liberalism of his day, however unintended.

Here we might recall the contemporary linguistic views of both Cuervo and Espinosa regarding the continuity of Peninsular Spanish in the Americas in relation to their conservative political orientations and concerns about tradition and societal order in the face of radical liberalism. Although Cuervo and Espinosa contemplated principally the diachronic dimensions of language while Saussure shifted the focus to *synchronie*, they all advocated for scientific method in linguistics, addressed questions of continuity and order, and shared similar right-leaning ideological orientations. As already noted, Hispanism in the Americas was generally associated with political conservativism.

In the US, the interdisciplinary paradigm of what would ultimately be called Latin American Studies began to coalesce among historians and Spanish language and literature scholars early in the twentieth century. By the mid-1930s, a Committee on Latin American Studies was convened, and the first volume of the *Handbook of Latin American Studies* was published. Enthusiasm for the field grew throughout the 1930s in response to President

26 The linguistic order of (post)modernity

Franklin D. Roosevelt's Good Neighbor Policy, the popularity of Pan-Americanism, and the ongoing crisis in Europe. In conjunction with the Office of Coordinator of Inter-American Affairs (CIAA), a federal agency that generously funded academic programs related to Latin American Studies, Hollywood's Production Code Administration was charged with presenting Latin Americans in a favorable light. Filmmakers should integrate Latin American themes and settings in film, project images of large modern cities, and ensure linguistic 'authenticity' (Rodríguez 2004; Adams 2007). The policy was also economically motivated, since Hollywood had to look increasingly toward Latin America during the 1930s as European markets fell under Nazi control (Adams 2007). Indeed, one of the key functions of the CIAA was to counter German and Italian fascist propaganda in Latin America. Soon, however, with the German Blitz of London in late 1940 and the Japanese bombing of Pearl Harbor in December of 1941, national focus turned toward Europe and the Pacific as concern for Latin America waned.

With the attack on Pearl Harbor, Japanese Americans fell under suspicion. In February of 1942, President Franklin D. Roosevelt signed an executive order that led to the relocation of some 120,000 Japanese Americans to designated concentration camps. As McWilliams (1990) observed, "it was a foregone conclusion that Mexicans would be substituted as the major scapegoat once the Japanese were removed" (181). Throughout the 1930s, the federal government had forcibly deported Mexicans in large numbers, and others returned to Mexico voluntarily given the hostile social and political environment of the Great Depression. From 1929 to 1935, according to the Immigration and Naturalization Service, about 82,000 Mexicans were formally removed from the US, some through voluntary proceedings (US Citizenship and Immigration Services n.d.). However, the number reported in 1936 by the US Consulate General in Mexico City for the years 1930–1935 was much higher: 345,839. Other historical estimates place the figure higher still (Koch 2006). The official website of US Citizenship and Immigration Services states that "in 1930, as the extent of the Depression became more clear, some Americans accused Mexicans, as well as other aliens, of holding jobs needed by U.S. citizens." McWilliams (1990) offers a detailed insiders' account of the targeting of the Mexican-origin population in Los Angeles by the mass media, police force, and judicial system leading up to the Sleepy Lagoon Case in 1942 and the Zoot Suit Riots in 1943. In the former case, several members of a committee that had worked to free a group of nine young Mexican American men wrongly convicted of murder were subpoenaed by the Committee on Un-American Activities in California, accused of having "communistic inclinations" (McWilliams 1990, 185–186). The basis of the riots in June of 1943 was also racial and political. Zoot suits originated among African Americans in Harlem but later became associated with 'pachuco' urban forms of dress and creative Spanish-language use among young Mexican Americans in the Southwest during the 1930s. The pachuco speech phenomenon, referred to as *caló*, was popularized in films featuring Germán Valdés, also known as

The linguistic order of (post)modernity 27

Tin Tan. Because *pachuquismo* became symbolic of resistance to mainstream Anglo-American culture, zoot suit wearers were targeted during several days of attacks following a physical confrontation with uniformed sailors in Los Angeles. Just twelve days after the Zoot Suit Riots in Los Angeles, a race riot erupted in Detroit largely as a result of social tensions provoked by wartime austerity measures and a housing shortage following the Great Migration, which had brought hundreds of thousands of Black and White southerners to the city.[2] Already established European-origin immigrants and a growing Ku Klux Klan presence exacerbated the tensions.

These political and racial confrontations of the 1940s reflect the linguistic order that had already emerged in the late nineteenth century. In the decades following the US Civil War, standard English (i.e. the variety prevalent among educated northern Whites) would become positioned not only as the gatekeeper of racial and socioeconomic privilege but also as the exclusive vehicle for capitalist industrialism and the purveyor of Western-style democracy. Silence was the only other viable linguistic option within this order. Indeed, during WWII, silence was advocated by the US government in a public poster campaign of the War Advertising Council with slogans such as "Silence means security" and "Loose lips might sink ships," a phrase that eventually became a popular saying. All other languages within this order, with the possible exception of French, were either inconsequential or regarded as threats or potential threats to the Western capitalist order.

Though US government interest in Latin America had waned during WWII, the interdisciplinary model of Latin American Studies ultimately proved integral to the mission of Area Studies programs that would proliferate afterward, in the interest of national security (Morton 1963). Most of those programs were concerned with Asia, the Soviet Union, and tension zones. There was general disinterest in Latin American Studies throughout the 1950s (Cline 1966), though US economic interests in the region remained active. For example, the US government began to fund the training of Chilean economists at the University of Chicago during the 1950s in an effort to counter left-wing tendencies; the efforts would come to fruition with the US-backed dictatorship of Augusto Pinochet during the 1970s (Harvey 2005, 8). With Fidel Castro's takeover of the Cuban government in 1959, "government and private organizations were moved to inventory the disarray in the hemisphere, to rediscover the area as a seething laboratory of rapid social change, whose possible loss to the Free World imperiled national security" (Cline 1966, 64). Once Castro's alliance with the Soviet Union formed, the topic of national security in relation to the Spanish language emerged. With the solidification of the Communist Bloc, Castro's rise to power, and the appearance of leftist political movements in Central and South America, the linguistic order maintained Spanish defensively outside US national boundaries. As McWilliams affirmed, the "fear, or near hysteria" of a communist takeover in Central America, which could potentially spread to Mexico and spill into the US, determined government policy toward Latin America throughout

28 *The linguistic order of (post)modernity*

the 1980s (1990, 333). Expressly because of this fear, the US established the notorious School of the Americas in the Panama Canal Zone in 1946, which remained active until 1984. Things would not change until the fall of the Berlin Wall in 1989, the ultimate effect of President Ronald Reagan's friendship with Soviet leader Mikhail Gorbachev. The reunification of Berlin and the collapse of the Communist Bloc brought significant changes to the political and economic world order. For many, this moment is symbolic of the start of postmodernity.

Language in postmodernity

Like other epochs in the written history of Western humanity—antiquity, the medieval era, the early modern period, and modernity—what some have begun to refer to as postmodernity will only be characteristically defined and understood in retrospect, many years into the future. Even in hindsight, the distinctive character of epochs is discernible only in the sense of a broad temporal span, i.e. there is no singular moment when the Middle Ages or the Renaissance 'began' or 'ended.' Rather, a series of occurrences, works, and social or political transformations over many years serve to mark the end of one epoch and the beginning of another. The same will necessarily be true of postmodernity. From our present viewpoint, there is some consensus that modernity—especially in its characteristic terms of nation-state formation and authority, industrialization, and scientific discourse of linear 'progress'—has begun to cede to a different order of things, especially in relation to capitalism (Jameson 1991).

Although some argue that there is no convincing indication that modernity is ending, i.e. rather, we are living in a radicalized 'late modernity' (Giddens 1990), 'liquid modernity' (Bauman 2000), or 'multiple modernities' shaped by increasing economic disparity (Geyer and Bright 1995), others—whose ideas are described in this section—suggest that we are witness to the incipient stages of a shift. That shift is evident in various phenomena that intersect and overlap: the increasing transcendence of nation-state entities by international organizations, NGOs, and multinational corporations; the rise of economic neoliberalism worldwide; consumerism on a global scale; the de-industrialization of the so-called 'First World,' leading to postindustrial societies with principally service- and information-centered or knowledge-based economies; the rapid proliferation of information and communication technologies (ICTs) and mass media flows that transcend local and national spaces; the perceptive overlay of local and national consciousness with a transnational or global consciousness created by ICTs, mass media, cyberspace, and accessible modes of rapid transportation; and concomitantly, cultural globalization. The latter is not to be understood simply as cultural homogenization or 'Americanization,' but as a complex interplay of global forces and local practices, allegiances to locality through the lens of globality, or the

The linguistic order of (post)modernity 29

presence of both universalizing and particularizing tendencies that some dub 'glocalization' (Robertson 1992).

If postmodernity is the confluence of all these phenomena, it is impossible to determine a particular moment of its origin. It could arguably emerge in the outcome of WWII, as the stratifying forces of industrial capitalism and the growing tensions between left- and right-wing ideologies culminated in a standoff of superpowers that divided the globe. One might also consider that the standoff of US-style capitalism and Soviet-style communism from the 1950s to the 1980s introduced several of the scientific and cultural phenomena that would be key to postmodernity. Those decades were characterized by the proliferation of nuclear weapons that could trespass national boundaries (from long distances in short amounts of time), outer space exploration, the vogue of futurism and minimalism, and the advent of television and computers. The ultimate triumph of capitalism over communism was symbolized by the fall of the Berlin Wall in 1989, followed by the disintegration of the Soviet Union and the acceleration of economic reform in China. Optionally, one could conjecture that the September 11, 2001 terror attacks symbolically mark the beginning of postmodernity. For Jean Baudrillard, that beginning happened with the collapse of the Twin Towers, televised around the world. Baudrillard reasoned:

All Manhattan's tall buildings had been content to confront each other in a competitive verticality, and the product of this was an architectural panorama reflecting the capitalist system itself. That image changed after 1973, with the building of the World Trade Center.... This architectural graphism is the embodiment of a system that is no longer competitive, but digital and countable, and from which competition has disappeared in favour of networks and monopoly.... The fact that there were two of them signifies the end of any original reference. If there had only been one, monopoly would not have been perfectly embodied. Only the doubling of the sign truly puts an end to what it designates.... They were not of the same breed as the other buildings. They culminated in the exact reflection of each other.... The collapse of the towers—itself a unique event in the history of modern cities—prefigures a kind of dramatic ending and, all in all, disappearance both of this form of architecture and the world system which it embodies.

(2002, 38–41)

Hutcheon (2006) observed that the term 'postmodern' came into currency in the field of architecture during the 1970s in works that were "doubly coded," i.e. new and modern(ist) yet at the same time historical, perhaps in parodic or ironic ways: "These hybrid buildings self-consciously took advantage of all the technical advances of modernist architecture, but their historical echoes of earlier traditions challenged the anti-historical emphasis on purity of form

30 *The linguistic order of (post)modernity*

alone that had resulted in those familiar stark, undecorated skyscrapers typical of what was called modernism's International Style" (115).

Just following the construction of the Twin Towers, Jean-François Lyotard published *The Postmodern Condition: A Report on Knowledge* (1984, French original 1979), considered by many as the first important epistemological treatise on postmodernity. Describing the encroaching functions of computerization in the construction of knowledge, Lyotard emphasized the imminent shift to a postindustrial, knowledge-based economy, i.e. from the so-called Industrial Age to the Information Age (Castells 2010). In this transformation, language—and in Lyotard's terms 'language games' inspired by the philosophy of Ludwig Wittgenstein—would take on a more crucial role than ever before in human history. Lyotard's (1984) main argument was that the 'grand narratives' of modernity were no longer credible, and had ceded to an array of *petit récits,* or little narratives. The teleological narratives of science and progress were of main concern to him. According to Lyotard, the Enlightenment project and modern nation-state concept based on the universalist discourse of rationality, unity and equality had proven unpromising. Both world wars and the ensuing Cold War were evidence that the scientific, industrialist notion of 'progress' had in some ways been disastrous. The rise of totalitarian regimes, exploitation of workers, and gross abuses of human rights—of which the Holocaust provided appalling evidence—had led to profound skepticism regarding modernity's democratic, capitalistic model. The linearity of modernity's metanarrative of 'development' began to cede to a more nonlinear and fragmentary account of social inequality and economic disparity.

During the late 1960s, amid growing rates of inflation and economic instability (Harvey 2005), the little narratives of disenfranchised sectors of Western society would move to the foreground of public discourse: in the US, racism and the civil rights movement, sexism and the feminist movement, the gay and lesbian rights movement following the Stonewall Riots, and the Chicano movement that decried racial and linguistic discrimination as well as the ongoing exploitation of migrant farm workers; in Mexico and Brazil, massive student demonstrations against authoritarianism; in Canada, the Quiet Revolution; in France, the May of 1968 protests; in the former Czechoslovakia, the Prague Spring of 1968; and in Northern Ireland, the civil rights movement; among others. These social and political facts were, for Lyotard, the basis of his simple definition of the postmodern condition: incredulity toward metanarratives. The skepticism of postmodernity, from an epistemological perspective, stemmed from profound doubt or even disbelief in the universal truth of the scientific rationalism of the Enlightenment project and the principled progress of the modern democratic industrial nation-state model, e.g. the US, France, and Great Britain. An emergent emphasis on *petit récits* that exposed the diversity of human experience and the relativity of truth for diverse sectors of humanity was, according to Lyotard, the key characteristic of the postmodern worldview. The relativity

The linguistic order of (post)modernity 31

of knowledge, meaning, and truth had already been painstakingly interpreted in Foucault's *The Order of Things* (1994, French original 1966) and Derrida's *Of Grammatology* (1976, French original 1967).

One might argue, however, that an incredulity toward metanarratives is symptomatic of modernity in its 'late' stages, or even that the metanarratives of modernity are gradually displaced by other metanarratives proper to postmodernity. Trainor (1998) suggested that the postmodern reflects a sort of return to medievalism. First, he maintained that postmodern environmentalism is a rebirth of medievalism's organizing principle of nature (as explained in Foucault 1994). While modernity invokes a narrative based upon mastery or subjugation of nature through technology and scientific progress, postmodernity reclaims the fundamental importance of nature through the narrative of environmentalism. The mainstream narrative about climate change, which emerged during the 1980s and 1990s parallel to economic globalization, stands to reorient the framework of history by undoing the modernist distinction between nature and humanity, i.e. 'man against nature' (Chakrabarty 2009).

Second, Trainor (1998) observed that growing allegiance to local communities is a postmodern return to the medieval order of feudalism, or what he calls a new medievalism, by which the nation-state is viewed as an impediment to the flow of the universal (i.e. global) into the particular (i.e. local): "At the present time 'nationhood' and 'being a people' seem to be drifting apart; the former is no longer regarded as being a prerequisite for the latter.... The nations and regional assemblies of Europe are beginning to look increasingly like the duchies and baronies of feudal Europe" (140). The contemporary cases of Scotland, Catalonia, and Northern Italy provide compelling examples. Even in the case of the US, where the notion of sovereignty has very different roots than in Europe, ever fewer people regard the 'nation' as the indispensable institution or ultimate expression of the sense of 'being a people' (Trainor 1998, 141). Data from the widely cited Harvard Youth Poll clearly reflect this trend: in 2001, following the events of 9/11, 89% of college students aged 18–24 called themselves "patriotic"; that figure dropped to 63% in the 2020 survey. Only about half of all those surveyed, both Republicans and Democrats, indicated that they supported "patriotism" (Harvard Youth Poll, Spring 2020). Trainor concluded that there is "in each of the industrial, liberal democracies of the world, an emerging sense of being 'parts' of a universal 'whole'.... This consciousness of living in a world which subsists within, and is enveloped by, ever wider worlds can... be best characterised and described as a 'modern medievalist' (or 'postmodernist') consciousness" (1998, 141).

In this section, I explain how a postmodern account of the situation of Spanish in Miami seems fitting. But first, I engage on a theoretical level with two defining features of postmodernity: neoliberalism and consumerism. I then consider the pervasive influence of imagery and the cultural imaginary in postmodern social reality, following Appadurai (1996): "The world we live

32 *The linguistic order of (post)modernity*

in today is characterized by a new role for the imagination in social life" (31). All three of these phenomena are consequential to the way in which language is conceptualized and, in some regards, put into practice. I believe that all are highly relevant to the changing situation of Spanish in the US and crucial to understanding the sociolinguistic reality of Miami.

Economic neoliberalism

In 1974, Friedrich Hayek won the Nobel Prize in Economic Sciences for his work on the fundamental importance of a decentralized market system. The crux of Hayek's argument in his bestseller *The Road to Serfdom* (1944) was that centralized state planning was detrimental to economic prosperity, i.e. markets should not be government-regulated but rather be given free rein to regulate themselves through principles of supply and demand. Such was the basis of 'liberty' in Hayek's (1960) view, limiting the role of government to the mere provision of a legal framework within which market enterprise should operate freely. As a native Austrian who experienced the turmoil of both world wars, Hayek regarded the situations of early twentieth-century Germany and the Soviet Union as evidence of the dangers of economies that placed too much decision-making power in the hands of government officials. Hayek felt that markets should hold that power, independent of whether society was governed by democratically elected officials or by a dictator. One example of the latter is the implementation of a free market economy in Chile under Augusto Pinochet, who had personal ties to Hayek and to the University of Chicago, where Hayek was a professor (Valdés 1995). Backed by the US, Pinochet's authoritarian regime conducted a radical privatization experiment in Chile during the 1970s that would anticipate the expansion of economic liberalization projects throughout the continent in the following decade. Pinochet's economists, referred to as the 'Chicago Boys,' were "seen as part of an international movement and, at the same time, as people offering new and distinct ideas superior to those of politicians and economists in the past" (Valdés 1995, 36). That movement gained impetus by the early 1980s with the liberal economic order enacted by Ronald Reagan in the US and Margaret Thatcher in Great Britain, both of whom held Hayek's proposals in high regard.

Reaganomics and Thatcherism came on the heels of Deng Xiaoping's move to liberalize the Chinese economy in 1978. From these three 'epicenters'—the US, Great Britain, and China—economic liberalization quickly expanded across the world as free markets emerged on a global scale, a phenomenon that soon came to be referred to as 'globalization' and 'neoliberalism' (Harvey 2005). The neoliberal order became the hegemonic global order by the new millennium, according to Harvey (2005), with "pervasive effects on ways of thought to the point where it has become incorporated into the common-sense way many of us interpret, live in, and understand the world" (3). In its translation of social good and human action as matters of the market,

The linguistic order of (post)modernity 33

neoliberalism drove the demand for ICTs capable of superseding local and national levels and thus displacing the institutional structures of modern governments (Harvey 2005, 3). The latter has produced what Brown (2015) considers one of four deleterious effects of neoliberalism on democracy: the ever-growing intimacy of corporate and finance capital with the state (28–30). The other three are intensified socioeconomic inequality (noted already in the Chilean case by the late 1970s), unethical commercialization (e.g. the growing corporatization of education and public infrastructure), and economic volatility due to the market fluctuations of finance capital (e.g. the 2008–2009 recession).

Brown (2015) echoed prior assertions by Harvey (2005) and Fisher (2009) about the pervasive nature of neoliberal economic rationality in all realms of human activity:

> Deregulation of industries and capital flows; radical reduction in welfare state provisions and protections for the vulnerable; privatized and outsourced public goods, ranging from education, parks, postal services, roads, and social welfare to prisons and militaries; replacement of progressive with regressive tax and tariff schemes; the end of wealth distribution as an economic or sociopolitical policy; the conversion of every human need or desire into a profitable enterprise, from college admissions preparation to human organ transplants, from baby adoptions to pollution rights, from avoiding lines to securing legroom on an airplane; and, most recently, the financialization of everything and the increasing dominance of finance capital over productive capital in the dynamics of the economy and everyday life.
>
> (Brown 2015, 28)

This trend, Brown argued, has reconfigured human beings as market actors, "always, only, and everywhere *homo oeconomicus*" (31). It is important to note that in what Brown characterized as the economization of humanity and society, profit is not the *sine qua non* of neoliberalism. There is also what we might call a marketization aspect that is principally discursive, a world in which every aspect of life—including social life and personal identity—is leveraged like assets. 'Likes' on Facebook are one obvious example. Brown affirmed that "human capital's constant and ubiquitous aim… is to entrepreneurialize its endeavors, appreciate its value, and increase its rating or ranking" (36).

Like everything else, language is reconceptualized in neoliberalist discourse. It goes from being thought of principally as a national or ethnic identity phenomenon during most of the nineteenth and twentieth centuries to being regarded also as an asset or imagined social marketplace phenomenon by the 1990s. This shift of ideological paradigm drove an exponential growth in the numbers of Spanish language learners during the 1980s and 1990s (Looney and Lusin, 2019), i.e. knowing Spanish will improve one's employment prospects because it is 'useful' in the marketplace sense of exchange

34   *The linguistic order of (post)modernity*

and competition. This is not the way that most students of Spanish in the 1950s and 1960s conceptualized their motivation for learning the language. Some have referred to this phenomenon as 'commodification' of language (Heller 2007; Del Valle 2007). But following Brown's argument carefully, the objective of commodification, or thinking in terms of commodities, is profitability. Speaking or knowing a language is not really so much about making money. It could be if one is actually paid more on the job for being multilingual, but that does not usually happen in most occupational fields in the US (Porras, Ee, and Gándara 2014, 246). Rather, speaking or knowing a language is thought of more as an asset (Coulmas 1992), an aspect of human capital that increases one's rating, ranking, or social worth. As Baudrillard (1988) affirmed in *The Consumer Society*, "In the same sense that labor power is no longer connected to, and even denies, the relation of the worker to the product of his labor, so exchange value is no longer related to concrete and personal exchange, nor the commodity form to actual goods, etc." (42).

Arguably, the idea that Spanish is 'useful' in the US relies more upon the asset value that one attributes to the language rather than its real utility. We can think of countless millions of native Anglophones in the US who choose to learn Spanish as a second language because they perceive it as useful or even potentially necessary (typically in work-related settings) yet who will never use the language—much less need to use it—in any meaningful or profitable way. There are also countless millions of native Spanish-English bilinguals who are functionally proficient in both languages yet choose not to speak Spanish in settings where they could. Neither of these important segments of the population (US Anglophone L2 Spanish speakers and US Spanish-English bilinguals) is motivated by a principle of utility per se but rather by a system of values that is articulated through the ideological guise of utility, i.e. "I need to speak Spanish / I don't need to speak Spanish." Ideologies of language naturalize this utilitarian discourse—ideologies which essentially manifest the 'othering' of Spanish in sometimes insidious ways. A proverbial double-edged sword becomes apparent: on one hand, Spanish appears to benefit ideologically from its construed market value in the neoliberal economic order of postmodernity but, on the other hand, the economization of the language has been concomitant with detachment from personhood and repoliticization: "Inclusion inverts into competition, equality into inequality, freedom into deregulated marketplaces, and popular sovereignty is nowhere to be found…. In their newly economized form, neoliberal states will shed as much as possible the cost of developing and reproducing human capital" (Brown 2015, 42). Hence Spanish in the US becomes an ideological matter of consumerism or, in Harvey's (2005) words regarding the motivation behind neoliberalism, "a political project to re-establish the conditions for capital accumulation and to restore the power of the economic elites" (19).

With the economic downturn of the 1970s, as interest rates fell and profit margins dwindled, the upper classes began to advocate for neoliberal policies based on what they viewed as an early success of Pinochet's Chilean experiment. Prior to WWII, the top 1% of earners claimed 16% of the US national income; by the end of the war, their share dropped to 8% and remained steady at that same rate into the 1970s (Harvey 2005, 15). Advocacy for neoliberalism was in part a response to the apparent failure not just of communism but also of Keynesian capitalism or the practices of 'embedded liberalism' in the US and dirigisme in France in the 1950s and 1960s, leading to 'stagflation' in the 1970s. By the new millennium, after two decades of neoliberal reform, the top 1% claimed 15% of national income; in 1970 the ratio of the median compensation of workers to CEOs was 30 to 1, increasing to nearly 500 to 1 by the year 2000 (Harvey 2005, 16). The loss of jobs to new technologies and the relocation of large sectors of the manufacturing industry overseas not only stunted the growth of the US middle class but also served to foment contemporary political narratives of xenophobia and nationalism (Tankersley 2020). This is the moment when, according to Fisher in *Capitalist Realism* (2009), capitalism must turn inward, no longer driven by the pressure to absorb externality that it had faced in the wake of the collapse of the Communist Bloc. How was the expansionist ideological mechanism of capitalism sustainable once there was no longer an outside to appropriate?

Within the US, the answer came, at least in part, in the creation of so-called niche markets, perhaps the most vital one being the Hispanic market. Mora (2014) argued that the pan-ethnic identity concept of 'Hispanic' was the product of cross-field effects between the US Census Bureau, social movements (e.g. National Council of La Raza), and media markets at the end of the twentieth century. Arguably, the presence of Hispanics—and concomitantly Spanish language—in the US was not just the result of mass immigration from Mexico, the Caribbean, and various other countries of Latin America during the last two decades of the twentieth century. Demographic facts do not represent proximate causes for the so-called boom of Spanish north of Mexico. Even the most carefree perusal of historical account reveals the substantial presence and importance of Spanish in the US since the nation's inception. Spanish was always already there. Rather, the demographic presence of Spanish speakers would begin to translate into the ideological importance of Spanish in the US because the time was right both economically and—because it served economic ends—politically.

One garners a sense of history repeating itself when considering the phenomenological parallelism of the 1920s/1990s and 1930s/2000s, periods when prosperity and a Latin cultural 'boom' were subsequently fractured by grave economic and political crises in which explicit Hispanophobia grew rampant. During the decade of the 1990s, a so-called 'Latin fever' swept the US: Ricky Martin, Enrique Iglesias, and Shakira topped the Billboard charts with songs partially or completely in Spanish; Jennifer Lopez rose to stardom with her Hollywood portrayal of popular Tex-Mex singer Selena, whose death was publicly mourned by millions in the US and Mexico; salsa outsold ketchup in US supermarkets for the first time in the nation's history; and Spanish language programs at schools, colleges, and institutions of higher learning across

36 *The linguistic order of (post)modernity*

the country expanded significantly. Jennifer Lopez was not the first Latina superstar, but rather Dolores del Río, who rose to Hollywood stardom during the early days of silent film in the 1920s. As I noted earlier, rather predictably, Del Río's appeal to producers and audiences quickly waned when her 'foreign'-accented English could be heard in talkies, within the context of the Great Depression. The career of Ramón Novarro, who was receiving 1,300 fan letters per week and earning roughly a million dollars a year in 1923, met a similar fate, along with Antonio Moreno, Lupe Vélez, and numerous others; by 1937, Novarro had lost imminence in Hollywood (Rodríguez 2004). The professional outcome of these prominent public personalities underscores the great vitality of the linguistic dimension of cultural imaginaries, and the primordial role that Spanish language and Hispanic-accented English play in the projection of Latinidad in the US context (Lippi-Green 1997). Both Novarro and Vélez were what we today consider heritage speakers of Spanish, having arrived in the US from Mexico at the ages of 14 and 13, respectively. As much as Hispanic-accented English became a liability for so many early Hollywood actors during the 1930s, it is equally true that, nearly six decades later, the lack of Spanish-language fluency was in some ways perceived as a liability for both Selena and Jennifer Lopez in their early days of fame (Aparicio 2003).

Clearly, something changed ideologically from the 1930s to the 1990s. First, communism no longer posed a real threat to the political-economic order. During the 1910s and 1920s, even despite economic prosperity and the cultural vogue of Hispanophilia, the Spanish language never attained any degree of legitimacy in US public life not just because of modernity's one nation–one language imperative or the political turmoil of WWI, but also because of the leftist threat linked to the use of non-English languages (Portes and Rumbaut, 2014). By the early 1980s, it seemed inevitable that the Berlin Wall would soon come down and China would pursue liberal economic reform. The Mariel crisis of 1980 provided further evidence that socialism had led to widespread discontent in Cuba. Operation Condor had eliminated the immediate possibility of leftist regimes in the Southern Cone by the late 1970s. Right-of-center governments were also firmly in control in the Dominican Republic and Mexico, and the US was actively intervening in military campaigns to quell leftist movements in Central America at the time—campaigns that produced gross abuses of human rights and led to the deaths of countless thousands (Chomsky 2015). The collapse of the Communist Bloc provided assurance that capitalism would prevail across the globe into the 1990s. Upon the eve of the new millennium, it was apparent that the US was "no longer the puppeteer of a world system of images but only one node of a complex transnational construction of imaginary landscapes" (Appadurai 1996, 31).

Second, there was a need for new markets. Baudrillard (1988) described the moment in the later twentieth century when the Western capitalist enterprise was confronted with market saturation, i.e. productivity outpaced product disposability. At that juncture, it became necessary not just to make products and market them, but to fabricate a consumer demand for those products by

The linguistic order of (post)modernity 37

conditioning and controlling market behavior: "It is clear that the whole economic and psychosociological apparatus of market and motivation research, which pretends to uncover the underlying needs of the consumer and the real demand prevailing in the market, exists only to generate a demand for further market opportunities. And it continuously masks this objective by staging its opposite" (39). In short, for Baudrillard, late capitalism shifts the focus away from production and onto consumption, i.e. consumption becomes the main protagonist and the market is the arena for its staging. Following this reasoning, we better understand the motives for staging the Hispanic market in the US during the 1980s and into the 1990s, and the scripting of the Spanish language as an essential feature of that market.

Finally, late capitalism was driving economic tertiarization, of which language is a key commodity (Heller and Duchêne 2012). Simply stated, in the workings of neoliberalism, the Spanish language in the US became ideologically relevant, necessary, and useful for the economic elite. Such a utilitarian, market-oriented view of Spanish actually emerged in relation to free market enterprise and a boom of Spanish language enrollments in the early twentieth century (Dulfano and Rubio 2014), as noted in the previous section. *New York Times* headlines during that time were illustrative: "European War Opens South America's Big Market to the US" (August 23, 1914); "Study of Spanish Making Big Gains: Now Leads All Other Languages in New York High Schools" (October 6, 1918); "Business Needs Extend the Study of Spanish" (June 14, 1925) (cited in Dulfano and Rubio 2014, 142). Of course, the liberal economic policies of the 1910s and 1920s would lead to the Wall Street Crash of 1929. But the political landscape was not rife for the recognition of Spanish in economic life, i.e. communism remained a clear and present ideological danger. By the 1990s, however, this was no longer true. At that time, neoliberalism willed Spanish into existence in the US in the interest of making money, undoing the previous linguistic order of modernity in a struggle against the limits of the market and in reconciliation with the need for expansion and for social control through organization of the system of production—the latter driven by respect for diversity as an ideological imperative in the postmodern era, i.e. civil rights, equality, social justice. We turn now to the social implications of this changing economic order, as viewed through the cultural lens of consumerism.

Consumerism

In his widely cited sociological treatise on consumerism in postmodernity, Baudrillard (1994) noted that consumption is "not a function of 'harmonious' individual satisfaction (hence limited according to the ideal rules of 'nature'), but rather an infinite social activity" (41). He described the process that intertwines functional value and symbolic value in consumer society:

> Within the field of their objective function objects are not interchangeable, but outside the field of its denotation, an object becomes substitutable in

38 *The linguistic order of (post)modernity*

a more or less unlimited fashion. In this field of connotations the object takes on the value of a sign. In this way a washing machine serves as equipment and plays as an element of comfort, or of prestige, etc. It is the field of play that is specifically the field of consumption. Here all sorts of objects can be substituted for the washing machine as a signifying element. In the logic of signs, as in the logic of symbols, objects are no longer tied to a function or to a defined need. This is precisely because objects respond to something different, either to a social logic, or to a logic of desire, where they serve as a fluid and unconscious field of signification.

(1994, 44)

To offer some historical context for Baudrillard's thinking, we recall Bernard Mandeville's *Fable of the Bees* (1724). In the incipient stages of the first Industrial Revolution in early eighteenth-century England, Mandeville underscored the growing tendency of purchasing goods as a means of pleasure rather than simply to meet a need, i.e. shopping for pleasure. Mandeville attributed this tendency to a general argument that sociability in humanity stems from desires and the attempt to satisfy those desires. Once directed toward objects available for purchase, human desires would have profound implications for industrial capitalism, the ideology of socioeconomic mobility, and the role of religion in society. Highly criticized at the time, *Fable of the Bees* suggested that these natural 'private vices' created 'public benefits,' i.e. trivial purchases yielded profits, employment opportunities, and economic growth. Wealth, in turn, brought a sense of security, fostered generosity and charity, and thus elevated the status and spirit of society overall. Business and government could, in turn, help the poor and improve public welfare in ways that the church had been unable to do. These ideas would later be taken up by Adam Smith in *The Wealth of Nations* (1776), a classic work in economic theory and a source of inspiration for Karl Marx's proposals.

While use value is tangible and stems from perceived need, exchange value is intangible and stems from value on a market, taken in abstraction, in relation to other objects on the market—causing fetishization of certain commodities. To these two values, Baudrillard (1994) added sign value, which stems from the relationship of the object to other objects in a web or network. Sign value supersedes use or exchange value, such that the value of an object depends not just upon its perceived functionality or worth but also its relative brand prestige (see Sebba 2015 on the ideological value of orthographic convention in relation to branding). The demand for inordinately priced designer clothing and luxury cars is illustrative of what Baudrillard defined as sign value. In the branding and advertising of such products, imagery and mass media are key, i.e. we desire to purchase objects that we associate with those whom we admire, with desired lifestyles, aspirational personalities, or places where we would like to be. According to Baudrillard, virtual production of signs via television, film, and internet gradually displaces the real

The linguistic order of (post)modernity 39

production of material goods as the prevalent force in social life and the political economy. Hence imagery and imagination become essential organizational features for the postmodern economic order. 'Hyperreality' is the result of what Baudrillard calls a 'simulation,' in which signifiers increasingly derive their meanings from other signifiers, rather than upon a material signified. In this intangible world of signs, copies are based increasingly upon other copies (rather than upon a referent that is perceived as original or tangible). This phenomenon gives rise to mediatization, which will be the theoretical focus of Chapter 2.

Baudrillard's (1994) notion of simulation is important to the present argument about language. As both Baudrillard and Lyotard argued, the world of signifiers acquires a proverbial life of its own in ICTs, mass media, cyberspace, and artificial intelligence. Indeed, the foundation of the so-called knowledge-based or tertiary economy is linguistic. In the service sector, codified and prescriptive language use is the *sine qua non* of success, leading to a market valorization of language itself (Duchêne and Heller 2012). In this process, language grows detached from personhood (Da Silva, McLaughlin, and Richards 2007), in the sense that for some purposes language exists in realms devoid of nationality, ethnicity, race, gender, socioeconomic status, or native speakerhood.

A fitting example is the local bank in my small hometown in the Blue Ridge Mountains of North Carolina, where Spanish was entirely a foreign language up until the early 1990s when I left to attend college. Seasonal migrant workers from Mexico came during the fall each year to help with the apple harvest, but very few people socialized with them. During a visit with my family for the holidays in 1995, I went to the only bank ATM in town to withdraw cash and was surprised by a prompt to choose between English and Spanish to make the transaction. How was Spanish possible at a little bank in a town of only two thousand Anglophone people in the hills of North Carolina in the mid-1990s? The answer was in the bank's recent corporate trajectory, of which I was unaware at the time. Headquartered in Charlotte some eighty miles away, North Carolina National Bank (or NCNB) had changed its name to NationsBank in a 1991 merger with Citizens and Southern National Bank, which was headquartered in Atlanta. In 1993, NationsBank purchased Maryland National Bank and also the Chicago Research and Trading Group, leading to their involvement in foreign exchange trading. In 1995, they acquired Bank South Corp, and with their subsequent purchase of St. Louis–based Boatmen's Bancshares in 1996, they became the largest bank in the southern US. The following year, they purchased Barnett Bank, the largest bank in Florida, as well as Montgomery Securities. In 1998, they acquired the San Francisco–based Bank of America corporation and decided to use that name but maintain headquarters in downtown Charlotte, in what is now the tallest building in the Carolinas. My surprise encounter with a Spanish-language option at the bank ATM in 1995 was obviously a top-down corporate decision taken for purposes of a macro-level market that extended across the

40 *The linguistic order of (post)modernity*

US and beyond. Similar corporate trajectories—enmeshed in the discourse of neoliberalism and the exigencies of global economic networks—introduced Spanish all over the country during the 1990s and 2000s, in public settings where it had previously either been erased or was altogether absent.

Simply stated, through consumerism, which quickly framed Spanish as a commodity or an asset in the late 1980s and early 1990s, the language garnered increasing legitimacy as it was reconfigured in the neoliberal economic and postmodern cultural imaginary of the US. Appadurai (1996) underscored the fundamental role that the imaginary of consumerism and mass media play in terms of social agency: "Consumption in the contemporary world is often a form of drudgery, part of the capitalist civilizing process. Nevertheless, where there is consumption there is pleasure, and where there is pleasure there is agency" (7). This idea leads us to the vitality of the consumer-driven and mass-mediated cultural imaginary in postmodern society, which, according to Appadurai, "is now central to all forms of agency, is itself a social fact, and is the key component of the new global order" (1996, 31).

The postmodern imaginary

Approaching the new millennium, Appadurai (1996) observed that the pervasive role of mass media in conjunction with migration had begun to produce what he characterized as a rupture or break with "all sorts of pasts" (3). He wrote that mass mediation and migration

> mark the world of the present not as technically new forces but as ones that seem to impel (and sometimes compel) the work of the imagination. Together, they create specific irregularities because both viewers and images are in simultaneous circulation. Neither images nor viewers fit into circuits or audiences that are easily bound within local, national, or regional spaces.... This mobile and unforeseeable relationship between mass-mediated events and migratory audiences defines the core of the link between globalization and the modern.... There has been a shift in recent decades, building on technological changes over the past century or so, in which the imagination has become a collective, social fact.
>
> (1996, 4–5)

As Appadurai explicitly recognized, imagination and cultural imaginaries have always been an inherent feature of human collectivities. But in recent decades, images and imagery have come to play a much more central role in the constitution and dynamics of social life.

Appadurai attributed the "newly significant role" of the social imagination in the 'postelectronic world' to three phenomena. First, he noted that the imagination is no longer principally confined to the realm of art, myth or ritual, but is now "a part of the quotidian mental work of ordinary people in many societies" (1996, 5). Different than in the past, there is now a necessarily

The linguistic order of (post)modernity   41

symbiotic relationship between mass mediation and migration, in that the imagery and discourse of mass media create imagined worlds and possibilities that concretely impel human motion: "For migrants, both the politics of adaptation to new environments and the stimulus to move or return are deeply affected by a mass-mediated imaginary that frequently transcends national space" (6). Second, Appadurai maintained that, different than modern fantasy, the collective social imagination is increasingly linked to agency and action in postmodern societies. He observed that the consumption of mass media "often provokes irony, selectivity and, in general, *agency*" and that images of the media "are quickly moved into local repertoires of irony, anger, humor, and resistance" (7, emphasis in the original). Third, he affirmed that the collective, mass-mediated imagination plays an agentive role that, different than in modernity, transcends the nation-state concept. He clarified that Anderson's (1983) 'imagined community' in relation to print capitalism is of the same principle and emphasizes that "electronic capitalism can have similar, and even more powerful effects, for they do not work only at the level of the nation-state" (8). He argued that the mass accessibility, fluidity, and mobility of all sorts of texts within what he calls diasporic public spheres "fold global pressures into small, already politicized arenas, producing locality in new, globalized ways" (9). In this way, texts 'in motion' and local events spread on a global scale to be reproduced in other distant localities. Some contemporary examples of this phenomenon would be the Occupy movement, the Arab Spring, A Rapist in Your Path performances, and Black Lives Matter protests. All of these are mass-mediated transnational communities of sentiment, i.e. "a group that begins to imagine and feel things together" on a global scale (Appadurai 1996, 8). Globalization might thus be characterized in Giddens' (1990) terms as an "intensification of worldwide social relations which link distant localities in such a way that local happenings are shaped by events occurring many miles away and vice versa" (64).

To be clear, the terms 'imagination' or 'imaginary' must not be interpreted in an oppositional sense of that which is 'real.' Quite to the contrary, the conditions that motivated each of the aforementioned movements and protests are real from a social ontological perspective, and the movements themselves were physically real. The concept of the imaginary is not antonymous to the concept of the real; rather, the collective social imaginary, now constructed and impelled through the discourse and imagery of the mass media in unprecedented ways, is increasingly the basis of reality from social ontological perspectives. Imaginaries are important to scholars of language because they give presence—and in a psychological sense, life—to language in society, and to 'imagined' speech communities on local, national, and global levels. Anderson (1983) affirmed that "all communities larger than primordial villages of face-to-face contact (and perhaps even these) are imagined. Communities are to be distinguished not only by their falsity/genuineness, but by the style in which they are imagined" (6).

42 *The linguistic order of (post)modernity*

Dawson (1994) defined the 'cultural imaginary' as "those vast networks of interlinking discursive themes, images, motifs and narrative forms that are publicly available within a culture at any one time, and articulate its psychic and social dimensions" (48). This is certainly the case when imaginaries are made concrete through institutionalized policies and practices, political and commercial discourse, architecture, place names, signage, advertising, literature, theater, music, film, and television shows. All of these cultural phenomena serve, semiotically, to create places and to situate language in context at both micro and macro levels. Images and thoughts of places and of characterological figures evoke in our social minds the use of particular languages, dialects or sociolects; likewise, language use may also evoke or serve to establish places and communities in the psychological, social, economic, and political sense. In this way, language usage becomes socially enregistered (Agha 2007). The terms 'model,' 'idea,' 'image,' 'discourse,' among possible others, "convey the notion of an enacted representation, a thing made somewhere through some activity conveying something about another.... These moments of being made, grasped, and communicated are the central moments through which reflexive models of language and culture have a social life at all" (Agha 2007, 2).

As I will highlight in Chapter 3, phenomena of reflexivity and social indexicality play a more transcendental role in the postmodern linguistic order of things (Blommaert 2010; Androutsopoulos 2014; Caravedo 2014). For the emergent sociolinguistic imaginary of Spanish in the US, both Madrid and Mexico City have been vital protagonists. The death of Francisco Franco in 1975 and Spain's democratic transition in the 1980s meant that, for the first time since the previous century, Spain began to experience economic prosperity. The confluence of Spain's democratic capitalist opening and global economic flows drove a burgeoning Spanish-language industry within which a pluralistic ideology was articulated and constructs of proficiency and assessment were enacted, e.g. the Instituto Cervantes' DELE (Diploma de Español como Lengua Extranjera) (Del Valle 2014). The imaginary of a normative variety of Spanish with a global reach quickly took shape as the Instituto Cervantes extended to the US and the Academia Norteamericana de la Lengua Española was revived in the interest of promoting normative Spanish usage among the US Latinx population (cf. Lynch and Potowski 2014). Madrid was not the only center, however. For mass media, Mexico City had already established itself as the industrial center for 'neutral' Spanish throughout Latin America during the mid-twentieth century; in 1951 the Mexican government took the initiative to establish the Association of Spanish Language Academies, cementing the country's leading role in the standardization and unification of Spanish in the Americas vis-à-vis Madrid (see Del Valle 2013).

During the 1980s and 1990s, the powerful television industry of Mexico City extended its reach northward to the US. In the highly lucrative Spanish-language television market that quickly came into existence in the US during the 1990s and early 2000s, the 'neutral' voice of the Mexican industry was

The linguistic order of (post)modernity   43

adapted as the norm (Valencia and Lynch 2016). The creation of a televised, media-centered imagined Spanish-speaking community in the US was concomitant with the propagation of a so-called Hispanic market (Dávila and Rivero 2014; Mora 2014) or, in media terms, a community with 'no sense of place' (Meyrowitz 1985). In the making of that market or community, a normative center for Spanish in the US was created in mediatic spaces through a process of social engineering that forges a 'voice from nowhere' (Woolard 2008), rather than on geopolitical grounds through a process of national institutional doing—an important break with the linguistic order of modernity (Lynch 2018b). The normative voice of Spanish-language television emanating from the US, in many regards, has no real-world referent within the US.

Baudrillard's (1994) concern with the profound influence and pervasiveness of the imitation in postmodern culture, or what he considered the substitution of the natural world by a fabricated one, led to his widely cited proposal regarding 'simulacra and simulation.' In a culture of simulation, the simulacrum—or copy—no longer links to a real referent, i.e. all that exists is the simulacrum itself. In this way, representations of reality themselves become constitutive of reality. A prime example of this 'hyperreality' is the increasingly symbiotic relationship between real events of political concern and the mass media representation of those events. Authority and authenticity are then increasingly contested, i.e. how does one discern between the 'original' and the 'copy,' or between what is 'real' and what is 'fake'? To what extent are our ideas, perceptions, desires and decisions based on mass media representations and mediated images versus real-world referents? In the realm of culture as politics, Yúdice (2004) prefers to conceptualize Baudrillard's notion of simulation in terms of performativity, "the processes by which identities and the entities of social reality are constituted by repeated approximations of models (i.e., the normative) as well as by those 'remainders' ('constitutive exclusions') that fall short" (31). Yúdice's observation that "to the degree that globalization brings different cultures into contact with each other, it escalates the questioning of norms and thus abets performativity" (2004, 31) is, I believe, highly relevant to theories of language variation and change in a postmodern sociolinguistics. I turn now to the sociolinguistic situation of Miami within a framework of postmodernity, as background for the analyses presented in this book.

The postmodern circumstance of Spanish in Miami

Miami bore the characteristics of a postmodern city even before the postmodern era and is arguably the first postmodern metropolis of the US (Nijman 2011). Already upon its inception, Miami's society and economy were fundamentally shaped by transiency, a key characteristic of present-day global cities: tourists and seasonal residents, outside investments, commercial and political flows with the Caribbean. Arguably one of the nation's most transient, stratified, and segregated cities (Croucher 1997; Nijman

44 *The linguistic order of (post)modernity*

2011; Aranda, Hughes, and Sabogal 2014; Mallet and Pinto-Coelho 2018), Miami also constitutes the only major metropolitan area of the US with a clear Hispanic/Latino majority population. Of Miami-Dade County's total population of more than 2.7 million (age 5+) in 2019, some 75% spoke a language other than English at home; the great majority of those were Spanish speakers (US Census Bureau, Miami-Dade County QuickFacts). The number of speakers of other languages paled in comparison: French Creole (some 106,000 speakers, mostly Haitian), Brazilian Portuguese and French (about 15,000 speakers each), Chinese (9,000 speakers), Russian (7,000 speakers), and Hebrew (6,000 speakers); Italian, Tagalog, German, and Arabic claimed just under 5,000 speakers each (US Census Bureau 2015 estimates). Although 44% of Miami's Hispanic/Latino majority population spoke English 'very well' according to the 2014 American Community Survey, only 10% used English exclusively at home (Pew Research Center 2016). These data alone suggest that there are higher levels of bilingualism among Hispanics in Miami than in other global US metropolitan areas, as reflected in Table 1.1.[3]

Although it is possible that lower rates of exclusive use of English in Miami homes is owed to recency of immigration (61% of the Hispanic/Latino population was born outside the US), a comparison of data from Washington suggests that birthplace is not the only factor at play. In the nation's capital, some 53% of the Hispanic population was foreign-born in 2014, yet the rate of English-only use at home was higher there than in New York, Chicago, or Los Angeles (which had foreign-born rates of 36–42%). This fact leads one to assume that higher rates of Spanish use in Miami are not merely a reflection of the percentage of foreign-born speakers but are owed to an array of social, political, economic, and cultural factors that bestow the language greater vitality there than in other cities of the US.

Probably one crucial factor that distinguishes the vitality of Spanish in Miami from other major urban areas is its prevalence across all socioeconomic

Table 1.1 Income, education, and language use of Hispanic population in global US metropolitan areas

City	Median household income	Living in poverty	University degree (bachelor's or higher, age 25+)	Less than high school education	Speak English 'very well'	Speak English less than 'very well'	Speak only English at home (age 5+)
Chicago	$49,600	19%	7%	19%	42%	29%	20%
Los Angeles	$45,700	23%	6%	24%	41%	32%	18%
Miami	**$42,000**	**19%**	**17%**	**14%**	**44%**	**40%**	**10%**
New York	$43,000	23%	11%	19%	39%	35%	17%
Washington	$66,000	11%	14%	21%	37%	30%	23%

American Community Survey 2014 (Pew Research Center 2016)

The linguistic order of (post)modernity 45

strata. Although Hispanics in Miami had a lower median household income ($42,000) than in Chicago, Los Angeles, New York or Washington in 2014 (Table 1.1), they also had the highest levels of education overall: 17% held university degrees (vs. 14% in Washington, 11% in New York, and only 6% and 7% in Los Angeles and Chicago, respectively), and 14% had less than a high school education (vs. 19% in Chicago and New York, 21% in Washington, and 24% in Los Angeles). Taking median household income and education level into account, it is evident that Spanish language use in Miami is not socioeconomically stratified. As shown in Table 1.2, a non-English language (i.e. principally Spanish in Miami) was spoken in the majority of homes across all areas of the city, ranging from about 58% in Coral Gables to over 94% in Hialeah at the time of the 2010 US Census.[4] A comparison of data from Hialeah, Doral, and Key Biscayne clearly reflects this fact: despite vast socioeconomic differences in terms of education level and income, a non-English language was spoken in the vast majority of homes in all three areas. The case of Key Biscayne—one of South Florida's most exclusive addresses—demonstrates that Spanish language use is as much associated with wealth as it is with middle-class status (e.g. Doral) or the working class (e.g. Hialeah) in Miami (Table 1.2).

Although Spanish is prevalent across the city's socioeconomic spectrum, English is inarguably the dominant language of second- and third-generation bilinguals (Portes and Schauffler 1994; Otheguy, García, and Roca 2000; Eilers, Kimbrough Oller, and Cobo-Lewis 2002; Porcel 2006; Gutiérrez-Rivas 2007; Lanier 2014; Carter and Lynch 2015; Pascual y Cabo 2015; among others). Most are firm in the conviction that English is 'the language of the US' and they present considerable bias in favor of English at both the individual and societal levels, yet at the same time they assert overtly positive attitudes toward Spanish (e.g. Lynch and Klee 2005; Lanier 2014; Pascual y

Table 1.2 Language use and socioeconomic status across Miami

Area	Hispanic/ Latino	Speak a non-English language at home (age 5+)	Median household income	University degree (bachelor's or higher, age 25+)
Miami-Dade County	64.5%	71.9%	$43,605	26.2%
Miami (city proper)	70%	77.3%	$29,621	22.2%
Hialeah	94.7%	94.2%	$31,648	13.5%
Miami Beach	53%	66.9%	$43,538	43.1%
Kendall	63.7%	69.5%	$61,266	41.5%
Doral	79.5%	88.8%	$69,300	55.4%
Coral Gables	53.6%	57.5%	$84,027	63.7%
Key Biscayne	61.6%	79.9%	$104,554	74.7%

(US Census 2010)

46 *The linguistic order of (post)modernity*

Cabo 2015; Carter and Lynch 2018b). English dominance and lack of formal education in Spanish among second- and third-generation bilinguals in Miami lead to patterns of linguistic simplification and convergence, as in all other areas of the US (Escobar and Potowski 2015). Cross-structural influence of English in bilingual Spanish in Miami has been attested in phonology (Alvord 2010a, 2010b; Alvord and Rogers 2014), morphosyntax (Lynch 1999; Zurer Pearson 2002), lexicon (Franco-Rodríguez 2007; Lynch 2017) and pragmatics (Gutiérrez-Rivas 2011a, 2011b). Because the majority of Miami's population is bilingual, there is also some influence of Spanish on the local urban variety of English at the phonological level (Carter, López Valdez, and Sims 2020) and in lexical patterns (Mullen 2015). The apparent cross-generational 'loss' of Spanish in Miami seems paradoxical in light of the ubiquity and relative prestige of the language in South Florida, a topic that I take up in Chapter 3.

In Miami, globalizing flows and language ideologies of economic neo-liberalism intersect with long-standing one nation–one language ideologies, which are continuously negotiated in the local on-the-ground dynamics of a highly transient, majority bilingual city whose inhabitants are mostly immigrants or the children of immigrants. On an everyday basis in Miami, the modern nation-state paradigm is confronted by the transnational flows of globalization. In what follows, I briefly frame the postmodern circumstance of Spanish in Miami in terms of Appadurai's (1996) concept of 'scapes,' which he defined as "deeply perspectival constructs, inflected by the historical, linguistic, and political situatedness of different sorts of actors: nation-states, multinationals, diasporic communities, as well as subnational groupings and movements (whether religious, political or economic), and even intimate face-to-face groups" (33). Appadurai affirmed that the individual actor is "the last locus" of these scapes, which comprise imagined worlds that are "navigated by agents who both experience and constitute larger formations" (33).

Financescape

One could argue that Miami's economic character was already postmodern during modern times. Founded in 1896, the city emerged with no manufacturing base during the industrial heyday of the early twentieth century. In this sense, from its beginning Miami was a 'postindustrial' city without ever having been industrial (Iglesias Illa 2010; Nijman 2011). As I explain in Chapter 2, the city began as an exclusive retreat for wealthy northern industrialists and soon morphed into a tropical playground for middle- and upper-class vacationing northerners who were attracted by warm weather and the unabashed flouting of Prohibition laws. During the mid-1920s, about 75% of tourists in Miami also visited Havana (*New York Times* 1926), solidifying the basis of the city's tourism and service-sector economy in relation to Cuba. The land boom of the 1920s established real estate and construction as another of the city's key economic sectors. After the crash of the Roaring Twenties, Miami's economy remained relatively stagnant during the years of the Great Depression and

The linguistic order of (post)modernity   47

WWII. In the 1950s, Miami Beach reemerged as a mecca for leisure and entertainment for celebrities and for the White middle and upper classes (as it had been during the 1920s), who drove Miami's consumer economy. Retail was in fact the city's largest employer in 1962 (Nijman 2011, 72). The city also became a center for illegal gambling and organized crime during the 1950s and 1960s.

By the early 1980s, illegal trafficking of marijuana and cocaine came to play a "major transformative role in the incipient stages of Miami's emerging trade and finance sectors" (Nijman 2011, 74). Legislation of the US International Bank Act and changes to Florida law in 1978 allowed for foreign banks to establish operations in the state; by 1984 Miami had 43 'Edge Act' banks engaging in foreign activity and an additional 45 foreign-owned banks (Nijman 2011, 80). During the early 1980s, annual revenues of drug trafficking were estimated between $7 billion and $12 billion, compared with the legitimate $9 billion generated by tourism and $12 billion by real estate; in 1980 alone, $1.3 billion worth of marijuana and $5.8 billion worth of cocaine were seized by law enforcement in and around South Florida (Nijman 2011). The Miami Federal Reserve Bank's surplus of $5 billion in 1980, mostly in laundered $50 and $100 bills, was more than that of all the nation's other Federal Reserve branches combined (Kelly 1981). Indeed, the passage of the Money Laundering Control Act by the US Congress in 1986 was driven partly by the findings of a high-profile undercover investigation conducted in South Florida, "the center of the drug trade" (Levi and Reuter 2006, 296).

As I highlight in Chapter 2, the economically motivated 'cocaine wars' during the early 1980s forged a cultural imaginary of Miami as a crime-ridden, Spanish-speaking tropical paradise astride the political and social borders of the US and various Latin American nations. This imaginary, captured in Didion's (1987) book *Miami* and projected in *Scarface* (1983)—to be subsequently glamorized in the internationally acclaimed television series *Miami Vice* (1984–1989)—served to position Miami on a global scene. According to Quiroga (2009), "*Scarface* and [Didion's] *Miami* signal the turn from the politics of the Cold War to cocaine politics, but they also propel the narrative toward the time when Miami ceases to be a Cuban city and becomes instead the 'Latin' city par excellence" (159).

In the years following Fidel Castro's rise to power, many Cubans in Miami "prospered as bankers, industrialists, real estate developers, sugar planters, merchants, and shop owners. They revitalized southern Florida. By the early 1970s they owned and operated nearly 20,000 businesses.... Spanish was the requisite language of employment" (Pérez 1999, 502). Throughout the 1980s, Miami's economic and demographic growth were concomitant with increasing social use and ideological legitimacy of Spanish in public life (Resnick 1988). The city's highly educated and entrepreneurial early Cuban exile population increasingly attracted Latin Americans—especially of the middle and upper socioeconomic classes—who were escaping political and economic instability in their home countries, e.g. Nicaraguans during the Sandinista Revolution;

48   *The linguistic order of (post)modernity*

Colombians and Peruvians fleeing political instability from the 1980s through the 2000s; Venezuelans following Hugo Chávez's rise to power in the 1990s; and Argentines in the wake of the 1998–2002 financial crisis. Despite the fact that Los Angeles County's Hispanic population was more than triple the size of Miami-Dade's approaching the new millennium, the number of Hispanic-owned business firms in Miami-Dade in 1997 (120,605) was not too far below the number in Los Angeles (136,678), an indicator of the marked difference in the general socioeconomic status of Hispanics between the two metropolitan areas. Moreover, receipts of Hispanic-owned firms in Miami-Dade totaled more than $26.7 billion, compared to $16.2 billion in Los Angeles, despite the latter city's greater number of firms.

In a survey of 245 metropolitan Miami businesses conducted by Fradd in 1996, 47 reported use of Spanish 11–25% of the time, 66 used it 26–50% of the time, and 33 used it 51–75% of the time. One in ten businesses surveyed said that Spanish was used in 76–100% of their communication, while one in four reported use of Spanish less than 10% of the time (Fradd 1996, 39). Nearly half of the businesses surveyed reported that 76–100% of their employees conducted business in English, yet one in three survey respondents said that English was used in business communication by less than half of its work-force. Of all the businesses surveyed, 96% agreed (60% said "strongly agree") to the importance of having an English-Spanish bilingual workforce (Fradd 1996, 42). Fradd's study made clear that both English and Spanish played vital roles in Miami's economy approaching the new millennium and that being bilingual was a requisite for employment in many sectors. I describe the emergence of the marketplace imperative of bilingualism in South Florida in Chapter 2. Today, roughly half of Miami-Dade County's employed popula-tion has a service-, sales- or office-related occupation (American Community Survey 2019), in which working abilities in Spanish and English are important.

Once established as a center for finance and trade between the US and Latin America, Miami's Brickell Avenue banking district came to be referred to as the 'Wall Street of Latin America.' Writing for *Forbes*, Beyer (2015) affirmed that Miami's Spanish-speaking majority makes it "a natural place" for Latin American people and firms to do business, "more than other emerging but nativist cities like Nashville, Atlanta, and Houston. Investors from Brazil, Argentina, Colombia and Venezuela have directed capital into Brickell's banks and real estate, with an estimated two-thirds of demand for neighbor-hood units coming from South America." But it is important to highlight that the economic power of Spanish language in Miami was already felt during the 1940s and 1950s. Miami's steadfast touristic and commercial exchange with Havana through the first half of the twentieth century had solidified the vitality and instrumentality of Spanish (Pérez 1999). The city reaped immense benefit from tens of thousands of Cuban visitors annually, who took advantage of shopping prices that were often substantially lower than in Cuba. A 1957 advertisement directed to Cuba by the Florida Development Commission read: "Florida has the solution to all your shopping needs,

The linguistic order of (post)modernity 49

whether you are a businessman buying specialized equipment or a housewife in search of famous wardrobe articles made in Florida or an entire family in search of a marvelous vacation. Florida is the closest place where you can obtain products and services of the U.S.A. And 'Se habla español' almost everywhere" (cited by Pérez 1999, 438).

Following Castro's rise to power, Miami's highly successful Cuban Spanish-speaking 'ethnic enclave economy' grew in relation to continuous immigration and commercial ties to the Caribbean and Latin America (Portes and Stepick 1993), a growth facilitated by the mobile character of Miami's capitalists and business leaders (Nijman 2011, 73). In this regard, one can affirm, as did Booth in a widely cited *TIME* article in 1993, that "Miami's fate... was sealed when Fidel Castro started reading Karl Marx at the University of Havana. The mass exodus of middle- and upper-class Cubans, driven into exile by communism in the 1960s, began a process that lifted the city from its utter dependence on domestic tourism into the global economy" (Booth 1993). Nonetheless, Latin American tourists presently remain a crucial source of revenue in Miami, which has important implications for the city's other scapes. For example, the national sales director for Miami-based Warner Music Latina explained that, prior to the digital revolution, the city's record sales were largely tied to tourism: "The Miami [music] market is often mis-read, because our No. 1 industry is tourism.... When we had physical sales [LPs, CDs and cassette tapes], Marc Anthony would sell a lot of records in Miami. But they weren't selling to locals. They were selling to tourists from Brazil or Mexico or Argentina" (Rodríguez 2016). In 2018, Miami hosted 16.5 million overnight visitors, 45% of whom came from Latin America (Greater Miami Convention and Visitors Bureau 2019). In 2021, Miami became a prime destination for Covid vaccine tourists from Latin America (Londoño, Politi, and Carneri 2021). Different than other US global cities such as New York, Los Angeles, Chicago or Washington, Miami has always been a place where Spanish was primordial for business—"*the* hemispheric city" of South and Central America and the Caribbean according to Nijman (2011, 202, emphasis in the original).

Ethnoscape

Transience—embodied by tourists and short-term or seasonal residents— is one of the main factors contributing to Miami's postmodern character. According to Nijman (2011), "Miami's various population groups, and the ways they relate to the city, are best understood in the broader context of glo-balization, transience, and identity of place" (139). Nijman identified three main segments of the city's population in sociological terms: locals, exiles, and mobiles. The first group he defined as those who have been born and raised in Miami and call it their 'hometown,' arguably only 15 to 20% of the population (140). Exiles, who constitute about a third of the city's popula-tion according to Nijman, are those who have made their way to Miami in

50   *The linguistic order of (post)modernity*

light of political or economic adversity in their home countries. He affirmed that exiles "do not consider Miami their hometown, or the United States their home country" and suggested that a major part of their identity is defined by "the future prospect of returning home, real or illusory" (140). Mobiles, who constitute roughly another third of the population, have no identity ties to South Florida and, like exiles, they consider that their stay is temporary. Importantly, they tend to be rather affluent: seasonal residents, long-term vacationers and regular tourists, entrepreneurs and investors, professionals who come to Miami for work assignments, wealthy Latin Americans drawn to Miami's opulence and glamour—a cultural imaginary that has been perpetuated in television and film. Because of the lifestyles that they demand and the money that they have brought to the city ever since the days of its founding, they have long exerted a fundamental cultural influence (140). Since most mobiles in Miami have ties to Spanish-speaking countries, Spanish language use is part and parcel of their identity profile. In terms of social indexicality, their vital and constant presence links Spanish to lavish lifestyles and great spending power in some sectors of the city. One must bear in mind that the ratio of wealthy foreigners in Miami is much higher than in other metropolitan areas of the US (Nijman 2011, 140). This is not to say that most Spanish speakers in Miami are wealthy, but rather that many of them are; and in cultural and linguistic terms, their presence is highly meaningful.

Celebrated Univision news anchor Jorge Ramos, who has lived in Miami since 1985, affirmed that "Miami has been incredibly generous to Latinos… As one of my first bosses here told me, 'It's the only city in America where we're not treated as second-class citizens'" (Finnegan 2015). In her acclaimed account *Miami*, Didion (1987) made a similar observation:

> The sound of spoken Spanish was common in Miami, but it was common in Los Angeles, and Houston, and even in the cities of the Northeast. What was unusual about Spanish in Miami was not that it was so often spoken, but that it was so often heard: in, say, Los Angeles, Spanish remained a language only barely registered by the Anglo population, part of the ambient noise, the language spoken by the people who worked in the car wash and came to trim the trees and cleared the tables in restaurants. In Miami Spanish was spoken by the people who owned the cars and the trees, which made, on the socioauditory scale, a considerable difference. Exiles who felt isolated or declassed by language in New York or Los Angeles thrived in Miami. An entrepreneur who spoke no English could still, in Miami, buy, sell, negotiate, leverage assets, float bonds, and if he were so inclined, attend galas twice a week, in black tie.
>
> (63)

Such observations about Miami's exceptionalism in the US context abound not only in personal anecdote but in sociological, literary, and cultural studies accounts as well.

The linguistic order of (post)modernity 51

Hence in Miami we contemplate a complex ethnoscape, a concept defined by Appadurai as "the landscape of persons who constitute the shifting world in which we live: tourists, immigrants, refugees, exiles, guest workers, and other moving groups and individuals [who] constitute an essential feature of the world and appear to affect the politics of (and between) nations to a hitherto unprecedented degree" (1996, 33). Diasporic communities—which are most communities in Miami—remain connected to the homeland and to other diasporic communities to an unprecedented degree, as well. Appadurai emphasized that because of this connectedness, the mobile populations of postmodernity "can never afford to let their imaginations rest too long, even if they wish to" (34). This is especially true in global cities such as Miami, where more than half of the total population is foreign-born (54.6%) and the children of immigrants comprise another substantial percentage (American Community Survey 2019). Of Miami-Dade County's foreign-born population, the overwhelming majority—93.2%—are of Latin American origin (American Community Survey 2019), meaning that most of the county's population was either born in Latin America or have parents who were born there. It is thus no surprise that the vast majority of the population (around 70%) identifies as Hispanic or Latino, of whom roughly half are of Cuban origin. According to the same estimate (American Community Survey 2019), Miami-Dade's non-Hispanic White population numbers 347,010 or 12.8% of the county's total. The non-Hispanic Black and African American population is just over 416,000 or 15.3% of the total, many of whom are of Caribbean origin (e.g. from Haiti, Jamaica, The Bahamas, and islands of the Lesser Antilles). Non-Hispanic Asians comprise only 1.5% of the county's total population. Of course, one must bear in mind the important presence and visibility of mobiles, as defined by Nijman (2011), who for the most part do not enter into census counts. Nonetheless, Miami-Dade is indisputably a minority-majority metropolitan area, in which the combined non-Hispanic White and Black segments of society—as typically understood in ethnic terms elsewhere in the US—constitute only about one-fourth of the total population. The traditional US White/Black distinction in American English is fundamentally reconfigured by various factors in Miami, among them the highly diverse dialectal and sociolectal backgrounds of Miami's White non-Hispanic minority (who for the most part are transplants from other regions of the country), as well as the fact that many Black speakers of English in Miami are of Caribbean origin and do not identify historically as African American (Carter and Lynch 2018a).

Here one must note the rather different contours of language, race, and ethnicity in Miami as compared to other areas of the US. For example, within the context of the Black Lives Matter movement, Alvarez (2020) affirmed: "The Latino experience in Miami-Dade is unusual for the United States.... Miami-Dade's rare bubble of Latino empowerment has desensitized us." Pasols (2020) also remarked upon Miami's "bubble" phenomenon:

> In South Florida in general, non-Black Latinos often have a blind spot when it comes to recognizing themselves as a minority in the United

52 *The linguistic order of (post)modernity*

States. Miami-Dade County is [majority] Hispanic, forming a protective demographic bubble around a populace that has grown accustomed to viewing itself as the dominant culture.... The reality is that non-Black Latinos, being minorities themselves, are subject to discrimination and prejudice as well. It may not be as apparent while living comfortably in the 305 [Miami's original area code]—but it does happen.

Because of this "bubble" phenomenon, racialization of language (Alim, Rickford, and Ball 2016; Rosa 2019) is more nuanced in Miami than in other parts of the country, or even in other major cities with large Spanish-speaking populations such as Los Angeles, Chicago, New York, or Houston. Alvarez (2020) observed personally: "As a white Latina here, I never considered myself a minority. I spoke Spanish and English freely. I was proud of my Cuban-ness and our role in shaping modern-day Miami. If some non-Hispanics bristled, they could leave. Many did, sprinting to English-speaking counties north of here, and that was fine with us. We are the establishment now."

Because Miami's racially diverse demographic majority does indeed speak Spanish, racialization of the language manifests rather differently than in the broader US context. Miami's Spanish-speaking political and economic establishment has historically identified as racially White; still today, 82.3% of Miami-Dade's population born in Latin America identifies as White (American Community Survey 2019). Mallet and Pinto-Coelho (2018) nonetheless documented intra-ethnic divisions along lines of race among Miami Latino immigrants, especially regarding indigenous versus European-descent phenotypic traits (105). The link between Whiteness and Spanish language use in Miami sometimes leads to the perception of Afro-Latinxs as English speakers. Less than 10% of Miami-Dade's population born in Latin America identifies as Black (American Community Survey 2019), thus some African Americans in Miami perceive Hispanics as "Whites who speak Spanish" (Grenier and Pérez 2003, 77).

Cuba's racialized social class divide extended to Miami during the 1960s and 1970s (Laguna 2017), as anthropologist Mercedes Cros Sandoval affirmed: "Para el exilio [antes] del año 1980, que era mayoritariamente blanco— está de más decirlo, eso nos distanció bastante de los negros" (2008). That distance oftentimes led the White majority among the early exiles to assume that Black individuals in Miami were African American and thus did not speak Spanish. In a chapter titled "It's Like Cubans Could Only Be White," Aja (2016) documented this phenomenon in ethnographic interviews with Miami Afro-Cubans: "there's 'no way' a Spanish-speaking Black Cuban could co-exist in proximity to white Cubans and Latinxs" (91). Following the Mariel boatlift in 1980 and the racial and national-origin diversification of Miami's Spanish-speaking population into the new millennium, Spanish-speaking Blackness became more integrated in the city's sociolinguistic landscape and cultural imaginary. But the prevalent notion of Whiteness in relation to Cubanness has in some ways persisted, as one of the Afro-Cuban interviewees in Aja's (2016) account observed: "Regardless of social setting... people hear my Cuban accent or hear me speak Spanish but still ask: where are you from? Colombia, Panama, Dominican Republic, they guess. I tell them I'm Cuban and they're shocked.... If you're black in Miami, you're either African American, Haitian, Bahamian or a black Hispanic from other countries, no one ever imagines Cuba" (93).

Many Black speakers of English in Miami are bilinguals of Haitian Creole or bidialectal speakers of other Caribbean English varieties (Carter and Lynch 2018a). Afro-Cubans sometimes note being ethnically marginalized not only by White Cubans but also by African Americans; the latter tendency gives title to another of the chapters of Aja's (2016) book: "You Ain't Black, You're Cuban!" (107). The important sociopolitical and ethnic rifts between Cuban and non-Cuban Black communities are also documented by Croucher (1997) on the occasion of Nelson Mandela's visit to Miami in 1990; the cultural tensions between African Americans and Haitians during the 1980s are poignantly related in Stepick et al.'s (2003) ethnography of Miami high school students; the "divergent fates" of African Americans and Cubans are described by Grenier and Pérez (2003).

In spite of the preponderance of Cubans in Miami, who constituted 52.3% of Miami-Dade County's Hispanic population in the American Community Survey (2019) estimate, the sociolinguistic import of Cuban varieties of Spanish is ambiguous. Colloquial Cuban Spanish variants appear to prevail in the Latinx imaginary of the city (Callesano 2020), but in terms of actual language practice, Cuban influence seems less substantial. Among local university students of diverse Spanish-speaking origins, Fernández Parera (2017) found that lexical particularities of Cuban Spanish (e.g. trusa [swimsuit], cake [cake], fruta bomba [papaya], jimaguas [twins]) were largely unfamiliar to and unused by second- and third-generation speakers of other varieties of Spanish. Although participants in his study tended to affirm the relevance of Cuban Spanish and Cuban culture in the city, the results of a lexical survey and image-naming task led him to conclude that "Cuban culture in Miami might not enjoy the hegemonic status that it is perceived to have" (Fernández Parera 2017, 224). Moreover, the 129 participants of Fernández Parera's study demonstrated a clear negative bias toward Cuban Spanish when asked to rate it according to 'correctness' and 'pleasantness' alongside other national varieties of the language, confirming Alfaraz's (2014) previous finding that Caribbean varieties in general garner relatively lower prestige in Miami.

Fernández Parera (2017), Alfaraz (2014), and Carter and Callesano (2018) have all confirmed that Miami Hispanics tend to attribute highest prestige to the Spanish of Spain, even though immigrants from Spain constitute an extreme minority in South Florida. In an implicit perception experiment, Carter and Callesano (2018) asked public university students in Miami to rate recordings of the voices of three young professional males living in Miami—one from Barcelona, one from Havana, and another from Bogotá—according to a series of personal characteristics such as personality (e.g. friendliness, dependability,

54 *The linguistic order of (post)modernity*

intelligence), language use, employment, income, and family background. In some cases, participants were given background information about the speaker they were hearing, including the parents' country of origin. The parents' national-origin label sometimes matched the speaker's actual country of origin, while in other cases, the background information and voices were mismatched, e.g. the participant heard the voice of the Cuban speaker but was told that his parents came from Spain, etc. On other occasions, no speaker background information (i.e. no national-origin label) was given. The authors argued that this manipulation permitted them to evaluate the influence of the national-origin label on the listener perceptions of the speech signal itself (i.e. the voice they were hearing). Of 292 participants who completed the study via an online survey platform, 67% ($n = 195$) identified as Hispanic or Latino/a, and 33% ($n = 96$) identified as non-Latino/a; 52% ($n = 152$) of the sample reported being 'native speakers' of Spanish. The results revealed a significant bias: the voice of the male from Barcelona was consistently attributed a much higher probability of holding a white-collar job (i.e. being a marketing executive or an attorney on the given scale) and a much lower probability of working in a coffee shop or a cell phone store, jobs which were more frequently attributed to the Cuban and Colombian voices (78–79). Figure 1.1 reflects the perceptual ratings for the combined white-collar professions in Carter and Callesano's study according to the voice and the given parent-origin label. In their statistical analysis, there were no significant interactions between the label and the speaker's voice. It is nonetheless noteworthy that when assigned a 'Spain' label, ratings of all voices were consistently higher; when assigned a 'Cuba' label, they were consistently lower. Indeed, the Cuban voice bearing a 'Cuba' label was attributed the least likelihood of being that of a professional.

Carter and Callesano (2018) concluded that their findings were "unsurprising in light of pervasive Eurocentric ideologies, colonialist ideologies that construct Spain as *la madre patria*, and the ideological workings of the Real Academia de la Lengua Española and other institutions that support 'purist' language ideologies" (84–85). They further affirmed:

> Because language varieties act indexically for other social meanings, and because this indexical link is tended to so carefully by language academies, educational systems, and in everyday discourse and interaction, perceptions of individuals based on speech are practically overdetermined. We believe this is especially the case in Spanish-speaking Miami-Dade not only because of the presence of the county's immense Spanish dialect diversity and the language ideologies from Spain and Latin America that attend it, but also because questions of language are already so fraught with signification in South Florida because of the presence of US-based language policies, politics, and ideologies that limit and problematize multilingualism while centralizing the assumption of English monolingualism.
>
> (Carter and Callesano 2018, 86)

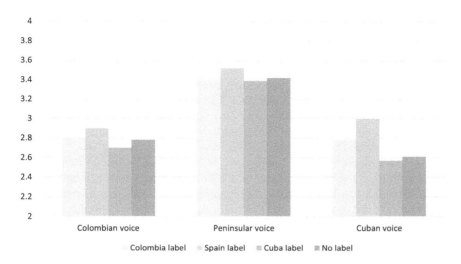

Figure 1.1 Perception of voice, national-origin label, and occupational status among university students in Miami, 1 to 5 Likert scale (1 = unlikely to hold a white-collar occupation; 5 = likely to hold a white-collar occupation)
Adapted from Carter and Callesano (2018, 80)

Following this reasoning regarding the indexical value of particular varieties and, within those varieties, particular variants (lexical, phonological, morphosyntactic, and discursive) of Spanish in superdiverse Miami, one begins to comprehend the complexity of the city's Spanish-speaking ethnoscape. In Chapter 5, I consider the social diffusion of Anglicisms in terms of dialectal variation and Spanish-English bilingualism at the local level. The global and 'glocal' character of Spanish in Miami manifests in the mediascape.

Mediascape

The media rapidly evolved from being one of various institutions of modern public life to being arguably the most central in postmodern societies (Thompson 1990; Androutsopoulos 2014). A product of the ubiquity and rapidity of media flows, the mediascapes of postmodernity play a vital role in human subjectivities (Appadurai 1996). In Miami's mediascape as well as its ideoscape, Spanish not only coexists with English, but also with an array of 'other places' where Spanish is spoken. Historically, the Cuban capital has played a crucial role in terms of sociolinguistic reflexivity and indexicality in Miami. Media flows between South Florida and Cuba have worked to shape the evolution of Cuban Spanish in the US and on the island, both in terms of linguistic and political 'othering' (i.e. Miami versus Cuba) as well as in a symbiotic fashion (i.e. Cubanness on common transnational ground). Because of

56 *The linguistic order of (post)modernity*

the constant communication and textual exchange between the two places, Spanish in Cuba is continuously influenced by the tendencies of Miami Cuban Spanish speakers, and varieties of Cuban Spanish are today sustained in South Florida in ways that were inconceivable for early exile immigrants of the 1960s (Laguna 2017; Valencia 2018).

Analyzing the discursive tropes and contents of numerous local television productions in Miami, Valencia (2018) concluded: "La *cubanía* no es solo un instrumento afectivo siempre en reformulación, también es un bien material, un recurso mercantilizado orientado a enfocar a un segmento de los hijos de la Revolución en Miami.... La transnacionalidad de los emigrados recientes está impactando las formas en que la sociedad estadounidense y los cubanos en la Isla se perciben entre sí" (114). In this regard, the imaginary of Cuban Spanish has become ever more transnational not only in relation to South Florida but also within the Cuban diasporic public sphere that includes Cuban emigrants across the globe. Valencia (2017) argued that within that imaginary, a sense of *cubanía* or "desire for belonging to a nationality beyond/ without a nation" is commodified through a hyperbolic *cubaneo* or "a performance of such desire in the public space" (46).

However, within the context of the lucrative pan-Hispanic television industry in Miami, which produces programming for national and international markets, some Cuban-origin actors consider that their participation is limited on the basis of linguistic discrimination. Language is thus characterized as "el otro muro" that blocks some varieties of Spanish from the industry. Gerardo Riverón, a Cuban actor in Miami who is well known for his participation in various telenovelas, remarked: "Esto del acento neutro es una gran mentira, algo que se han inventado para proteger ciertos intereses y llevar a todo el mundo a hablar con acento mexicano" (González and Liste 2017). Alain Cabrera, a producer who worked for Univision in Miami, confirmed Riverón's experience:

> The variant of Spanish that is mandatorily and inviolably demanded is Spanish with a Mexican accent. The euphemism of 'neutral' is used to eliminate any possibility of accusation of racism or discrimination. The reasons are that the largest population of Latinos in the United States is from Mexico. It is completely forbidden to try to impose or even propose to use an accent that is not Mexican. More tropical accents like the Dominican, Puerto Rican or Cuban cannot appear on the screen in a soap opera. Even the Colombian accent, which is much 'smoother' and more correct, is equally censored. This criterion, although decided by casting directors or producers of programs, is a criterion imposed by the network.
>
> (cited in Valencia and Lynch 2020, 92)

Theater actress Vivian Acosta alleged that the neutral accent has gone viral in Miami, "lo cual convierte a esta ciudad en un lugar muy despersonalizado,

The linguistic order of (post)modernity 57

sin identidad" (González and Liste 2017). Acosta's words recall the notion of a Spanish-speaking voice detached from personhood (Da Silva, McLaughlin, and Richards 2007), which I highlighted earlier.

Home to the headquarters of both Univision and Telemundo—the nation's two largest Spanish-language television networks—as well as a substantial film industry, Miami has been dubbed the 'Hollywood of Latin America.' Univision's commitment to "empowering audiences" reflects the ideological roles of Spanish-language mass media in the creation of a Latino/Hispanic market category in the US, as defined by Mahler (2018): activist, reactivist, and culturalist. The activism of Chicanos (e.g. La Raza) and Puerto Ricans during the civil rights movement evolved into a more inclusive identity category for political purposes by the 1980s (Mora 2014) and the unifying concept of the so-called Hispanic consumer (Dávila 2001). 'Reactivist' refers to the effect of this unification on mainstream US culture: "Paradoxically, the more Hispanics unify, the greater they can be, and are likely to be, perceived as a threat and vilified" (Mahler 2018, 8). Finally, the 'culturalist' dimension reveals cultural distinctiveness vis-à-vis mainstream culture and other segments of the population (Valencia and Lynch 2020, 76).

The executive vice-president of NBC Universal Telemundo Enterprises stated in relation to the company's futuristic global media megacenter, recently constructed in Miami: "We want to create a sense of community here, internally and externally…. When you walk into this building, throw out your perception of what you thought about Hispanics in this country. This is what we are and we want the world to know about it." (Rodríguez 2018). Telemundo's mandate after being acquired by NBC Universal and Comcast was to overtake their competitor, Univision, to claim the most viewers in the US market. As leading global media conglomerates based in Miami, both networks aim to legitimate the place of Spanish language and advance the image of the Hispanic population in the US. Linked to studio facilities in Mexico and Colombia, Miami thus emerges as a strategic node in global media flows, a locus for the world Spanish-language mediascape, for the articulation of a Latinx identity, and for Latin American cultural production (Yúdice 2004; Valencia and Lynch 2020).

Technoscape

Intricately bound up with the mediascape is the technoscape, the product of "the global configuration, also ever fluid, of technology and the fact that technology… now moves at high speeds across various kinds of previously impervious boundaries" (Appadurai 1996, 34). Global cities such as Miami are nodes for such movement across boundaries. Appadurai offered an example: "How is one to make a meaningful comparison of wages in Japan and the United States or of real estate costs in New York and Tokyo without taking sophisticated account of the very complex fiscal and investment flows that link the two economies through a global grid of currency speculation

58 *The linguistic order of (post)modernity*

and capital transfer?" (34). The Telemundo Center is a good example of the ways in which flows beget flows. Constructed in suburban Miami in 2018 at the cost of $250 million, the center employs some 1,200 people who work in the company's corporate offices, news departments, creative and production facilities, and recording studios. The enterprise produces content for markets in the US and throughout Latin America (Rodríguez 2018). In addition, the complex contains 495,000 square feet of stores, restaurants, gyms, and other commercial services. This technological center involves not only retail and restaurant industries, but also national real estate and construction companies, transnational bankers and brokers, and local state and city agencies (Rodríguez 2018).

Before Miami's emergence as a global center for Spanish-language television and film production, it was already home to a vital music industry (Yúdice 2004). In 1979, Miami Cuban American Juan Estevez helped launch Discos CBS, which later became Sony Discos. Estevez explained that during the 1970s Miami became the center for Latin music production in the US: "A lot of the big hits at the time—Julio Iglesias, Raphael, Camilo Sesto—came from Spain. Miami became a focal point for them because they could own property here, use it as a home base for tours to Latin America and they didn't even need to speak English. At the same time, we had Univision and later on Telemundo" (Rodríguez 2016). In 1979, Estevez offered a recording contract to a local band called the Miami Sound Machine—featuring lead vocalist Gloria Estefan—who would quickly accrue international fame as their distinctive "Miami sound" entered mainstream music. Other chart-topping artists followed: Jon Secada, Exposé, Willy Chirino, and Enrique Iglesias (Julio's son) by the 1990s. All of these Miami-based artists produced music in both English and Spanish, and sometimes used both languages in the same songs. Global superstar Shakira moved from her native Colombia to Miami in 1997, when she enlisted Emilio Estefan as her manager and the producer of her hit English-language crossover album *Laundry Service* (2001). In the year 2000, the city became home to the Latin Grammys. Music moguls such as the Estefans, Marc Anthony, and Pitbull all call Miami home. Currently, each of the three major US record labels—Sony, Warner, and Universal—have two separate labels based in Miami: one that caters to the US market and another to the markets of Latin America and the Iberian Peninsula.

The transition from physical (i.e. LPs, CDs and cassette tapes) to digital (i.e. downloading and streaming) technologies has impacted growth substantially, especially because of widespread piracy throughout Latin America and the region's lag in terms of internet availability (Rodríguez 2016). Leila Cobo, executive director of Latin content and programming for Billboard, explained that although there is no longer a particular "Miami sound" or distinctive brand for the city, it now constitutes a central creative and technological node in the world's Spanish-language music industry: "There's no Miami Motown. But there are a lot of Latin artists who live here full time—singers, producers, musicians—and the city does seep into their work. All

The linguistic order of (post)modernity 59

these different influencers are here: the best Colombian producers, the best Argentine producers, the best studios" (Rodríguez 2016). Although revenues experienced a decline with the digital revolution, Miami's importance in the music technoscape actually grew as a result. Tomas Cookman, director of the Los Angeles–based Nacional Records, explained that digital technology drove Miami's growth "because you can do the same thing from Brickell [as you can] from Buenos Aires. Anyone who is running a record label has to have a good perspective of what is happening in Latin America, just the way it's good to know what a Pop-Tart is if you're selling music in the U.S. And Miami gives you a better avenue to Latin America than any other city in the country" (Rodríguez 2016). This has certainly been the case of reggaeton and Latin trap over the last two decades, as I will note in Chapter 6. In sum, Miami's position as a technological center for music and television production is a prime example of the ways in which technoscapes emerge in intimate relationship with mediascapes, financescapes, and ethnoscapes. These scapes generate ideoscapes, which in turn drive and, in some ways, (re)create them.

Ideoscape

In principle, ideoscapes can be conceptualized in terms of political discourse and state ideologies, consisting of concatenations of images and Enlightenment keywords such as 'freedom,' 'welfare,' 'rights,' 'sovereignty,' 'representation,' and 'democracy.' Appadurai argued that, within the global flows of the four previously described scapes, such terms have become more highly nuanced through the political narratives of the differential diaspora:

> As a result of the differential diaspora of these keywords, the political narratives that govern communication between elites and followers in different parts of the world involve problems of both a semantic and pragmatic nature: semantic to the extent that words (and their lexical equivalents) require careful translation from context to context in their global movements, and pragmatic to the extent that the use of these words by political actors and their audiences may be subject to very different sets of contextual convictions that mediate their translation into public politics…. This creates ever new terminological kaleidoscopes, as states (and the groups that seek to capture them) seek to pacify populations whose own ethnoscapes are in motion and whose mediascapes may create severe problems for the ideoscapes with which they are presented.
>
> (1996, 36–37)

Since the city's inception, Miami's ideoscape has been articulated in relation to the Caribbean, in particular Cuba. Language contact between Spanish and English was an integral aspect of the history of *La Florida*, which is depicted in early colonial navigational charts as part of the same landmass as Cuba (Portes and Stepick 1993, 63). In 1894, only 73 years after the Spanish Crown

60 *The linguistic order of (post)modernity*

officially ceded Florida to the US, the author of a *Scribner's Magazine* article on "Subtropical Florida" wrote that nearby Key West was "a thoroughly Spanish city, there being less than a thousand English-speaking Whites out of twenty-five thousand inhabitants"; he reported having "made inquiry of four persons as to the locality of the post-office before receiving a reply in English" (Dodge 1894, 351). Miami, not incorporated until 1896 when Cuba's War of Independence was already well underway, readily manifested an intimate political and economic relationship with its southern neighbors: "With foreign [Spanish] agents off its coast, contraband in its harbors, refugees on its streets and arms merchants checking into its hotels, Miami, in its first year of existence, had already realized the significance of its emotional and geographic proximity to Cuba" (Sicius 1998, 11). Sicius affirmed: "Although it would take the federal government a few more years to learn these lessons, Miami already knew that for better or worse its future was tied to Cuba's and that a part of its population would always claim the heritage of 'Cuban-American'" (1998, 13). Throughout the second half of the twentieth century, the symbiotic relationship between South Florida and Cuba would prove essential to the identity of Miami, as I will explain in Chapter 2.

Of course, that relationship is fundamentally characterized by the tension between communism and capitalism, which is the theoretical focus of Chapter 4. Within this standoff, which has persisted to the present day, three decades after the collapse of the Communist Bloc, notions of 'democracy,' 'human rights,' 'freedom,' and 'sovereignty' are contested and continuously rearticulated. Perhaps the term that has been key to Cuban Miami's ideological conceptualization is *la lucha* [the struggle], referring to the desire to restore a democratic government and capitalist economy to the island. Cámara (2003) affirmed:

> Thinking that "Castro is about to fall" is a kind of collective delirium, a firm desire that keeps people united in their identification as a community of exiles. Precisely this phenomenon is one of the factors that make Miami a difficult enclave in which to work for political choices and cultural alternatives. It is not an apt space for accepting and cultivating difference or dialog. Even so, I think that the city, for reasons of historical legitimacy, is an indispensable space for reconstructing the map of our fragmented [Cuban] nation.... Miami, apart from its expressways and McDonalds, has created and maintained the important language of memory, whose oppressive orality is at the same time a guarantee of its perpetual renovation.
>
> (164)

The fervent pro-capitalist right-wing ideological orientation that became the *genius loci* of exilic Cuban Miami during the 1960s and 1970s, concomitant with the rapid economic and demographic growth of urban South Florida, made the city a magnet for similar political exiles from other Latin American

The linguistic order of (post)modernity   61

countries. As a 1987 *New York Times Magazine* exposé on Miami's troubled social environment affirmed, "Nowhere else in America is local politics so permeated with foreign policy, which in Miami has sometimes meant an almost hysterical anti-Communism" (Sherrill 1987, 18).

Nicaraguans were the first major exile group to follow on the heels of the Cubans. As with the Cubans, Nicaraguan immigration occurred in three major waves. The first wave of nearly 15,000—overwhelmingly composed of the upper socioeconomic class (including the Somoza family)—arrived in Miami in the years immediately following the overthrow of the right-wing Somoza regime by the Sandinistas in 1979. Most of the immigrants, tied to the purse strings of the Somoza government, were political dissidents and entrepreneurial elites who brought with them much wealth. Nicaragua saw continued conflict and unabated political violence throughout the 1980s as the Reagan administration supported the Contra war. As civil war ensued, members of the middle class began to arrive in Miami in the second wave, settling primarily in the western suburb of Sweetwater in an area which later would be called Little Managua. Many established social networks and found economic and employment opportunities among Cubans and the previously arrived Nicaraguan entrepreneurial elite (Portes and Stepick 1993, 153). The third wave of Nicaraguan immigration in Miami took shape in the mid-1980s and peaked in 1989. Between summer 1988 and early 1989, an estimated 300 Nicaraguan refugees settled in Miami-Dade every week, according to the US Immigration and Naturalization Service (Portes and Stepick 1993, 150). But what some had thought was to be a Nicaraguan "repeat performance" of Cuban exile did not occur, due to several factors: the Nicaraguan influx happened in a much more compressed period of time and involved fewer people; the US federal government was more hostile toward Nicaraguan immigration than in the Cuban case; and, unlike Cubans, most Nicaraguans never fully closed the ideological door to their homeland: "A mythical Nicaragua could not be constructed in exile, as the Cubans had done with their island, because the real Nicaragua was too accessible" (Portes and Stepick 1993, 169–70).

Political and economic strife in several Latin American nations brought new waves of immigrants to Miami through the 1990s and into the 2000s. Colombians fled the longtime conflict between the national elected government, the leftist FARC, and right-wing paramilitary groups. Venezuelans became exiles of the leftist military regime of Hugo Chávez, whose election led to massive protests and human rights abuses, as well as state censorship of the mass media. Because of Chávez's intimate alliance with Castro, centrist and right-leaning Venezuelans garnered the sympathy and support of Miami Cuban exiles. By 2002, locally published Venezuelan newspapers were accessible throughout Miami, denouncing the tyranny of Chávez and his lack of respect for democracy and individual freedom, reminiscent of Cuban exile literature against Castro. Economic instability in early 2002 brought the closure of Argentina's banks and led to violent riots and looting in the streets of Buenos Aires. By summer of that year, Argentina had gone from having the

62   *The linguistic order of (post)modernity*

highest per capita income in Latin America to being the sixth poorest country in that region of the world, preceded by Nicaragua, Bolivia, Paraguay, Ecuador, and El Salvador. As a result of these events, hundreds of thousands of middle- and upper-class Colombians, Venezuelans, and Argentines established a vital presence in Miami that was Spanish-speaking and politically right-leaning. Other substantial contingents of Peruvians, Ecuadorians, Dominicans, and Hondurans have settled in Miami as a result of political turmoil and economic instability since the 1990s. More recently, economic crisis and the destruction caused by Hurricanes Irma and Maria in 2017 brought substantial numbers of Puerto Ricans to South Florida, where they joined a rather more centrist or right-leaning diaspora than in other urban areas: "[Edwin] Meléndez [director of the Center for Puerto Rican Studies at Hunter College] said that while you can count on Puerto Ricans in New York or Chicago to vote Democrat, the vote in Florida is not as secure. 'The party affiliation of Puerto Ricans in Florida is much more contested…. It's more up for grabs'" (Boryga 2019).

All of this is not to suggest that Miami's Hispanic majority constitutes a right-wing monolith that is largely conservative in their positions on social issues, e.g. abortion or LGBTQ rights (Iglesias Illa 2010, 200). Actually, Democratic US presidential candidates have consistently won the popular vote in Miami-Dade County since the 1992 election of Clinton; in 2020 Biden secured 53.3% of the vote (miamidade.gov). What is important for our purposes, however, is the prevalence of right-wing politics in the ideoscape of Miami and its seemingly unquestionable commitment to neoliberal economic practices. Despite the left-leaning sentiment and liberal social tendency of South Florida's slight majority, the right-wing legacy of the early Cuban exiles—who were nonetheless predominantly secular (Grenier and Pérez 2003, 42)—remains a key characteristic of Miami's ideoscape. A 2010 story in *Miami New Times*—the city's leading free weekly "independent source of local news and culture" targeted toward a young and upwardly mobile demographic—playfully reminded readers that "Latin American Dictators Love South Florida" (Elfrink 2010): "Put down that glossy guidebook to Orlando hotel bargains before we sic our guerrillas on your pastel-pants-wearing ass. This is South Florida, *muchacho*, the retirement home of army strongmen, torturers, and every other unsavory character from the Southern Hemisphere. We make Casablanca look like a Daffy Duck cartoon." The story named numerous right-wing politicians and military leaders accused of gross human rights violations who ultimately migrated to South Florida, among them former Cuban presidents Gerardo Machado and Fulgencio Batista; Nicaragua's Anastasio Somoza; Guatemalan military sergeant Gilberto Jordán; Peruvian military lieutenant Telmo Ricardo Hurtado; and former Bolivian defense minister Carlos Sánchez Berzaín, nicknamed "Bolivia's Dick Cheney." Iglesias Illa (2010) affirmed Latin American leftists' dislike of the city: "Miami ha sido en las últimas décadas tan hospitalaria con personajes nefastos de las derechas latinoamericanas… que es natural para una persona

The linguistic order of (post)modernity   63

que se considera de izquierda sentir asco por ella.... Sería difícil imaginar una mayor falta de química ideológica como la que ha habido históricamente entre Miami y el progresismo sudamericano" (200–201).

In sum, opposition to left-wing ideologies and progressive Latin American political agendas—fundamentally linked to political tensions in the Caribbean and Latin America—and fervent advocacy of free market enterprise and consumerism arguably constitute the master narratives of Miami's ideoscape, narratives for which Spanish is the matrix language (Iglesias Illa 2010). In the ideoscape, the cultural prevalence and economic prominence of a decidedly right-leaning historical contingent has eclipsed the presence of other political identities among the city's Spanish-speaking majority. By virtue of their highly outspoken anticommunist stance and *laissez faire* economic agenda, Miami's evolving Cuban exile community secured a privileged and—from the political perspective of the mainstream US—permissible space for the use of Spanish in public life. But that space, vis-à-vis English, would not go uncontested, as we will see in Chapters 2 and 3.

Scapes and the scope of the present argument

One might assume that the exceptional or peculiar status of Spanish in Miami within the context of the US was merely the result of immigration. Such an assumption would be naïve, however. Through the lens of Appadurai's (1996) concept of scapes in postmodernity and Baudrillard's (1994) argument that mass media and global consumerism are reshaping cultural and political realities, the current sociolinguistic situation of Miami might have been predictable already in the 1970s. As in the Southwest, Spanish was always already there (Sánchez 1994), and was metaphorically ushered into an increasingly legitimated cultural and political existence through the workings of neoliberalism, consumerism, and the flows of globalization. In this respect, the vitality of bilingualism in South Florida is not surprising, nor is the perceived prestige of Spanish in Miami.

Though languages in the postmodern era are resources to be exploited agentively by the individual (Heller 2011)—communicative repertoires that are institutionally misconstrued as 'named entities' to deleterious effects (Otheguy, García, and Reid 2015)—they are also conceptualized as objects by practically everyone for diverse ideological interests, including those of linguistics as an intellectual discipline (Varra 2018). People think of 'English' and 'Spanish' as bounded entities that can be contemplated, described, discussed, and debated sometimes in highly fraught yet unapologetic ways. Language exists because we presume to isolate it from other facts of reality, as a naturally occurring phenomenon that we perceive and process, to which we react and respond. This argument follows upon the philosophical premise developed in Anderson's (1983) *Imagined Communities* and Appadurai's (1996) extension of that inquiry to the postmodern reality, i.e. imagination and perception are fundamental features of humanity and, as such, influence

64 *The linguistic order of (post)modernity*

the construction of reality writ large: society, economy, politics, identity and, of course, language. Especially within the flows of postmodernity and the volatile spaces of global markets, the objectification of Spanish in the US appears to be a nonteleological activity driven by rather nearsighted social, economic, and political motives.

In light of this tendency, this book centers on the ideas that people have about language, how language 'works' or should (not) work, and the ways in which their ideas and perceptions serve to substantiate language as a social ontological reality (Lakoff and Johnson 1980; Searle 1995, 2007). Ideology, language, and social reality are all intricately bound up together, as Thompson (1984) affirmed:

> To study ideology is, in some part and in some way, to study language in the social world.... The theory of ideology, thus enriched and elaborated through a reflection on language, enriches in turn our view of language. For it directs our attention towards aspects of language use which have been neglected or suppressed by some perspectives in linguistics and the philosophy of language. To explore the interrelations between language and ideology is to turn away from the analysis of well-formed sentences or systems of signs, focusing instead on the ways in which expressions serve as a means of action and interaction, a medium through which history is produced and society reproduced.
>
> (2)

Each of the chapters in this book contemplates the relationship between ideology and language within the various scapes of postmodernity. In the remaining pages, we venture along the multifarious paths through which history is produced and society reproduced in ideas and perceptions regarding language, examining postmodernity's potential to forge novel sociolinguistic realities for Spanish in the US.

Notes

1 Some content of this section appeared in Lynch (2018a).
2 I have opted to follow the recommendation of the American Psychological Association and the MacArthur Foundation regarding the capitalization of both 'Black' and 'White' in reference to constructs of racial identity. At the time of this writing, varying stances were being taken by institutional organizations and media outlets. In citations containing these terms, I have maintained the original form as written by the author(s).
3 I use the terms 'Hispanic' and 'Latina/o/x' interchangeably throughout this book to refer collectively to individuals who trace their heritage to the Spanish-speaking countries of Latin America or Spain and who identify with any of those labels in US Census data and in sociological and cultural studies. This choice is not meant to reflect any sort of political position on my own part; I have no personal preference regarding use of any of the above terms. I note that in a survey conducted by Pew

The linguistic order of (post)modernity 65

Research Center, half (51%) of said individuals indicated having no preference for either term. Among those who did express a preference, 'Hispanic' was favored by most (33%); only 14% chose to call themselves 'Latino' (Taylor et al 2012). Some 70% of those surveyed affirmed that 'Hispanics' represent many different cultures, and most indicated using their family's country of origin to describe their identity (e.g. Mexican, Colombian, Cuban, Mexican American, Cuban American, etc.). In my own research endeavors and personal observations, I have noted that after country-specific terms, the collective label 'Hispanic' is most commonly used in South Florida, as I document in Chapter 3. I have not yet heard the term 'Latinx' used outside of academic circles or for purposes other than cultural institutionality in Miami.

4 US Census 2020 results for Miami-Dade County were still unavailable at the time of this writing.

2 Imagining Spanish in Miami

> Miami, for both better and worse, has captured the imagination of America.
> —T. D. Allman, *Miami: City of the Future* (1987)

The same year in which Emmy Awards went to *I Love Lucy* for Best Situation Comedy and Lucille Ball for Best Comedienne, the Hollywood star was subpoenaed by the House Committee on Un-American Activities. The Congressional Committee, created in 1938, was charged with investigating potentially subversive elements of US society. Beginning in 1947 and continuing through the 1950s in an effort to expunge the television and motion picture industry of leftist influences, the committee investigated hundreds of Hollywood producers, directors, screenwriters, and actors. Ball had been reported by a former Communist Party member who claimed to have attended a meeting at the actress's home in 1937. During her hearing in 1953, Ball admitted that in the 1930s she had registered to vote under the Communist Party affiliation to appease her ailing grandfather, a fervent socialist. She testified: "I am aware of only one thing I did that was wrong, and that at the time wasn't wrong, but apparently now it is, and that was registering because my grandfather wanted us to" (cited in Battistella 2014, 111). Ball declared that she had no sympathy for communism and had never supported the party's activities, although there was some evidence to suggest that she had indeed done so during the 1930s. Although the committee exonerated her, the hearings came to public light. Eager to defend their top new moneymaker, CBS officials released a statement affirming: "Miss Ball is not and has never been a communist. People seem to feel this thing is silly, not serious, and they all love Lucy" (cited in Árvay 2016, 41). Realizing the potential threat to their public image, Desi Arnaz addressed the live studio audience before beginning shooting of the first episode of *I Love Lucy*'s third season on September 11, 1953. In defense of his wife, he affirmed that her hair was "the only thing red about her, and even that's not legitimate," and also confessed: "I was kicked out of Cuba because of communism. We both despise communists and everything they stand for" (cited in Árvay 2016, 42).

DOI: 10.4324/9780429438363-2

Imagining Spanish in Miami 67

Arnaz was born into a wealthy aristocratic family in Santiago de Cuba. His father was a senator and Liberal Party ally of President Gerardo Machado (in office 1925–1933), often characterized as a dictator because of his violent response to critics and political insurgents. When Machado was ousted in 1933, Arnaz's father was imprisoned, and leftist insurgents ransacked the Arnaz family home. Like thousands of other Cuban exiles affiliated with the Machado regime, Arnaz and his father both fled to Miami (Arnaz 1977). There, he would finish high school along with friend and classmate Al Capone, Jr., learn English and later begin his career as a musical performer. In his 1977 biography, he reflected upon the situation of Spanish in the city: "In 1934 there were very few Cubans in Miami.... The only ones who were there then were the exiles from the Machado regime. A week later I found one small restaurant with a sign which said, '*Se hable Español*' [*sic*]. Today, with the half million or more exiles in that same area of Miami [southwest], you are lucky if you can find one that says 'English spoken'" (37).

Cuban discontent with Machado had been related to Cuba's relationship with the US under his direction, the economic policies he implemented following the Wall Street Crash, and ultimately, his authoritarian style of rule. During Machado's time in office, US investment in Cuba surpassed $1.5 billion, equal to the amount of US investment in all other Caribbean and South American countries combined during the same time period (Sicius 1998, 16). Having borrowed large sums of money from US banks to fund major public works in Cuba, Machado began an aggressive promotional campaign in Miami in 1930 to attract US commerce and tourism to the island. Not only had Machado made an agreement with automotive entrepreneur and Miami Beach real estate mogul Carl Fisher to market US-manufactured automobiles in Cuba, he had also established English-language schools in Havana and had begun to run a weekly five-page special section of the *Miami Herald* to tout US business opportunities there. In consequence, the center of Cuban revolutionary activity shifted from Key West and Tampa to the city of Miami during the early 1930s, reinforcing its symbiotic relationship with Havana.

After a failed coup attempt against Machado in 1931—the same year in which the recently formed Pan American Airlines began regular service between Miami and Havana, former president Mario García Menocal (in office 1913–1921) fled along with a cadre of wealthy followers. García Menocal's home on Miami Beach became the focal point for high-profile organized opposition to Machado's administration in Cuba and the symbolic center of an elite exile community. Just across the bay in downtown Miami, García Menocal found an unlikely ally in the much younger leaders of the leftist Directorio Estudiantil Universitario, among the ranks of whom figured two would-be presidents of Cuba: Ramón Grau San Martín (in office 1933–1934, 1944–1948) and Carlos Prío Socarrás (1948–1952). More than a thousand in number, the student revolutionaries were active demonstrators

68 *Imagining Spanish in Miami*

who shared García Menocal's stance against US intervention in Cuba and his dislike of Machado (Sicius 1998). Successful in their goal of ousting Machado in August of 1933, the exiles met Machado's wife and his Secretary of State in Miami as they fled the uprising in Cuba. When physical conflict ensued, Miami Police used force to contain the demonstrators, and Captain L. O. Scarboro publicly declared: "No more demonstrations will be tolerated. If they want to fight and raise hell, let them go back to Cuba!" (cited in Sicius 1998, 24).

García Menocal, like most of the anti-Machado revolutionaries, did indeed return to Cuba. Ironically, Machado would end up in the same city where his overthrow had been orchestrated, finally laid to rest in Miami's Woodlawn Cemetery in 1939, where his former opponent Prío Socarrás was also buried in 1977. Prío Socarrás had again taken exile in Miami in 1952 after his presidency was toppled in a US-backed coup staged by Fulgencio Batista, who had also lived in Florida following his first presidency (1940–1944). Like most Cuban political dissidents, Fidel Castro also went to Miami, seeking support from the Batista exile community in 1955. After a rousing speech at the Flagler Theater, he collected several thousand dollars (Elfrink 2010). Castro's July 26 Movement, orchestrated along with Marxist revolutionary Ernesto "Che" Guevara, gained traction in Cuba as economic disparity grew and social unrest was violently repressed under Batista in his second mandate (1952–1958). Meanwhile, US-based companies and Mafia members reaped extraordinary profits on the island, as did some Cubans, many of whom visited and shopped in Miami.

During the 1950s, nearly 50,000 Cubans visited Miami annually, up from about 40,000 annually in the 1940s (Pérez 1999, 435). An article appearing in the *New York Times* in 1948 noted that, during the summer of that year, Cuban travel brought in as much as $500,000 each month to the city's economy, and Spanish language was ubiquitous: "Almost as much Spanish as English is heard on the streets and in business establishments. *'Se habla español aquí'* appears in the show window of almost every store, and it is not uncommon to find most of the customers inside speaking Spanish" (Phillips 1948, X11). In 1948, the Miami Police Department required new recruits to take at least forty hours of Spanish language lessons and continue with forty additional hours once in uniform (Phillips 1948). In 1949, Spanish language became the most popular subject of winter courses for seasonal visitors at Florida's colleges and universities (Davidson 1949, X17). That same year, an article appearing in *Newsweek* observed: "In the summer planes from Havana wing in bringing Cubans by the thousands: rich Cubans, poor Cubans, clerks, professional men, skilled workers, even domestic servants.... The Cubans are leaving their mark on Florida.... Last summer it sounded as if as much Spanish as English was being spoken on Miami streets. Shops hired Spanish-speaking clerks and the city broke out with a rash of signs reading 'Se habla español'" (cited in Pérez 1999, 435). By 1957, celebrated journalist Eladio Secades would affirm: "All we Cubans have gone to Miami by now.... Spanish

Imagining Spanish in Miami 69

is spoken everywhere in Miami: in restaurants, in the shops, in the hotels, on the streets. There are moments in which the foreigner could think that what is not spoken in Miami is English" (cited in Pérez 1999, 439).

Although only five to six thousand Cubans permanently resided in Miami in 1958, the many Cubans who emigrated to Miami after Batista fled Havana on New Year's Day of 1959 did not arrive in unknown environs. As Portes and Stepick (1993) affirmed, "When the Cuban middle class did start to exit the island, it went to a social environment made utterly familiar by years of proper travel.... Cuba's exiles did not really move to a foreign land" (101). Similarly, Pérez (1999) observed that "powerful economic and cultural forces had set in place the basic structures that would facilitate and, indeed, foster the gigantic migration after 1959. The more Miami became familiar, the more it became Cuban" (444). More than four centuries after Ponce de León's exploration of the Florida coastline, history seemed to come full circle in Coral Gables as "the Andalusian settings so presciently built by George Merrick half a century earlier now became populated by people who knew their origins and could pronounce the street names correctly" (Portes and Stepick 1993, 88). With a population of "sun-seeking retirees, part-time tourists, and newly arrived farmers... by the mid-twentieth century, Florida, though no longer a vacant frontierland, was still in search of an identity and far more permeable to outside influences than the older societies of its erstwhile Confederate partners" (Portes and Stepick 1993, 83).

On sociolinguistic grounds, the societal porousness of South Florida would prove highly consequential for post-Castro Cuban immigration. Because Miami had remained a highly diverse and transient city, and because its political and economic structures were mostly familiar to upper-class Cubans who began to arrive in 1959, Spanish readily made broad inroads into public life. Assuredly, however, there was resistance on the part of the Anglophone majority. An article about the presence of 105,000 dissident Cubans in Miami published in *New York Times Magazine* in 1963 clearly reflected an anti-Cuban narrative. Highlighting their "disenchantment" and political tendency "to subdivide like amoebas," the author affirmed that "the only true unifying factor in the refugee community is the yearning to get back to a liberated Cuba" (Bracker 1963, 106). Emphasizing the exiles' dissatisfaction with John F. Kennedy's response to the Castro regime and, in particular, his lack of support for the Bay of Pigs invasion two years earlier, the article painted Cubans as somewhat contrary to predominant Anglo-American culture. The journalist pointed out that Miami's new residents eat *arroz con frijoles*, drink "countless small cups" of dark coffee, wear tight-fitting skirts "because [their] men like them that way," blare their radios too loudly, and cause a disproportionately high number of car accidents, which a Cuban was quoted as attributing to the "different system" that exists on the island: " 'In Cuba you blow your horn and keep going' " (Bracker 1963, 106).

Two important themes are apparent in Bracker's (1963) article. The first may be characterized as a 'danger' narrative, which would lead to an outright

70 *Imagining Spanish in Miami*

'battle' to defend ethnolinguistic boundaries by the 1980s, as I describe in the following section. Bracker affirmed that "the mere presence of the agency [US State Department's Coordinator of Cuban Affairs] here is evidence of the extent to which the fiery and thwarted Cubans have involved Dade County in a potentially deadly international drama," turning "one of the nation's greatest resort areas into a hot point in the cold war" (1963, 7). This narrative is also reflected in the above observations regarding the mayhem wrought on Miami streets by Cuban drivers and their ostensible lack of constraint concerning caffeine intake. The second narrative theme regards the danger of Spanish language use: "Boiling less with physical activity than with the pent-up feelings that have no true outlet, Miami's Cubans flood the town with Spanish" (7). This notion of sociolinguistic siege would come to occupy the public discursive forefront during the 1980s.

For the early exiles, however, Anglophone resistance seemingly did not pose a major sociological obstacle, as Iglesias Illa (2010) cynically remarked: "Los cubanos decidieron ignorar todo eso. En lugar de conquistar Miami, se dedicaron a construir otra paralela, al lado de la anterior.... En 1959, Miami era una ciudad amorfa, dócil y, comparada con La Habana, pueblerina. Nadie que viniera de La Habana rutilante y glamorosa de los 50 podía sentir miedo o fascinación por la Miami de los 60" (85). Importantly, Miami's early 1960s exiles held political gravitas given their legal status as asylum seekers—an artifact of Cuba's centrality in the escalating Cold War between the US and the Soviet Union. They also boasted generally high levels of formal education and had extensive entrepreneurial experience, having worked within the context of US business in Cuba. Indeed, Castro once remarked that Cuban entrepreneurialism was an impediment to socialism on the island: "We are a nation with a shopkeeper mentality" (cited in Grenier and Pérez 2003, 42). It seemed rather natural, then, that a cohort of the early exiles would soon establish businesses—in which Spanish would be the vehicular code of communication—once they settled in Miami. Those businesses provided a network of employment opportunities for continuously arriving Cubans and kept capital within the Spanish-speaking sectors of the city through the 1980s, a phenomenon often referred to as Miami's 'ethnic enclave economy' (Portes and Stepick 1993). This phenomenon facilitated rapidly growing trade and commerce with Latin America during the 1980s and 1990s, and "established a legitimacy of Spanish language use that was to have a lasting impact on South Florida" (Resnick 1988, 96).

In this chapter, I consider two principal metaphors that served to construct the ideological 'place' of Spanish in Miami during the final decades of the twentieth century: battleground and marketplace. The former is a narrative continuation of the modern national boundary and the struggle to maintain it in ethnic and linguistic terms; the latter has become the prevailing trope of postmodern economic neoliberalism. The 'battleground' metaphor in Miami has not only been employed to conceptualize and express the social realities of immigration, language contact, and ideologies of language—as in other parts of the US—but it has in ways served to create the image of the city itself, as we will see in the following section. The postmodern rise of Spanish in US public life in the 'marketplace' metaphor during the late twentieth century was not a novel phenomenon within the context of Miami, but rather the salient swell of a cultural current that characterized the city's foundation. Miami was never an industrial manufacturing center, as other major US cities have historically been. The city's economic livelihood always depended substantially upon the commodification of leisure and entertainment (Nijman 2011) and, concomitantly, upon strategies of image-making and marketing (Sherrill 1987), which are necessarily discursive in nature (Blommaert 2005).

In its historically symbiotic relationship with Cuba and its great distance—both geographically and socially—from the rest of the US, Miami was always unique. This has been true even within the context of Florida, as Sherrill (1987) posited in a *New York Times Magazine* exposé on the societal upheaval of Miami caused by violent drug wars, ethnic tensions, and immigration crises during the 1980s: "Many people in Tallahassee, the state capital, thought of Miami as an alien land even before it became known as the nation's largest cocaine transshipment point and before its felons became the inspiration for *Miami Vice*.... Tallahassee is 500 miles from Miami—which means that Miami, both in spirit and distance, is twice as far from the capital of Florida as from the capital of Cuba." The 'trouble in paradise' imaginary of Miami created by the mass media during the 1980s—with *Miami Vice* as the paragon—ironically drew tourists to South Beach in great numbers once again, precipitating a 1990s boom similar to that of the 1920s. What made the 1980s and 1990s different than the 1920s, however, was the vital impact of several key components of postmodernity: mass migration, the emergence of global financial networks, the power of mediascapes, and a transnational—rather than local—conceptualization of language.

According to Coupland and Kristiansen (2011), contemporary media "are increasingly flooding our lives with an unprecedented array of social and sociolinguistic representations, experiences and values, to the extent that... it is inconceivable that they have no bearing on how individuals and communities position themselves and are positioned sociolinguistically" (31). Because mass media can reach vast audiences in terms of both size and scope, they have the potential to shape popular perception and ideas about language. In postmodernity, the sensations produced by an increasingly rapid flow of text—both visual and discursive—taken together with heightened human mobility, i.e. movements and migrations, destabilize traditional subjectivities of modernity (Appadurai 1996, 4). Imaginaries are the fundamental characteristic of this sociological phenomenon, in the sense that mediascapes "tend to be image-centered, narrative-based accounts of strips of reality, and what they offer to those who experience and transform them is a series of elements (such as characters, plots, and textual forms) out of which scripts can be formed of imagined lives, their own as well as those of others living in other places" (Appadurai 1996, 35).

72   *Imagining Spanish in Miami*

As Androutsopoulos' (2014) volume cogently demonstrates, the media (i.e. mass media, new media, media representations, and media engagement) have great relevance for contemporary scholarship on language, globalization, and transnational flows. There is growing consensus that the notion of language change in sociolinguistic theory must move beyond structural considerations, widening the traditional—and exclusive—focus on change in linguistic systems to include a contemporary focus on change in the relationships between language and society (Coupland 2014). For our purposes, I wish to emphasize Androutsopoulos' (2014) affirmation that "sociolinguistic change is not limited to spoken language in the community, but also examines language practices and linguistic flows across media and institutional contexts" (6). As this chapter will suggest, the shift from (modern) ethnolinguistic boundary to (postmodern) marketplace asset in mass media representations of Spanish in Miami at the end of the twentieth century provides evidence of sociolinguistic change in the language ideological sense, i.e. change not at the structural level of linguistic variability but rather in terms of cultural reflexivity and the societal configuration of language in terms of role and place (Coupland 2014).

At the crux of the matter for us is cultural representation, an examination of narratives, discourses, actors, and characters in media text and talk from a sociolinguistic perspective, one that transcends mere formal analysis of linguistic structure in the media (Androutsopoulos 2014, 9). Several phenomena come into play: the construction of social and political identities in patterns of language use; the representation of linguistic heterogeneity in the portrayal of particular communities or societies, which produces "increasingly blurred boundaries between media language and community language"; the representation of change in language and society itself through metalinguistic discourse; and the construction of typical or 'exemplary' speakers through mediatized performance, which also heightens cultural reflexivity regarding language and identity (Androutsopoulos 2014, 9). All of these phenomena create the potential for mediatization: the historical, ongoing process by which media—mass media and increasingly new media (e.g. social media)—continue to proliferate and pervade all aspects of social life, not only influencing but also in some ways serving to construct social relations, especially on perceptual grounds (Krotz 2009; Lundby 2009). Appadurai's (2015) more recent thinking links mediation and materiality as mutually constitutive phenomena: "Mediation may be seen as an *effect* of which some sort of materiality is always the condition of possibility. But this materiality does not preexist mediation, any more than speech preexists language, pictures preexist images, or the eye preexists vision. The two sides of this relationship always exist and work together, as two sides of the same thing" (225, emphasis in the original).

In what follows, I take a critical discourse perspective (Blommaert 2005) on the metaphors of Miami as 'battleground' and as 'marketplace' in mass media representations of the sociolinguistic situation of the city. The former serves to construct the cultural imaginary of an Anglophone society ostensibly

Imagining Spanish in Miami   73

struggling to defend itself against the invasive threat of Spanish during the socially turbulent 1980s, and the latter offers a sociolinguistic staging ground for economic neoliberalism's rise to prevalence during the 1990s. Each of the award-winning and critically acclaimed television shows that I will comment on in this chapter had an immense and widely diverse viewership in its day, well into the millions of people in the US and abroad. These shows all remain highly popular still today, generating continued sales and playing in rerun to substantial audiences. The *Miami Herald*, which I also consider, has long been the most widely read newspaper in South Florida and was one of the largest newspapers in the nation in terms of readership during the latter part of the twentieth century; from 1946 until 2009 its international edition also circulated in more than twenty Caribbean and Latin American countries. It has won 22 Pulitzer Prizes, including the awards for Feature Writing in 1980, National Reporting in 1987, and Public Service as well as Commentary in 1993—years which will be of particular interest to the present discussion. The discourse of these mass media sources thus not only reveals much about actual sociolinguistic change in Miami in the language ideological sense, but it also had the potential to shape patterns in language-and-society relations during the transformative years of interest to us.

My objective is to shed some light on the language representational dimension of mediatization, i.e. what Jaffe (2011) defined as "representational strategies and choices involved in the production and editing of text, image, and talk in the creation of media products about language" (565). Metaphor is a crucial aspect of perspective-taking in text production (Derrida 1976); it not only does the work of organization and orientation on perceptual grounds, relating the 'real' physical world to the social ontological world of institutional, political, and cultural realities (Lakoff and Johnson 1980), but it also serves to foreground particular aspects of those realities. In the present consideration of the discursive representation of Spanish and English in Miami, I do not purport to make empirical claims about language in the sense of canonical social scientific method. As Jaffe affirmed, "We must begin from the premise that many media consumers know that representations of people depicted in broadcast, print, and web media are mediated, not 'direct' and that they also know the conventions through which sociolinguistic verisimilitudes (of 'true,' 'spontaneous' speech, reflecting essential qualities of identity) are mediatized" (2011, 567). Our interest is thus in the mediatization of language through representational worlds—which, by virtue of being realistic, in turn impact the perception of lived reality and, potentially, the course of sociolinguistic change in the poststructuralist sense of the term (Androutsopoulos 2014).

Defending modern ethnolinguistic boundaries: Miami as battleground

The initial idea of Miami was predicated upon South Florida's year-round warm climate, idyllic beaches, tropical sensuality, and relative geographic

74 *Imagining Spanish in Miami*

isolation. This environment lured thousands of the northern elite—among them John Jacob Astor, Andrew Carnegie, and John D. Rockefeller—to Henry Flagler's Royal Palm Hotel at the turn of the century. Because the hotel was the city's "whole reason for being" (Parks and Bush 1996, 28) in its early days, one can assume that the idea of a "*dolce-far-niente* existence in this dreamland" (Dodge 1894, 360) was the primordial element of the city's foundational narrative and the centerpiece of its original imaginary. Parallel to—and perhaps concomitant with—this dreamland or paradise narrative ran a narrative of pleasure and vice. Redford (1970) affirmed that Miami was "one of the first instances where the pleasure industry, rather than farming, mining, or lumbering, did the pioneering" (31). In its pioneer days, the Magic City—called such because early residents boasted that it had sprung from the tropical wilderness "as if by magic"—was a "rough and tumble place" where saloons, gambling dives, and brothels soon thrived just outside the official city limits, beyond the reach of Henry Flagler and Julia Tuttle's mandates on morality (Parks and Bush 1996, 28).

The newly incorporated city also found itself quickly embroiled in the escalating Cuban independence movement and subsequent Spanish-American War. As a strategic point in the clandestine arms trade with Cuba leading up to the war in 1898, the city reaped substantial illicit profits (Sicius 1998). The nearly 7,200 troops stationed in Miami at the time not only brought business to the saloons and brothels, but also social unrest and racial tensions with the local 'colored' community (Parks and Bush 1996, 41). Alcohol consumption figured prominently in Miami's early economic success. In 1913, the same year in which Henry Flagler died and the *Miami Herald* declared that he had "created an empire out of what was a barren and hopeless wilderness" (cited in Parks and Bush 1996, 51), Miami was legally declared 'dry.' During the national Prohibition Era (1920–1933), Miami profited immensely from bootlegging and rum-running as a principal point of entry and consumption of Bahamian and Cuban rum, earning it the dubious title of "leakiest spot in America" (Chepesiuk 2010). Indeed, Miami Beach openly flouted Prohibition laws and thus emerged as one of the country's premier vacation destinations during the 1920s.

Hundreds of thousands of northerners flocked to Miami in the early years of the 1920s, doubling the city's population and generating one of the greatest hotel and real estate booms in US history (Parks 1991; Portes and Stepick 1993). Miami's image as playground of the rich would evolve into that of America's playground as the middle classes began to join them. Speakeasies and brothels proliferated, as did organized crime and corruption; murder rates reached a historic high during 1925–1926 (Redford 1970; Chepesiuk 2010). The booming economy would soon falter, however, beginning with construction gridlock and a rapid decline of land values in 1925, followed by a devastating hurricane in September of 1926 and yet another in 1928, and finally the Wall Street Crash in 1929. Although South Florida's permanent population continued to grow significantly in the following decades, its economy

Imagining Spanish in Miami   75

remained largely tied to tourism, leisure, and entertainment, as well as an important underground financial current created by gunrunning and gambling (Nijman 2011).

When Prohibition ended in 1933, gambling assumed alcohol's previous position as the mainstay of Miami's tourist industry and its underground economy during the 1940s and 1950s, a phenomenon captured in the television series *Magic City* (2012–2013). Some of the nation's most notorious gangsters of that time migrated to South Florida, among them Meyer Lansky, who became the overlord of Cuba's casino industry with intimate ties to Fulgencio Batista (Redford 1970). In 1928, Al Capone purchased a Spanish Revival–style estate on Miami Beach's Palm Island, where he spent the final years of his life after his release from prison in 1939. Carl Fisher's early efforts to have Capone removed from Miami Beach proved futile because, as a detective hired by Fisher concluded, bringing incriminating evidence against Capone would lead to "exposing the whole rotten mess involved in running a wide-open town," i.e. bringing to public light the illegality and corruption that pervaded all levels of economic and political life in Miami (Redford 1970, 195). By the late 1940s and into the 1950s, Miami was not only described as a "plunderground" for the Mafia and a focal point for gangster activity according to FBI director J. Edgar Hoover, it was also characterized as "the underground capital-in-exile for the plotters of revolution in the Caribbean and throughout Latin America" in a 1958 *TIME* article (cited in Nijman 2011, 42).

Because of the central place the city occupied in US organized crime networks, the US Senate Special Committee to Investigate Crime in Interstate Commerce held its first hearings in 1950 in Miami; from there the proceedings continued to thirteen other major cities. Over 600 people were called to testify, including Frank Costello and others of the nation's most notorious mobsters. The televised hearings drew an estimated 30 million American viewers in March of 1951 (US Senate Historical Office, n.d.). A *Life* magazine article affirmed that "never before had the attention of the nation been riveted so completely on a single matter.... The Senate investigation into interstate crime was almost the sole subject of national conversation" (cited in US Senate Historical Office, n.d.). At the center of that national conversation was South Florida; the committee chair concluded in his report, which also implicated Florida's state governor in illicit gambling activities: "If ever we found concrete evidence of the interstate nature of organized crime it was in the Miami area." Still eighteen years later, a *Miami Herald* reporter wrote in 1968: "Organized crime ruled South Florida. Almost every racket known to man was operating.... Syndicate gangsters owned major hotels, restaurants, nightclubs, and were heavy investors in service industries. Corruption was nearly complete" (cited in Redford 1970, 228).

During the 1970s, two new products—imported from Latin America— came to dominate the underground economy: marijuana and cocaine. Because of its geographic proximity to South America and its open borders, i.e. surrounded almost entirely by seawater or wetlands, Dade County

76 *Imagining Spanish in Miami*

emerged as the epicenter of the drug trade. Miami's infamous 'cocaine wars,' vividly captured in the documentaries *Cocaine Cowboys* (2006) and *Cocaine Cowboys: The Kings of Miami* (2021), established the city as America's most violent by 1979 (Nijman 2011, 63), and in 1980–1981 it purportedly had the highest urban homicide rate in the world (Sherrill 1987). A defining blow for the city's image would be dealt by *TIME* on the highly publicized cover of its November 23, 1981 issue, which read "Paradise Lost? South Florida" (Kelly 1981). The inside feature story exposed Miami as the nation's most crime-ridden city, highlighting the "burden" posed by the 1980 Mariel boatlift and the mass arrival of boatloads of Haitian refugees, the significant rise in crime and violence due to drug trafficking, and the extraordinary homicide rate. Among the statistics cited in the article were these: 70% of all cocaine and marijuana imported into the US went through South Florida, and about 220,000 guns had been sold in Dade County over the previous five years—an average of more than seven guns for every new household.

Metaphors of battle pervaded Kelly's now infamous 1981 story, which constitutes one of the most influential pieces of journalism in terms of its relationship to the imaginary of Miami. Some examples are:

- "Consider what South Florida is **up against**."
- "If you stay here, you **arm yourself** to the teeth, put bars on the windows and stay at home at all times," says Arthur Patten, a Miami insurance executive. "**I've been through two wars and no combat zone is as dangerous as Dade County**."
- "As terrified residents search for **protection**, the region is beginning to be as **armed as a military base**."
- "Besides buying such **standard gear as pistols and window grates**, residents are purchasing **attack dogs**, alarms that scream out "Burglar! Burglar!" and even **armor-plated cars usually made for export to the war zones of Central America**."
- "**Battling** the dope runners are the combined **forces** of the U.S. Customs Service, the Coast Guard and the Drug Enforcement Administration, as well as local lawmen. But they all are **fighting a losing battle**."
- "With the arrival of the Marielitos, Blacks feared that they would **lose out** in the scramble for the few low-skill jobs available in the region."
- "Through boom and bust, hurricanes and real estate development, the mangrove has **stood its ground**. South Floridians surely will too."

This metaphor would soon be extended to the sociolinguistic imaginary during the 1980s in the mediatization of rapidly evolving language-and-society relations in Miami. The extension of the 'battleground' metaphor to the language use debates of the time was highly consequential: because criminality and physical violence in Miami had become mediatized on local and national levels, speaking Spanish would concomitantly become mediatized violence.

Imagining Spanish in Miami   77

The battle over Miami: Language about language in the mass media

Although there had been links to Cuba during the days of rum-running and gambling, it was not until the late 1970s that Miami's underground economy would come to depend—almost exclusively—on a Latin American import: cocaine. At that time, Miami's already established reputation as a place of great wealth where criminality and corruption ran rampant became inextricably bound up with its characterization as a Spanish-speaking city. The battles waged by and against criminals, mobsters, rum-runners, smugglers, crooked politicians, and corrupt law enforcement officials in South Florida since the early 1920s provided a ready-made metaphor not only for discourse about the problem of the city's drug trade and ethnic tensions during the early 1980s, but also for the conceptualization of societal debates around language policy issues. In this regard, we might personify the Spanish language as an innocent bystander who became an unfortunate casualty of mediatized violence.

Enacted in 1980, Miami-Dade County's English-only ordinance was also commonly referred to as the 'anti-bilingual ordinance' because it repealed a previous 'bicultural and bilingual' ordinance of the County Commission dating from 1976. The 1980 measure was explicitly interpreted in journalistic and academic treatises as a symbolic ethnic backlash to the Mariel boatlift and a mass influx of Haitian refugees—a backlash that had physical manifestations as well. Heightened ethnic and racial tensions were kindling for riots that would erupt on May 17, 1980 in Liberty City and Overtown after the acquittal of four White Miami Police officers charged in the brutal beating death of a Black motorcyclist who had led them on a high-speed chase, but had surrendered and been handcuffed. It was revealed that the officers had fabricated evidence at the scene. The ensuing riots paralyzed the city for three days. More than 3,000 National Guardsmen were called in to quell the unrest. Eighteen people died, nearly 200 were left injured, and 1,100 were arrested. In the aftermath, Miami was declared a federal disaster area, having sustained an estimated $80 million in property damages (Porter and Dunn 1984).

Although drugs, crime, and violence were clearly the focus of his "Trouble in Paradise" exposé, Kelly (1981) also drew the attention of *TIME* readers to South Florida's relationship to Latin America, the growing presence of Spanish-speaking immigrants, and the use of Spanish. Undeniably, the author sought to establish a definite—albeit implicit—relationship between criminality and Spanish language use in Miami. He pointed out that, in the previous year, Dade County voters had approved an English-only ordinance by a 3-to-2 margin. Tellingly, Kelly prefaced his mention of this potently symbolic piece of language legislation alluding to conflict, at the start of the respective paragraph: "Just beneath that cosmopolitan veneer, ready to erupt, are tensions between the Cubans and their fellow Floridians." The author detailed how, since the 1960s, Miami had "undergone a Latin-flavored business boom," becoming home to the Latin American headquarters of at

78 *Imagining Spanish in Miami*

least one hundred multinational companies and playing host in the previous year to some 12.6 million foreign visitors, "most of them Spanish-speaking." After affirming that "the Latins are gradually turning the region into their own colony," he noted that Dade County was 39% Hispanic, 44% White, and 17% Black at the time, and would become majority Hispanic by 1985. The "exodus" of Anglos from Miami was attributed to "the shocks of crime, drugs and cultural tensions," yet the only factor cited in that same paragraph was specifically language-related: "Says Jeff Laner, 26, a native of Miami who moved this year to work as a stockbroker in Kansas City: 'I was going to be damned if I had to learn a foreign language to get a job where I had lived all my life'" (Kelly 1981).

Noting that $4 billion of Latin American exile money was banked in Miami at the time, Kelly offered a list of several high-profile figures living there, including the widow of Anastasio Somoza and the son of Fulgencio Batista. He cited "one leading political exile, alive and well in Key Biscayne" as saying: "God, all I have to do is go out to the pool and I find everyone I knew there here. They are all speaking Spanish and walking around in their bathing trunks." The author highlighted not just the growing presence of Spanish speakers in Miami, but also the expansion of Spanish-language mass media, arts, and entertainment venues. He declared that early 1960s Cuban exiles had "transformed Miami from a resort town into an international city where 'buenos días' and frijoles negros are as familiar as 'good morning' and hamburgers." Kelly's appraisal of recently arrived Mariel Cuban immigrants was much less favorable: "Next to crime and drugs, South Florida's most pressing problem is refugees. The 125,000 Marielitos who fled Cuba last year have strained the area's economy and aggravated its racial tensions, perhaps irretrievably." He then offered statistics linking Marielitos directly to Miami's soaring rates of crime and murder, and posited ostensible cultural differences between the Cuban and Colombian cocaine cartels, clearly based on stereotyped notions: "Cuban dealers favor Mercedes Benzes and bodyguards dressed in dark suits and carrying two guns.... The Colombians are the most secretive of all, preferring to keep the business in the family."

The battleground metaphor of the so-called cocaine wars was appropriated not just by journalists and broadcasters who reported on the language controversy but also by politicians and ordinary citizens when speaking about it. Stories appearing in the *Miami Herald* related to the 1980 Dade County English-only ordinance, the 1988 Florida legislation establishing English as the state's sole official language, and the ultimate 1993 repeal of the county's ordinance all clearly reflect how this metaphor was used to cast the debate discursively. One of the first articles published after the enactment of the county's English-only ordinance explained that its vague language made actual application difficult. The story explained the frustrations faced by assistant county attorney Greenberg, who was charged with making case-by-case decisions. For example, he determined that Metrorail train schedules and brochures about fire prevention and the care of newborn infants could be printed only

Imagining Spanish in Miami 79

in English, but he allowed the posting of bilingual signage at Metro Zoo and the purchase of Spanish-language books by Dade County Public Libraries. The article stated: "Greenberg says his job is to 'walk a delicate line between enforcing the law and **protecting** the people.' Neither side of the bilingualism **battle** likes the route Greenberg has chosen" (Fisher 1983, 1B).

In 1984, commissioners voted unanimously to "liberalize" the ordinance by passing an amendment to permit the use of non-English languages to promote tourism, provide medical and emergency services, and serve the elderly and handicapped. A *Miami Herald* story highlighted the "bitterness and ethnic divisiveness" that marked the public hearing over the amendment, where leaders "reached a compromise to spare Dade another bitter referendum **battle** over the issue… 'It's a heck of a lot of work we're glad to get out of,' Benson [of Citizens of Dade United] said Tuesday, referring to the threatened referendum **fight**" (Dugger 1984, 1D). Another article published in the month prior reported:

> With the elections over, Metro Commissioner George [Jorge] Valdes… said he is now ready to **fight the fight** he has promised for four years: to change Dade's anti-bilingualism ordinance. The issue that **violently divided** Anglo from Hispanic, neighbor from neighbor, in the aftermath of the 1980 Mariel boatlift has been nagging at Valdes since he took office that year…. After South Florida was inundated with Cuban and Haitian refugees in 1980, the Citizens of Dade United… proposed to **fight back against the foreign tide** with a new law…. When Valdes' 1982 talk of modifying the anti-bilingualism ordinance raised **fear** of another lengthy, bitter community **battle**, he dropped the issue.
>
> (Fisher 1984, 1B)

A story about a private bilingual school in Hialeah published four months later began with the same metaphor: "Edison is a Latin bilingual school. It is one of 10 in Dade that have **banded together to fight one battle**: assimilating into the American way of life without being assimilated into the American melting pot. **Their weapon**: an accrediting agency called the Council of Bilingual Schools" (Asayesh 1985, NW10).

By summer of 1987, the same year in which the *Miami Herald* launched a separate all-Spanish daily newspaper called *El Nuevo Herald*, County Commissioner Valdes again considered the possibility of repealing the English-only ordinance. He ultimately chose not to do so. An article (Gillis and Feldstein Soto 1987) on Valdes' dilemma recurred once again to the notion of battle:

- "Metro-Dade Commissioner Jorge Valdes **retreated** Monday from his call for a public vote to repeal Dade's English-only law."
- "Monday's news conference marked the first strong public statement by Hispanic leaders on the anti-bilingual **battle**, which for several weeks had been a **lone crusade** by Valdes."

80 *Imagining Spanish in Miami*

- "It has also provoked **outrage—threats of violence** and almost 2,000 telephone calls to commission offices—from **backers** of the law."
- "[County Commissioners] James Redford and Harvey Ruvin said an instant repeal would **trigger** the same controversy Valdes wants to avoid. 'If we repeal the existing law, then we're just **sure-shot** going to get another petition drive' by anti-bilingual **forces** to put the law back on the ballot, Redford said."
- "Valdes said Monday: 'I've been a **fervent defender** of bilingualism, and I continue being a **fervent defender**. I'm going to **continue the fight** to remove the anti-bilingual ordinance.'"
- " 'If they do that, it's going to **tear this community apart** again,' said Terry Robbins, head of Dade Americans United. 'If they didn't like it in 1980, they're not going to like it in 1988.'"

At that time, attention turned to the state level. Leading up to the 1988 elections, when a proposed constitutional amendment would appear on the ballot to make English the official language of Florida, the *Miami Herald* ran a continuing series of stories. Predictably, they titled the series "Florida's battle over language." This key term had already appeared in at least two separate story headlines in the previous year:

- "Official English Push **Sparks Battle of Words**" (March 8, 1987)
- "English Is a **Losing Battle**, Say Two Who Won Bias Case" (August 17, 1987)

As one would suspect, the stories published in the *Herald*'s 1988 special series featured the battleground metaphor quite prominently. A July 31 article began by framing the controversy entirely in such terms, personifying language as "a live issue":

> Language in Miami is rarely **neutral ground**. It is not just a means of communication, but a live issue, the subject of some of the nastiest **civic battles** in Dade County in the past decade. English, Spanish and Creole coexist in a **fragile peace**. Friction over politics, economics, even simple courtesy often takes language as its **flash point**.
>
> (Viglucci 1988a, 1A)

Several related vignette stories recounted the personal experiences of people on both sides of the ethnolinguistic divide in Miami.

Featured in one of the vignettes was an elderly Anglo couple described as "survivors of another era," English monolinguals (Viglucci 1988b, 14A). Residents of Dade County since 1935, the Eakers had moved to the small town of Hialeah in 1948. At that time, Hialeah was almost exclusively non-Hispanic White and English-speaking. When it became Florida's fifth largest city in 1988, it was more than 80% Hispanic and, according to the story, the Eakers had been left isolated by their inability to communicate with their neighbors. Evelyn Eaker, age 70, affirmed that although her husband had been pressuring her to move to North Carolina, she wanted to stay in Hialeah. Her reason for staying invoked the 'tropical paradise' narrative: " 'I thought this was heaven and still do.... I have the sun, the flowers and the ocean, all those things that help me pretend it doesn't matter what language the neighbors speak.'" Her only reason for ever leaving invoked the narrative of battle: " 'The other day my husband asked me what it would take to make me go. I told him, when Castro is on the top step **with a gun pointed at my nose**, then I'll pack.'" (Viglucci 1988b, 14A).

The personal perspective of a Cuban American *Miami Herald* staff writer had appeared a few months earlier, a reflection on the reality of language shift to English in the second generation at the expense of bilingualism (Veciana-Suarez 1988). Like Eaker, Veciana-Suarez also constructed the language debate in terms of a battleground. She wrote:

> As the Florida English Campaign whips itself into a tizzy collecting signatures for its petition, I am busy **waging a language war** of my own.... Florida English, a group that wants to make English the official language of the state, is big time.... My **battle** pales in comparison. There are five of us, and the **battle** has yet to move from the **minefields** of home, sweet home.... I bet mine is not the only Hispanic household facing the dilemma. My children rarely speak Spanish. It's a **battle** to get them to practice. They are more comfortable in English.... By the second generation, it's an uphill **battle** to keep the language.... Miami's future, America's future, is international. Those of us who can communicate in more than one language will be successful, leaders of a new generation. The sad part, I believe, is that in Miami we emphasize—and inexplicably fear—only Spanish.... Forcing my children to speak Spanish is just part of the **battle**.
>
> (Veciana-Suarez 1988, 1B)

Several prominent local Hispanic politicians and businesspeople opted out of the state-level debate. In an article bearing the headline "Top Latins Sitting Out the Language Fray" (Viglucci 1988c), Miami banker Raul Masvidal explained: "We all think it's a losing **battle**. I don't see the practical effects of **leaving the ring with a black eye** after **getting punched around** for the next two months." The article also cited Jon Weber, the executive director of English Plus, a national organization opposed to the English-only movement. Weber urged that to be successful in South Florida, the opposition must "move away from the ethnic recriminations that marked the **language battles** of the early 1980s" and "cast their message in business terms," since language use restrictions would "**hurt** tourism and international trade" (Viglucci 1988c, 1B). Weber's words about the economic dimensions of language forespoke an ideological shift in terms of how Spanish would be imagined in Miami by the early 1990s, as I explain later.

82 *Imagining Spanish in Miami*

Article II, Section 9 (the Official English amendment) was added to the Florida State Constitution following the elections of November 8, 1988, having won the support of 84% of Florida voters: "(a) English is the official language of the State of Florida; (b) The legislature shall have the power to enforce this section by appropriate legislation." Osvaldo Soto, president of SALAD (the Spanish American League Against Discrimination), affirmed that the amendment "would bring chaos to Miami" (cited in Ramos 1988, 2D). One week after the vote, a *Miami Herald* headline read "Official English Now Draws **New Battle Lines**" (Ramos 1988), referring to differences between Hispanic advocacy groups who vowed to block language laws and monitor cases of discrimination and, on the other hand, pro-English-only advocates who would seek to pass legislation to enforce the amendment. The article stated that two days after the amendment was approved, a local supermarket cashier had been suspended from work for speaking Spanish, and SALAD received dozens of calls from people reporting that store clerks would not assist them in Spanish. There were then complaints that a high school principal in West Palm Beach allegedly told students that they could not speak Spanish in the hallway, though school administration denied the claim (Ramos 1988).

Several South Florida legislators affirmed they would try to stop the passage of further laws that would enforce the Official English amendment, to which a spokeswoman for Florida English responded: "There are 67 counties in the state, and South Florida does not rule. Don't assume this won't pass because some Hispanic legislators are upset. This state doesn't run like a **junta** in South America" (cited in Ramos 1988, 2D). One month later, two Hispanic organizations in Miami announced that they would monitor Official English to prevent "perverse interpretation and discriminatory application" of the amendment (Wallace 1988, 2B). Relying upon metaphors of criminality, leaders of the organizations urged that "as Floridians and responsible citizens, we must all be careful not to encourage an irresponsible minority of individuals to become the language **vigilantes** of Florida, who **deputize** themselves with puritanical self-importance to **stomp out** the speaking of Spanish **as if it were some crime**." They declared: "We will **fight fire with fire**." The *Miami Herald* reporter clarified that they were referring to going to court "to **do legal battle** if needed" (Wallace 1988, 2B).

Kelly's (1981) *TIME* narrative still reverberated years later. In 1987, the *Orlando Sentinel* made explicit reference to it in a report—with a notable physically charged tone—about a Dade County Commission meeting regarding the imminent repeal of the local 1980 English-only ordinance:

> Tension was so thick that Commissioner James Redford screamed "Shut up!" at a woman opposed to the repeal who interrupted him. The woman, Pat Keller, vice president of the group responsible for putting the anti-bilingual ordinance on the ballot in 1980, made no attempt to hide her disdain for Valdes or temper her opinion of what Miami will become if the ordinance is repealed. "They won't say, 'Miami, paradise lost,'" Keller

said, referring to a 1981 *TIME* magazine article. "They'll say, 'Miami, Spanish-speaking hellhole.'"

(Bell 1987, D1)

The author of a similar article appearing in the New Jersey newspaper *The Record* that same year observed: "People tend to think of Miami as the U.S. capital of crime and drugs. But that melodramatic reputation (even if it's deserved) isn't really central to the lives of most Miamians. When I visited last week, the land of 'Miami Vice' was in a furor not over cocaine or corruption but over a county ordinance: a law about language" (Corcoran 1987, B13).

In April of 1993, the headlines of the *Miami Herald* would once again evoke the battleground: "**Battle Lines Drawn** over English-Only at Metro" (Morales and Filkins 1993). The story reported that SALAD had announced plans to repeal Dade County's English-only ordinance. SALAD's president declared the ordinance "an insult to the Hispanic community," and County Commissioner Alex Penelas, who would subsequently become Executive Mayor of Miami-Dade County in 1996, affirmed: "We have entered a new era when the community must come together. This ordinance is something divisive." The authors of the article observed: "Some people speculate that the new 13-member Metro Commission… might be **inclined to kill** the ordinance. The new commission has six Hispanics, four blacks and three non-Hispanic whites. A **battle** seems certain" (Morales and Filkins 1993, 1B). A spate of stories, editorials, and opinion pieces appeared in the *Herald* leading up to the County Commission's vote. Days before, the newspaper's editor Jim Hampton urged commissioners to "bind up anti-bilingual wounds" by repealing the policy, asserting that "the resentment against Spanish is, in my experience, expressed almost wholly by people who won't try, or don't feel they should need to, learn Spanish" (1993, 2M). The 13-year-long English-only ordinance was unanimously repealed by the Dade County Metro Commission on May 19, 1993. The Official English amendment remains in the Constitution of the State of Florida.

Although it would be difficult to establish a causal link between mediatization and the outcome of language policy debates in the case of Miami, the potential cognitive effect of the mediatized violence of Spanish language use on readers cannot be dismissed. Contemporary studies suggest that extensive exposure to television portrayals of violence can create a heightened or exaggerated perception of violence in the real world (McQuail 2005) and lead to more aggressive behavior (Anderson and Bushman 2002). Research has also demonstrated that contemporary school shootings are a mediatized phenomenon, and that mediatization can have significant effects on the outcome of actual events during and after the rampage (Muschert and Sumiala 2012). It is thus not a far reach to hypothesize that journalists' and commentators' choice of the battleground metaphor in discussions of language practices and preferences during the 1980s did indeed antagonize social tensions and, ultimately, condition more pro-English-only attitudes.

84 *Imagining Spanish in Miami*

The effect could be true regardless of ethnolinguistic identity. Perhaps note-worthy in this regard are the results of a randomized telephone survey of 592 Miami residents conducted by the *Miami Herald* in 1988 (in English or Spanish per respondents' preference). The poll found that 43% of Hispanics (vs. 75% of non-Hispanics) supported Florida's Official English amendment to the State Constitution; 73% of Hispanics (vs. 78% of non-Hispanics) agreed with the statement that "All people should show that they can speak and read English before being allowed to vote"; and 41% of Hispanics (vs. 61% of non-Hispanics) agreed with the statement that "Taxpayers' money should not be spent to print bilingual versions of government documents such as ballots and meeting notices" (*Miami Herald* 1988, 20A). Interestingly, 62% of non-Hispanics agreed that "All children in South Florida should learn both English and Spanish" (versus 88% of Hispanics), a majority sentiment that was seemingly erased in the mainstream discourse of Miami's ethnic battleground.

Ways to tame a wild imaginary: Ethnolinguistic dimensions of Miami crime drama

'Battleground' provided a key metaphor not only for the imaginary of Miami being constructed in the news media during the 1980s, but it was also exploited creatively by the television and film industry. At the height of the drug wars, Hollywood greatly capitalized on Miami's dubious reputation as the nation's most murderous and crime-ridden city and the intrigue of a Spanish-speaking tropical paradise plagued by social ills. The best examples of this are Brian de Palma's now cult classic film *Scarface* (1983) and the iconic television series *Miami Vice* (1984–1989), marketed in the Spanish-speaking world as *Corrupción en Miami* and *Vicio en Miami*. These two wildly popular productions inspired a quasi subgenre of Miami crime drama, corresponding in particular ways to the city's imaginary. In the 2000s, three such crime drama series reached great popularity and critical acclaim, both nationally and internationally: *CSI: Miami* (2002–2012), *Burn Notice* (2007–2013), and most remarkably *Dexter* (2006–2013), slated to return in November of 2021. In what follows, I place special emphasis on *Dexter* because of the immense popularity of the show and the greater presence of Spanish in its script. First, a bit about *Scarface* and *Miami Vice*, iconic Hollywood productions set in Miami that have an enduring cultural value in terms of mediatization.

The defense of the linguistic order

A remake of a 1932 film with the same title, which was based loosely on the story of Al Capone in Chicago, the 1983 film *Scarface* portrayed a fictitious Mariel Cuban refugee named Tony Montana (played by Al Pacino speaking English in a highly affected Cuban accent) who rises to the top of Miami's cocaine trafficking industry. The film not only garnered an initial X rating

Imagining Spanish in Miami   85

because of extreme violence, drug use, and graphic language, but also a disclaimer by leaders of Miami's Cuban community because of its negative representation of Cuban immigrants. Before shooting began in Miami, the film's content caused controversy among some Cuban exiles, including a city commissioner, leading De Palma to relocate to Los Angeles. Many who had championed the production in South Florida were left disappointed, including Florida Governor Bob Graham and the Miami Chamber of Commerce, who had appealed to the movie's producer, as well as the City of Miami Beach, which had passed a formal resolution welcoming the film. Quiroga (2009) argued that Cuban exiles' original injunction not to film *Scarface* on location in the city where the story would take place marked the beginning of what he considered to be Miami's prime narrative: "a city that in itself seems to beckon other people's projections and other people's ideas" (151); "a city that is neither known nor unknown, but rather a canvas, a project, a kind of abstract topography" (155). Quiroga suggested that by forfeiting claim to their own representation, Miami Cubans lost much of the symbolic capital they had held as a model immigrant community prior to the Mariel crisis, "for *Scarface* turned narrative and personal history into culture, and thus cemented what would later be called the 'Latin Americanization' of Miami…. Over time, and as a result of processes that came to the forefront during the *Scarface* production, Cubans became the minority that it was politically correct to defy" (2009, 155–56).

As for the controversy surrounding the potential harm that *Scarface* would do to Miami's image, producer Martin Bregman told the *Miami Herald*, "If they don't want us there, we'll leave. Believe me this is not going to give Miami or that area a bad image. It already has that image" (cited in Meltzer 2007). Nijman's (2011) sociological account would support Bregman's affirmation. At the time, *Miami Vice* executive producer Anthony Yerkovich told *TIME* that he had been collecting information on Miami prior to the show's conception. He noted that the city "seemed to be an interesting socioeconomic tide pool: the incredible number of refugees from Central America and Cuba, the already extensive Cuban-American community, and on top of all that the drug trade…. Miami has become a sort of Barbary Coast of free enterprise gone berserk" (Zoglin and Worrell 1985). That image would inspire the setting and plot for the gun battles fought by Crockett and Tubbs (played by Don Johnson and Philip Michael Thomas), two undercover Metro Dade Police Department detectives who bust drug traffickers and prostitution rings, and propel *Miami Vice* to become one of the most critically acclaimed television series of all time. The *TIME* article observed that although "some civic leaders were originally unhappy at the prospect of a network TV series blaring the city's crime problems into living rooms across the nation," the revenue generated by the show—which was actually shot on location in Miami—and its boost to the tourist trade had seemed to quell the concern. Miami's then mayor, Puerto Rican–born Maurice Ferré, was cited in the article affirming that "it shows Miami's beauty," and William Cullom, president of the Greater

86 *Imagining Spanish in Miami*

Miami Chamber of Commerce, stated that "it has built an awareness of Miami in young people who had never thought of visiting Miami" (Zoglin and Worrell 1985).

Many credit the imaginary created by *Miami Vice* with the high fashion and tourism boom of South Beach in the 1990s, as well as the revival of its historic Art Deco District, which was physically deteriorated and blighted by crime and poverty by the early 1980s (Rieff 1987). In fact, the exteriors of rundown buildings were often painted and restored to serve as sets bestowing a highly characteristic look to the show. In this instantiation of mediatization in its finest sense, the imaginary of the television series actually lent itself to construct a reality for South Beach by the late 1980s and into the early 1990s. Upon the release of the 2006 film adaptation of *Miami Vice*, an Associated Press article seemingly evoked Lynch's (1960) classic urban studies treatise *The Image of the City* in a reflection on the physical and cultural evolution of Miami's image since the mid-1980s, when the original television series was shot there: "Television was helping to create a new image for South Beach and Miami, and reality wasn't far behind" (Associated Press 2006). A longtime Miami Beach resident recalled: "They created a lot of the glitz and the glamor—the Miami that we saw in *Miami Vice* sure wasn't where we lived. It became this synergistic relationship where *Miami Vice* was painting its own buildings and using architecture as a character in the show, and millions were seeing this on television" (Associated Press 2006).

Iglesias Illa (2010) remarked upon the relationship of the series' imaginary to the city's real social transformation and its ephemeral quality:

> Para Miami, que en los 80 estaba velando a su vieja ciudad... y le estaba abriendo paso a su nueva versión, global, conflictiva y multilingüe, los intentos de Crockett, Tubbs y Castillo por frenar este proceso representan la última batalla de Miami por resistir el cambio.... *Miami Vice*, que entendía el trauma de Miami con su obsesión por lo efímero y su incapacidad para sostener una identidad en el largo plazo... transmitía bien, aunque quizás a su pesar, la idea de Miami como una ciudad que está siempre a medio hacer, atada con un alambre, a un día del próximo huracán.
>
> (72–73)

As I noted in Chapter 1, Baudrillard proposed in his seminal work *Simulations* that, in the postmodern context, reality dissolves into simulation, "a hyperreal henceforth sheltered from the imaginary, and from any distinction between the real and the imaginary, leaving room only for the orbital recurrence of models and the simulated generation of difference" (1988, 167). In this condition of 'hyperreality,' simulacrum supersedes the principle of equivalency between representation and reality, i.e. the notion that the representation reflects or stands in for a real-world referent: "Miami, que nunca fue industrial, fue postindustrial antes que nadie: desde sus primeros días vivió

Imagining Spanish in Miami 87

de vender una idea de sí misma que no siempre coincidía con la realidad" (Iglesias Illa 2010, 221). In this respect, the relationship of the *Miami Vice* imaginary to the social reality of Miami exemplifies the complexity of postmodern society in terms of mediatization. According to Agha (2011), "social processes in any complex society derive their complexity from practices oriented to forms of mediatization" and "an account of mediatization is... not a theory of the media but an account of the social processes that the media construct obscures. Mediatized practices occur inside the media but also outside them" (163–64).

The inside-outside dynamic of mediatization is not only important to interpreting sociolinguistic change in South Florida through the lens of the 'battleground,' but it also captures the problem of presence and the uncertainty of reality in Miami. The illusory nature of identity is posed already in the first season of *Miami Vice*. In episode 2, Crockett first finds out that Tubbs is not really who he said he was (but is using his dead brother's name to avenge his death), then he learns that his lieutenant, whom he looked up to, is on the take, and also discovers that his former partner, whom he greatly trusted, is being paid off by the cartel as an informant. After having his former partner apprehended, he calls his ex-wife and asks her, "I need to know something, Caroline. The way we used to be together—I don't mean lately, but before—it was real, wasn't it?" Throughout the series, Miami is represented as a place where identities seem fake, a leitmotif that perhaps inspires the virtualization of the city as backdrop in *CSI: Miami* (West 2009). Dexter himself declares in the eponymous show's first episode that "People often fake a lot of human interactions, but I feel like I fake them all"; later in the first season an officer comments that "the whole fuckin' city of Miami reinvents itself every five years" (episode 4). In their widely cited accounts of Miami, both published separately in the same year, Rieff (1987) and Didion (1987) emphasized the enigmatic character of the city. Didion affirmed: "Miami seemed not a city at all but a tale, a romance of the tropics, a kind of waking dream in which any possibility could and would be accommodated" (1987, 33).

According to Quiroga (2009), the "sense of strangeness and dissolution" that Didion experienced in Miami may be partly attributable to the presence of Spanish in "fashionable places," unlike in Los Angeles or other major US cities where its use was relegated to the periphery (158). Indeed, Didion commented on the widespread use of Spanish across all sectors of Miami, and noted the perception that Spanish pervades Miami even before arriving: "I never passed through security for a flight to Miami without experiencing a certain weightlessness, the heightened wariness of having left the developed world for a more fluid atmosphere.... At the gate for such flights the preferred language was already Spanish" (1987, 23). The ubiquity of bilingualism undoubtedly contributes to Miami's fluid—if not deceptive—identity in the cultural imaginary. Already in Bracker's (1963) *New York Times Magazine* article, previously cited, the dubious character of early Cuban exiles was attributed in part to bilingualism: "One 8-year-old was asked if he wanted to

88 Imagining Spanish in Miami

return to Cuba. 'I wanna stay here', he said. Later, his mother asked why he had said that. 'He was an American man', the boy replied in Spanish. 'That's what he wanted to hear me say'" (106). Forty years later, expert pollster and political campaign strategist Sergio Bendixen affirmed: "Miami is like polling two or sometimes three different worlds.... And we're moving in the direction of the number of worlds expanding. You poll the Hispanics in Spanish and the Hispanics in English and they give you two different answers to the same question" (Dudley 2003).

It is noteworthy in *Miami Vice* that criminal characters are often Spanish speakers. Tubbs is shown speaking and understanding Spanish at times, but never his White Anglo partner Crockett, the show's main character. Ramírez Berg (2002) observed that the conventional and socially dominant Hollywood protagonist is a non-ethnic White, vaguely Protestant, healthy, handsome, middle-aged, upper-middle-class, heterosexual, Anglo male who is intelligent and excellent at problem solving, but not intellectual (25). To Ramírez Berg's description sociolinguists would add English-speaking, preferably monolingual—in a mainstream variety of US English, i.e. having no marked regional or ethnic accent. This description surely fits Crockett in *Miami Vice*, as well as the protagonists of more recent hit crime drama series set in Miami: Horatio Caine (played by David Caruso) in *CSI: Miami*, Dexter Morgan (played by Michael C. Hall) in *Dexter*, Michael Westen (played by Jeffrey Donovan) in *Burn Notice*, and Jim Longworth (played by Matt Passmore) in *The Glades*.

In all these popular television series, as in *Miami Vice*, there is a predominance of White Anglo characters whose knowledge of Spanish and friendly acquaintance with Spanish speakers are next to none, reflecting Hollywood's unyielding ideological insistence to erase Spanish from the US ethnoscape, even in Miami. As Lippi-Green (1997) demonstrated, in Hollywood cultural productions, likeable characters overwhelmingly are speakers of mainstream varieties of English. Conversely, use of other languages or nonmainstream varieties of English, including 'accented' ones, is largely observed in characters with dubious or negative motivations and actions (101). Few would disagree that Tony Montana in *Scarface* is, for the most part, meant to be an unlikeable character whose motivations and actions are negative. According to Ramírez Berg, the formulaic Hollywood narrative, entrenched in the industry for ideological purposes, begins with an equilibrium (i.e. tranquil status quo) that is somehow disrupted (i.e. the status quo is threatened) and then ultimately restored by the WASP male protagonist (2002, 67). So that this protagonist can display his preeminence socially, characters of other cultural, ethnic, racial, class—and to this list I would add linguistic—backgrounds play supporting or minor roles, often antagonistic: "Not just Latinos but all people of color represent an inherent threat to the status quo simply because they are markedly different from the established WASP norm" (67). This is certainly the portrait that *Scarface* paints of Tony Montana, who speaks English with a marked accent.

Typically, in Miami-imagined crime dramas, Spanish is heard very infrequently in brief dialogues with or between menial service workers (e.g.

housekeepers, gardeners, or low-level assistants), criminals, their victims, and family members. On rare occasions, supporting characters speak a few words of Spanish to each other. For example, the only Spanish heard in the pilot episode of *The Glades* is when Carlos Gómez, the bilingual Latino medical examiner—who plays a supporting role to Jim, the show's monolingual Anglo protagonist—translates Jim's instructions to the Spanish-speaking golf course groundskeepers not to move his golf ball from a particular spot. In the pilot episode of *Burn Notice*, the only reference made to the Hispanic presence in Miami is in a line uttered to the protagonist, Michael, by Mr. Pyne, a wealthy Anglo-American who suspects his estate caretaker, Javier, of stealing a valuable work of art from him. Mr. Pyne says: "This is Miami. Any incident and the police blame the nearest Cuban or Haitian. You should've seen the way they were all over my gardeners." *CSI: Miami* presents a similar sociolinguistic imaginary, with extremely little use of Spanish relegated to minor or supporting roles.

Similar to Horatio Caine in *CSI: Miami*, Dexter Morgan serves to (re) stabilize Anglo-American identity within majority Hispanic and Spanish-speaking Miami as it is represented in the series. West (2009) explained that for Caine, who was inspired to join the police force to protect "his city" after his mother was murdered by a drug dealer during the violent 1980s, the "Miami community is a cosmopolitan and diverse space that is, however, anchored to the racial identity he owns as a white American" (121–122). West argued that, in Caine, the viewer perceives a sense of anxiety about ethnic and racial diversity that is counteracted by "a liberal tolerance of difference so long as it is framed by the hegemony of white, patriarchal identity" (123). With regards to *Dexter*, Kirkland (2011) observed that the multiethnic cast of the show serves to place the protagonist's 'Whiteness' in relief:

> Dexter, the white heterosexual male, seems at first to be devoid of character. He has no political ax to grind. He has no distinct accent. He is polite, unobtrusive, and quietly professional. He has no sexual peccadilloes, as far as anyone knows. And at the same time, just as white paint is only noticeable when placed on a non-white surface, this 'colourful' environment allows Dexter's ethnicity to become visible.
>
> (201–2)

Linguistically, Dexter was the only one of the protagonists named above who actively demonstrated any knowledge or use of Spanish. For this reason, and because of its immense popularity and viewership, I turn to a more detailed consideration of the presence of Spanish in *Dexter*.

Linguistic (mis)representation and mockery in a murderous city:
Spanish in Dexter

The imaginary of Miami as a violent city provides the ideal backdrop for the character of Dexter in Showtime's award-winning series precisely because it

90 *Imagining Spanish in Miami*

is one of the elements that permit the viewer to justify the protagonist's murderous behavior and empathize with his 'code' of killing other killers who have escaped the police. As Michaud (2011) remarked, "It seems we think that what Dexter is doing isn't really that bad; as a matter of fact, it might be a good thing" (35). In its annual Best of Miami issue, the *Miami New Times* named it the Best TV Show Set in Miami for 2008 and again for 2013, stating that *Dexter* is "still the best illustration of that old saying about Miami: 'sunny days, shady people'" (Volume 28, Issue 12, 68). A *Miami New Times* reporter wrote in 2012: "Shows about Miami are notorious for misrepresenting the city's look and layout. But if ever there were a show that got Miami right, *Dexter* would be it. The equatorial light streams in hard.... Touches of saturated color—blood reds, hot pinks—make white, otherwise boring rooms pop.... And, of course, there's all the crazy crime that could only happen in South Florida" (Hiatt 2012). In the show's first episode, Dexter, whose voice serves always as background narrator, comments on the artificializing effect that Miami daylight has on murder scenes: "There's something strange and disarming about looking at a homicide scene in the daylight of Miami. It makes the most grotesque killings look staged, like you're in a new and daring section of Disney World: Dahmerland" (season 1, episode 1).

The seeming artificiality of nature cast in the daylight of South Florida and the imagined ubiquity and mundaneness of violent crime in Miami are arguably what make the protagonist and plot of *Dexter* palatable to so many viewers. Despite his being a self-confessed sociopathic serial killer, Dexter's self-indulgent crusade for justice in a highly unjust environment—in which nature appears imbued with artificiality—somehow seems justifiable. Smith (2011) explained the connection between the show's lighting and the everydayness of violence in Miami as created in *Dexter*: "This careful attention to the lighting and the camerawork aestheticizes the violence and makes it compelling and interesting, if unnerving. These techniques are used not only during scenes of violence and actual gore but throughout the series, suggesting that there is an undercurrent of violence and malevolence in the everyday" (398). After declaring in the opening narration of the show's pilot episode that "Miami is a great town" and that he "love[s] the Cuban food," Dexter points out to the viewer that the great majority of murderers in Miami go unpunished: "With the solve rate for murders at about twenty percent, Miami is a great place for me—a great place for me to hone my craft. Viva Miami" (season 1, episode 1). After Dexter murders the series' first victim in this episode and is disposing of the body in Biscayne Bay, Beny Moré's classic ballad "Conocí la paz" plays, the first of many Spanish-language songs that would provide ambient background music throughout the series.

Like the music, lighting, and imagined pervasiveness of violence in Miami, Dexter's own occasional use of Spanish, as in the line "Viva Miami," makes his existence seem all the more mundane in a city where Spanish looms large. For Dexter to appear a natural and normal resident of Miami, he would be expected to hear and possibly use Spanish to some extent in everyday life,

Imagining Spanish in Miami 91

particularly given the fact that he works for the Miami Police. Likewise, if the city of Miami and its police force as (re)created and (re)presented in the series are to seem convincing, thus naturalizing the protagonist's true character, Spanish should be part of the sociolinguistic landscape. In the pilot episode, basic Spanish is indeed used in interactions with Detective Angel Batista (played by David Zayas), Dexter's bilingual Cuban American colleague. Angel addresses both Dexter and his fellow forensics expert Vince Masuka, a Japanese American, in code-switched English and Spanish. When viewers first meet Angel and Vince, already at the crime scene where the dismembered and bloodless corpse of the "Ice Truck Killer's" first victim is found, Angel points out to Dexter and Vince that the killer apparently did not complete what he had set out to do: "He didn't finish. No terminó" (season 1, episode 1). After a few moments, when Dexter turns to walk away and leave the scene, Angel asks him, "Dex, ¿adónde vas? Where are you going?", to which Dexter—the team's blood spatter expert—responds, "No blood, no trabajo." Back at the police station, Dexter's customary offer of a doughnut to Angel occurs in Spanish: "¿Uno más?" (Dexter) / "Gracias" (Angel, taking a doughnut) / "De nada" (Dexter). Later in the episode, at another crime scene, Angel greets Dexter in Spanish ("¿Cómo estás? What are you doing here?"), then begins to point out to him the particularities of the murder that has occurred using a Spanish deictic ("Mira esto"). As Angel explains what he believes the murderer has done, Dexter responds, "muy bien."

These brief interactions, in which very basic phrases that most anyone who has taken an elementary Spanish course would comprehend, give the impression that code-switching is part of everyday language at the fictional Miami Metro Police Department, both in work-related and personal conversations. Angel also uses Spanish frequently with Lieutenant Maria LaGuerta (played by Lauren Vélez), another bilingual Cuban American character in whose office viewers see an art piece inscribed with the phrase "No es circunstancial que esta noche comuniquemos." Angel's interactions in Spanish with Maria are discursively a bit more complex than those with Dexter. For example, in season 1, episode 2, during a late night at the office, Maria asks Angel how his daughters are:

LAGUERTA: "¿Y tus hijas cómo están?"
BATISTA: "Están maravillosas."
LAGUERTA: "Tú sabes que ellas también te necesitan. Angel, vete a tu casa."

This short dialogue, entirely in Spanish with no subtitles, likely would not be understood by viewers who do not have some basic knowledge of the language. The same is true of what Angel states to Maria in season 7, episode 12, regarding her insistence that Dexter is the so-called Bay Harbor Butcher: "Eso es lo más ridículo que yo ha [*sic*] oído en mi vida, Maria." Curiously, Dexter's own use of Spanish with his friend and colleague Angel disappears altogether after the first few episodes of season 1, never to recur, and Angel's use of

92 *Imagining Spanish in Miami*

Spanish is relegated mostly to dialogue with Maria. Indeed, by the eighth and final season, Angel admonishes Vince, the Japanese American colleague with whom he uses occasional phrases in Spanish during the first season, for saying a few words to him in his native language: "It's weird when you try to speak Spanish" (season 8, episode 1).

Throughout the series, Angel and Maria—both played by actors of New York Puerto Rican background—pronounce each other's names with Spanish phonology and, in various scenes, briefly speak to each other in notably Puerto Rican–accented Spanish or insert occasional Spanish words into their English discourse. Although the show's producers laudably aspire to represent Miami's Spanish-speaking reality through these two characters, however ethnically stereotyped (Aguiló Mora 2010), they seemingly ignore the fact that Spanish phonology varies across Latin America and in the US. To anyone familiar with Caribbean Spanish, Angel and Maria do not sound Cuban or Cuban American, much less Miami Cuban American. Some side characters who are supposedly Spanish-speaking immigrants are portrayed by actors who are clearly heritage speakers, i.e. they present particular phonological and discursive tendencies typical of US-born, English-dominant Latinos. For example, while in pursuit of a suspect in season 5, officer Debra or "Deb" Morgan (who is Dexter's sister, played by Jennifer Carpenter) stops to ask a street vendor which way the car she was chasing had gone, only to discover that he speaks only Spanish (episode 12). She apparently comprehends much of what he says to her in Spanish, and produces some very basic phrases herself, such as "¿Adónde fue?" and "¿Qué?" when asking the man what could be found along the street the suspect had taken. The man responds, "Nada mucho, un campamento." For a Spanish-dominant speaker, the phrase "nada mucho" (calqued on English "not much") would be ungrammatical, if not altogether incoherent ("nada" meaning 'nothing' and "mucho" meaning 'a lot,' a semantic contradiction in Spanish grammar).

The Hollywood tendency to homogenize varieties of Spanish language—including those of heritage speakers and Spanish-dominant immigrants in the US context as well as highly distinctive dialects of the language—is concomitant with lumping all Spanish speakers into a single and ostensibly monolithic category of 'Latino.' This ideological practice also gives rise to cultural misappropriations across different national and ethnic groups within the US. For example, in season 5, a series of murders in Miami is attributed to the practice of Santa Muerte, which is apparently widespread in Hispanic Miami. In reality, however, this practice is characteristic of Mexican-origin communities in the US, especially in the Southwest and Los Angeles; indeed, the origins of Santa Muerte are Mexican. The prevalent occult ritual practices to be found in Miami actually stem from Caribbean-origin belief systems such as Santería, Palo Mayombé, or Voodoo. This cultural confusion is readily apparent in a scene in which Deb, in the company of a Spanish-speaking detective, enters a local botanica to find out if the store sells an iconic Santa Muerte figurine previously found at a crime scene (season 5, episode 3). A large

Imagining Spanish in Miami 93

image of the Mexican icon La Virgen de Guadalupe adorns the store's outer wall, but inside Cuban *son* music plays in the background. The attribution of Santa Muerte to Miami's highly predominant Caribbean cultures is thus not only unconvincing on sociocultural grounds but is altogether unlikely in demographic terms. Indeed, the Mexican-origin segment of Miami's Hispanic population is very small: just 2.2% in the 2019 US Census estimates (American Community Survey 2019).

Another noteworthy demographic discrepancy is that the vast majority of Dexter's targets are non-ethnic Whites, with the important exception of Miguel Prado, an upper-class Cuban American who becomes Dexter's ally in season 3. In reality, non-Hispanic Whites constituted only 12% of metropolitan Miami-Dade's population in the 2010 US Census, at the time the show was being produced. In mere demographic terms, it would be significantly more likely that Dexter's victims would be Hispanic or Latino, as nearly 70% of the area's population identified as such; another 18% identified as African American in the 2010 US Census, yet this segment is scarcely reflected in any of *Dexter*'s storylines. In this regard, the show appears whitewashed, in that it portrays a majority of non-Hispanic Whites both in negative (i.e. criminal or morally corrupt) characters as much as in positive (i.e. law-abiding and morally upstanding) ones. On the surface, one might interpret this demographic misrepresentation as a commendable effort on the producers' part to avoid stigmatizing Latinos within the broader US context. For example, Kirkland (2011) affirmed that the series treats the subjects of racial or ethnic tensions and illegal immigration "with sensitivity and respect" (200).

Although Kirkland's characterization of the show seems true for Dexter, who never appears to profile or stereotype particular ethnic identities, occasional dialogue among other characters on the show reveals an anti-immigrant bias, notwithstanding the humoristic tone perhaps intended in the script. For example, Deb begins as a vice cop working a prostitution sting during the first few episodes of season 1. Her relationship to then Lieutenant Maria LaGuerta is highly contentious. Maria's obvious liking for Dexter, whom she frequently flatters and even flirts with at times, stands in stark contrast to her equally strong disdain for his sister, whom she publicly disses and insists on relegating to menial assignments. In the show's pilot episode, Deb's personal disregard for Maria is conveyed in an anti-immigrant comment that she makes to Dexter in reference to the lieutenant's inability to recognize a killer's *modus operandi*: "She's dumber than the boat people. Throw her a fuckin' raft" (season 1, episode 1). In season 7, as Maria, by then promoted to captain, grows suspicious that Dexter may actually be Miami's notorious Bay Harbor Butcher, she seeks the help of the former captain Tom Matthews, of Anglo background, who has a distant personal relationship to Dexter. When she approaches Tom, who is having a morning scotch on his boat and now on forced retirement because of Maria's previous inside political maneuvers, his response is imbued with a clear anti-immigrant ideology: "Go home, Maria. The only help you'll get from me is a lift back to Cuba" (season 7, episode 9).

94 *Imagining Spanish in Miami*

In a later scene of the same episode, Maria and Tom agree that she will reinstate him long enough to earn his full retirement pension in exchange for his assistance investigating the possibility that the Bay Harbor Butcher could be someone other than James Doakes—Maria's former lover, now deceased. "Personally, I think that she's had one too many *mosquitos* [with affected Hispanic accent], or whatever they call that goddamn drink," Tom utters to Dexter in a subsequent conversation some episodes later in which he reveals to him that Maria suspects that Dexter might be the killer (season 7, episode 11). Two elements of this utterance clearly reflect ethnic posturing in the show's writing. First, there is the attribution of mojitos—which Tom playfully misnames ("mosquitos") yet authentically pronounces with Spanish-like phonology—to the Cuban American character, in contraposition to the attribution of Scotch whisky to the Anglo character, Tom, who is shown drinking it in the morning on several occasions. Second, Tom's taste for Scotch whisky seems to imply, in oppositional fashion, not only his disdain for mojitos but also his trivialization of its Spanish-origin name ("whatever they call that goddamn drink"). After discovering evidence that Dexter had planted to incriminate Doakes, Tom tells Maria that she must now consider the case closed. Because the Christmas holiday is approaching, he then says to her in an affirmative and dismissive tone, "Feliz Navidad, Maria" (season 7, episode 11). Such instances of language play, and what Hill (1998) has called 'mock Spanish,' occur in numerous episodes of the show. For example, while at a nightclub attempting to meet women, Vince gives Angel the following advice in season 1, episode 10: "Don't talk about the divorce unless they ask, *comprendo*? [with English phonology] Oh, and eighty-six the ring." Also in season 1, in the pilot episode, Deb comments to Dexter regarding a blunder that she made in procedure: "Say *adiós* [with English phonology] to my career. I'm gonna die a meter maid."

Unlike her brother Dexter, who never finds himself confronted in any way with the use of Spanish throughout the series (except for his own voluntary use of it in season 1), Deb faces recurrent communicative obstacles because of Miami's Spanish-speaking population. On several occasions in the series, she is either disadvantaged or ridiculed by her lack of knowledge of Spanish. In season 2, when she finds herself unable to communicate with the Spanish-speaking mother of a homicide victim, a bilingual child interprets the woman's snub of the police for Deb (episode 2):

MOTHER: Cada semana, cada noche hay violencia en mi vecindario. Y ¿por qué? Porque la policía no hace nada.

DEB: Please, señora, más despacias [*sic*]. Please slower.

MOTHER: It's más despacio! [gestures dismissively and walks away]

CHILD: She's saying the fucking cops aren't doing nothing.

DEB: Grandma really talks like that?

CHILD: Not exactly, but you get the point, right, bitch?

DEB: Fuck! The people don't wanna help.

Imagining Spanish in Miami   95

In season 3, Deb is publicly humiliated by her lack of understanding of the words of a song dedicated to her by Anton, a local musician with whom she had become romantically involved after coercing him into being a police informant. Because she has manipulated him, Anton playfully insults her with the song "Puta, flaca, mala," performed in a crowded bar:

ANTON [SINGING]: Es una puta, flaca, mala. Eso es exactamente lo que es. Te agarra por los cojones y después, te arrastra a la cárcel. Se reirá por todo el camino de ti. ¿Por qué? [chorus] Puta, flaca, mala, puta, flaca, mala, puta, flaca, mala…
DEB [SMILING AND BRAGGING TO A GROUP OF WOMEN DANCING BESIDE HER]: He wrote this for me!
WOMAN: You're the puta, flaca, mala?
DEB: Yeah, that's me!
WOMAN [LAUGHING, TO HER FRIENDS]: She's the skinny mean bitch.
[Deb looks at Anton scornfully]

While investigating the Santa Muerte–related murders of season 5, Deb is accompanied to a botanica by Detective Cira Manzón (played by April Hernández Castillo; season 5, episode 3). As a brief exchange occurs entirely in Spanish between Manzón and the elderly woman attending the store counter, Deb stands in the background in silence, linguistically alienated. Manzón later interprets into Spanish the questions that Deb poses to a man working in the darker back section of the store, who explains that he does not personally believe in Santa Muerte ("Yo ni siquiera creo en esta mierda"). Deb then asks why he has a large tattoo of Santa Muerte on his arm, but before Manzón can interpret the question for him, he responds to Deb entirely in Hispanic-accented English: "I got drunk one night, woke up, and it was there. You tell me." After a pause, the man turns to Manzón and asks her, "¿Te llamas Manzón?" Manzón responds, "Sí." And the man says, "¡Coño, eres la hija de Andrés!" Deb then says, "Hey, hey [clicking her tongue to call the man's attention], we're doing great in English!", to which he responds, "You live in Miami! Why you no learn Spanish?" Curiously, his grammar in the previous utterance was entirely correct, yet he appears unable to form a simple negative syntactic structure in the phrase "Why you no learn Spanish?" Deb's response is mocking: "Because me too busy, making a living." Deb is once again challenged to learn Spanish for work purposes in a later episode of the same season. When she loses sight of the alleged killer's car while following it (season 5, episode 12, the same scene mentioned earlier), she stops to get information from a Spanish-monolingual street vendor. During the interaction, in which she resorts to hand gestures and mock Spanish (e.g. 'trunko' for car trunk), she frustratedly declares: "I fuckin' swear I'm takin' Spanish after this!"

In sum, although the presence of Spanish in _Dexter_'s cultural imaginary of a murderous Miami is not tied to criminality per se, it is on numerous

96 *Imagining Spanish in Miami*

occasions ideologically posed as a social obstacle for Deb, while her brother—the show's White male antihero—never finds himself in such situations. The protagonist's Anglophone monolingualism appears entirely a non-issue for his social life in Miami and his work with the Miami Police. His active use of colloquial Spanish with his colleague Angel in various initial scenes of the show disappears altogether after season 1, and his interactions with everyone else throughout the series are entirely in English. As I have pointed out, where Spanish is present and for the characters who use it, the language and its speakers are oftentimes culturally misrepresented or socially mocked, even through language play. Nonetheless, and rather importantly, Spanish is present in *Dexter*, unlike most other popular Hollywood cultural productions. This is especially true in dialogues between Angel and Maria, both of whom have roles of relative social power in the context of the Miami Police and are of great affective importance in Dexter's life. But the idea of Spanish-language ability as societal or workplace asset appears only in storylines involving the protagonist's sister, perhaps in her projected vulnerability as a woman. The idea of Spanish as instrumental asset is key to the 'marketplace' metaphor of the postmodern linguistic order, a trope to which I now turn.

Valuing Spanish: Miami as marketplace

In the years immediately prior to the Mariel crisis and the race riots of Liberty City and Overtown, as Miami began to emerge as the center for drug trafficking in the Americas and so-called murder capital of the US, the quiet and comical life of one fictional Cuban family in Miami's Little Havana neighborhood captured the imagination of television audiences across the nation. As the protagonists of *¿Qué Pasa, USA?*, three generations of the Peña family brought bilingualism to mainstream US audiences for the first time in the nation's history. Produced and recorded by a local PBS affiliate, the show was originally intended only for the South Florida viewing public when it began in 1977 but soon became one of the nation's most widely acclaimed sitcoms of the decade. By the series' end in 1980, it had won six regional Emmy Awards and was broadcast on 121 stations across the US and Puerto Rico (Frías 2017). Still today it has an enthusiastic following. Bilingualism is presupposed in the storylines that relate the plight of an immigrant family who confronts the social and cultural dilemmas of 1970s Miami from a cross-generational perspective. In all 39 episodes, English predominates in the young Miami-bred generation, while Spanish and English alternate fluidly in the Cuban-accented discourse of their parents, and their grandparents speak exclusively in Spanish. In this regard, *¿Qué Pasa, USA?* was, on one hand, intended as a representation of linguistic and cultural assimilation (Rivero 2012), but on the other hand, it unapologetically confronted Anglophone viewers with a social reality in which Spanish was not only normal but also valuable. Undoubtedly, the show's script—as much as its success in national television ratings—was

Imagining Spanish in Miami 97

an unequivocal intimation of the postmodern linguistic order of things to come, not only in South Florida but across the US.

Key to normalizing Spanish in *¿Qué Pasa, USA?*, beyond merely making the language fully present in dialogues, was casting it as a valuable resource on social and economic grounds. In various episodes, the vitality of Spanish beyond the Peña household projects the idea of bilingualism as an asset—an idea that would proliferate by the late 1980s and, as we will see, gain discursive traction in South Florida by the early 1990s. From the prevalent local battleground narrative of bilingualism during the 1980s and following the officialization of English in the Florida State Constitution in 1988, Spanish quickly evolved into a valuable economic resource or marketplace asset in the mainstream imaginary of the 1990s. This changing perception of Spanish in public life was concomitant with the rise of economic neoliberalism all across the US, as explained in Chapter 1. In Miami, however, this ideological trope had extraordinarily strong resonance, in that it placed front and center a discourse around the value of Spanish that had been present in Miami since its early days, albeit more subtly. In the following section, I explore representations of this idea in the popular US television sitcoms *¿Qué Pasa, USA?* and *The Golden Girls*. In the subsequent section, I highlight the explicit reliance upon the marketplace metaphor in *Miami Herald* accounts of the indispensable value of bilingualism in the 1990s, as well as in other national journalistic accounts.

Television sitcom narratives of bilingualism as asset in South Florida

In his groundbreaking analysis of the performances of Cuban exile comedian Álvarez Guedes during the social turbulence of early 1980s Miami, Laguna (2017) argued that the artist's humorous characterizations of relations between Cubans in exile and between *americanos* and *cubanos* "illustrate the role of diversión [fun] in forging a narrative of Cuban exile identity that privileged whiteness and heteronormativity while simultaneously speaking back to discrimination from Anglo Miamians" (29). According to Laguna, the language of 'choteo' in Guedes' highly popular "Clases de idioma cubano" subverted ethnic power dynamics in Miami by turning the burden of bilingualism on its head, i.e. the Cuban audience was urged to pity "those poor Americans" who could not speak Spanish; as Cubans 'defended themselves' or 'got by' in English, the *americanos* must "fulfill the literal meaning of what it means to live in a bilingual city where *everyone* speaks two languages" (2017, 49, emphasis in the original). In this way, Guedes' performances not only provided a pleasurable filter for social anxieties at the time, but also forged the space of 'home' in cultural, political, and sociolinguistic terms: "Miami must become home; what could not be done in Cuba will be attempted here. Imagining Miami through the narrative form of choteo is just one step towards making Miami 'home'" (Laguna 2010, 524).

98 *Imagining Spanish in Miami*

I suggest that the popular sitcoms *¿Qué Pasa, USA?* (1977–1980) and *The Golden Girls* (1985–1992) served a similar function of interpreting the dynamics of language and power in South Florida through a comical lens, though not through any sort of discursive strategy of subversion. Both shows represent the mundane lives of common people, i.e. neither criminals nor those who pursue criminals, who call Miami 'home.' In the cultural imaginaries of domesticity that they project, the orientational roles of English and Spanish within the broader bilingual context of Miami are contested, extensively and explicitly in *¿Qué Pasa, USA?*, and rather more reservedly and subtly in *The Golden Girls*. Of course, the former was a local series created by Cuban Americans that was originally intended only for South Florida PBS viewers, and the latter was a mainstream Hollywood production destined for the national television market on the NBC network. As I will observe, both shows present situations that cast Spanish seemingly in terms of net asset value, projecting its important worth in spite of its potential liabilities within a broader societal framework of Anglophone hegemony. Their representation of Spanish as marketplace asset foreshadows—from the 'local' perspective of Miami—the national marketplace boom of Spanish in the emergent neo-liberal economic order of postmodernity (Mora 2014).

It is worth nothing that, at a more macro or meta discursive level, the ideational increasingly became a commodity with the growth of mass media over the twentieth century, and, concomitantly, ideological processes must be interpreted through the lens of commodification (Thompson 1990). The reflexive link between communication and commodification is, according to Agha (2011), the basis of mediatization: "In linking communication to com-moditization, mediatized institutions link communicative roles to positions within a socioeconomic division of labor, thereby expanding the effective scale of production and dissemination of messages across a population, and thus the scale at which persons can orient to common presuppositions in acts of communication with each other" (163). In this way, for our more micro-level purposes, the marketplace metaphor of Spanish in Miami not only serves an organizational function in the metalinguistic commentary about the roles of language as portrayed on these two shows, but it also orients viewers to a common presupposition—or what Strauss (2004) defined as 'cultural standing'—regarding the 'common sense' relational value of Spanish vis-à-vis English. In essence, then, these shows provide early evidence of the mediatization of Spanish in postmodern US society, i.e. the commodification of the idea that Spanish is a commodity.

Living with Spanish: Bilingualism in ¿Qué Pasa, USA?

America's first bilingual television sitcom began with a local proposal for funds from the Emergency School Aid Act (ESAA-TV), a federal grant program that sought to foster awareness and appreciation of racial and ethnic diversity among US schoolchildren through television formats. Manny Mendoza, a social science professor at Miami-Dade Community College and fan of the iconic sitcom *All in the Family*, invited the college's director of bilingual programs, José Bahamonde, to join him in the proposal to produce a show targeting South Florida teenagers (Frías 2017). Once funding was secured, Luis Santeiro, also a Miami Cuban American with PBS experience, joined as head writer. With a meager budget of $25,000 per episode, the producers brought on board several professional Cuban radio and television actors in exile in Miami, including Velia Martínez in the role of the grandmother Adela, Luis Oquendo as her husband Antonio, and Ana Margarita Martínez-Casado as their daughter Juana. Manolo Villaverde joined the cast as Juana's husband Pepe, along with Ana Margo and Steven Bauer (then called Rocky Echevarría) in the roles of their children Carmen and Joe. Bauer would later join the cast of *Scarface* as the only Cuban American actor in the movie, playing Tony Montana's best friend and confidant.

Ana Margo stated that, in her role as Carmen, the show mirrored her own life as a teenage bilingual Cuban American in Miami: "I personally was living the situations that I was portraying in *¿Qué Pasa, USA?*.... Real life and the studio were the very same situations and topics.... We were doing real life, as it was at the time in Miami" (Delgado and Veraldi 2007, 51–52). A fundamental aspect of the 'real life' quality of the series was its bilingual format: English predominated for Carmen and Joe, while Spanish and English alternated in the discourse of their parents Juana and Pepe, and their grandparents Adela and Antonio spoke in Spanish. Bahamonde's training in comparative linguistics guided him in devising an original format of 60% Spanish and 40% English, which later changed to 40/60% in favor of English after the show met national success (Delgado and Veraldi 2007, 48). Color-coding the script and counting words at times to make sure that the percentages added up, Bahamonde and Santeiro took care to present plot points in both languages yet avoid excessive repetitions (Delgado and Veraldi 2007, 48). In character dialogues, misunderstandings abounded—mostly on the grandparents' part—as well as malapropisms and bilingual language play, as when Adela interprets the name Peter Hill as 'perejil' [parsley] (episode 33).

Like the protagonists of popular mainstream sitcoms of the 1970s, e.g. *All in the Family*, *Maude*, *Good Times*, *One Day at A Time*, etc., the family in *¿Qué Pasa, USA?* confronted prominent national social issues of the time, especially women's rights and social and cultural diversity, but with traditional Cuban versus mainstream US mores and practices placed under scrutiny. Interestingly, questions of Cuban politics or US-Cuba relations never entered the dialogue; as Rivero (2012) observed, "The Peñas lived in a 1970s Miami that was at the forefront of US socio-cultural changes but that concomitantly coexisted in an imagined Cuba framed in a temporal stasis, a place where the post-revolutionary nation-state and its citizens were absent" (102). Because the Peñas were apparently apolitical and lived a working-class existence, the show might be viewed as a challenge to contemporary mainstream media constructions of "a singular, economically solvent, right-wing, and

100 *Imagining Spanish in Miami*

anti-Castro, Cuban exile community" (Rivero 2012, 105). Assuredly, the economic concerns of the family and the value they place on bilingualism are prominent features of the show's storylines.

Indeed, the commodification of language constitutes the resolution of episode 17, "Abuela Adela Speaks English," in which Joe dreams that family language roles are reversed: his grandparents are highly fluent bilinguals while he and Carmen are only able to speak Spanish. The devil (enacted by his father Pepe) appears to Joe, informing him that he will be punished for his bad deeds: "Bad deed number one: You have changed the television channel to watch a rerun of *I Love Lucy* when your grandparents wanted to watch *Romances guajiros*.... Punishment: You will watch one hundred programs of *Romances guajiros*." The grandparents propose as punishment the sole use of English with Joe and Carmen, "como hacían ellos con nosotros." Abuela Adela affirms, in native-like English: "You kids think you're so smart.... Antonio, isn't it a drag to communicate with someone who you have to translate everything for?!" When he wakes from the dream, Joe begs his grandparents' forgiveness and promises to speak to them only in Spanish from then on, to which Abuela replies, "No, mi cielo. Háblanos en inglés. Nosotros queremos aprender."

In the opening scene of the episode, before Joe falls asleep, Carmen attempts to teach the grandparents basic English—much to comic effect—so that they can gain employment, Abuela aspiring to be a cook and Abuelo a gardener. In his dream, the grandparents make Joe aware of everything they do for him (cooking, cleaning, doing his laundry, etc.), all in symbolic exchange for the use of Spanish at home. After Joe awakes and as the episode ends, Pepe points out to Juana that if her parents begin to work outside the home, they will need to hire a maid, which will be quite expensive. At that moment, Antonio says to his wife, "Mira, Adela, yo creo que aquí en este país, nadie considera nada si no lo pagan. Así que, ¿qué te parece si nos declaramos en huelga?" Adela responds, in highly accented English, "You right. No money, no work-y no more." As the credits roll, the grandparents begin to compile a list of their fees for everyday domestic tasks, quoting prices in English: "Merendar—snack: 25 cents; dinner: one dollar; una quarter por cada cama; 75 cents for cleaning room; cortar la hierba, five dollars; por cleaning the bathroom, two dollars— no, three dollars." In sum, their lack of ability to speak English kept them at home, where they performed costly and much-needed domestic labor; in exchange for this work, they should be spoken to in Spanish.

Similarly, in "We Speak Spanish" (episode 4), three language-related phenomena are highlighted: Joe and Carmen's lack of respect toward their grandparents by speaking in English; their lack of ability in Spanish, exposed in the use of numerous Anglicisms in the episode's dialogue (prompting Antonio to characterize his grandson's Spanish as being found in the latest edition of the dictionary of the 'Real Academia de la Sagüesera,' a colloquial reference to Miami's Calle Ocho neighborhood); and their embarrassment regarding their parents' limited and highly accented English. The latter leads an indignant Pepe to prohibit the use of English in the house, forcing Joe and Carmen to communicate only in Spanish. Joe, seeking a part-time job as a bilingual typist, is told by Carmen that not only will he need to learn to type, but also to speak Spanish. Joe responds, "Español—no problem, pero sí tengo que aprender a taipear," at the moment when Antonio walks into the room. When his grandfather asks, "¿Aprender a qué?", he replies, "Typing, taipear." Antonio then scolds him, "¿Taipear? ¡Mecanografiar! ¡Qué horror! Ya estos muchachos no saben hablar su propio idioma." Joe retorts, "I speak Spanish perfectly well. Yo hablo más mejor [*sic*] que nadie en el colegio," prompting Antonio to comment to Adela, "No quisiera yo oír a los otros, ¿eh?" I take up the matter of Anglicisms in Miami in Chapter 5.

In the same episode, during a visit with Joe's school counselor Mrs. Peabody (whom Joe jokingly refers to as "Cuerpo de chícharo" in a literal translation of her last name), Juana learns that her son has not been informing her of the school's regular PTA (Parent Teacher Association) meetings because he is embarrassed by his parent's limited English ability. Mrs. Peabody informs Juana that the school has this 'problem' with all the Cuban parents, i.e. they do not participate in the school's meetings. When Juana returns home and confronts her son in the presence of his grandparents, she affirms that Joe has a language complex: "It looks like this Cuban accent complex is a very contagious disease. It's being spread all over the Cuban community." At the same time that Joe and Carmen's overall lack of ability in Spanish is pointed out by their parents and grandparents, their vital role as English language brokers for the family is brought to the forefront through a series of comical misunderstandings with a Goodwill worker who visits the house to pick up a donation, a cosmetics saleswoman, and Joe's school counselor Mrs. Peabody, all of whom only speak English. The crux of the argument is that, without the capacity to communicate in English, the household would soon flounder. Ultimately, Joe is disqualified from the job as bilingual typist not because he fails the typing test, but because he fails a Spanish language test as part of the interview. Clearly, the message is that both Spanish and English are invaluable assets of life in Miami, not just at home but in institutional and professional settings as well.

In this regard, the notion of bilingualism as asset conveyed in the show seemingly stands in counterpoint to Rivero's (2012) suggestion that the show reflected "an ideological push towards assimilation" (97). Rivero maintained that the show's educational and political goals of exposing the "self-containment of the Cuban subculture" and the inter- and intra-ethnic pressures confronted by contemporary young Cuban Americans were achieved in part through its bilingual format. In her interpretation that cross-generational shift to English language dominance is synonymous with assimilation, Rivero perhaps overlooked the apparent metalinguistic debate around Spanish versus English in the show's storylines, which placed value on both languages independently. Curiously, however, she noted that many critics at the time remarked that the delivery and comical effects of Spanish in the show's

102 *Imagining Spanish in Miami*

dialogues were superior to those of English (2012, 103). The fact that some Anglophone critics lamented their own inability to understand what appeared to be the dialogue's funniest lines (Rivero 2012, 103) and the observation that monolingual viewers often said they "understood only half" of the show (Delgado and Veraldi 2007, 52) might also mean that the message was not about 'assimilation' per se. *New York Times* reviewer Les Brown wrote: "The use of two languages may be bothersome to viewers at first—especially when the laughter of the studio audience is triggered by the Spanish dialogue—but it soon enough becomes natural, as indeed it is in a bilingual household" (cited in Rivero 2012, 103–4). *Newsday* critic Marvin Kitman, though praising the show, stated in 1978: "Listening to the first episode of a sitcom that I only half understood was an epiphany. At first hearing the live, Spanish-speaking audience laughing at the jokes is a culture shock. You get angry. You bunch of elitist snobs on public TV. You're already speaking British English that I don't understand. What will you do next to keep me out of it—Molière, in the original French?" (cited in Rivero 2012, 104).

The series arguably provided US audiences with the first mainstream jolt of full-fledged, unabashed Spanish-English bilingualism in public life. Situating the Peñas' life in the cultural imaginary of Miami likely afforded the show its widespread appeal and surprising success, i.e. for viewers this sort of linguistic behavior would have been conceivable and acceptable in the imaginary of Miami although perhaps not so in the contexts of New York, Los Angeles, or Chicago. As Delgado and Veraldi (2007) observed, in the show's dialogue "both sides struggle to understand and to be understood. Neither 'Anglo' nor 'Cuban' culture or language is mainstream or marginalized" (52). I believe that in the bilingual stasis of the show's script, the Peñas appear forward-looking in terms of the societal and economic value of Spanish-English bilingualism that would come to the fore of US public discourse by the early 1990s, in the context of cultural 'Latinization' and with Miami as the nation's paragon. The idea of Spanish as asset would re-appear on mainstream US television just a few years later in a rather unlikely household in South Florida: that of *The Golden Girls*.

Living around Spanish: Anglophone monolingualism in The Golden Girls

First aired in 1985 and ending in 1992, *The Golden Girls* was among the top ten most watched television programs in the US for six consecutive seasons according to Nielsen ratings. The show's global popularity inspired remakes and adapted versions in various countries, including Great Britain, Greece, Turkey, Russia, Chile (titled *Los años dorados*) and Spain (called *Las chicas de oro*, starring acclaimed actresses Carmen Maura and Concha Velasco). Though set in Miami, *The Golden Girls* was made in Los Angeles, as was *Dexter* (with the exception of its first season). Residing in a four-bedroom house on fictional Richmond Street in a quiet neighborhood, Blanche (played by Rue McClanahan), Rose (Betty White), Dorothy (Bea Arthur), and her elderly mother Sophia (Estelle Getty) confronted controversial social issues of

Imagining Spanish in Miami 103

their time, including poverty and homelessness, race relations, sexism, lesbian and gay rights, the AIDS crisis, assisted suicide, urban environmentalism, and US-Soviet relations. US immigration policy under the Reagan administration was poignantly critiqued in "Dorothy's Prized Pupil" (episode 46), about the deportation of an undocumented adolescent (played by Mario Lopez) whom Dorothy tutors.

In seeming antithesis to the concurrent series *Miami Vice*, the city represented in the storylines of *The Golden Girls* appeared an entirely mundane place, with a few possible exceptions: their home is once burglarized though nothing is stolen (episode 8); they are shaken up when two police detectives use their house to spy on their neighbors who are suspected jewel thieves (episode 49); Dorothy jokingly observes that in Miami "all the single men under 80 are cocaine smugglers" (episode 1), and also later laments that she has been "turned down for every available part-time job in Dade County that didn't involve selling cocaine" (episode 34). Despite the great attention given to drug trafficking and criminality in Miami mass media and especially in the hit series *Miami Vice* during the 1980s, the *Golden Girls'* city appeared unremarkably similar to most other urban areas of the US. And despite Miami's demographic reality, the overwhelming majority of their friends and acquaintances, like the people they casually encountered, were non-Hispanic White and entirely Anglophone.

Although Spanish was generally erased in the imaginary of Miami that the show created overall, there were allusions to its important presence. For example, when Sophia first arrives to the house in the pilot episode, she states that a Cuban cab driver had attempted to charge her an additional fee for being bilingual; in episode 9, when Rose finds out that her 80-year-old mother, who is visiting, has left the house to explore the city by herself, Sophia reassures her there is nothing to worry about because she is carrying $400 and a Spanish-English dictionary; on another occasion, Sophia returns home later than expected and says that the city changed the number of her usual bus route, leaving her in an area where the only person she could find who spoke English had tried to blame her personally for the Bay of Pigs debacle (episode 35). Recovering from a romantic heartbreak in episode 160, Blanche asks the others if they know how to say "vulnerable" in Spanish as she heads to Hernando's Hacienda for 'Gringo Night'—a humorous wink to the fact that Miami was by then a Latinx majority city. Curiously, despite Blanche's liberal attitude toward sex, which is an ongoing aspect of the show's comical storylines, only one Latino appears among her multiple exploits and romantic interests over the series' 180 episodes. Fidel Santiago, who courts Blanche and Sophia simultaneously in episode 77, is a Cuban immigrant of the traditional Hollywood 'Latin Lover' mold who speaks English with a notable accent, probably for purposes of playing to cultural stereotype (cf. Lippi-Green 1997). Spanish appears racialized in a few brief scenes, as in episode 8, when Rose is frightened by a "swarthy" man outside their house; Dorothy later identifies him as their gardener and yells to him offscreen, "Buenos días, Fernando."

104 *Imagining Spanish in Miami*

The protagonists' stereotypes regarding Spanish speakers are brought into critical focus for audiences later in the series, however, prompting viewers to reconsider their own possible language-based prejudices. In episode 94, Sophia invests in a prizefighter who ostensibly does not speak English. After she introduces him to the others, she asks him to leave the room to "do some road work" so they can talk in private about their expected profit if he wins an upcoming match. When he asks her, "¿Qué?", she replies with an excited tone, "Immigration! Immigration!", prompting him to run out the door as the audience erupts in laughter. Sophia then explains that of the $10,000 they will be paid for his participation in the match, "Kid Pepe" will receive only 20%, and they will keep the remainder. Blanche asks if that percentage is standard for a boxer, and the audience laughs at Sophia's reply: "It is if he doesn't speak English." To their surprise, they later find out that Pepe is actually a professional violinist about to audition for The Juilliard School, and he indeed speaks English fluently, "better than Sylvester Stallone" according to Rose. They ask for an explanation:

DOROTHY: Why did you pretend to only know Spanish?
PEPE: It's part of the image. Cuban boxers are supposed to know their right from their left, nothing else.
DOROTHY: And you think we are that narrow-minded and prejudiced that we actually felt that way?
PEPE: You bought into it, didn't you? Hey, I didn't invent Kid Pepe. I just conformed to your image of a simple-minded Hispanic fighter. But I am a Cuban.

Ultimately, Pepe is unable to play violin for the audition because his memory is impaired by a concussion he receives during the fight. Instead, he takes the opportunity to perform a Shakespeare monologue for the board members, who immediately admit him to Juilliard's acting program. Hearing their decision, Sophia declares, "When was the last time you saw a Cuban Macbeth? He'll get out of school and spend his whole career getting arrested on TV cop shows." Sophia's prediction would have likely proven accurate for fictional Pepe's acting future: a 2001 *TIME* story described the "brownout" of US television, noting that Latinos constituted only 2% of characters on prime time shows that year, despite a 58% growth of the nation's Hispanic population during the 1990s (Poniewozik 2001).

The television image of Hispanics would subsequently be brought into more prominent focus in episode 106 through the character of Enrique Mas. In that episode, Rose is informed that her deceased husband's employer has declared bankruptcy and, as a result, she will no longer receive his pension check. The others encourage her to denounce the company to the local television consumer affairs reporter, whom Blanche describes in the following terms: "Enrique Mas is a great champion of the people. Besides, he has all that gorgeous black hair, and those swarthy Latin good looks, and the sexy way he rolls his 'r's, 'Enrrrique' [with affected Spanish language accent]." After the audience laughs, Blanche continues with lustful eyes and seductive tone of voice, "Boy, I'd love to get him on a couch made out of Corinthian leather," likely an allusion to the iconic television advertisements for the Chrysler Cordoba that featured Mexican-origin actor Ricardo Montalbán. Because of his Hollywood 'Latin Lover' image, elegant persona, and Hispanic-accented English, Montalbán popularized Chrysler's marketing term "rich Corinthian leather" for the automobile's seats during the 1970s. The success of the commercials subsequently launched him into a starring role as Mr. Roarke in the highly rated television series *Fantasy Island* (1977–1984) (Montalbán 2002).

Although Rose does not turn to Enrique Mas regarding the loss of her pension check, she does eventually seek his help regarding the age discrimination she experiences while applying for jobs (episode 106). At the WSF-TV station, she learns that Mas is seeking a production assistant and tells him that she would like to apply for the position. When he responds that someone of her "advanced age" would not have the level of energy required for the job and she calls out the irony of the situation, Mas defends himself by explaining that there are actually two of him:

> Oh it is not me, it is 'Enrrrique Mas' [with affected tone of voice and Spanish-language trilled 'r'].... You see, there are two 'me's. There is Enrique Mas [with normal tone and no trilled 'r,' as with English-language phonology], the dedicated consumer advocate fighting for justice and equality. And then there is 'Enrrrique Mas' [with affected tone and trilled 'r'], the television personality who wants to get out of this local station and onto the network so he can become a really big fish in a big pond. It is 'Enrrrique' [with affected tone and trilled 'r'] who has reservations [again with trilled 'r'].

Rose then accuses him of being "a fake" because of this apparent duplicity, perhaps evoking the illusory and fluid nature of identities in Miami mentioned in the previous section. Mas in turn defends his apparent duality to Rose by explaining that he had always wanted to be on television but found no mainstream characters with whom to identify: "Do you know what that's like for a Hispanic kid? Who were my role models? Zorro and Ricky Ricardo." When she calls him "Mister Mas" when thanking him for the opportunity to try out for the job finally, he insists to Rose, "You can call me 'Enrrrique' [with trilled 'r']." She replies with a quizzical look, "No, I don't think I can."

It is noteworthy that the role of Enrique Mas was played by Chick Vennera, the same actor who portrayed Pepe the Cuban prizefighter in episode 94. Vennera was born in upstate New York and has an entirely mainstream US education and career trajectory, including appearances in major Hollywood films. While Pepe's voice is undeniably that of a mainstream English speaker, Enrique Mas speaks English with an accent seemingly typical of a

106 *Imagining Spanish in Miami*

Spanish-dominant speaker who has acquired English as a second language during adulthood. Following Lippi-Green's (1997) argument, one might suppose that Pepe did not have a discernible 'accent' because it was intended that viewers empathize with the plight of Spanish-speaking immigrants in the US and the stereotypes they must confront. Enrique's noticeably accented character, on the other hand, was symbolic of the rise of Spanish in US public life and the pressure placed on English monolinguals, like Rose, to learn Spanish for workplace purposes. In this regard, the character of Enrique Mas exemplifies Lippi-Green's observation that, in US cinema and television, accent constitutes an easy link to broader questions of dominance, race, and socioeconomic status (1997).

Spanish had already been presented as an insurmountable challenge for Rose in the storyline of a previous episode (61), in which she begins to take Spanish classes as a requirement for a promotion in her job as a grief counselor. She declares to the others in the opening scene: "From now on I'm only speaking Spanish. I'm eating Spanish food, I'm wearing Spanish clothes, and I'm rereading the covers of my Julio Iglesias albums really, really carefully." In the following scene, she appears in a Spanish shawl and speaks mock Spanish, greeting Dorothy with "Buenas [*sic*] días, Dorotheo" and commenting on Blanche's lowcut apparel, "mucho mucho bazoomas." In a later scene, she and Blanche accompany Dorothy to a pawn shop to sell various belongings. Upon entering, Blanche explains that they must negotiate the sale carefully. When the attendant greets them in Spanish ("Buenos días, señoritas"), Rose enthusiastically replies on their behalf, "Buenos días. ¿Cómo está? Quieremos [*sic*] todo tu dinero." Frightened, the attendant places his hands in the air and urges in English, "Please, don't hurt me! Just take my money!" Rose apologizes: "I must have confused my verbs." By the episode's end, Rose declares that she has given up on the possible work promotion because of her inability to learn Spanish, which she attributes to her Scandinavian heritage: "Norwegians are notoriously bad at Spanish."

In sum, of *The Golden Girls'* four protagonists, all Anglophone monolinguals (with the exception of Sophia's purported heritage language ability in Italian), only Rose confronts the exigency of Spanish in Miami, similar to Deb in *Dexter*. In two episodes of *The Golden Girls* in which Spanish is prominently featured in the storyline's metacommentary (61 and 106), viewers are urged to reflect upon the growing workplace value of the language in Miami. The bilingual imperative for the South Florida workforce was cited in national mass media at the time, e.g. Sherrill's (1987) exposé, which mentioned that in 1980 about one-third of Hispanics in Miami spoke primarily Spanish at work according to a corporate survey; by 1987 the number reportedly rose to 50%. In a general sense, the character of Enrique Mas represents not only a workplace present but also a mass media future, for South Florida and for the US more broadly. Viewing that 1989 episode in retrospect (episode 106), the "big pond" envisioned by Enrique Mas augurs the exponential growth of the Spanish-language

Imagining Spanish in Miami 107

television industry, with Miami as its national and global center (Yúdice 2004; Valencia and Lynch 2020). By 2014, the industry had become so prominent that the father of the main character of *Jane the Virgin*, The CW Network's award-winning dramedy series (2014–2019), was portrayed as a global star of Spanish-language telenovelas made in Miami. Headlines of the *Miami Herald* regarding the expansion of the Spanish-language television industry increased from only a handful during the late 1980s to nearly fifty during the 2000s, reflective of the trend. At the same time, there was an ideological shift from language as ethnic identity marker to language as economic asset in news stories about Spanish, from the region as a 'community' to the region as a 'marketplace' (Lynch 2018b). This shift is the topic of the following section.

From community to marketplace: Spanish and economic globalization in the news

In Miami, the pressure to speak Spanish faced by fictional characters like Rose in *The Golden Girls* and Deb in *Dexter*—or the imagined *americanos* in the comedy act of Álvarez Guedes—was expressed repeatedly in news stories from the late 1980s through the 2000s, the period of economic globalization characteristic of postmodernity already described in Chapter 1. A United Press International (1987) article observed that "Whites who have left said they were put off by Miami's crime and drug problems, by its congestion and by the perception that few jobs are available for those who don't speak Spanish." That same year, *New York Times Magazine*'s exposé of the social crisis in Miami stated:

> If you don't speak Spanish, you may need an interpreter to deal with hotel help or store clerks. You may even have trouble negotiating with the city and county governments. A couple of years ago, when the county offered free English lessons to those on the public payroll, one-third of the 4,500 Hispanics working for the county admitted they had difficulty speaking and reading English. This makes a lot of Anglos uncomfortable and angry. They find it hard to adjust to a city where the immigrants seem more at home than they do.... Cubans gained power, culturally and, later, politically, mostly because they moved in, but partly because the Anglos moved out. Those who left thought it cute to sport bumper stickers that read, "Will the Last American to Leave Miami Please Bring the Flag?" But in fact it was a quip of surrender. As Mayor Ferré said at the time, "The Anglos can't adapt. They can't take it, so they're moving."
>
> (Sherrill 1987)

So-called White flight was indeed a demographic reality (Boswell 1994). According to US Census data, the non-Hispanic White population of Miami-Dade County steadily decreased from 80% in 1960 to less than half in 1980,

108 *Imagining Spanish in Miami*

then to just under 24% by 2000 (Demographic Profile Miami-Dade County 1960–2000 2003).

In 1975, the same year when Miami-Dade Community College professors Manny Mendoza and José Bahamonde prepared an ESAA-TV grant proposal for *¿Qué Pasa, USA?*, Southeast Bank and WQBA Radio conducted two market surveys about the growing Latin presence in Miami. In a front-page feature story with the headline "Miami Is Changing," a *Miami Herald* reporter—striking a tone similar to that of Didion (1987)—noted the "monied style" of the event he had attended at an upscale hotel where the surveys' results were revealed to an interested public: "The women were gorgeously groomed and mostly wearing pants suits, and the men were impeccable in dark hued designer suits with slash pockets.... Altogether it was the kind of crowd that travels these days under the label 'beautiful people.' And as they sipped coffee and nibbled Danish and clustered in a number of very energetic and animated conversations, almost everyone was speaking Spanish" (Elder 1975, 1A). At the event, Mayor Maurice Ferré asserted: "The challenge of the 1980s... for Dade County may well be the ability of various cultural groups to get along well, or at least reasonably well, with each other.... We are a multi-ethnic community. You may or may not like that. But the fact is there" (Elder 1975, 1A). The reporter observed that the mayor's comment apparently went directed to several "Anglo businessmen" in the audience. Several predictions were highlighted: continued growth of the "Latin influence" concomitant with the city's dwindling Anglo population, dispersion of the Hispanic population well beyond Little Havana, and the emergence of general societal bilingualism in the coming decade. The author observed that "the oversimplified reaction to all this—sometimes expressed in the statement 'The Cubans are taking over the place,' is as frustrating to many Latins as it is alarming to some Anglos" (Elder 1975, 1A).

As previously noted, the County Commission declared Miami-Dade officially 'bilingual' the following year, a resolution that would be overturned by an English-only ordinance just four years later, in 1980. By 1993, in editorials and columns published in the *Miami Herald* during the weeks of the commission's repeal of the restrictive policy, positions both for and against maintaining the thirteen-year ordinance were noticeably stated more in economic terms than along ethnic lines, rather different than the debates of the previous decades. Some examples are:

- "Our community not only is multicultural and multilingual, it's also a primary tourist destination.... We need to reach out... to visitors, our **economic mainstay**—in any language in addition to, *not instead of*, English." (Hampton 1993, 2M, italics in the original)
- "Dade is the natural 'Gateway to the Americas,' and **its future lies in international trade, tourism, and investment**. It's impossible to count the number of times this theme is repeated.... Yet when the subject comes up before the Metro Commission—which is often, what with the airport's

Imagining Spanish in Miami 109

and seaport's **expansion** plans—there is always an underlying irony. While commissioners agree heartily with the logic behind major **expenditures to meet growing trade needs**, they're doing so in a county that forbids official use of any language but English." (Editorial 1993, 10A)

- "While we talk in Washington about the need to simplify government and **cut the deficit**, Dade County will **spend millions of dollars** to translate county documents, court records, and other complex papers into Spanish.... **Payers of high taxes**, whom they call 'Anglos,' have been leaving. The county will become even more **Third-Worldized**." (Geyer 1993, 19A)
- "There is a concomitant, gnawing feeling in South Florida that encouragement of the further use of Spanish in public enterprises and **in the marketplace** will produce likenesses to the bicultural hang-ups of French Quebec.... To encourage greater ethnicity **in the public marketplace** is highly divisive stuff." (Katzberg 1993, 19A)

Concurrently, numerous *Miami Herald* headlines announced the corporate vitality of Spanish language in South Florida's rapidly expanding economy that same year (1993):

- "Sprint to Sell Spanish-Language Phones in S. Florida" (October 2, 3C)
- "Blockbuster Offers Growing Selection of Films in Spanish" (June 19, 1C)
- "Carnival Starts a Fiesta: New Line Offers Cruises in Spanish" (January 21, 1C)
- "Bookstore Chains Going after Spanish Readers" (October 18, BM13)
- "Expect More Cable Programs en Español" (October 12, 1E)
- "Spanish-Language Networks Spread Around World" (October 2, 1C)

Assuredly, as the notion of the so-called Hispanic or Latin market began to coalesce nationwide in the early 1990s, Miami would emerge as the center of US economic globalization in relation to Latin America.

In a November of 1993 special issue on "The New Face of America," *TIME* featured an article explaining that "the new ethnic consumer is forcing U.S. companies to change the ways they sell their wares" (McCaroll 1993), and another bearing the title "Miami: The Capital of Latin America" (Booth 1993). Just three weeks later, Fidel Castro's photo would appear on the cover of the same magazine with the headline "Castro's Cuba: The End of the Dream" (December 6, 1993). The inside story, titled "Cuba Alone" (Mcgeary and Booth 1993), explained the capitalistic measures being taken by Castro to readjust the Cuban economy in the wake of the collapse of the Berlin Wall, the symbolic death knell of the global twentieth-century communist movement. Just a few months later, during the summer of 1994, Miami would face the 'Balsero crisis' when some 35,000 Cubans fled the dire circumstances of the so-called Special Period on improvised rafts destined

110 *Imagining Spanish in Miami*

for South Florida. As the 1990s ensued and the neoliberal economic order established itself on a global scale, the marketplace metaphor of the economic vitality of and consumer-based demand for Spanish prevailed in the headlines of the *Miami Herald*. Two themes in the city's emergent 'global' economic imaginary would come to the fore, both of which shifted the representation of language away from ethnic identity concerns and more toward marketplace issues approaching the new millennium: the lack of bilingual ability among Miami-born Hispanics, which I describe in what follows; and the boom of the locally based Spanish-language mass media industry.

The ideological shift from anxieties about linguistic assimilation in South Florida during the 1980s to the worry of dwindling bilingual ability in the 1990s is readily apparent in the pages of the *Miami Herald*. In both decades, local trends animated national debates, and those, in turn, further shaped the discourse in Miami. In reality, the origin of the US Official English movement during the 1980s can be attributed to Dade County's English-only ordinance of 1980, which Castro (1992) described as a "harbinger and model of future language struggles" in the national sphere (180). He affirmed that Miami's 'anti-bilingual' campaign "provided the first test of the extent of voter sentiment against government recognition of language pluralism and thus of the potential for a national English Only movement" (180). It seemed suiting that Phil Donahue would air a 1986 episode of his highly popular talk show dedicated to the national language debate from a stadium in Miami, where some 4,000 audience members "engaged in verbal warfare" according to a *Miami Herald* reporter (Meluza 1986, 1B). Prior to 1980, only two US states had official English language policies; by 1988, when Florida voters approved English-only legislation at the state level, the number had grown to fourteen, and then to half the nation by 2000. Although the title of Fishman's (1992) article characterized the fervor of the movement as "displaced Anglo-American anxieties," its leading proponent at the national level was California Senator S. I. Hayakawa, the Canadian-born son of Japanese immigrants who was a trained linguist and scholar of semantics; as founder and chair of the national organization U.S. English in 1983, Hayakawa was succeeded by Mauro Mujica, a Chilean immigrant. Motivation for the movement was and remains, in large part, opposition to bilingual education.

Miami holds a distinct honor as the home of Coral Way Elementary School, where bilingual education was revived in the US following its demise in the xenophobic backlash against German during the period of WWI. The bilingual program at Coral Way Elementary was instituted in 1963 at the request of early Cuban exiles, who argued that their children would require literacy in Spanish upon their imminent return to a post-Castro Cuba (Gándara and Escamilla 2017). This program gave impetus to the Federal Bilingual Education Act of 1968 within the broader context of the civil rights movement, followed by the landmark *Lau vs. Nichols* Supreme Court ruling and the Equal Educational Opportunities Act of 1974. However, these legislative actions, like most state-level initiatives, left the notion of 'bilingual'

Imagining Spanish in Miami   111

loosely defined, and subtractive programs with the goal of transitioning immigrant students to English language dominance would by far prevail, excluding literacy development in other languages (Gándara and Escamilla 2017). Following on the heels of the English-only movement, bilingual education became an object of national political scrutiny during the 1990s, culminating in voter approval of Proposition 227 in California in 1998, which eliminated state funding for bilingual models in public schools. Similar propositions were passed in Arizona in 2000 and Massachusetts in 2002. Nearly 40% of Latino voters in California supported Proposition 227 according to an exit poll conducted by CNN and the *Los Angeles Times*, and other prior polls found overwhelming support for mainstream English language education—at the expense of Spanish—among Spanish-speaking parents (Pedalino Porter 1998).

Immediately following the passage of Proposition 227, the *Miami Herald* reassured readers that bilingual education in Miami-Dade schools was "far different" than in California, in that "immigrant students struggling with English are placed in classes where 80% of their lessons are taught in English," while in California they spent "the majority of the school day" in their native languages (Mailander Farrell 1998, 8A). The article noted that students of English for Speakers of Other Languages (ESOL) were mainstreamed into all-English courses in less than three years on average in Miami-Dade, whereas their California counterparts spent six to nine years in ESOL courses. Yet despite the obvious fact—given the figures presented—that the bilingual model of Miami-Dade schools was entirely subtractive, the article went on to tout the success of recent efforts to expand bilingual programs in the county: "The community in Miami-Dade has largely embraced bilingual offerings in schools, with business leaders pushing the School Board... to expand the program." The county's executive director of bilingual education was quoted regarding the rationale of Miami-Dade's programs: "In Miami, it is not a political issue because being bilingual here is an economic advantage.... It is way beyond the sentimental or the cultural effort to maintain our roots. It's at a level where people are aware, 'Hey, this is going to pay me'" (Mailander Farrell 1998, 8A).

Miami-Dade County Public Schools' efforts to expand bilingual programs came on the heels of a 1996 study commissioned by the Greater Miami Chamber of Commerce that had concluded that the great majority of high school seniors lacked the sort of Spanish language proficiency required for the bilingual workforce (Fradd 1996). A *Miami Herald* story relating the initial findings of the study bore the headline "Is Dade's Bilingual Advantage at Risk?" and affirmed: "Dade County's future economic growth as an international marketplace could be in jeopardy.... If young people continue to forgo learning Spanish or don't learn it well...Dade could experience a dangerous decline in its bilingual workforce" (Santiago 1996, 1B). Just three months later, the newspaper's front-page headline emphatically warned readers of the impending crisis: "VANISHING SPANISH. Only 2

112 *Imagining Spanish in Miami*

in 100 Dade kids graduating fully fluent" (June 14, 1996, caps in original). In the following years, numerous *Herald* headlines emphasized the economic consequences of language shift for Miami's young Hispanic population and the value of bilingual abilities in the workplace, among them:

- "Bilingualism a Huge Asset in Job Search" (September 7, 1997, 1F)
- "Experts: Bilingualism Vital to Economy" (March 31, 1998, 1B)
- "Language Returns Dividends to Those Who Pay Attention" (September 10, 1998, 14A)
- "Business Leaders Worry that Language Skills Aren't at Suitable Level" (June 27, 1999, 3L)

A 1998 editorial urged that, given unemployment figures in Miami and the city's potential to become the commercial hub of the Americas, "It would be unconscionable for the School Board to ignore this wake-up call" (*Miami Herald* 1998, 16A).

Based on 1990 US Census data, Boswell (2000) demonstrated that the ability to speak both Spanish and English brought definite personal economic advantages in metropolitan Miami. He showed that Hispanics in Miami-Dade County who indicated that they spoke English 'very well' and lived in homes where 'mostly Spanish' was spoken earned an average of $7,000 more per year than Hispanics who spoke 'only English' at home. He concluded that "Hispanics who speak English very well and speak Spanish have higher incomes, lower poverty rates, higher educational attainment, and better-paying jobs than Hispanics who only speak English"; and added that "one of the most important reasons that so much Spanish is heard in Miami is that there are economic incentives for knowing Spanish as well as English there" (2000, 422–23).

Twenty years later, however, the *Herald*'s urgent calls for increased Spanish language education in the public schools appeared to have gone unheeded and, for the most part, the school board's bilingual initiatives never materialized. In 2018, Coral Way Elementary School remained one of only a few schools in the county to offer bilingual or dual language education. In the 2017–2018 school year, only 8% of Miami-Dade primary schools offered education in Spanish that went beyond a separate language-specific block of time, i.e. a traditional subject labeled as 'foreign' or 'world' language education (Miami-Dade County Public Schools 2018a). Fewer than one out of five children (19.4%) were enrolled in a dual language program in any language, i.e. Spanish, French, German, Italian, Chinese, or Portuguese (Miami-Dade County Public Schools 2018b). In that same school year (2017–2018), 53.9% of all students claimed to speak mostly Spanish at home, and more than 67,600 students were enrolled in ESOL programs, meaning that about 20% of the public school population in grades K–12 lacked functional academic abilities in English, despite the system's predominantly English-only medium of instruction (Miami-Dade County Public Schools 2018b). That year's results of statewide standardized testing for English Language Arts (Florida Standards Assessments) yielded a score at or above the 'satisfactory' level for only 54% of all tenth-grade Miami-Dade School students; nearly a quarter (24%) of students rendered an 'inadequate' performance on the test, while just one in ten achieved 'mastery' (Florida Department of Education 2018), further evidence in support of Rosa's (2019) argument about institutionally constructed 'languagelessness' among US Latinx youth.

In sum, in light of the real outcomes two decades later, the 1990s discourse of the economic imperative of Spanish for Miami youth and the purportedly apolitical future for bilingual public education in South Florida might appear, in retrospect, a fitting example of what Didion (1987) meant when she remarked that "to spend time in Miami is to acquire a certain fluency in cognitive dissonance" (99). Although we might have expected 'on the ground' ideologies about the essential value of Spanish language education in Miami to have been shaped to some extent by the mass media, such links are difficult to apprehend: "Like social behaviours it is not clear how ideological shifts might relate to structural shifts" (Stuart-Smith 2011, 230). It could be that, in this case, modern nation-state discourse simply prevailed over postmodern global economic discourse (Heller 2013), or even that the 'state' in the globalization-era sense of the concept (Blommaert 2005, 218) imposed material authority by suppressing bilingual education models in practice, confounding 'bilingual education' with acquisition of English as a second language for purposes of mainstreaming (Rosa 2019, 135). Another possibility is that the decoding of media language about the marketplace value of Spanish in Miami was constrained by the incongruence between the readers'/viewers' existing sociolinguistic frames of knowledge and what they were actually experiencing (Stuart-Smith 2011, 229), hence education in Spanish did not garner the support one would have anticipated in a place such as Miami. Census data such as that analyzed by Boswell (2000) does not include important sociolinguistic variables: it is possible that the monolithic concept of 'Hispanics' obscured the actual experiences or conscious perceptions of the value of bilingualism across different segments of the population, a matter I take up in Chapter 3. Although the empirical criteria chosen to determine the economic value of Spanish in the US are debatable (Dulfano 2013), it seems safe to assume that the worth of any language is a fundamentally ideological—and in our times, mediatized—matter.

Conclusion: A postnostalgic identity

Mediatization is not a new phenomenon. Rather, the pervasiveness and extent of media flows, taken together with mass migrations and the incipient reworking of nation-state economic paradigms, have led to potentially novel effects of media in recent decades. Mediascapes have indisputably become a fundamental aspect of our lived social realities, although their measurable effects on sociolinguistic behavior remain difficult to gauge (Stuart-Smith

114 *Imagining Spanish in Miami*

2011; Androutsopoulos 2014), and the relationship between representational and 'real' worlds grows rather more elusive (Baudrillard 1994). The Second Red Scare of the McCarthy era, which brought Lucy and Desi's integrity as 'Americans' into question in 1953, was a mediatized affair. The global sense of panic felt during the days of the Cuban Missile Crisis in October of 1962 was also driven by the media. Some argue that mediatization played a decisive role in the success of the July 26 Movement in Cuba, ultimately leading to Castro's government takeover (DePalma 2006). During the following decades, the plight of Cubans in Miami was also mediatized, with important implications in terms of cultural production, urban politics, and postmodern immigrant identities, as we have seen in this chapter.

A hallmark media feature of Cuban Miami has been the construction and continuous (re)production of nostalgia (De la Torre 2003; Grenier and Pérez 2003; Laguna 2017; among others). During the 1960s and 1970s, the longing for a return to a post-Castro Cuba was the basis of nostalgia, which functioned to create solidarity among exiles who perhaps previously had little in common in Cuba. The Marielito crisis of 1980 exposed the fault lines in that nostalgic sense of solidarity, in terms of race, social class, and language (Alfaraz 2002, 2014, 2018; Lynch 2009a, 2009b), though all remained united in their opposition to—or at least personal dissatisfaction with—Castro's communist regime. In the hope that the regime would falter following the collapse of the Communist Bloc in the early 1990s, there was a renewed and by then rather different sense of nostalgia. As previously mentioned, various measures taken by Castro, including the reopening of the island to tourism and the legal introduction of the US dollar in Cuba's currency, served to restructure the economy as tens of thousands of 'balseros' emigrated to South Florida. According to Laguna (2017, 93–96), these events marked the beginning of a highly commodified renewal of nostalgic *cubanía* that manifested not only at the local level, i.e. among older exiles and their US-born offspring in Miami, but also at national and global levels, e.g. the wide popularity of the music of Buena Vista Social Club and the great success of Gloria Estefan's 1993 album *Mi Tierra* as well as of Cristina García's 1992 novel *Dreaming in Cuban*.

Arguably, for second- and third-generation Miami Cubans, many of whom had never set foot on Cuba, the sense of nostalgia was based upon the nostalgic experience of their parents and grandparents, meaning that the referent of their nostalgia was nostalgia itself. Baudrillard (1994) might suggest that at that juncture in Cuban Miami, "when the real [was] no longer what it used to be"—neither for the early exiles and their US-born offspring nor for the recently arrived 'balseros'—"nostalgia assume[d] its full meaning" (6). Recalling not a 'real' past but an imagined history, with a drastically changed Cuba now as the backdrop, Cuban Miami entered a 'postnostalgic' phase. A key feature of this highly commodified, consumer-driven postnostalgia was *herencia* (Laguna 2017), which has an important sociolinguistic dimension. It was in the 1990s that the third generation of Miami Cubans, all of whom are

English-dominant, began to come of age. As the Cuban Spanish-dominant majority increasingly became Cuban American English-dominant, Spanish in Miami appeared within the emergent heritage language paradigm at the national level (Lynch 2000; Otheguy, García, and Roca 2000). In Miami's cultural imaginary, that generation would be the children of Carmen and Joe from *¿Qué Pasa, USA?*

In a 2007 interview, the head writer of *¿Qué Pasa, USA?*, Luis Santeiro, attributed the show's continuing appeal and renewed popularity among young Cuban Americans to nostalgia: "*Qué Pasa* represents a period of the Cuban immigration when the large bulk of Cubans was landing in the melting pot. *Qué Pasa* is like a graphic testimony of the period. We have changed from then. We are at a different level. At the time of *Qué Pasa*, we were still naïve. I believe people watch it today as a remembrance of an era…there is comedy, but the series is also nostalgic…what we had…it is like a record of that time" (Delgado and Veraldi 2007, 51, ellipses in the original). Santeiro did not qualify his remarks about having changed and being "at a different level," nor did he explain what he meant by having been "still naïve" at that time, but one might assume that he was alluding to the dramatic transformations that would begin to occur as the show's last season aired in 1980, the year of the Marielito crisis.

¿Qué Pasa, USA? is perceived as a concrete or 'real' referent—a "graphic testimony" or "record of that time," as Santeiro affirmed—and thus constitutes an authoritative and authentic resource for Cuban American identity. Still today, young US Latinx viewers, Cuban and non-Cuban alike, tend to find the dialogues sociolinguistically authentic, or 'real,' as Ana Margo observed when she was playing bilingual English-dominant Carmen in the late 1970s (Delgado and Veraldi 2007, 51–52). Thus, for the Miami-born, the show's appeal perhaps has to do with Laguna's (2017) observation regarding the nostalgia phenomenon of the 1990s, i.e. "the desire to make sense of their ethnic identities," which is "heightened by the possibility of change in the air" (96). This desire became all the more meaningful within the context of the 'new Miami' described by Yúdice (2004), characterized by intensified transnational flows, the emergence of global Latin American cultural industries based in South Florida, and the rapid diversification of the city's majority Hispanic population—half of whom now are not of Cuban origin.

Iglesias Illa (2010) attributed the continued social, political, and cultural prevalence of Cubans to the dispersion and fragmentation of other groups (185), much smaller in number, whom he characterized rather facetiously: "Están los venezolanos, recién llegados; los colombianos, ya mimetizados con el paisaje; los argentinos, nunca convencidos de su propio exilio; los nicaragüenses, invisibles" (25). Although a cultural commentary, Iglesias Illa's observation could perhaps find some support in purposeful anthropological or sociological inquiry, though I am unaware of any such studies to date. I nonetheless note that Portes and Stepick (1993) attributed a relative lack of political voice and community cohesion among Nicaraguans

116 *Imagining Spanish in Miami*

to their open reception by the Cuban majority during the 1980s (i.e. they were assimilated in a certain sense), and to the active links they maintained with their home country, as previously noted in Chapter 1. I also note Sorenson's (2016) sociolinguistic finding that Miami Argentines tend to maintain *voseo* rather than accommodating to the societal majority *tuteo*, a pattern that he attributed possibly to their resistance to "being viewed simply as part of a largely monolithic Hispanic population.... It is conceivable that many Argentines in places such as Miami not only fail to accommodate, or converge, toward the behavior of other Hispanics, but may actually attempt to exaggerate their 'Argentine-ness'" (192).

I speculate that the prevalence of Cubans relative to other Latinx groups in Miami has to do mostly with historical presence and the evolution of the city's cultural imaginary as a Cuban stronghold. Other large Spanish-speaking contingents such as Colombians, Nicaraguans, Puerto Ricans, Dominicans, Venezuelans, Peruvians, and Argentines arrived to a city that was 'already' Cuban, not just in demographic, political, and sociolinguistic terms but also in popular cultural perception. Undoubtedly, Cuban and Cuban American ways of speaking prevail across Miami in terms of the popular cultural imaginary (Callesano 2020), despite the general sociolinguistic stigmatization of Cuban accents in Miami in terms of 'correctness' or standard acceptability (Alfaraz 2014; Fernández Parera 2017; Carter and Callesano 2018). This probably suggests that Cuban vernacular speech carries a sort of covert prestige as being 'Miami authentic' in everyday social contexts and informal registers, to the exclusion of the many other varieties of Spanish spoken across the city. This is especially true in humoristic discourse—perhaps a vestige of the functional value of Cuban 'choteo' in coping with the difficulties of immigration, politics, and ethnic tensions in Miami, as described by Laguna (2017). Hence, Cuban postnostalgia may well set the general tone for Latinidad among Miami's local resident population. For the highly substantial transient or transnational Latin American population in Miami, which Nijman (2011) characterized as 'mobiles,' the contours of Latinidad are a much more complex matter. In this respect, Iglesias Illa's (2010) *Miami*, written from an Argentinean 'outsider' perspective, is highly insightful in terms of the city's social reality vis-à-vis its cultural imaginary as "la última frontera de América Latina."

One of the more remarkable aspects of the *¿Qué Pasa, USA?* success story was its broad linguistic appeal beyond Cuban Miami, not just among other Latinx groups but among US mainstream and even some Latin American audiences at the time (Delgado and Veraldi 2007). On sociolinguistic grounds, the show transcended the Miami Cuban experience, offering an early glimpse into the coming mediatization of bilingual Spanish-speaking identities within the US mainstream. In this regard, I believe that Miami—always already postmodern—was likely the first ideological 'location' of mediatization of Spanish in the US, from the Peña family in the 1970s to the ethnolinguistic battleground of the following decade and then the emergent neoliberal economic marketplace approaching the new millennium. The course that ideologies of Spanish and English took in the 'new Miami' during the 2000s is the focus of the next chapter, which explores the attitudes and perceptions of high school students born in the 1990s. The perspectives of these Miami Latinx millennials reveal much about the ideological process of sociolinguistic change in South Florida thirty years after the battle over English-only, even though our possible apprehension of the consequences of mediatization remains far on the postmodern horizon.

3 The postmodern paradox of Spanish in Miami

> Not only is there no resolution (false or otherwise) of contradictory forms in postmodern parody, but there is a foregrounding of those very connotations.
> —Linda Hutcheon, *The Politics of Postmodernism* (2002)

In 2011, a Twitter account and web series called *Shit Girls Say* went viral. By 2012, the original video, which parodied women's speech and conversational styles, had garnered 30 million views and inspired many imitations. Among them was *Shit Miami Girls Say*, which also went viral in South Florida. Each episode of the video series parodied sociolinguistic particularities of English-speaking Miami Latinx young adults, e.g. widespread use of 'literally,' 'supposably,' 'irregardless,' and 'like' with a characteristically Hispanic light /l/ and backed vowel quality (Carter, López Valdez, and Sims 2020); Cubanisms such as 'eating shit' [wasting time or doing nothing]; Spanish-origin lexemes like 'dale,' 'chancleta,' 'pata sucia,' 'tiqui tiqui,' and 'caca'; as well as brief code-switches into Spanish. In a special Halloween episode (2017), a "White girl" called Amber from Davie in nearby Broward County visits Miami and finds herself in "A Nightmare on Calle Ocho," where she is force-fed croquetas, accosted by a Spanish-speaking "Papi chulo," and interrogated about her identity by a group of translanguaging Hialeah "chongas," a term commonly used in reference to young Miami Latina women of lower socio-economic status with highly stylized dress and speech (see Hernández 2009). The "chongas" mock Amber's dress and hairstyle, calling her a "papa sin sal" and asking her, "Do you even have a plancha, bro?" When she tells them she is from Davie, they laugh and affirm emphatically that they are from Hialeah, to which she exclaims in an exasperated tone, "Is this America? I should have learned Spanish!"

Hialeah became the bastion of Cuban exile during the 1980s as growing numbers of recently arrived Central Americans began to settle in Little Havana or Calle Ocho, the historic neighborhood along Southwest Eighth Street near downtown Miami where many Cuban immigrants of the previous two decades had settled. Comprising much of Miami's northwestern metro area, Hialeah boasts the highest percentage of Spanish-speaking households

DOI: 10.4324/9780429438363-3

The postmodern paradox of Spanish in Miami   119

in South Florida: nearly 95% according to US Census estimates. Because it is solidly working-class and the vast majority of the population is foreign-born, Hialeah bears the brunt of local jokes and stereotypes regarding recently arrived immigrants and, particularly, Miami Cuban urban popular culture. An independent city located within the already majority Hispanic and Spanish-speaking Miami metro, Hialeah is thought of as 'the' Spanish-speaking place in South Florida and the epicenter of Cubanisms (Lanier 2014; Callesano 2020). In Miami's sociolinguistic landscape and cultural imaginary, both Hialeah and Calle Ocho thus constitute prominent 'places' in Blommaert's (2005) terms: spaces onto which a complex array of social, cultural, and affective attributes is mapped and senses of rights, belonging, and authority are projected (222). Blommaert reminds us that "people speak *from* a place. Given the deep connections between forms of language and par-ticular places, the use of specific varieties 'sets' people in a particular social and/or physical place, so to speak, and confers the attributive qualities of that place to what they say" (2005, 223).

When Amber from Davie ended up on Calle Ocho, she was undoubtedly in a different place, one where Spanish expressed belonging and the "chongas" from Hialeah held authority. Although a parody—a politically incorrect one in some ways—based upon sociolinguistic stereotypes and the popular 'Cubans are taking over' narrative that circulated in Miami during the 1970s and 1980s (as we saw in the previous chapter), the Halloween episode of *Shit Miami Girls Say* forefronts a question sometimes posed by Anglophone visitors from other parts of the US, some in jest and others half seriously: "Is this America? Where am I?" In the introduction to her widely cited 'global city' concept, Sassen (2005) put it another way: "The global city particularly has emerged as a site for new claims: by global capital, which uses the global city as an 'organizational commodity,' but also by disadvantaged sectors of the urban population, frequently as internationalized a presence in global cities as capital. The 'de-nationalizing' of urban space and the formation of new claims by transnational actors, raise the question: Whose city is it?" (39).[1] The response to these questions, however jokingly one might attempt to articulate it, delves into an entirely serious and socially high-stakes matter for the children and grandchildren of Spanish-speaking immigrants in a majority Spanish-speaking immigrant city that has been dubbed 'The Capital of Latin America.'

In unconscious yet also highly conscious ways, Miami Latinx youth must negotiate sociolinguistic identities that are much more complex than those of their monolingual Anglophone counterparts just to the north or their monolingual Spanish-speaking counterparts just to the south. On one hand, they are in the US, geographically speaking, and they consider themselves 'Americans,' politically speaking. On the other hand, they are not 'really' or 'fully' in the US, culturally speaking, and they consider themselves 'Cubans,' 'Colombians,' 'Nicaraguans,' etc., ethnically speaking. Many young Miami-born Latinxs echo the following young woman's perspective: "I'm American

120 The postmodern paradox of Spanish in Miami

because I was born here and I grew up here, but I'm Colombian because of all this other stuff.... I mean, everybody here in Miami might feel that way because Miami's the midpoint. Living here you kind of get a little bit of American life and you kind of get a little bit of your family's culture, so you're somewhere in between" (interviewee in Lanier 2014[2]). The intense pressure young Miami Latinxs face to assimilate to a monolingual Anglophone mainstream, which emanates from national discourse spheres and is institutionally enacted in formal education (Valenzuela 1999; Rosa 2019), must be reconciled with the pressure—equally intense at times—to speak Spanish, which circulates in familial and local societal domains, including commerce and the workplace, as well as in the macro-level discourse of globalization more abstractly. These are two principal language ideological dimensions of a complex vertical scalar order of Spanish in Miami, reflective of a postmodern sociolinguistic situation that might be characterized as paradoxical. As I will argue, the local expediency and transnational exigency of Spanish in Miami synchronically contest the diachronic prevalence of English along an apparent cross-generational axis. This axis, however, is continuously intercepted or crossed by the flows of globalization in a Spanish-speaking sociolinguistics of mobility (Blommaert 2010).

The vitality of Spanish in Miami is a crucial element of local identity on the ground, given that people speak not only *from* a place but also *in* a place (Blommaert 2005). The human, media, financial, cultural, and commercial flows that make Miami an integral part of Latin America, as described in the previous two chapters, serve to keep Spanish highly present in the cultural imaginary as much as in lived sociolinguistic reality. Practically speaking, Spanish is everywhere. As a locus of dynamic migratory flows within the broader context of Latin America, Miami's globalization has been concomitant with rapid sociolinguistic diversification, creating a condition of Spanish-speaking 'superdiversity,' i.e. "a dynamic interplay of variables among an increased number of new, small and scattered, multiple-origin, transnationally connected, socio-economically differentiated and legally stratified immigrants" (Vertovec 2007, 1024). The superdiversity of Spanish vis-à-vis the generalized norm of bilingualism in English, which is the result of English-language hegemony both nationally and globally, leads to complex orders of social indexicality (Blommaert 2010). Various dimensions of horizontality and verticality are confronted on multiple levels: the local (i.e. Miami or neighborhood within Miami), regional (East Coast US and the Caribbean), national (US-Cuba, US-Colombia, Cuba-Colombia, Colombia-Venezuela, etc.), and international (the world English speaker versus the world Spanish speaker). In the ideological processes of confrontation and contestation within these complex social orders of indexicality, distinctive features of Spanish and English, and their concomitant dialects and sociolects, are brought into sharper relief in the sociolinguistic landscape. As speakers of Spanish move, the varieties of Spanish they speak move across different orders of indexicality: "Mobility, sociolinguistically speaking, is therefore a

The postmodern paradox of Spanish in Miami 121

trajectory through different stratified, controlled and monitored spaces in which language 'gives you away'" (Blommaert 2010, 6).

In Miami, as "boundaries of inclusion and exclusion, of belonging and otherness, of 'us' and 'them'" are constantly and intimately negotiated (Brah 1996, 209), the confrontation of Spanish and English within a continuous process of cross-generational language shift gives impulse to a sort of fractal recursivity (Irvine and Gal 2000), which inevitably implicates Spanish-speaking superdiversity. In other words, varieties (regional or national) and variants (lexical, phonological, etc.) of Spanish in Miami are ideologically conditioned—at least in part—by Spanish-English bilingualism among the local majority and the hegemony of English (Lynch 2019). In Miami, exemplary of the sort of intersectional 'diaspora space' described by Brah (1996) and the sociolinguistic 'mental space' elaborated by Caravedo (2014), the differentiation of Spanish and English is fractally projected onto processes of contestation and social stratification of diverse varieties of Spanish, which in turn condition the perception and evaluation of particular variants or forms within and across Spanish varieties themselves, e.g. Cuban variants in the speech of distinct groups of Cubans, Cuban variants in Nicaraguan repertoires, coastal versus highland variants among Colombians, etc. The latter process at times indexes values that have been transplanted from other areas of the Hispanic world, such as the idea that Caribbean varieties of Spanish are less 'correct' than Latin American Mainland varieties (Lynch 2019). I will return to this phenomenon in more detail in Chapter 5. Through such elaborate and at times enigmatic ideological channels, Spanish language use is negotiated and patterns of language variability and change are conditioned in Miami. Visitors and recently arrived immigrants often find this sociolinguistic scenario quite bewildering. For recent-arrival youths in school settings, the scenario is particularly concerning.

In this chapter, I discuss the paradox of Spanish in Miami, to wit: Spanish is spoken by a local majority who positively value it and accord it political and economic prestige, yet it is oftentimes culturally and socially stigmatized by the youth of successive generations who appear reluctant to speak it (Porcel 2006). Given the nearly exclusive use of English in formal education and its hegemonic status in popular culture, sociolinguistic discontinuities emerge in Spanish already among first-generation speakers who have lived in Miami for some time, and among all speakers of successive generations (Lynch 2013). Hence, there is cross-generational 'loss' of Spanish in the classic sociological sense, despite pervasive use of the language across all sectors and domains of the city, and despite its vital role in the city's economic, cultural and political life. One could rightly assert that the observable discontinuity of Spanish among third- and fourth-generation speakers in Miami merely reflects the continuation of modern one nation–one language ideology and the hegemony of English in the global era, which is indeed an unremarkable and frankly uninteresting fact. What interests us for present purposes, however, is the necessity of the preposition 'despite' in the case of Miami. This is perhaps

122 *The postmodern paradox of Spanish in Miami*

more apparent in a reversed clausal order of the foregoing sentence: the use of Spanish is pervasive across all sectors and domains of the city, and it plays a vital role in the city's economic, cultural, and political life despite cross-generational loss of the language.

In the first section of this chapter, I explore the roles and values that local bilingual Latinx youth *from* Miami attribute to Spanish and English *in* Miami. Based upon the results of a language use and attitudes survey, I observe the differential ways in which the paradox of Spanish manifests according to social class. In the second section, I offer a theoretical explanation for the apparently paradoxical situation of Spanish in Miami, relying principally upon Blommaert's (2005, 2010) notion of scalar orders of indexicality in a sociolinguistics of mobility. As I will suggest, upper-middle and especially upper-class speakers of Spanish orient to vertical scalar sociolinguistic orders rather differently than those of the lower socioeconomic strata, notwithstanding the highly positive attitudes toward the language to be found across all sectors of the city. Widely cited Cuban American sociologist Alejandro Portes explained the perspective of Miami Cubans in spatial terms of Hialeah vis-à-vis Coral Gables, one of Miami's most affluent areas, which lies to the south: "La gente que llega [de Cuba] va derecho a Hialeah, un lugar completamente distinto a Coral Gables.... La gente de Hialeah no sabe que es pobre, vive en un mundo aparte. No saben dónde están colocados en la escala norteamericana. Lo único que saben es que están ellos allí y que hay otros cubanos más al sur que no quieren saber nada con ellos" (cited in Iglesias Illa 2010, 205). Within these distinct realities or 'mental spaces' (Caravedo 2014), not only are the roles and values attributed to Spanish rather different, but so are those attributed to English. This social fact reflects the salient divide between the so-called 'haves and have-nots,' a key characteristic of the postmodern social condition of global cities such as Miami.

Socioeconomic class presents itself as a crucial dimension of Spanish-speaking Miami for various reasons: Miami is the only major city of the US where Spanish is spoken by a majority across all socioeconomic strata (Carter and Lynch 2015); South Florida society reflects a neoliberal, highly consumerist—not to say materialistic—mainstream (Iglesias Illa 2010; Nijman 2011); and socioeconomic status overshadows racial dimensions of Spanish language use in most contexts because the vast majority of Miami's Latin American-born population identifies as White (82.3% according to American Community Survey 2019). Hence the city offers us a compelling glimpse not only into processes of Spanish language variation and change through the lens of English language contact (e.g. Silva-Corvalán 1994; Zentella 1997) in tandem with socioeconomic class differentiation, but also into patterns of sociolinguistic change in ideological representation (Androutsopoulos 2014). For the present purposes, I prefer to think of social class in terms of 'multiaxiality,' i.e. "multiple axes of power that crisscross our daily lives and the identities and relations that we form and re-form as we move through

The postmodern paradox of Spanish in Miami   123

them" (Fiske 1996, 65). In hyperliterate, postindustrial societies such as that of South Florida, modes of representation play a crucial role in the creation of social alliances and the construction of identities, which increasingly disrupt the stability of traditional categories such as class, race, and gender. Such categories, according to Fiske, may be better regarded "as terrains upon which alliances are formed and strategies deployed, not as fixed determinants," i.e. what he terms 'social formations' (1996, 67). I highlight Fiske's proposal to convey my recognition that the use of the term 'social class' is problematic; it is not a fixed determinant of stance, attitude, or posture.

That stated, the heightened perception of class in response to the growing socioeconomic divide in economic globalization is an incontrovertible social fact (Appadurai 2013), one that is blatantly obvious if one traverses Miami from north to south and talks to people who live on either side. The ideas that those people have about Spanish are rather different, in very important albeit highly nuanced ways, as we will see in this chapter. I will ultimately attribute the class-driven paradox created by a higher-level prestige order of indexicality of Spanish to postmodern parodic practice—not in the eighteenth-century sense of ludic imitation, but rather in the critical sense explained by Hutcheon (2002), which I relate to language ideological modes of representation: "a value-problematizing, de-naturalizing form of acknowledging the history (and through irony, the politics) of representations" (90).

The meaning of bilingualism: Differential views of Spanish and English among Miami Latinx youth

I have already noted the observations made by Didion (1987) and Iglesias Illa (2010) regarding the greater amplitude of Spanish on the socioauditory scale in comparison to other Hispanic-majority areas of the US. An observation made by a young Cuban-born woman whom I interviewed is highly illustrative. She described the 'culture shock' of Spanish language use that she experienced at age 16 when she moved to Miami from Los Angeles, where she had lived since immigrating from Cuba at age 5:

Nosotros vivíamos en la ciudad de Los Ángeles, y casi todo el mundo son hispanos. Porque yo diría que en mi escuela el 98% de todos los estudiantes eran hispanos. Pero en Los Ángeles no es como aquí, que en la calle se habla mucho español. Así no es allá [Los Ángeles]. Cuando tú sales de tu casa, se murió. Nadie habla español. Cuando yo llegué aquí [Miami], yo estuve, para mí fue más difícil acostumbrarme, créelo o no, más difícil acostumbrarme a la vida cuando vine de California a Miami, que cuando fui de Cuba a California cuando tenía cinco años, aunque yo no sabía el inglés. Yo nunca había oído inglés en mi vida, so lo tuve que aprender, un idioma completamente diferente. Pero cuando vine a Miami fue un culture shock tan grande porque yo me acuerdo que llegué a la escuela y todo el mundo estaba hablando español. Cuando vivía en

124 *The postmodern paradox of Spanish in Miami*

> California mi español era atrocious, pero se ha puesto mucho mejor desde que vivo aquí [Miami].

These personal observations highlight the perceptual salience of Spanish in public high schools in Miami. In a city where Spanish is highly prevalent and migratory flows are continuous, English, which is the unequivocal code of formal education in Miami, acquires immeasurable symbolic value as social differentiator in terms of the place students come *from* and the place they are *in*.

The pressure to speak English among adolescents and young adults is compounded by the stigmatization of particular monolingual varieties of Spanish among their bilingual majority peers. Several participants in Lanier's (2014) qualitative study of language use and perceptions among young adult Miami Latinxs recounted the social stigma of speaking Spanish in high school. One recalled: "When you're in school, it's like if you speak Spanish, you feel like you're outcasted in a sense because they're like oh, you speak Spanish, you're right off the boat" (57). Another interviewee described the phenomenon in similar terms: "In my high school, 96 percent Hispanic—everyone's Hispanic, the kids who spoke Spanish, we used to call them 'refs.' 'Refs' as in refugees. That's the name we had for people who spoke Spanish.... It's just they were new arrivals, or like, people who hadn't acclimated into American culture.... There was a certain cultural rift between you and them" (58). This rift, so to speak, reflects a meaningful social divide between recently arrived immigrant students and those who are *from* Miami. In the context of school populations that may be 80% to 95% Hispanic and from Spanish-speaking homes, as in Hialeah, English acquires an indispensable symbolic value in terms of social differentiation.

In what follows, I take up this matter based upon responses to a language use and attitudes questionnaire completed by students at two vastly different high schools during the early 2010s: a public institution in Hialeah where the majority of students are from families of low to lower-middle socio-economic status; and a private school located in a highly affluent neighborhood of the much wealthier southern part of Miami, attended principally by students from upper-class families. I will refer to the former as 'Northside' and the latter as 'Bayview.' Like Miami in general, both schools were majority Hispanic. As we will see, students in both locations viewed Spanish positively and disagreed with suggestions to restrict or limit the use of Spanish in society. However, within this general trend, there appeared differential degrees of orientation toward the ideology of 'language as commodity,' which became discursively prevalent during the 1990s, as we saw in Chapter 2, and which I will characterize as a higher-level scalar order of indexicality (Blommaert 2010) in the second section of this chapter. Elite private school students appeared to have gotten the proverbial message about the value of bilingualism (i.e. not the value of Spanish or English per se) more than their working-class counterparts in Hialeah. For the latter, Spanish appeared to be as much a marker of cultural authenticity (Woolard 2008)—as in the case of the Halloween episode of *Shit Miami Girls Say*—as it was a marketplace asset. Although students at both schools disagreed with pro-English-only statements, upper-class-background students disavowed them significantly more than working-class students, reflecting the symbolic value that Hialeah teens attribute to English as a social differentiator with respect to immigration and as the vehicle for upward socioeconomic mobility—a much more real concern for them than for their wealthy counterparts.

The study and its participants

Students at both schools, all of whom self-identified as Hispanic or Latina/o, responded to a written questionnaire. In the first section, they provided information regarding their age and gender, family origin (Cuban, Colombian, etc.), birthplace and time of immigration, and their identification with the terms 'Hispanic' or 'Latina/o.'[3] They were asked to estimate their own abilities to speak Spanish and indicate the frequency with which they used Spanish and English with their mothers, fathers, grandparents, siblings, and friends based on a Likert scale with values from 1 to 5, as in Example 3.1. Based upon the same scale, they were also asked to estimate the frequency of the two languages in television programs and movies they watched, and in their usual music choices.

Example 3.1

What do you estimate to be the percentage of your use of English and Spanish with your **friends**? (Please CIRCLE)

1	2	3	4	5
English almost always	Mostly English / some Spanish	Half English / half Spanish	Mostly Spanish / some English	Spanish almost always

In the second section of the questionnaire, students were asked to indicate their level of (dis)agreement with a series of 54 statements concerning social and cultural roles and values of Spanish and English. These responses were also based on a Likert scale with values from 1 to 5, as in Example 3.2.

Example 3.2

It would be difficult to have a close friend who only spoke Spanish.

1	2	3	4	5
I totally disagree	I disagree somewhat	I neither agree nor disagree	I mostly agree	I totally agree

126 *The postmodern paradox of Spanish in Miami*

Everyone responded to the questionnaire in English, which was the language of instruction at both schools (i.e. neither offered a bilingual or International Baccalaureate program). Teachers opted to participate in the study, offering their regular class time for students to respond on a voluntary basis. Official permissions were previously obtained from the administration at both locations and from Miami-Dade County Public Schools.

A total of 254 students comprised the present sample: 137 males and 117 females, with an average age of 16.3 years. Those born and raised in Miami constituted 72% of participants; another 20% were born in Latin America but immigrated to Miami as children, sometime before age 11; the remaining 8% arrived sometime after age 11. As would be expected, there was greater diversity of national origins at Bayview due to Miami's status in Latin American finance and commerce, i.e. the city attracts professionals and wealthy people from all over Latin America (Nijman 2011). At Bayview, students attributed their origins to fifteen different Spanish-speaking countries of Latin America; 30% were of Cuban origin, and there were also three students whose families were from Spain. At Northside, on the other hand, the majority of students' families hailed from Caribbean and Central American nations, with Cubans representing about half; Colombians and a few students of other South American nationalities were also present.

All of the questionnaire data was entered into SPSS (Statistical Package for the Social Sciences). To understand the structure of the data first in an overall sense, exploratory factor analysis was conducted on all 54 Likert-scale items of the second section of the questionnaire. Factors were extracted with principal axis factoring and promax rotation was used, as factors were expected to be correlated. While there were nine factors with eigenvalues greater than one, the screen plot and pattern loadings suggested extracting fewer factors. Therefore, solutions extracting three to seven factors were explored. Based on the pattern of loadings, a three-factor solution was retained. Each of these so-called factors can be thought of as a thematic grouping of questions according to patterns in the responses. For each of the three factors, composite scores were then calculated upon which to test for significant differences between the two schools.

In a general sense, the three themes that emerged in the factor analysis were: roles and values of Spanish; ideological orientation to English; and personal affective dimensions of Spanish and English. In what follows, I present results for each of these three main factors or general themes, in separate sections. Within each one, I discuss particular items of the questionnaire, noting important differences between the two schools.

Roles and values of Spanish: Language through the lens of cultural authenticity

In the statistical analysis, 24 items loaded onto this first main factor, all related to roles and values of Spanish (α = .83). An independent samples *t*-test revealed no significant differences between the two schools for this factor ($t(252) = 0.11$, $p = .909$), which suggests that, in the composite sense, Spanish was viewed similarly among high school students of upper socio-economic status in the highly affluent neighborhoods to the city's south ($M = 3.08$, $SD = .55$) and those of lower-middle-class backgrounds in generally working-class areas of the northwest ($M = 3.08$, $SD = 0.56$). It is important to note upfront that an independent samples *t*-test revealed no significant differences between the two schools in terms of oral competence in Spanish ($t(252) = 0.69$, $p = .493$): students at both schools overall indicated having 'good' to 'very good' abilities to speak Spanish, Northside ($M = 3.52$, $SD = 1.12$), Bayview ($M = 3.61$, $SD = .1.03$). About a quarter of students at both schools indicated having 'excellent' ability in the language: 23% at Northside and 25% at Bayview. There were no important differences in self-reported ability to speak Spanish according to gender; this variable did not prove significant for any of the three main factors. Nor were there any significant differences between the two schools in terms of bilingual patterns, combining data from responses to all questions in the first part of the questionnaire about extent of Spanish and English language use with different interlocutors ($\alpha = .774$) ($t(252) = 0.99$, $p = .325$). As reflected in Table 3.1., the strong preference for English with siblings and friends, as well as in television and movies, reflects an intergenerational shift to English language dominance among students at both schools.

Already in 1975, Solé (1979, 1982) affirmed that shift to English was evident in the responses to a questionnaire study that he conducted in Miami with 268 public secondary school students of Cuban origin, despite their overtly positive attitudes toward Spanish. Twenty years later, in a survey of 2,843 eighth- and ninth-grade students (not all of Hispanic backgrounds) in Miami-Dade and Broward Counties, Portes and Schauffler (1994) observed a general preference to speak English among everyone, but noted that only about one-fourth of the Hispanic students included in their study reflected 'foreign language loss'; this figure dropped to only 11% among Cuban

Table 3.1 Reported language use among students at Northside and Bayview ($N = 254$) (1 = English almost always; 3 = half English / half Spanish; 5 = Spanish almost always)

Reported language use	Northside	Bayview
With mother	3.24	3.17
With father	3.33	3.10
With grandparents	4.59	4.43
With siblings	1.84	2.12
With friends* ($p = .05$)	1.70	1.94
In TV and movies watched* ($p = .04$)	1.54	1.75
In music choices* ($p = .000$)	2.13	2.55

128   *The postmodern paradox of Spanish in Miami*

private school students. The authors concluded that "Cuban and other Latin American-origin youth in South Florida are mostly bilingual" (651). Lynch (1999, 2000) also noted high levels of bilingual ability among private university students in Miami; Roca (1991) and López Morales (2003) commented on the tendency to 'maintain' Spanish among Miami Cuban Americans in general. Porcel (2006) and Pascual y Cabo (2015) described 'loss' of Spanish among young adult Miami-born Cubans, and both Lynch (2013, 2017) and Gutiérrez-Rivas (2007, 2011a, 2011b) observed patterns of sociolinguistic discontinuity in Cuban Spanish across adult first-, second-, and third-generation speakers. All of these prior studies suggest that bilingualism among Hispanic youth in South Florida is the majority norm, with English dominance and clear preference for English in peer and sibling interactions as a function of time of arrival in the US. Miami-born Hispanics who do not actively speak Spanish are not altogether uncommon, especially among the third generation. In the present survey, extremely few students indicated having 'poor' ability to speak Spanish: 4% at Northside and only 2% at Bayview. Another 14% and 10%, respectively, indicated having 'fair' oral ability in the language, meaning that 82% of teenagers surveyed at Northside and 88% at Bayview estimated their abilities in Spanish to be 'good' to 'excellent.'

It is noteworthy that Northside students indicated using Spanish slightly more with parents and grandparents than their Bayview counterparts, yet the pattern was reversed in the case of siblings: 1.84 at Northside vs. 2.12 at Bayview. Although this difference did not reach statistical significance ($t(236) = 1.72$, $p = .087$) it nonetheless seems important, especially in light of the fact that it inverts the cross-group differential pattern between the two schools with respect to other family members. One might suppose that this tendency could be attributed to more recency of immigration among students at Bayview, but this is not supported by demographic data: 7% of Northside students indicated arriving in Miami after age 11, and 9% of Bayview students indicated the same. Furthermore, recency of immigration would also likely condition greater use of Spanish with parents and grandparents, which was not the case for Bayview students. Ability to speak Spanish did not appear to be the key variable in this instance, either: among the US-born, Miami-raised respondents of the sample ($n = 183$), 42% at Northside reported having 'very good' to 'excellent' oral abilities compared to 29% at Bayview. In this regard, the significantly greater use of Spanish with friends among Bayview students and in their music, television and film choices surely calls our attention (Table 3.1). I return to this matter below in the following two sections. As I will argue in this chapter, the trend among Bayview students of slightly more use of Spanish with siblings and significantly more use of Spanish with friends and in consumption of cultural products may be indicative of a more 'bilingual' ideological orientation in comparison to their Northside counterparts.

In an overall sense, though, the responses to items regarding language use patterns and ability to speak Spanish, taken together with the lack of any significant difference between the two schools for the items of this first

The postmodern paradox of Spanish in Miami   129

factor in the composite, support the popular impression (e.g. Didion, 1987) that Spanish is not socioeconomically stratified in Miami, i.e. it is as widely spoken and, as we will see, positively valued among wealthy people as much as those of the working class. As I noted in Chapter 2, this sociolinguistic reality is generally erased in mainstream Hollywood television and film, which tend to project a predominantly—and in some cases almost exclusively—Anglophone city. Students at both schools agreed that "It would be strange to live in a city where people did not speak Spanish" ($M = 3.52$, $SD = 1.43$ at Bayview; $M = 3.54$, $SD = 1.32$ at Northside). They also mostly agreed that "Latin culture is what makes Miami such a cool city," although upper social class students at Bayview agreed with this statement somewhat more ($M = 3.95$, $SD = 1.04$) than their counterparts at Northside ($M = 3.73$, $SD = 1.00$). In relation to Chapter 2, it is noteworthy that students at both schools mostly agreed that "When people elsewhere in the United States think of Miami, they think of people speaking Spanish," with a mean response of 3.7 at both schools ($SD = 1.0$ at both as well). They also tended to agree with the suggestion that "Miami is as much a part of Latin America as it is the United States," with a mean response around 3.5 at both schools ($SD = 1.2$ at both).

The particular ideological lenses through which students at both schools positively valued Spanish appeared to be rather different in some regards. There is evidence that Northside students perhaps perceived Spanish language use more in terms of speaker authenticity (Woolard 2008) than their much wealthier Bayview counterparts. The latter, on the other hand, sometimes appeared to perceive the value of Spanish more through the discourse of language commodification, as I will suggest in the following section. Perhaps the first and most obvious 'authenticating' criterion of Latinx identity would be the ability to speak Spanish, as Scott Shenk (2007) observed among Mexican Americans in California. Students at neither school appeared to have a firm opinion regarding the affirmation that "To be 'Hispanic' or 'Latino' in Miami, you have to be able to speak Spanish," though students at Northside agreed with this statement more ($M = 3.41$, $SD = 1.27$) than students at Bayview ($M = 3.14$, $SD = 1.31$), a difference that was not statistically significant. In response to the open-ended question "Do you consider yourself Hispanic or Latina/o? Why or why not?", the majority referred to their family's geopolitical origins in a 'Hispanic' or 'Latin' country; most did not refer to Spanish language per se. The majority indicated identifying with both terms, though many indicated a preference for 'Hispanic.' This finding aligns with that of a 2013 Pew Research Center survey, which found that most of the US population in question did not have a preference. Among those who did, however, 'Hispanic' was preferred to 'Latino/a' by a 2-to-1 margin: 33% vs. 15%, respectively (López 2013). Among those who indicated identifying exclusively as 'Hispanic' in the present survey, there was a tendency to associate that term with Caribbean identity, especially among Cuban-origin respondents. For example, a respondent from Northside who was born in Miami to Cuban

130　The postmodern paradox of Spanish in Miami

parents wrote: "I consider 'Latinos' people from Latin American countries, not those from the Caribbean islands such as Cuba." Another Cuban-background student at Northside wrote that "Latino is a label given to those that come from Mexico." A young Miami-born Venezuelan American interviewed by Lanier (2014) made a similar remark: "I feel like 'Latino' is a very California thing—I think it's very Mexican-centered. I feel like in Miami we say 'Hispanic' more" (cf. Rosa, 2019).

In response to the statement that "It's annoying when people who know Spanish act like they only speak English," students at Northside tended to agree more ($M = 3.71$, $SD = 1.36$) than their counterparts at Bayview ($M = 3.49$, $SD = 1.32$), a difference that was not statistically significant. These slight differences regarding speaking Spanish in relation to 'Hispanic' or 'Latina/o' identity seem indicative of an ideological pattern that did indeed prove statistically significant in responses to three other items suggestive of cultural authenticity. The first such item was: "Telenovelas in Spanish have more likeable characters than most television dramas in English." Students at both schools tended to disagree with this statement somewhat, but the noteworthy finding was that students at Bayview disagreed significantly more ($M = 2.46$, $SD = 1.16$) than students at Northside ($M = 2.90$, $SD = 1.34$) ($t(252) = -2.63$, $p = .009$). On the surface, this seems a matter of little intrigue, but one is led to venture possible reasons as to why the statement elicited significantly different responses at the two schools. One possibility could simply be that Northside students engaged more with telenovelas and hence indicated perceiving their characters as more likeable than those of English-language dramas.[4] Another possibility, not exclusive of the first, would relate to the matter of cultural authenticity in television representations. The fact that a greater percentage of Northside students found the Spanish-speaking characters of telenovelas more likeable than their Bayview counterparts—leaving aside the question of English—could suggest that they attributed greater authenticity to Spanish-speaking television characters. Of course, the presupposition in such case would be that the likeability of characters in television dramas is a function of their 'authenticity' in terms of personality and motives.

Clearly, authenticity is more at stake in television portrayals than the appeal of a character's personality per se. This interpretation seems rather more convincing in light of the fact that there was no difference whatsoever in responses to a separate item that proposed that "Spanish speakers often have more interesting personalities than English speakers." The mean response for that item at both schools was 3.1 ($SD = 1.25$ at Bayview and 1.22 at Northside), suggesting that everyone felt that Spanish and English speakers have equally interesting personalities, i.e. 'neither agree nor disagree.' Students at both schools also responded similarly to the idea that "People who switch back and forth between English and Spanish in conversations are more interesting than people who speak the whole time in just one language," with a mean response of 2.81 at Bayview and 3.01 at Northside (SD of 1.21 for both), a slight difference that was not significant ($t(252) = -1.30$, $p = .193$).

The postmodern paradox of Spanish in Miami   131

Hence, the significant difference with respect to dramatic television portrayals seems more likely attributable to the perceived authenticity of Spanish rather than the idea that Spanish speakers have more interesting personalities in general.

The case for Spanish-speaking cultural authenticity among Northside students appears more unequivocal in responses to two items about denial or refusal to speak the language, both of which yielded significant differences between the two schools. The first of these propositions was that "A Hispanic teenager from Miami who claims not to know Spanish is probably lying." In response, Bayview students disagreed (M = 2.65, SD = 1.19) significantly more than Northside students (M = 3.04, SD = 1.27) ($t(252)$ = −2.45, p = .015). At the same time, students at both schools tended to disagree with the suggestion that "Hispanic teenagers in Miami who refuse to speak Spanish are 'sell-outs,'" but Northside students disagreed more (M = 2.44, SD = 1.43) than their counterparts at Bayview (M = 2.83, SD = 1.26), a difference that also proved to be statistically significant ($t(252)$ = 2.17, p = .03). In other words, Northside students were significantly less likely to believe a Hispanic teen in Miami who claims not to know Spanish, but they were also significantly less likely than Bayview students to call that individual a 'sell-out.' This latter proposition is more ideological, abstract, and political in identity terms, while the former seems less so. The notion of the 'sell-out' is obviously linked to the discourse of consumerism and upward mobility. Those who 'sell out' consciously deny or actively repress some aspect or trait of their identity that others would consider as inherent, natural, or expected, for some sort of social capital or economic gain. But in postmodernity the 'sell-out' also alludes to being fake or inauthentic; in Hutcheon's (2002) sense of parodic practice, the 'sell-out' problematizes the value of Spanish in a politically ironic way. Working-class Northside students may be less judgmental of a Hispanic teen who refuses to speak Spanish than upper-class Bayview teens because, for the former, English language use is tied to upward socioeconomic mobility more strongly than for the latter. In middle- and especially upper-class sectors, the ideology of language commodification appears more firmly entrenched, as I will argue in the following sections. This hypothesis garners some support from the pattern of responses to the proposition that "People in Miami who don't know Spanish are missing out on a lot." For this item, Bayview students indicated significantly more agreement (M = 3.86, SD = 1.09) than Northside students (M = 3.44, SD = 1.16) ($t(252)$ = 2.83, p = .005). Like 'selling out,' the notion of 'missing out' alludes to gain or benefit, of which Bayview students appeared to be more acutely cognizant.

The pervasiveness of Spanish in Miami likely conditioned responses to two other items that were related to pragmatic functions of the language. There was indifference to the suggestion that "Family values are better expressed in Spanish than in English": the mean response was 3.1 at both schools (SD of 1.1 at both schools as well). This finding appears perhaps contradictory to the popular cultural perception—not to say stereotype—that the expression

132 *The postmodern paradox of Spanish in Miami*

of family values via Spanish is symbolic of Latinidad in the US (Rodríguez 2009), as evident in some dialogues of television shows, e.g. interactions between Maria LaGuerta and Angel Batista in *Dexter*, or in literary representations, e.g. *Dreaming in Cuban* by Cristina García. Perhaps because Spanish is heard in practically all spheres of Miami public life, these students did not associate the language as strongly with home or family life as might Latinx teens in other areas of the country. This tendency may also be related to the high degree of bilingualism among Miami Latinx youth, meaning that family values, or any sort of values for that matter, could be expressed equally well in either language. The same might be assumed regarding the expression of humor. In light of Laguna's (2017) analysis of the social value of 'choteo' among Miami Cubans, as well as my own personal observation that US Latinx bilinguals often use Spanish for humoristic purposes in code-switched discourse (e.g. *Shit Miami Girls Say* or the social media site Only in Hialeah 305), I supposed that students would strongly agree that "Joking around is funnier in Spanish." That was not the case, however. There was only slight agreement with this statement at both schools, with a mean around 3.3 (SD = 1.20 at Northside; SD = 1.13 at Bayview). In sum, responses to these two items regarding family and humor—both symbolic cultural dimensions of Latinidad—are perhaps unsurprising in light of Miami's reality as a Latinx majority city where Spanish is so widely spoken.

Despite the pervasiveness of Spanish, however, a majority of students at both schools tended not to agree with the suggestion that "Spanish should be an official language in Miami," with a mean response of 2.8 at Bayview and 2.75 at Northside (SD of 1.37 at both). However, students at both schools disagreed even more emphatically with the proposal that "English should be the only official language in the United States," as we will see in the next section, focused on English language orientation.

Ideological orientation to English: Socioeconomic mobility and language commodification

In response patterns for the 13 items that loaded onto this factor in the statistical analysis (α = .69), it was clear that students at both schools thought of Miami as a bilingual, Spanish-speaking city, and they generally eschewed English-only practices and policies. What was interesting in statistical terms was the differential extent of their agreement regarding the former and their disagreement regarding the latter, as we will see in this section. The differences between the two schools in the composite sense for this second factor of the analysis proved to be highly significant ($t(252)$ = 5.74, p = .001).

There was overwhelming rejection of the idea that "English should be the only official language in the United States," but Bayview students rejected it more (M = 1.97, SD = 1.27) than their counterparts at Northside (M = 2.29, SD = 1.36), a difference that approached significance ($t(252)$ = −1.83, p = .068). A highly significant difference indeed emerged in response to the suggestion

The postmodern paradox of Spanish in Miami 133

that "Miami would be a better place if everyone spoke only English" ($t(252) = -3.32\ p = .001$). Though students at both schools disagreed, those at Bayview were significantly more emphatic in their opposition ($M = 1.53$, $SD = 0.92$) than those at Northside ($M = 1.99$, $SD = 1.16$). The same trend played out in response to an item related to language use in the school setting. Bayview students objected almost categorically ($M = 1.11$, $SD = 0.45$) to the affirmation that "Students should not be allowed to speak Spanish on school grounds, except in Spanish class," while Northside students appeared rather more attenuated in their disagreement ($M = 1.58$, $SD = 1.08$), a difference that was highly significant ($t(252) = -4.04$, $p = .000$).

Speaking Spanish at school reflects an important social division between recently arrived immigrants and the English-speaking US mainstream. Differential language choice among friends in the high school setting involves social variables that do not enter into language choice with family members or patterns of acquisition and use in the home. In socialization among teenagers at school, language practice becomes much more culturally loaded, and ideologically charged (Eckert 1989). Numerous teachers in Miami-Dade's public high schools have commented to me that there is a marked social divide between students who have been born or raised principally in Miami—who clearly prefer to speak English—and students who are more recent arrivals to Miami, all Spanish-dominant speakers typically enrolled in ESOL courses. This is particularly the case in lower-income areas. The division is exacerbated by the reluctance that ESOL students sometimes have to speak English, thus distancing themselves even more from their US-born bilingual peers. Indeed, as we will observe in the next section, students at Bayview appeared significantly more receptive of friendships with Spanish monolinguals than their counterparts at Northside. One must bear in mind that distinctions between lower versus upper social class in Miami are not drawn along the lines of Spanish versus English, since in both sectors of society there are positive attitudes toward both languages, and both are spoken extensively. Rather, limited English language ability and perceived variety of (monolingual) Spanish both carry symbolic value as markers of social class in Miami, among numerous other attributes related to habitus and worldview (Bourdieu 1991). The ideological preeminence of English is concomitant with a broad cultural, societal distinction between recently arrived immigrants and those who have spent most or all of their lives in the US. The school setting is likely a microcosm of this broader societal trend.

Beyond the school setting, asked if "Only English should be spoken in stores and businesses in Miami," students at both locations disagreed with the statement, but Bayview students disagreed more emphatically ($M = 1.72$, $SD = 1.03$) than their Northside counterparts ($M = 2.13$, $SD = 1.13$). This difference was highly significant ($t(250) = -2.87$, $p = .004$). Following the same trend, Bayview students disagreed more strongly ($M = 1.85$, $SD = 1.09$) with the notion that "It's offensive when salespeople or restaurant servers in Miami speak to customers in Spanish" than those at Northside ($M = 2.22$,

134 *The postmodern paradox of Spanish in Miami*

$SD = 1.06$), again yielding a highly significant difference between the two schools ($t(252) = -2.62, p = .009$). Responses to several other items reflected a differential ideological orientation toward English between students at the two schools. Bayview students tended to disagree ($M = 2.37, SD = 1.14$) with the idea that "English is the true language of success in Miami," while Northside students neither agreed nor disagreed ($M = 2.96, SD = 1.17$), yielding a highly significant difference ($t(252) = -3.91, p = .000$). In response to the proposition that "The best way to get around in Miami is by speaking Spanish," students at Bayview agreed significantly more ($M = 3.48, SD = 0.94$) than those at Northside ($M = 3.17, SD = 1.0$) ($t(252) = 2.47, p = .014$), a result that would perhaps seem surprising in light of the latter's location in Hialeah.

Viewed through the ideological marketplace lens of language as asset, however, these significantly differential patterns make sense. For upper-class teens, bilingualism is perceived as key to professional and economic success, perhaps a characteristic of global citizenship, reflective of the generally mobile profiles of their families, i.e. people who travel often and have ties to various countries. For working-class teens, many of whom rarely travel beyond the US or even Florida, English garners rather more exclusive attention as the vehicle of upward socioeconomic mobility. It is important to reiterate that the emphasis on English among Northside students, already evident in their responses to the various pro-English-only items just mentioned, does not condition a negative view of Spanish. Students at both schools agreed equally that "Spanish is necessary to be truly successful in Miami," with mean responses around 3.5 ($SD = 1.06$ at Bayview, 1.10 at Northside). Students at both schools also agreed that "Spanish is necessary for a good job in Miami," even slightly more so at Northside ($M = 3.89, SD = 1.15$) than at Bayview ($M = 3.78, SD = 1.08$), a difference that was not significant ($t(252) = -.747, p = .456$). There was also equal agreement with the following statement: "A lack of school instruction in Spanish is the reason that some Hispanic teenagers in Miami are not fully bilingual"; for both Bayview and Northside students, the mean response was 3.5 ($SD = 1.1$ at both schools). I will return to these matters in the second part of this chapter.

All of this evidence suggests that the ideological discourse of Spanish as asset, which became so prevalent at the time these teenagers were born in the 1990s, has been assimilated in both socioeconomic sectors of the city. For students at both schools, there appears little doubt that Spanish is valuable and that the ability to speak it is a good thing. The meaningful difference between these two groups is in the way that this ideological 'fact' about language as commodity is sociologically processed by each. For those of lower or lower-middle socioeconomic backgrounds, the value of Spanish seemingly stands apart from the imperative of English in the US and their view that English is the main vehicle for upward socioeconomic mobility. For Bayview students, on the other hand, upward socioeconomic mobility is probably less of a concern, since they come from wealthy families—extremely wealthy

The postmodern paradox of Spanish in Miami   135

in some cases—and live in the most opulent areas of the city. For wealthy teenagers, the principal message has been about the value of bilingualism, i.e. not Spanish or English per se, each viewed in isolation. This interpretation finds some support in two items containing the term 'bilingual,' for which Bayview students offered more emphatic responses. Bayview students demonstrated near categorical agreement with the proposition that "Being bilingual is a good thing" ($M = 4.89$, $SD = 0.34$), while Northside students were in somewhat less emphatic agreement ($M = 4.72$, $SD = 0.75$), a difference that was statistically significant ($t(252) = 2.08$, $p = .038$). In response to the suggestion that "Miami is a bilingual city (Spanish and English)," there was again overwhelming agreement at both schools, but Bayview students agreed more emphatically ($M = 4.71$, $SD = 0.70$) than students at Northside ($M = 4.47$, $SD = 1.0$), a difference that was again statistically significant ($t(252) = 2.06$, $p = .040$).

These findings align well with those of a previous study conducted by Lambert and Taylor (1996) regarding socioeconomic class differences in Miami. Based on interview data from 108 first-generation Cuban-born mothers who were asked to estimate the level of fluency and use of both Spanish and English for themselves and for their Miami-born children, those authors observed significant differences between working-class and middle-class families. In the latter, there were statistically significant correlations between mothers' Spanish fluency and that of the first- and second-born children, suggesting that "these mothers are oriented towards an 'additive' form of bilingualism/biculturalism for their children.... [They] appear to realize that the maintenance of a solid Hispanic identity, along with English fluency, is necessary if their offspring are to rise to occupational prominence in Miami's multi-ethnic community" (1996, 496). Among working-class mothers, on the other hand, Lambert and Taylor observed a general pattern of 'subtractive' bilingualism, i.e. a more prevalent orientation toward English, which they attributed to the concern of upward socioeconomic mobility. Different than in middle-class families, there was no significant correlation between working-class mothers' Spanish fluency and the Spanish fluency of any of their children, leading the authors to conclude that outside-family influences likely constitute the major factors conditioning the high level of Spanish ability among working-class second-generation speakers in their sample. A quote from a young Cuban American woman whom I interviewed in 1998 reflects this tendency. Born and raised in Hialeah by working-class Cuban immigrant parents who did not speak English well, she told me: "Mi high school la llamaban Habana High porque todos éramos latinos.... Todas mis amistades eran cubanas. Y todo el mundo que yo conozco son latinos, todos los novios que he tenido na' más que hablan español, y eso es como un debate— a mi mamá le molesta, porque ella dice que yo tengo que buscarme a alguien que hable inglés para americanizarme más." Lambert and Taylor (1996) concluded that, in working-class families, "social forces operating in Miami's Hispanic community may temper or even override parental orientations by sustaining and nurturing Spanish language

136   *The postmodern paradox of Spanish in Miami*

skills, particularly for the first-born child, who in turn can have determining influences on the development of Spanish skills of younger siblings" (496).

Curiously, Lambert and Taylor (1996) observed more significant correlations between working-class siblings than between middle-class siblings with respect to Spanish language ability, while the present questionnaire data reflected greater use of Spanish with siblings among upper-class teens at Bayview than among their working-class counterparts at Northside, as noted above. Although the present study did not inquire into sibling order and language use patterns, it is possible that in the time transpired between Lambert and Taylor's research during the early 1990s and the present inquiry some twenty years later, the postmodern conditions of Spanish language use and perception coalesced socially in South Florida. As described in Chapter 2, there was a rapid sociolinguistic change in the ideological representation of Spanish in the *Miami Herald* and other national mass media from the late 1980s into the early 1990s, corresponding with the so-called 'Latin boom' of the 1990s. For the parents of the teenagers of upper socioeconomic class backgrounds in the present study, the emergence of postmodernity in the 1990s would likely have been more readily meaningful than for their working-class counterparts. Here I allude to a plethora of factors that would have impacted middle and upper socioeconomic sectors of society earlier on, during the 1990s: access to internet and international Spanish-language cable TV programming in their homes, more widespread entry into higher-level education that had begun to place strong ideological value on bilingualism in relation to globalism, greater participation in professional spheres and workplaces where the discourses of globalization began to circulate in the late 1980s, and generally increased mobility and sustained ties with (including travel to and from) the Spanish-speaking world beyond Miami. In this respect, it is possible that their children (i.e. the sample surveyed at Bayview) would be more predisposed to speak Spanish with siblings and friends, and concomitantly more likely to choose Spanish-language cultural products and sources of entertainment, than the children of their working-class contemporaries. As already pointed out, despite speaking slightly more Spanish with parents and grandparents, Northside students appeared significantly less likely to use Spanish with friends, choose Spanish-language music, or watch television and movies in Spanish (Table 3.1). In the following section, I attribute this in part to the so-called 'ref' phenomenon in lower-income schools and in popular Miami urban youth culture in general.

The stronger orientation to English among Northside students in the present study points to the same conclusion reached by Lambert and Taylor (1996) twenty years earlier:

> Emphasis on the heritage language [Spanish] may well arise because the families of middle-class mothers have been more successful in 'making it' in America and therefore feel less pressure to pursue English at the expense of Spanish.... The values and expectations of working-class families may

The postmodern paradox of Spanish in Miami   137

encourage them to emphasize English competency over Spanish for their children whereas another set of values and expectations, based more on heritage culture and language pride, may encourage middle-class families to emphasize Spanish more.

(1996, 487)

Following this reasoning, I hypothesize that the 1990s global discourse of language as commodity perhaps bolstered the ideological prevalence of English (as the global language par excellence) among working-class families and, at the same time, conditioned rather more insistence on the idea of the value of bilingualism among middle- and upper-class families. This argument rests upon notions of scales and orders of indexicality in a sociolinguistics of mobility (Blommaert 2010), as I will explain in the second part of this chapter.

Personal affective dimensions of Spanish and English: Identity and language use

The hypothesis that teens of lower- or lower-middle-class backgrounds regard English as requisite to upward socioeconomic mobility emphatically more than their wealthier counterparts garners further support from two items insinuating English as the language of authority, both of which loaded onto the third main factor of the statistical analysis ($\alpha = .65$). This factor, which included ten questionnaire items related to personal affective dimensions of language, yielded significant differences between the two schools ($t(252) = 3.15$, $p = .002$). The first such item suggested that "English is a more serious language than Spanish." While Northside students showed relative indifference to this statement ($M = 2.86$, $SD = 1.23$), their counterparts at Bayview mostly disagreed ($M = 2.44$, $SD = 1.14$), a pattern that was statistically significant ($t(252) = -2.67$, $p = .008$). The same pattern emerged in response to the statement that "People give you more respect in Miami if you speak to them in English," to which Northside students showed relative indifference ($M = 2.85$, $SD = 1.05$) yet their counterparts at Bayview tended to disagree with ($M = 2.51$, $SD = 0.92$), a difference that was again statistically significant ($t(251) = -2.58$, $p = .010$).

The greater importance accorded to English by Northside students was also evident in responses to two personal affective items regarding Spanish monolingualism. The first proposed that "It would be difficult to have a close friend who only spoke Spanish." Bayview students showed much more emphatic disagreement ($M = 2.18$, $SD = 1.29$) with this statement than their Northside counterparts ($M = 2.88$, $SD = 1.44$), a difference that was highly significant ($t(251) = -3.83$, $p = .000$). Divergent attitudes also appeared in response to the notion that "People who speak only Spanish in Miami are annoying." Again in this case, Bayview students disagreed more emphatically ($M = 2.23$, $SD = 1.25$) than their Northside counterparts ($M = 2.63$, $SD = 1.36$), a difference that was significant ($t(252) = -2.36$, $p = .019$). Responses to the suggestion that "It's easier to make friends in English than

138   *The postmodern paradox of Spanish in Miami*

in Spanish" provided further support: Northside students tended toward agreement (M = 3.42, SD = 1.28), while Bayview students showed relative indifference (M = 2.98, SD = 1.12). Once again, the difference between the two schools was highly significant ($t(252)$ = -2.78, p = .006). And finally, Northside students tended to disagree (M = 2.73, SD = 1.10) significantly more than Bayview students (M = 3.04, SD = 1.16) with the affirmation that "People in Miami are nicer to you if you speak to them in Spanish" ($t(252)$ = 2.15, p = .032). The differential pattern of responses for these four items related to personal affect and friendship seems to confirm that teenagers of working-class backgrounds in Miami tend to place greater emphasis on English than those of upper-class backgrounds. Not only did Northside students disagree significantly less than Bayview students with a series of pro-English-only statements regarding language in society, as described in the previous section, but they also appeared to be significantly less inclined toward friendships with people who do not speak English, and they viewed Spanish monolingualism less favorably in affective terms.

Different than their Bayview counterparts, the working-class students of Northside were confronted with a meaningful sociocultural division within their school in relation to recently arrived immigrants, which extended beyond the school setting: the so-called 'ref' phenomenon. One need not be privy to many conversations in English among Miami Latinx teenagers to overhear the term 'ref.' At the time I carried out this study, I was living in the neighborhood where Northside is located. Although I did not conduct formal interviews with anyone at the school, various teachers who were close personal acquaintances explicitly called my attention to this social division. Through my own family and friends, I also knew personally various students who were attending or had recently graduated from Northside. In their casual conversations, references to 'refs' and 'balseros' abounded, as did the adjective 'reffy' to describe particular places, individuals, social behaviors, and material items. Among various definitions of 'ref' found in Urban Dictionary (urbandictionary.com) are: 1) "Someone in Miami who recently arrived from Cuba, legally or illegally. Although, an immigrant and a ref are two very different things. Refs are loud, obnoxious and try to be as American as possible, failing miserably. A ref usually wears tight jeans, tight shirts, Gucci, designer sunglasses, etc." 2) "Short for 'refugee,' e.g. *Omg those refs are so friggin loud.*" 3) "An immigrant abnormally louder and [more] annoying than regular people. Speaks no English, or if so very little with a heavy Spanish accent. Mostly found in Miami, FL." In its general usage among adolescent and young adult Miami Latinxs who are English-dominant bilinguals, the term is undoubtedly derogatory, although it is sometimes used playfully in a rather less derogatory way, as in *Shit Miami Girls Say, Part 2* (2012). In that episode, a "guy" who is "always at Tootsie's," a local strip club, is described as "mad reffy"; in the immediately following scene a question is posed regarding a local annual holiday festival that features carnival rides and food stands: "Who goes to Santa's Enchanted Forest? That's so reffy."

The postmodern paradox of Spanish in Miami 139

A personal acquaintance who attended another public high school located near Northside in Hialeah during the early 2010s described the phenomenon to me in this way:

> The refs were ESOL kids. They were maybe bullied sometimes and kind of looked down upon. They were definitely isolated in their own groups. I mean, sometimes a ref would actually be someone's cousin, or like someone would start dating a ref or whatever, or there would be sports and refs would be on the teams and all—they'd be in our AP math or science courses because they were super smart, but for the most part people didn't cross lines. Of course, it wasn't really because we couldn't communicate with them. Like 90% of us spoke Spanish well and we'd talk to them sometimes, so it was more of a cultural thing—the way they dressed and the way they acted, some of them were obnoxious. They just didn't act like the rest of us. We all spoke English—or mostly English—to each other, and they always spoke Spanish to each other. Some of them really struggled with English, others just didn't really try, I think, and so we looked down on them. It wasn't because of their race or where they were from or anything like that—I mean, we were all Cuban or Nicaraguan or Colombian or whatever. They came from the same place we did. We're all Hispanic and we all speak Spanish. But they don't really speak English. Now, when they'd learn English after a couple of years or whatever—most of them—then they'd transition into being more like everybody else, like normal. They weren't always refs for life.

This individual seems to echo Urban Dictionary's definitions of 'ref' as a habitus: style and volume of speech, manner of dress, dispositions, practices of consumption, etc. (Bourdieu 1991). This distinction appears similar to the identity practices observed by Rosa (2019) among Mexican and Puerto Rican high schoolers in Chicago, i.e. the use of 'jíbaro/a/x' by Puerto Rican US mainlanders in reference to those whose language use and cultural practices were stereotypically associated with the island, regardless of gender or skin tone; and the use of 'brazer' among US-based Mexicans to refer to recently arrived Mexicans who appeared unsuccessful in their attempt at cultural assimilation, e.g. form of dress. Rosa noted that these students were " 'uncool' from the perspective of young people who asserted 'cool' US-based Mexican identities on the South Side of Chicago" (2019, 87). The above personal account also confirms my observation, supported by comments made to me by numerous other students and teachers over the years, that such social divisions are generally characteristic of public schools in Miami that are located in lower-income areas.

Another personal acquaintance recounted his own experience. Although born in Miami, he only spoke Spanish at home with his immigrant parents and was placed in ESOL when he began elementary school in a lower-income

140   *The postmodern paradox of Spanish in Miami*

neighborhood. He observed the class-based nature of the divide and attributed it to lower socioeconomic status:

> I grew up really poor in [Miami neighborhood] with only Spanish-speaking parents and was in ESOL in elementary. Whenever I had to go get my time restriction for testing, I remember hearing, "We just gotta wait for the reffy kids to finish first" when standardized testing would go on. I picked up English quickly and was able to get into gifted classes, and then it became, "Why are you dressed so reffy?", from my classmates. Later, we moved to the south and I went to [a magnet school] and kinda like switched into my English self, and it's a strict magnet school, so the ref archetype disappeared, and I was only around people who poked at the ref. It sucked. Because there's rich kids in private schools here that are Hispanic and they have only Spanish-speaking parents too, but they're totally saved all this face.

A crucial point made here is that in public schools serving middle- to upper-income neighborhoods of Miami, and in magnet schools or private schools, the 'ref' phenomenon appears not to occur, or at least not markedly so. Teachers at Bayview with whom I spoke told me that they had never observed such social division there, although there was an ESOL program at the school that served a fair number of students. At Bayview, according to teachers with whom I spoke, other recently arrived students had attended bilingual schools or American or British schools in their countries of origin, so they already had a good command of English for academic purposes. These observations lead me to conjecture that, because the sort of class-within-class divisions observed in low- to lower-middle-income schools like Northside do not manifest in more affluent school settings such as Bayview, students of the latter were probably more inclined to speak to and ultimately become friends with Spanish-dominant peers. Hence Bayview students perhaps indicated using Spanish with friends significantly more than their counterparts at Northside (Table 3.1). This hypothesis goes beyond the scope of the present study, and merits school-based ethnographic research in the future.

Fundamentally, where economic resources are more limited, the investment in cultural difference is greater; a more high-stakes cultural differentiation manifests based upon immigrant arrival flow. In a chapter titled "Just comes and cover-ups," Stepick et al. (2003) described a similar phenomenon among Haitian-background students in Miami's lower-income public high schools, where rigid social boundaries were drawn between US African Americans and Haitian immigrants. In the social hierarchy apparent in the schools that those authors studied, English monolingual African Americans were viewed (and viewed themselves) as being superior, compelling many Haitian-origin students to become 'cover-ups' who struggled to pass as African Americans (rather than Haitian Americans) and who greatly looked down upon the 'just comes,' i.e. those students who were more recently arrived from Haiti and

The postmodern paradox of Spanish in Miami 141

whose ways of dressing and speaking were noticeably Haitian. The authors explained that socioeconomic status was key to interpreting this phenomenon:

> Miami Haitians with enough resources to live in the middle-class African American or ethnically mixed suburbs encounter a more prosperous and optimistic America. They interact with more adolescent peers who believe that education promises a better future…. They live in an environment that more readily permits positive expressions of their Haitian culture. Middle-class Miami Haitians are more likely to retain pride in their national origins and become hyphenated Haitian-Americans.
>
> (Stepick et al. 2003, 122)

Although the racial, economic, and demographic situation of Hispanic high school students in Miami is rather different than that of Haitian-origin students, the role of social status in patterns of English language use appears to carry equal weight for both. As noted in the above comments regarding 'refs,' similar to the case of Haitian 'just comes,' the peer-group discrimination of recently arrived immigrant students does not generally appear to be based upon race or national origin, or even language use per se. It appears principally a matter of cultural assimilation through the lens of US Anglophone hegemony. As the necessary requisite for education and perceived upward socioeconomic mobility, English language ability is an obvious marker of this process and is thus symbolically implicated (Valenzuela 1999). In other words, although not all Spanish-speaking teens in Miami would be characterized as 'refs' (especially not those of middle or upper socioeconomic status), those who are cannot escape the condition of being perceived as 'refs' without having the ability to speak English. Nonetheless, one may continue to be perceived as a 'ref' based upon social behavior or manner of dress, even after acquiring the ability to speak English.

Such peer-group discrimination in school settings would still likely occur even without the social stigma of a stark political and ideological divide between Cuba and South Florida, which has endured for six decades. Good evidence of this comes from Rosa's (2019) study of Mexicans and Puerto Ricans in Chicago, in which he observed "fraught relations between bilingual adolescents who were born and/or raised in the US and their ethnoracial counterparts who had more recently arrived to the US and/or were viewed as possessing limited English language skills" (127). In a study of perceived within-group discrimination among foreign-born and US-born Latino youth in Los Angeles and Trenton, New Jersey ($N = 170$), Córdova and Cervantes (2010) also noted that "many foreign-born participants expressed experiences of discrimination by US-born Latinos because of their English proficiency, documentation, and generational status" (271). They urged that future research should consider "the ways in which, and the extent to which, discrimination occurs between Latino ethnic subgroups and… possible mechanisms or models to explain within-group distinctions between different Latino subpopulations

142 *The postmodern paradox of Spanish in Miami*

that contribute to behaviors and attitudes toward discrimination" (271). In the case of Miami, I believe that the ideological divide between island Cubans and US Cubans is one of the "possible mechanisms" of discriminatory attitudes toward recently arrived immigrants in secondary schools, as I will point out in the following section. This is a hypothesis that should be taken up in future ethnographic research. One must nevertheless bear in mind that 'refs' are not necessarily Cuban; individuals might be described as 'reffy' irrespective of their national origin or dialectal background.

One of the cultural phenomena associated principally with 'refs' twenty years ago was reggaeton. Prior to the 2000s, reggaeton was generally considered as vulgar or lower class by mainstream Miami Latinx youth. In the mid-2000s, however, this musical subgenre began to gain broader popularity with songs like "Gasolina" by Daddy Yankee and "Ven Báilalo" by Angel y Khriz. It boomed by the 2010s, bringing artists such as Bad Bunny to celebrity status. The rise of reggaeton and Latin trap in mainstream music—not only in the US but on a global stage—has meant that Latinx youth now listen to music in Spanish much more than they did at the start of the millennium; students at both Northside and Bayview listened to music in Spanish much more than they watched television or movies in Spanish (Table 3.1). As might be expected based upon everything we have seen thus far, Northside students placed greater emphasis on English in their attitudes toward music. In response to the affirmation that "Music is better in English than in Spanish," Northside students tended to agree ($M = 3.39$, $SD = 1.15$) while their counterparts at Bayview tended to disagree ($M = 2.84$, $SD = 1.27$), a difference that was highly significant ($t(251) = -3.55$, $p = .000$). While students at both schools mostly agreed that "Music in Spanish is better for dancing than music in English," students at Bayview appeared a bit more emphatic ($M = 4.00$, $SD = 1.07$) than those at Northside ($M = 3.74$, $SD = 1.19$), a trend that did not quite reach statistical significance ($t(251) = 1.75$, $p = .082$). Interestingly, students at Bayview not only listened to significantly more music in Spanish than those at Northside, but they also indicated watching significantly more television and films in Spanish (Table 3.1). Because I was unable to conduct interviews with any of the students surveyed, I do not know which particular musical genres, television shows, or sorts of movies they preferred in Spanish.

Although I cannot speculate as to why Bayview students would have consumed significantly more cultural products in Spanish than their Northside counterparts, I assume that the tendency is probably related to their stronger disposition to speak Spanish with friends and siblings (Table 3.1), and hence concomitantly to their social class status.

In sum, the significant differences between teenagers of lower-income and upper-income backgrounds observed in this questionnaire study likely reflect differential degrees of orientation toward the 'language as commodity' ideology that became so discursively prevalent during the 1990s, as we saw in Chapter 2. Bayview students appeared to have gotten the proverbial message about the value of bilingualism (i.e. not the value of Spanish or English per se) more

The postmodern paradox of Spanish in Miami   143

than their working-class counterparts at Northside. For the latter, Spanish was unequivocally valued, but English appeared more emphatically as the vehicle for upward socioeconomic mobility, a concern that was much more present for them than for their wealthy counterparts. Evidently, Northside students' firm stance regarding English extended beyond social divisions within the school setting, as they were less emphatic in their disagreement with pro-English-only propositions, as noted in the previous section. In the remainder of this chapter, I venture a theoretical explanation for the social class-based differences that we have observed thus far within the paradox of Spanish in Miami. To this end, I rely principally upon Blommaert's (2010) proposal regarding scalar orders of indexicality within a sociolinguistics of mobility.

Sociolinguistic mobility and the paradox of Spanish in Miami

One might wonder why a Miami-born, proudly self-identified Cuban teenager at Northside who speaks fluent Spanish would, on one hand, shun recently arrived immigrant peers for speaking Spanish yet, on the other, affirm the positive value of Spanish on a personal level and the necessity of Spanish for a good job in Miami. This sort of stance may appear duplicitous or contradictory if viewed through the lens of modernity, which conceptualizes migration as unidirectional and language choice as intimately bound up in the nation-state construct. In the tradition of modernity, language varieties are understood in a horizontal fashion, i.e. principally organized across bounded dimensions of geographic or geopolitical space (e.g. highlands vs. lowlands, north vs. south, Mexico vs. the US, etc.). In postmodernity, through the flows of globalization, a vertical scalar dimension emerges more prominently (though not to the exclusion of the horizontal): space as stratified and invested with power (Blommaert 2010, 34). I would interpret theoretically the situation of Spanish in Miami from that perspective, in terms of what Blommaert defines as scales within a sociolinguistics of mobility, i.e. levels or dimensions "at which particular forms of normativity, patterns of language use and expectations thereof are organized" (36).

The notion of 'scale' offers an analytic vertical image of the stratified nature of society, of lower- and higher-order indexical values of language in a spatiotemporal sense. For any given utterance or language form, not only are micro-level (i.e. momentary, local, or situationally immediate) indexical values invoked but also, simultaneously, more macro-level (i.e. timeless, translocal, or widespread) values enter into play. Lower-level scalar values are more highly contextual and dependent upon the individual, while higher-level values are more decontextualized and societally collective (Blommaert 2010, 34–35). Arguably, the fact that Spanish could be eschewed in one space or situation (e.g. with a peer at school) yet positively valued in another (e.g. with a customer in a commercial setting)—by the same individual within the same community—is reflective of complex vertical scalar orders of the language in Miami. Such an apparent contradiction does not occur in the case of

144 *The postmodern paradox of Spanish in Miami*

English, as it not only holds hegemonic status in the US but is also the global language par excellence. In this respect, I argue that the complex sociolinguistic situation of Spanish in Miami is characteristically more postmodern than that of English in Miami. This understanding of Spanish relies upon a sociolinguistics of mobility, meaning that moves across scales are inherent and inevitable, and the same linguistic resources may invoke different values according to those moves. In this section, I explain how this notion can elucidate the so-called paradox of Spanish in Miami.

Complex vertical scalar orders

In postmodernity, as linguistic space is increasingly crisscrossed by mass migratory, economic, and media flows, the process of language expropriation highlighted by Bakhtin more than a century ago becomes all the more complex, not in terms of actual substance but rather in terms of scale. Bakhtin argued: "Language is not a neutral medium that passes freely and easily into the private property of the speaker's intentions; it is populated— overpopulated—with the intentions of others. Expropriating it, forcing it to submit to one's own intentions and accents, is a difficult and complicated process" (2000 [1934], 278). In rebuttal to Saussure's structuralist proposal that all individuals of a speech community "will reproduce... the same signs united with the same concepts" in a mind-to-mind linkage (2000 [1934], 23), Bakhtin suggested that the meaning of any given utterance is understood always "against the background of other concrete utterances..., a background made up of contradictory opinions, points of view and value judgments" (2000 [1934], 273). Such phenomena of voicing, intertextuality, and polyglossia described by Bakhtin early in the twentieth century move more surely to the definitive forefront of sociolinguistics in the postmodern era, especially in the ethnoscapes, ideoscapes, and mediascapes created by the intensified flows of globalization (Appadurai 1996), and most obviously in global cities (Sassen 2007). In other words, what is 'new' in postmodernity is the scalar configuration of language varieties and sociolinguistic variants in the perceptual sense, not linguistic substance itself in the material sense (Blommaert 2005, 2010).

Caravedo (2014) makes a similar argument with her concept of 'mental spaces' in urban sociolinguistics. In relation to Andean migration in Peru, Caravedo (2014) posits that Lima—like other major urban centers of migration—must be thought of rather less in terms of geopolitical space and more in terms of perceptual space for purposes of sociolinguistic inquiry. Similar to the situation of local speech varieties characteristic of Mexico City, London, New York, Barcelona, or Madrid, the notion of 'el habla de Lima' has become highly complex over the past thirty years within the context of mass migratory and communication flows because "el desplazamiento espacial de los hablantes no solo traslada su variedad a un *locus* en que no existía, sino que además la transforma al insertarse en un nuevo escenario social" (Caravedo 2014, 260). In other words, geographic space as traditionally defined—and

The postmodern paradox of Spanish in Miami   145

as a category *de rigueur* in dialectology—should be rethought on perceptual grounds, since a majority of inhabitants are not 'natives' of the city nor are they 'from' the geopolitical space under scrutiny: "Al considerar los espacios en la migración hay que replantear la conexión tradicional entre variedad lingüística y espacio establecida como si fuera inmutable, privilegiando la movilidad como un factor esencial" (260). For Caravedo, habitation thus usurps birthplace as a key criterion for interpreting sociolinguistic variables, and inhabitants' ideas, beliefs, and perceptions play a fundamental part, perhaps similar to Brah's (1996) proposal regarding the construction of 'home' in *Cartographies of Diaspora*. It is important to point out that the notion of mental space, which brings together material, social, and perceptual or cognitive orders, is not exclusive of physical coordinates or geopolitical boundaries. Rather, the crux of Caravedo's argument is that the sociolinguistic spaces of postmodernity are perceived rather less in terms of generational continuity within a fixed geographic space and ever more in terms of mobility and symbolic value, "pues constituyen producto de una construcción mental en la que los hablantes del lugar y también los ajenos a él tienen una participación activa" (2014, 260).

Caravedo's concept seems highly sensible in the context of Miami, where the great majority of the city's inhabitants are *from* somewhere else, i.e. habitation usurps birthplace in the perception and ideological construction of language in Miami. However, different than Lima, where Spanish and Quechua are historically national languages, Miami reflects a dynamic transnational urban space where two 'big' global languages come into intimate contact: English as the global language par excellence as well as the *de facto* national language and the institutional language of local public life; Spanish as a language of globalization (Moreno Fernández 2016) as well as a valuable resource in a vital Hispanic national marketplace and the language spoken by a majority of the local population across all socioeconomic strata. Importantly, different than Quechua in the Peruvian context, Spanish in the US setting—especially in Miami—is in some ways viewed as an economic asset, as we saw in the previous chapter. This neoliberal economic orientation casts Spanish in a rather contradictory or even precarious light vis-à-vis US nationalism, as localism conspires with transnationalism.

In some ways, and in some areas such as South Florida, US nationalism as understood in modernity arguably acquires a new sense of 'statism'—and here is where Blommaert's (2005, 2010) argument about language scales becomes highly relevant to the situation of Spanish in Miami. One of the state's crucial functions is to organize transnational flows in relation to locality in the sociolinguistic landscape, serving as a sort of switchboard between various scales. The education system, mass media, and culture industries are key to this organizational process (Blommaert 2005, 219). Bearing in mind that postmodernity carries a discourse of demand and respect for diversity of all sorts, the postmodern state facilitates the construction of discourses of diversity, i.e. differences between the norms of 'others' and those that are legitimated

146 *The postmodern paradox of Spanish in Miami*

principally through the state-supported educational system. As Rosa (2019) affirmed in his ethnographic account of a Latinx majority high school in Chicago, "students' worlds were saturated with stereotypes about and signs of Mexican-Puerto Rican difference" (94). Ethnolinguistic identity is thus a vital aspect of indexical positioning in relation to the contemporary state, in that it marks "all kinds of contrasts with indexicalities operating both at higher and at lower levels of the polycentric system. It will also, and simultaneously, have to be seen as a discourse of power and (often) of coercion *by* the state or its apparatuses *about* the (ascribed) ethnolinguistic identity of its citizens" (Blommaert 2005, 220, italics in the original).

Heller (2013) reminds us that in contemporary global capitalism, the state is re-positioned from the national welfare state to a neoliberal one in which economic discourses prevail over political concerns (21). Postmodern statism thus functions rather differently than modern nationalism, in that transnational flows—particularly economic ones—disrupt some of the nation's traditional centering institutions or even nationalism itself (Blommaert 2005), in much the same way that tactical uses of social categories such as class, gender, or race in postmodern identity discourses disrupt the stability of those categories themselves: "Hyperreality dissolves stable categories of modes of representation" (Fiske 1996, 65). Within the context of centering institutions such as formal education and mass media, sociolinguistic complexity derives from this sort of contestation—in some ways, critical—of historical practices of modes of language representation. We might think of this process as the 'parodic practice' of modern one nation–one language ideology on a higher-level scalar order. Here I once again allude to Hutcheon's (2002) contemporary concept of parody and reiterate that her definition of the term should not be confused with its more common meaning as ludic or ridiculing imitation, derived from eighteenth-century wit. In the framework of postmodernity, Hutcheon defines parody in the sense of politically ironic acknowledgment of the history of representation, "both deconstructively critical and constructively creative, paradoxically making us aware of both the limits and the powers of representation—in any medium" (2002, 94).

This contestation or disruption occurs on local, translocal, and global scales in a vertical sense, i.e. within the same geopolitical space. The process engenders critical self-reflexivity, which I have previously characterized as "placing in sharper relief" the ideological contours of minoritized languages vis-à-vis Spanish and English throughout the Spanish-speaking world (Lynch 2018b). The growing global presence of English ideologically recasts or reconfigures minoritized languages in the sociolinguistic landscape of Latin America and Spain. So-called 'Americanization' appears to have a similar effect vis-à-vis 'Japanization' in Korea, 'Indianization' in Sri Lanka, or 'Russianization' in the Baltic States, among other examples (Appadurai 1996, 32). The incursion of English has provided an ideological arena for resistance and the reworking of identities, as bilingual/bicultural repertoires are (re)politicized and relocated in some ways beyond the 'local' spaces previously

The postmodern paradox of Spanish in Miami   147

drawn by modernity. Mediatization plays a vital role in the ensuing complexity (Agha 2011). In other words, the institutional, mediatic, and commercial legitimization of a language other than Spanish, i.e. English, engenders reflexivity with regard to local languages, which historically have been subordinate to Spanish (Lynch 2018b).

For example, an incipient bilingual (Spanish and English) education policy at the behest of governments throughout Latin America has created greater consciousness of policy and educational practice regarding indigenous languages. In Mexico, proposals to implement English language education are sometimes framed in terms of the competing value of local autochthonous languages. In the Peruvian Andes, the growing prominence of English in education and in the region's vital tourism industry has led to a revalorization of Quechua and Aymara through cultural production and the affirmation of ethnolinguistic pride (Zavala 2019). In Chile, one of Latin America's more potent economies, the English-language imperative is explicitly bound up in political discourse regarding progress, i.e. ability in English is synonymous with economic development and social advancement (British Council Chile 2014), a discourse that has indirectly emboldened the urban Mapuche identity movement in Santiago (Merino et al. 2020; Sadowsky and Aninao 2020). The perceived necessity of English for economic success has motivated bi- and trilingual models of public education in Spain over the past decade as well. The legislation of a trilingual model in the Balearic Islands (with Spanish, English, and Catalan in equal thirds) motivated the largest street protest in the history of the Balearic Islands in 2013 (*ABC* 2013), when some 90,000 people took to the streets of Palma de Mallorca to voice their concern that the curricular space afforded to English may be a renewed Spanish nationalist affront—and political setback—to the due space of Catalan in the educational system. In his response, then President José Ramón Bauzà (Partido Popular) advocated for the differentiation of Catalan—with Barcelona as its normative center—from the more 'authentic' varieties spoken in Mallorca, Menorca, Ibiza, and Formentera (cf. Heller 2013), thus disavowing mainstream Catalan language education by appealing to local language pride and all the while emphasizing the role of English in the islands' vital tourism and service industries (Aguiló Mora and Lynch 2017).

Clearly, the re-positioning of the state and the ideology of consumerism give impetus to such discourses. Within the framework of economic neoliberalism and the global economy, commercial interests assume a centering institutional power of their own, arresting the determining influence of one nation–one language ideology. For example, Pujolar (2007) cited Spanish Telefónica's decision in 1998 to provide customer services in Catalan following a local government call for bids. Prior to the liberalization of telecommunications in 1997, Madrid-based Telefónica provided services exclusively in Spanish. When the company was privatized and state language policy no longer applied, they were pressured to reconsider their monolingual policy. They initially refused to offer service in Catalan, but ultimately agreed under pressure from Catalan

148　*The postmodern paradox of Spanish in Miami*

authorities who advocated for Catalan, at least in part, from an economic marketplace perspective. Telecommunications giant Movistar would subsequently offer services in Quechua and Aymara in Peru as well, following the same marketplace ideology. In this regard, "the medium is the message," as Marshall McLuhan famously affirmed in 1964. Language—as choice or commodity—is attributed an economic value in the postmodern neoliberal marketplace of global corporations that it previously did not have within the ideological framework of the modern nation-state (Heller and Duchêne 2012; Heller 2013). This does not mean that languages lose their symbolic national value in the process, but rather that national value appears as secondary to perceived market value in some contexts or circumstances. Pujolar affirmed that "this situation effectively erodes the capacity of nation-states to control public linguistic practices, define their conditions of social legitimacy and, as a result, to maintain the procedures for the enactment and reproduction of the national speech community" (2007, 75). As I suggested in Chapter 1, the growing legitimacy of Spanish in the US in recent decades can be attributed in part to this neoliberal economic tendency.

In essence, the heightened complexity of the social meaning of language varieties in the global era—and in global urban centers in particular—stems not just from amplified mass migratory and media flows, which bring a multiplicity of voices and images into contact. Other phenomena such as postmodern statist centering institutions, an increasingly nuanced relationship between global and local language varieties, and the marketplace legitimacy of Spanish as a language of public life in the US create a complex vertical scalar sociolinguistic order of things in Miami. In the first part of this chapter, we saw that teenagers in an elite private school located in a highly affluent neighborhood of Miami appeared significantly more emphatic than their working-class counterparts when indicating disagreement with suggestions to restrict the use of Spanish on schoolgrounds and in public spaces such as stores and restaurants. Wealthy teenagers also showed significantly more opposition to the idea that "Miami would be a better place if everyone spoke only English", and they disagreed with the affirmation that "English is the true language of success in Miami," while their working-class counterparts appeared mostly indifferent, a highly significant differential pattern ($p = .000$), as noted above. Working-class high schoolers also disagreed somewhat less than wealthy ones with the suggestion to make English the sole official language of the US. Yet at the same time, both groups agreed equally that "Spanish is necessary to be truly successful in Miami," and the working-class students even showed slightly more agreement with the affirmation that "Spanish is necessary for a good job in Miami."

I argue that this ostensible paradox of Spanish in Miami is actually a critical, self-reflexive contestation of the historical mode of representation of the language vis-à-vis English, bearing in mind that all forms of representation are inherently political (Hutcheon 2002). In a complex vertical scalar order, Spanish is, on one hand, a symbol of immigrant status and all its concomitant attributes at the local level, and, on the other hand, a desirable marketplace asset at the global level. It is both things at once at the national level. Here we recall Appadurai's (1996) argument that globalization processes unfold principally on local levels, as well as Sassen's (2007) affirmation that "the global—whether an institution, a process, a discursive practice, or an imaginary—simultaneously transcends the exclusive framing of national states, yet partly inhabits, and gets constituted inside, the national" (1). Sassen emphasized that, in good part, what distinguishes the present era from previous 'global' eras is the existence of the nation-state; globalization does not undo or occur outside of the national, but rather leads to a rescaling of the national (2007, 6). Similarly, Heller (2013) affirmed that "our contemporary era is characterized more by continuity than by rupture, albeit in ways which destabilize our taken-for-granted assumptions about language, identity, culture, nation, and state" (21). Hutcheon's (2002) characterization of the postmodern as "resolutely contradictory and unavoidably political" seems applicable in this respect (1).

I would venture that in what is now the incipient stages of cultural postmodernity, framed by the global economy and the imperative of consumerism, the so-called paradox of Spanish in Miami—especially pronounced among the working-class teenagers of the study discussed here—may well not appear so paradoxical by next century. Tölölyan (2012) affirmed: "The paradoxical combination of localism and transnationalism, the fierce aspiration to achieve economic and social success and... the oscillation between loyalty and skeptical detachment that characterizes the performance of diasporic lives is... an example of the way everyone, including nationals, will have to live in an increasingly heterogeneous and plural world. It is a world in which diasporas have been living for a while" (13). This affirmation serves as a reminder that what is novel in a sociolinguistics of mobility is not linguistic substance but rather the perception and scale of sociolinguistic phenomena (Blommaert 2010), and that the re-positionings, rescalings, or parodic practices of today may well be next century's conventional *doxa* (Bourdieu 1991).

In other words, in this parodic practice (in Hutcheon's [2002] sense of the term), Spanish critically garners authority and legitimacy through the subversion of English within the neoliberal economic discourse of globalization, i.e. language as commodity. In this respect, I would extend Hutcheon's argument that "parody can be used as a self-reflexive technique that points to art as art, but also to art as inescapably bound to its aesthetic and even social past" (2002, 97) to the postmodern ideological terrain of language in the case that concerns us: the discursive representation of Spanish as commodity or asset engenders a critical self-reflexivity that not only objectifies and synchronically points to language as language, but also exposes the aesthetic and social contours of Spanish vis-à-vis English in a temporal sense. Here we recall, by way of example, Laguna's (2017) argument regarding the aesthetic and social value of 'choteo' for early exile Cubans (described in the previous chapter) and the evolution of a 'postnostalgic' manifestation of *cubanía* in Miami

150 *The postmodern paradox of Spanish in Miami*

following the collapse of the Communist Bloc. One might also recall (from Chapter 2) the representations of language in popular sitcoms such as *¿Qué Pasa, USA?* and *The Golden Girls*, which portrayed the use of Spanish as reifying and at the same time undermining Anglophone power, "to reconnect the representational strategies of the present with those of the past, in order to critique both" (Hutcheon 2002, 101).

In any case, as Hutcheon (2002) reminded us, there is always the problem of a lack of access or a "very real threat of elitism" in postmodernity (101); Blommaert (2010) was also concerned with inequality in terms of language resources; and Heller (2013) affirmed that "new minority elites mobilize the bilingualism that was once the hallmark of oppression in attempts to reposition the value of their cultural capital, in economic conditions which newly value it" (21). Assuredly, the higher-level indexical value of Spanish in Miami is nuanced: it has different ideological interpretations and real repercussions depending upon one's socioeconomic status. In light of Heller's (2013, 21) observation, it is unsurprising that Bayview students would appear emphatically more oriented toward an ideology of the value of bilingualism.

In her classic Marxist account of the dynamic border situation of Spanish among Chicanos in the US Southwest, Sánchez (1994 [1983]) observed in the early 1980s the apparent paradox of English language dominance in relation to upward socioeconomic mobility and group solidarity. She wrote:

> Second- and third-generation Chicanos... develop varying attitudes towards language shift. These Chicanos, who are fluent English speakers, have remained locked in the lower-wage levels of the occupation scale.... The myth of English acquisition as the vehicle for upward mobility begins to fade. At this point, the imposed residential and economic segregation can trigger a negation of the negative context, resulting in a positive social value as an ingredient for solidarity. This mechanism of defense serves to unite the community, at a rhetorical level.... At this level, then, use of the minority language [Spanish] is seen as a sign of loyalty to the group.... Language loyalty is widespread among those who reside in low-income areas with a high concentration of Chicanos, although it is also here where persons interested in social mobility and assimilation prefer shifting to English.
>
> (58)

Certainly, the ideological situation and socioeconomic context of Spanish in Miami in the new millennium is, in some ways, vastly different than in the Southwest during the 1970s and early 1980s, the time of Sánchez's observations. In present-day South Florida, Spanish language use is not relegated to low-income areas, nor is it particularly a symbolic resource for the construction of in-group solidarity or family values (as noted above in the questionnaire results). However, in terms of English, the situation is quite similar: English in Miami is unequivocally viewed as the vehicle of upward

The postmodern paradox of Spanish in Miami 151

socioeconomic mobility, emphatically so among the working classes. This ideological 'fact' must be reconciled with the asset value of Spanish within postmodern discourse of economic globalization and marketplace ideology.

The present-day sociolinguistic paradox of Spanish in Miami reflects the consonance of lower- and higher-level scalar orders that give local and transnational impetus to Spanish not only in a postmodern diaspora sense of belonging but also a neoliberal economic sense of value. At the same time, and within the same scalar orders, however, with regard to the hegemony of English, there is no sort of "dialectic resolution or recuperative evasion of contradiction" (Hutcheon 2002, 102). Since the time of Sánchez's writing, the so-called Hispanic or Latino market emerged very prominently in the US financescape and ideoscape, and perhaps foremost in Miami, as pointed out in Chapter 1. Based upon the views of high school students revealed in the present survey study, Miami Latinx bilinguals of middle and upper socioeconomic status appear to reposition the values of Spanish and English within the neoliberal discourse of language as commodity more so than those of lower socioeconomic status (Heller 2013). In a survey of South Florida adolescents conducted in the 1990s, Portes and Schauffler (1994) already noted this tendency among middle- and upper-class respondents who attended private schools: "Retention of the parental language... reflects the presence of a large and diversified ethnic enclave where Spanish is the language of daily intercourse for all kinds of transactions. Respondents in private bilingual schools are mostly the children of middle-class Cuban exiles who represent the core of this ethnic economy. It is not surprising that they have the lowest propensity to give up Spanish" (651). Among this sector of the population, which now includes wealthy migrants from all over Latin America (as observed in the questionnaire data from Bayview), Spanish appears in a rather less paradoxical situation vis-à-vis English; for them, the postmodern ideology of bilingualism is rather more normalized than for their working-class counterparts who attend public schools in lower-income areas such as Hialeah. There, in the lower socioeconomic strata, English holds important symbolic value in a hierarchical social order that is based principally upon length of time in the US. In Chapter 5 we will see this trend manifest again in the perceived use and acceptability of Anglicisms among Spanish speakers of all national-origin groups in Miami.

In sum, Miami offers us an intimate glimpse into the complex vertical scalar orders of language contact situations in postmodernity, and into the rescalings or reconfigurations that characterize Spanish vis-à-vis English in the global era (Lynch 2018b, 2019). Within the mental space of this emergent global city, superdiverse Spanish-speaking migratory flows crisscross hegemonic English language use across all socioeconomic strata, but as we have seen in this chapter, the perception of Spanish 'on the ground' is conditioned in important ways by the ideological discursive construction of Spanish 'in the marketplace' on a higher-level vertical scalar order, i.e. its relative value in the local, national, and global economies. This crisscrossing

152 *The postmodern paradox of Spanish in Miami*

constitutes what might be characterized as a parodic practice (Hutcheon 2002) or a paradoxical combination of localism and transnationalism vis-à-vis nationalism (Tölölyan 2012). One must bear in mind that neoliberal economic marketplace ideology extends well beyond mere commercial or financial concerns, as explained in Chapter 1. It is undergirded and sustained by the pervasive logic of neoliberal economic practice in all aspects of contemporary life (Brown 2015), by centering institutions such as education and mass media (Blommaert 2010), and by the consumerist orientation of cultural (re)production in postmodernity (Baudrillard 1994). This more abstract marketplace realm, in which language is conceptualized as commodity (Heller 2007, 2013), constitutes a higher-level location, so to speak, for Spanish in the vertical scalar order of things in Miami. In this way, on one level, Spanish may be stigmatized, yet on another, it may index prestige—by the same individual, in the same place. As we have seen so far in the first section of this chapter, the power of Spanish in the vertical scalar order is somewhat relative to socioeconomic status. Obviously, Spanish use is perceived as perpetuating inequality for some more than for others, and particular varieties of Spanish are also perceived as less equal than others, as I noted in Chapter 1. In what remains of this chapter, I describe the crisscross of Spanish-speaking migratory flows and English-language hegemony in relation to 'scale jumping.'

Jumping scales: Vertical movement across linguistic space

Thus far, we have seen how the complex sociolinguistic vertical scalar orders of globalized societies such as Miami reflect inequality, differential access, and a growing divide between the 'haves' and 'have-nots.' One particular sociolinguistic manifestation of inequalities is 'scale jumping': discursive movement between the level of the local or national, individual, and immediately situated to the translocal or transnational, collective, and decontextualized (Blommaert 2010, 35). Such movement is always semiotically ordered—i.e. not chaotic—and invokes practices of normative validity. In this respect, 'upjumping' (from a lower indexical level to a higher one in the vertical sense) is a power move, because it relies upon a collective, normative order that is not necessarily accessible to all. Not all instances of 'upjumping' are societally hierarchical, however; higher scales may dominate in some situations, while lower scales prevail in others (Blommaert 2003). In the case of human migratory movement, much is at stake for identities in the process of contestation and reconciliation of indexical orders, precisely because one individual or social group makes a metaphorical incursion into the space of another. This is especially the case in a global city such as Miami, where the majority population is migrant. In the face of mass migratory flows and diminishing national control over 'hard' domains such as the economy and international relations, language and culture remain crucial arenas for the construction of identity (Blommaert 2005; Heller 2007).

The postmodern paradox of Spanish in Miami   153

For those of working-class backgrounds, higher-level scalar orders link English with notions of progress or 'getting ahead' economically, as echoed in the following quote from a young Cuban American woman whom I interviewed in Hialeah:

> El inglés es muy importante aquí, pero el español es como—aquí es como una cosa de cultura, you know, como un pride de tu país, de donde tú viniste, y entonces para ellos como siempre han sabido, oh, el inglés, en los United States lo que se habla es inglés. Pa' adelantar, el inglés. Entonces ellos a veces creen, que yo creo que es naïve de la parte de ellos, pero ellos creen que al saber el español están atrasando a los hijos, pero yo creo que aquí saber los dos idiomas es un beneficio grandísimo. Cualquiera que sepa los dos idiomas tiene más adelanto que una persona que no más que sepa uno.

This young woman's remark concerning the different view that she takes in comparison to her parents is noteworthy: being bilingual is a great benefit and bilinguals have the possibility to 'advance' more than someone who only knows one language. Although she was born and raised in Hialeah to working-class immigrant parents, she had just begun her university studies at a selective private institution and was undeniably privy to the neoliberal economic discourse of the value of Spanish. Her own perspective, different than that of her Cuban parents, is articulated in terms of bilingualism as asset. She thus appears discursively more similar to Bayview students than to working-class teens from Hialeah, despite being from and having been schooled in Hialeah. In this way, one could say that she 'upjumps' in the vertical scalar order of indexicality regarding Spanish in Miami.

By 'upjumping' here, I do not mean 'up' in terms of social class but rather in terms of contextualization or immediacy, i.e. she locates the indexical value of Spanish on the more abstract or macro-level of the neoliberal discourse of commodification and consumerism, while her parents relegate that higher-level value almost exclusively to English. In counterpoint to her parents' characterization of Spanish as 'atraso,' she articulates bilingualism as 'adelanto.' In this instance, one must bear in mind Blommaert's (2003) observation that scales are not necessarily arranged in a fixed hierarchical order but are invoked dynamically in situational practice. Blommaert, Westinen and Leppänen (2015) emphasized that "while scale does matter to the participants, their scaling practices, and their views on what would even count as high/low or center/periphery are quite dynamic" (121).

As I have previously pointed out, Spanish in Miami is not associated with any particular socioeconomic class; it is widely spoken and positively valued across all sectors of the city. However, the generalized use of Spanish across the local majority population—as would be the case in any other Spanish-speaking city of Latin America—occurs within the national, institutional hegemony of English—unlike anywhere else in Latin America.

154 *The postmodern paradox of Spanish in Miami*

This configuration is contradictory in that, on one hand, Spanish is vital to the local economy and constitutes the everyday language of the majority across all socioeconomic strata, yet, on the other hand, English is preferred by US-born bilinguals and is in a superior position ideologically, given its uncontested prestige as *de facto* national and global language par excellence. Various studies, previously cited, have demonstrated that English indisputably has the proverbial upper hand, in a cross-generational sense and in institutional domains. This is not to say that Spanish lacks prestige, however. In truth, Spanish language use is associated with political power and with some of the most ostentatious, opulent lifestyles found in Miami; it is the language of substantial wealth.

Seemingly duplicitous yet parallel discursive imaginaries thus emerge: Spanish as the language of the economically disadvantaged immigrant who must learn English to 'get ahead'; and Spanish as the language of wealth, of local, national, and international politics, and of Miami's highly lucrative retail sector and cultural industries. This duplicity is reflected in a comment made by a young middle-class Colombian-born woman who moved to Miami with her parents at age 5. In an interview with Lanier (2014), she recalled her experience attending high school in a socioeconomically mixed area of Miami:

> A lot of my friends spoke in Spanish. Most people spoke Spanish to be honest. Generally, I enjoyed it, but sometimes there was like the pompous, arrogant version of the Hispanic group that I wasn't too fond of, though overall, I like Spanish-speaking people.... You'd have like the different groups: the think-alikes, you'd have like the modelesque type—yeah, like the more money, affluent—and then you'd also have your—like your chonga group, I guess.

It bears repeating that, for the economically privileged Spanish-speaking sectors of the city, bilingualism in English appears as the ideological goal, as it appears to be for most of Latin America's urban wealthy. For the economically underprivileged in Miami, on the other hand, the desirability of Spanish is often overshadowed by the exigency of English. Nonetheless, the importance of the historical legacy of Spanish-speaking (Cuban) Miami as an economic powerhouse cannot be underestimated. As previously affirmed, Miami's emergence as a global city is linked to the economic and political clout of early exile Cubans, who were unabashed in their use of Spanish (Cros Sandoval 2008) and, as Resnick (1988) pointed out, established a public legitimacy for Spanish in South Florida that remains still today.

Scale jumping with regard to Spanish is thus a complicated—not to say confusing—affair or parodic practice, in that Spanish use on the ground may happen in consonance with a higher-level order that casts it as a language of prestige, wealth, and the global economy; or it may happen in apparent divergence from a higher-level order that casts English as the language of

The postmodern paradox of Spanish in Miami   155

the US, as the vehicle of upward socioeconomic mobility, and as the global language par excellence. In working-class sectors of Miami, as in the case of Northside students in Hialeah, Spanish monolingualism tends to index economically disadvantaged recent-arrival immigrant status, as in the archetype of the 'ref' in youth culture. Within this ideological frame, English has strong symbolic value as social differentiator. In those sectors, English use is tied to acculturation through a process of consumption, in the same way described by Sánchez for Mexican immigrants in the US Southwest in the early 1980s:

> The Mexican immigrant is... not automatically coming from a counter or purely antagonistic culture but in most instances from a culture already controlled and influenced by United States multinational corporations, a culture already permeated by the dominant ideology of the United States. The degree of acculturation of the immigrant is largely determined by his degree of consumption of this ideology through his acquisitional power of cultural goods. The more middle class, the greater the acculturation. The lower the income, the less the acculturation. This phenomenon is repeated in the United States among first-generation immigrants. Consumption of the dominant ideology is thus synonymous with acculturation, a process promoted through the consumption of goods and services according to one's class status.
>
> (1994, 22)

Despite the temporal, economic, and geopolitical expanse between the context of Sánchez's remarks and the situation that concerns us, the growing influence of consumerism on ideological orientations toward Spanish and English in the US is indisputable.

As noted in Chapter 1, consumerism is an essential feature of postmodernity. Consumption replaces production in postindustrial societies (and here I remind the reader of Miami's always already postindustrial character), allowing desire for consumer goods to assume a more operative role in social class distinctions (MacCannell and Flower MacCannell 1993, 127). Baudrillard argued that consumption "is a complete system of values, with all that the term implies concerning group integration and social control.... In other words, this is a new and specific mode of *socialization* related to the rise of new productive forces and the monopolistic restructuring of a high output economic system" (1988, 49, italics in the original). This transformation is of vital consequence to the situation of Spanish in the US, especially in Miami. It is, in my view, the means or mechanism by which the modern value of Spanish as community or ethnic identity marker, in the sense of 'authenticity' (Woolard 2008), gradually begins to parallel the value of a more 'anonymous' Spanish-speaking voice within the culture of consumerism in US postmodernity and economic globalization. I return briefly to this phenomenon in Chapters 5 and 6.

156 *The postmodern paradox of Spanish in Miami*

Solidarity remains key in this language ideological process, but in a rather different sense than in modernity. Baudrillard (1988) argued that in postmodern consumerist society, the community or affective solidarities characteristic of modernity are displaced by 'mega-solidarities' that emerge from the desire of consumption. MacCannell and Flower MacCannell (1993) explained:

> Baudrillard can lead us to an examination of the foundation of the solidarity of large-scale, highly complex societies, the kinds of societies that are not geographically transfixed and which cannot command primary loyalty from all, or even any, of their members. Obviously, the solidarity of such entities must be able to draw upon detachment, disaffection, and atomization as primary resources. Nothing is better suited to this end than a collective drive to satisfy desire. This cannot be desire for another human being, which would only reproduce older forms of solidarity, or even for *objects* such as consumer goods, but the desire for desire itself. The desire for desire can never be satisfied because it is founded on lack in the first place and must always return to lack at the moment of its seeming fulfillment. Thus the foundation is laid for mega-solidarities not precisely in *consumption* but in a kind of behaviour modeled on consumption that might, in fact, properly be called *consumerism* once its requisite *impossibility* is understood.
>
> (127, italics in the original)

In this respect, Baudrillard thus calls our attention to the transformative role of consumerism in the ways in which solidarity is reimagined in postmodernity. Within the global market spaces, migratory flows, and complex communication networks that emerge at the end of the twentieth century, languages begin to be disentangled from personhood (Da Silva, McLaughlin, and Richards 2007). Personally, I do not find compelling evidence for this with regard to societal majority languages, which indisputably remain the symbol of national identity and belonging, e.g. English in the US or Spanish in Mexico. But if we look to the present-day situation of minority or minoritized languages, the workings of postmodernity are laid bare. Such appears to be the case of Spanish in Miami.

The sort of local ethnic group solidarity associated with 'authentic' Spanish language use throughout the US during most of the nineteenth and twentieth centuries, as observed by Sánchez (1994 [1983]), is theoretically transformed into a more 'anonymous' mega-solidarity (i.e. the so-called Hispanic or Latino market) within the logic of consumerism (Baudrillard 1988). Within this logic, Spanish is objectified as a commodity that, by virtue of its intangibility as a consumer good, is cast as a desirable asset, as I suggested in Chapter 1. In other words, Spanish has evolved into an object of desire in the US setting on a higher-level scalar order. Miami probably reflects the earliest site of this evolution and is the prime example of this crucial ideological transformation

The postmodern paradox of Spanish in Miami   157

of the sociolinguistic situation of the US. I think the evolution of a market-based sense of mega-solidarity rooted in the ideology of consumerism is perhaps what led Bayview students to be significantly more likely than Northside students to characterize Hispanic teenagers in Miami who refuse to speak Spanish as 'sell-outs,' as previously noted.

But we are still left with the questions "Where am I?" and "Where are you from?" As people move about, they are led to reevaluate orders of social indexicality according to linguistic spaces or settings other than those to which they are accustomed. In these circumstances, they may be engaged in jumping scales in ways that are perceptually less deliberate or ideologically more nuanced than the power moves defined by Blommaert (2010). By way of example, one could think of a second-generation speaker of Cuban Spanish in Hialeah who enters into online gameplay with an upper-social-class Argentine Spanish speaker in Recoleta, Buenos Aires—a not so uncommon scenario. Their private off-line chat enters into topics of local popular culture in both cities and, inevitably, metalinguistic commentary about local, national, and transnational variants of Spanish and English. In such an interaction, both would be actively involved in jumping scales in a language ideological sense, as vertical scalar orders relative to Hialeah enter into contestation and reconciliation with those relative to Recoleta. Polycentricity and intertextuality are crucial to understanding each other. In this hypothetical case, both interlocutors remain in their 'own' physical, geopolitical spaces, meaning that neither has 'entered' the sociolinguistic space of the other.

In Miami, the matter of where one is *from* is highly important for identity practices. A young Miami-born Colombian American interviewed by Lanier (2014) observed: "When you talk to people here in Miami, and they ask you, 'Where are you from?', they don't mean like what part of the city you're from. They mean what Latin country are you from. And it's really funny, because you just automatically know what they're referring to, so you'll be like, 'Oh, I'm Colombian.'" Rosa (2019) observed a similar tendency among Mexican- and Puerto Rican-origin teens in Chicago. Lanier's (2014) interviewee went one step further, explaining that when she is in a majority Colombian setting in Miami, her answer must be more specific: "If you're in like a Colombian club or a Colombian scene and somebody asks you where you're from, then, you know, they're asking you what city in Colombia you're from." At the same time, she observed that when Colombian-born friends in Miami learned that she was born in Miami, they sometimes told her she was American, not Colombian: "And it was kind of like half joking, but at the same time, there is the mentality that you weren't born there, so you're American. You're not full Colombian. So I'm like, okay, sometimes I don't know what to say. Somebody will ask me where I'm from, and I'm like, 'Miami,' and then they'll be like, 'But what country are you from?'" (73; cf. Scott Shenk 2007). Over the years, I have found myself in similarly awkward social encounters in Miami when my response to the question "Where are you from?" has been simply, "The United States." Although this happens in English-speaking encounters, it

158   *The postmodern paradox of Spanish in Miami*

seems all the more awkward when the conversation is in Spanish, and I am then sometimes pressed a bit further: "But where are your parents from?" Clearly, in Miami the reference point of a normatively valid response to the question regarding one's origin is another country.

In part, I would attribute this tendency to the fact that Miami is a majority (im)migrant city, i.e. demographic reality is that most people have either been born in another country or are the children of (im)migrants. In Miami, the fact that people regularly ask "Where are you from?" seemingly remains a holdout of modernity within Caravedo's (2014) proposal that habitation usurps birthplace in the sociolinguistic construction of postmodern mental space. There is another important facet of this tendency, however, which might be explained in terms of scale jumping. Typically, in modernity's higher-level scalar orders, birthplace indexes national identity, e.g. Colombian. As the intense migratory and media flows of globalization make birthplace rather less relevant to the shape of sociolinguistic repertoires, as Caravedo (2014) cogently argued, the higher-level scalar order is necessarily and more actively contested, in the sense of semiotic practice. This dynamic process of contestation of place thus becomes a key variable for identity construction in global cities such as Miami. Proof of this phenomenon is found in the further questions that usually follow the 'one nation' response to the query regarding one's origin: "Where in Colombia?" Almost always, such further questions when speaking Spanish in Miami suggest that a national-origin response is not the end goal, but rather a more localized response along the lines of sociolinguistic repertoire, as our young interviewee explained: "When I speak Spanish here [Miami], people can tell I'm *paisa*. They'll be like, 'Oh, you're from Medellín.' But then when I go to Colombia and speak Spanish they're like, 'You're not from here.' ... I would say the way I speak Spanish is a little bit more—umm, I guess neutral? Because I don't speak with such a heavy accent in Spanish. But it's still—it has the traits of the *paisa* accent, from Medellín.... I'm not from anywhere. I'm from Miami. It's normal."

For Cubans in Miami, distinctions are sometimes drawn not only in geographic space but also temporal space. Another of Lanier's (2014) interviewees, who attended a high school in Hialeah at the same time the Bayview-Northside survey was conducted (2010–2011), reiterated that worldview and habitus are principal factors in the perception of social differences among Cubans, which he attributed to the effects of Castro's regime. He said:

> You have the Cuban refs that are right off the boat, that are super like Fidel Castro type Cubans. 'Cause there are two types of Cubans: there's the Cuban that was before Fidel and people that are from Fidel Castro's time that grew up with Fidel.... I'm Cuban and I will tell you straight up. They come to America and they think they're el papi chulo. They think that—they speak Spanish really fast, sometimes you can't understand them. And it's like, yo, shut up, I can't understand what you're saying. I'm Cuban and I can't understand you.... And they have these really

weird cocky attitudes, which is really bad. And then they have different mannerisms. I mean, not all of them, of course.

Such negative perceptions regarding some recently arrived Cuban immigrants—"not all of them, of course"—by more long-standing Cubans in Miami, as expressed by this individual, are not limited to teenagers or school settings. The social stigmatization and stereotyping of successive waves of Cuban immigrants, which lead to perceived divisions across Miami's diverse Cuban communities, have been observed in various academic inquiries (e.g. De la Torre 2003; Alberts 2005; Lynch 2009b; Alfaraz 2014, 2018; Portes and Puhrmann 2015; Laguna 2017; among others).

In his cultural commentary, Argentine journalist Iglesias Illa (2010) described the broad social distinctions among Miami Cubans as follows:

> En Miami circulan cientos de historias sobre el supuesto maltrato de los exiliados históricos hacia los marielitos de los 80 y los balseros de los 90. Una primera conversación típica entre dos cubanos que no se conocen incluye a menudo las siguientes preguntas y respuestas: '¿Usted es cubano?' 'Sí, señor.' '¿De dónde?' 'De La Habana.' ... 'Ajá. ¿Y cuándo llegó?' Esta es la pregunta bisagra, cuya respuesta ubicará al interrogado en una férrea escala social de la que se predicarán todo tipo de deducciones: '1961' es una respuesta prestigiosa; '1974', un poco menos prestigiosa; '1980', dramática; '1994', balsera; '2005', inmigrante.
>
> (203–4, ellipsis in the original)

Although I cannot say with certainty that the societal tendency among Miami Cubans to stigmatize later or more recent arrivals from the island is the basis of the sometimes discriminatory 'ref' phenomenon observed in lower-income school settings, I hypothesize that it does play a part. As Alfaraz (2018) affirmed, "Viewing the diaspora and the homeland [Cuba] through the lens of socio-political and language ideologies, the diaspora is able to assert its authenticity and legitimacy, its Cubanness, even though it is not in Cuba. The homeland variety is perceived as a highly stigmatized, corrupt version of the diaspora variety, which is accorded a high degree of prestige" (67). The comment that "I'm Cuban and I can't understand you" from the interviewee in Lanier's (2014) study, cited above, echoes this perceptual tendency. Sociolinguistic differences among chronologically distinct groups of Cubans will be the focus of the next chapter.

In closing, I would point out that the identity boundaries drawn in such discursive distinctions sometimes appear less rigid in the practices of everyday life in Miami, just as Rosa (2019) noted in Chicago. In his study, a young Puerto Rican woman affirmed that "Puerto Ricans stay with Puerto Ricans, Mexicans stay with Mexicans…," but Rosa observed that she had dated Mexicans and had several Mexican cousins: "There was a marked disconnect between her way of talking about difference and her actual lived experience of

160 *The postmodern paradox of Spanish in Miami*

intimate relationships across lines of Puerto Rican–Mexican difference" (94). He remarked upon this same sort of "disconnect" between the discourses and actual experiences of the high schoolers whom he studied in Chicago, noting their long-standing shared personal histories and sustained intimate interactions (95). I recall the words of a personal acquaintance, previously cited above: "They weren't refs for life," meaning that after a time in school, mutual understandings were forged and perceptual differences generally disappeared as recently arrived students acquired English. I would also note that the meaning of the term 'ref' is quite broad and highly contextual, and the division that young people in Miami make discursively between refs and nonrefs is not always as rigid in social practice as it would appear in ideological principle. In Chicago, Rosa (2019) concluded: "Discursive differences in Puerto Ricans' and Mexicans' articulations of their respective political and economic positionalities must always be considered in relation to linked subjectivities and forms of frictive intimacy that emerge from shared experiences of exclusion. These experiences place Chicago Mexicans and Puerto Ricans alongside one another in marginalized residential, employment, and educational spaces" (100).

What makes Miami particularly compelling in this regard is that the demographic majority identifies as Hispanic or Latina/o/x and actively speaks Spanish, not just at home but in public life, across the full socioeconomic spectrum. It thus seems to me that the high currency use of the term 'ref' among the city's majority Latinx youth perhaps serves the purpose of discursively portraying socioeconomic class stratification more than ethnic, racial, or raciolinguistic boundaries. However, in a qualitative study, Mallet and Pinto-Coelho (2018) concluded that Latino immigrants in Miami "experience secondary marginalization from their peers, who display a form of social separatism across lines of national origin, race, and class, which can translate into discriminatory acts and segregation based on socioeconomic status as well as physical criteria (e.g., skin color), legal status, and preconceived ideas about other groups" (109). As we have seen in this chapter, such divisions are recast in terms of language choice in the school setting, which is perhaps the only institutional space where Spanish is unabashedly marginalized in Miami.

Here I recognize the limitations of the present questionnaire-based research, and I emphatically reiterate that ethnographic inquiry is needed in Miami's diverse Spanish-speaking communities. Nonetheless, there can be little doubt that Spanish is marginalized in formal education in Miami and in South Florida society more broadly within national-level discourse, just as it is in New York, Los Angeles, or Chicago, bearing in mind Rosa's (2019) argument that "Latinx identities are produced as part of a US settler colonial history and broader histories of European colonialism," which in turn shape perceptions of "Latinx communicative practices in relation to an imagined linguistic spectrum from Spanish to English" (4). The hegemony of English in the US and the relative atomization of Spanish-speaking identity in Miami, i.e. Spanish language use as a means of recognition of intra-Latinx difference

The postmodern paradox of Spanish in Miami 161

rather than similarity (Rosa 2019, 148), are concomitant with the social stigmatization of particular varieties of Spanish among the city's Latinx majority. These phenomena contribute to important sociolinguistic discontinuities in the language (Lynch 2013) and, ultimately, near monolingualism in English for some third- and fourth-generation speakers.

Conclusion

Upon the release of the Halloween special of *Shit Miami Girls Say* in 2017, a *Miami New Times* critic affirmed that it "skewers South Florida stereotypes in typical funny-because-it's-true fashion" but noted that this particular episode "adds a new layer of social commentary" by mocking the White girl, Amber, for her reaction to the characters she encountered on Calle Ocho: "Yes, the *papi chulo*'s gross gesturing is creepy, especially in this #MeToo era. But equally off-putting is Amber herself. 'Is this America?' she whines, later admitting, 'I should have learned Spanish.' No shit, honey. By the end of the video, you'll have laughed at, and with, the ridiculous Miami characters, but you'll be glad you're not some white girl who can't handle a couple of croquetas" (Lavelle 2017). Clearly, this video captures both senses of parody: the common eighteenth-century concept of ridiculing, playful imitation as well as the postmodern notion of value-problematizing, ironic acknowledgment of the history of representations (Hutcheon 2002). It is this latter postmodern sense of parodic practice that I have attempted to scrutinize in this chapter in relation to higher-level vertical scalar orders, which are at times apparently contradictory.

I conjecture that the postmodern paradox of Spanish in Miami stems from the socioeconomically fraught representation of Spanish vis-à-vis English in higher-level orders of indexicality that works to denaturalize the historical relationship between the two languages, in politically ironic fashion. The globalizing discourse of economic neoliberalism, which has saliently objectified or commodified Spanish as marketplace asset since the early 1990s, provides the contours of the acknowledgment of the language, which is complicated by the dynamic tensions of intense migratory flows. At the same time, there is another facet of the value of Spanish that—also perhaps ironically—jeopardizes its continuity in Miami: the atomization of Spanish-speaking identity. This process conforms ideally to the structural effects of consumerism traced by Baudrillard (1988):

> Whereas the directed *acquisition* of objects and commodities is individualizing, atomizing, and dehistoricizing.... the structures of consumption are simultaneously fluid and enclosed.... That is because consumption is primarily organized as a discourse to oneself, and has a tendency to play itself out, with its gratifications and deceptions, in this minimal exchange.... The object of consumption creates distinctions as a stratification of statuses: if it no longer isolates, it differentiates; it *collectively*

162   *The postmodern paradox of Spanish in Miami*

assigns the consumers a place in relation to a code, without so much as giving rise to any *collective solidarity*.

(54–55, italics in the original)

Following this reasoning, in the consumerist framework of Hispanic or Latinx identity in the US, the sort of collective solidarity implied in the mono-lithic concept of a 'Hispanic market' (Mora 2014) never emerges. Instead, the object of consumption—Spanish language, in our case—"creates distinctions as a stratification of statuses" in an atomizing, value-problematizing, denatur-alizing fashion, one which appears parodic in the postmodern sense defined by Hutcheon (2002). By reducing Spanish-speaking identity to locale-specific criteria, i.e. local articulation of the global through a rescaling or reworking of the national (Appadurai 1996; Sassen 2007), English ends up being favored, further reinforcing its status as global language par excellence, in spite of the undeniable presence, prestige, and pervasiveness of Spanish locally and trans-nationally in Miami. Thus, no such thing as 'Miami Spanish' or 'US Spanish' has yet appeared, at least not from the social ontological perspective of those whom I have interviewed and observed—formally and informally, person-ally and impersonally—over the past two decades. When speaking Spanish in Miami, the question of where one is *from* is not expected to garner the response: 'Soy de Miami.' That expectation is paradoxical, indeed.

Notes

1 Morales (2018) affirmed: "By claiming the right to the city as a living space, urban Latinx are demanding the right to the global center, the center of commercial activity and wealth accumulation, a claim that would logically come from migrants from the periphery" (245).
2 Quotes attributed to Lanier (2014) were taken from unpublished transcripts of interviews that she conducted with Latinx bilinguals in Miami. Where no page number is indicated, the quote was not included in her published thesis. All of the quotes presented in this book have been used with Lanier's express permission.
3 The questionnaire did not include the term 'Latinx,' which came into more common currency just after the time this study was conducted. A small number of students who completed the questionnaire at both schools self-identified as non-Hispanic/non-Latino. Their responses were excluded for purposes of the present analysis.
4 Gender was not a significant variable for this item.

4 Power and solidarity across the Miami/Havana divide

> Mode of address intrudes into consciousness as a problem at times of status change.
>
> —Roger Brown and Albert Gilman, "The Pronouns of Power and Solidarity" (1960)

In late October of 1998, a tropical storm named Mitch formed in the southwestern Caribbean Sea. Over the following two weeks, it would become the deadliest and most costly hurricane of the twentieth century as it passed over Central America, devastating parts of Honduras and Nicaragua, before crossing the Gulf of Mexico to impact South Florida. One of the little-known casualties of the storm occurred on a small uninhabited island off Cuba's southern coastline, where it toppled a bust of the island's namesake Ernst Thälmann. The nine-mile-long key was called Cayo Blanco del Sur until 1972, when Fidel Castro officially renamed it in honor of the legendary German Communist Party leader (1925–1933) upon ceremonially gifting the island to the German Democratic Republic during a diplomatic visit to East Berlin. The gift was symbolic of the intimate political relationship between Cuba and East Germany, one that would endure until the fall of the Berlin Wall in late 1989. By then, the wall had blocked communication between East and West Berliners for nearly three decades, with the only point of passage controlled by the US Army at Checkpoint Charlie. Earlier in the same year that the Berlin Wall went up, another political standoff culminated in the division of a national population across the Atlantic. Just a few miles from Cayo Blanco del Sur, in the Bay of Pigs, the failure of a US-backed exile attempt to overthrow Castro in April of 1961 symbolically served to construct a wall of its own sort. Less than a year after the debacle, the US government imposed an embargo on all exports to Cuba, and the State Department subsequently banned travel to the island in 1963, entrenching a divide that remains to the present day.

As Castro's regime in Havana worked to dismantle the capitalist class-based structure of the Cuban economy during the 1960s, nationalizing industry and expropriating private property, the island's exiled wealthy elite

DOI: 10.4324/9780429438363-4

164 *The Miami/Havana divide*

in Miami set out to establish a free-market enclave economy of their own as Cuban migrants continued to arrive. According to Cuban American sociologist Guillermo Grenier, this enclave reproduced in Miami "a class system that feeds on its own" in which "Cubans exploit Cubans, basically, all the way down the line," especially in terms of recency of immigration (2015). As Portes and Stepick (1993) affirmed, "in political defeat, success in business gradually emerged as a source of collective self-esteem and as proof of the correctness of the refugees' ideological stance: while Cuba went down economically..., the Miami enclave flourished on the energies of exile entrepreneurs and the social capital created by their solidarity" (137). The spirit of the early exiles was characterized similarly by Rieff (1993): "What has been a temptation for all immigrant groups in America—that is, the safety afforded by an intensified tribal solidarity—became a command for Cubans marked as much if not more by the injustice of their exile as by the inevitable travails of the immigrant" (39). In this respect, the Miami/Havana divide was not just economic or political, or about the reproduction of Cuba's class system in South Florida, but it was also about ultimately proving who was right, and who would end up on the proverbial right side of history.

As with all social divisions, language use would become symbolically implicated in the Cuban case, just as happened in Germany. Berlin dialect clearly came to reflect the physical and ideological division of its speakers by the 1980s, when Dittmar, Schlobinski, and Wachs (1988) observed that colloquial variants of *Berlinerisch* were more frequent in everyday usage in East Berlin, while in middle-class areas of West Berlin those same variants were eschewed. They suggested that, in the East, communist ideology had a particular favoring effect on what were considered popular or informal ways of speaking at the time of the Cold War, while in the West, capitalism entrenched the practice of *Hochdeutsch*, or Standard High German: "In West Berlin the Berlin dialect is associated with a value system (vulgar, insolent, proletarian, uneducated) that is virtually nonexistent in East Berlin.... The orientation to the standard [in West Berlin] as a matter of principle reflects the relationship between the controvertibility of linguistic capital into economic capital, profit and profit maximization" (42). During the reunification process in 1991, the 'Word of the Year' of the Gesellschaft für deutsche Sprache, Germany's foremost government-sponsored language society, was 'Besserwessi'—a compound of 'besser' [better] and 'Wessi' [someone from West Germany], which played on the word 'Besserwisser' [know-it-all or smart aleck]. This term referred to the common perception among East Germans that those from the West viewed them as inferior and their achievements under communism as valueless. Indeed, the culturally charged term 'Ossi,' which 'Wessis' used to denote their Eastern counterparts, was used pejoratively though sometimes playfully, similar to the present-day use of 'ref' among Miami Cuban youth in reference to recently arrived Cuban immigrants (described in Chapter 3).

For Cubans in Miami, capitalistic class-based ideologies constitute the social and cultural fabric of everyday life, a reality in stark contrast to that

The Miami/Havana divide 165

of Havana, where socioeconomic classes were ostensibly abolished under communism. In South Florida, Cuban migrants and their US-born children and grandchildren position themselves against Castro's communist order of things, placing social classes among Miami Cubans in sharp relief and drawing identity boundaries according to time of arrival (De la Torre 2003; Alberts 2005; Portes and Puhrmann 2015; Laguna 2017; among others). The first major schism within Miami developed in 1980 with the arrival of the Marielitos, whom many 1960s and early 1970s Cuban exiles viewed with disdain, principally because the Marielitos were the product of two decades of Castro's Cuba and their ideological views did not unequivocally align with those of the earlier exiles (García 1996; Grenier 2015). As López Morales (2003) affirmed, "no eran pocos—nativos y refugiados asentados ya—los que se preguntaban si aquellas gentes, nacidas y criadas bajo otro sistema, serían capaces de adaptarse a un régimen democrático" (29). Iglesias Illa (2010) documented this tendency as well: "Para los viejos cubanos, los exiliados nuevos representan lo que para ellos es la Cuba destruida por el castrismo, personas sin los modales de la Cuba señorial de su recuerdo mítico y que 'no han tenido nunca un trabajo serio en su vida'" (204).

Although the vast majority of Marielitos were socioeconomically and educationally quite similar to the previous wave of Cuban immigrants in the 1970s (Portes, Stepick, and Clark 1985), a minority element with criminal records was highly publicized. As we saw in Chapter 2, local and national mass media portrayed the city as a 'battleground' plagued by ethnic tensions and drug-related violence in the wake of the Mariel crisis; *Scarface* and *Miami Vice* popularized a stereotyped criminality among the city's immigrant population. Although it is estimated that some 26,000 of the more than 125,000 Marielitos indeed had prison records in Cuba, only 4% to 6% of those were hard criminals (Portes, Stepick, and Clark 1985). Racism was an important dimension of the discrimination (Cros Sandoval 2008). After three years in the US, 75% of Marielitos indicated that they had been clearly discriminated against by 'older' pre-1980 Miami Cubans; 21% reported frequent experiences of anti-Mariel discrimination within the Miami Cuban community (Portes, Stepick, and Clark 1985, 8).

A Cuban American writer who had immigrated to Miami from Cuba in 1970 as a teenager described the chasm created by the Mariel crisis in a 1998 interview with me. She explained the divide not only in terms of the negative view that early exiles had of Marielitos, but also the "militant" cultural position that some Marielitos took toward the early exiles:

Los marielitos eran despreciados al principio. Decir que tú eras de Mariel no era muy buena referencia. Entonces empezaron a hacer—a establecer una distinción entre la gente que había venido antes de Mariel y después de Mariel…. Yo noté un gran conflicto entre los marielitos a su vez. Asumieron una posición militante ante eso, ¿no? Entonces ellos quisieron apropiar—muchos de ellos quisieron decir que eran ellos los que habían

166 *The Miami/Havana divide*

> traído la cultura cubana aquí a Miami, o la "gran cultura," o que ellos eran los escritores, y que aquí no había nada, que esto era un desierto. Se armó toda una—Y al mismo tiempo esta gente acusaba a aquellos de haber sido criados con Castro, y que eran malos o que eran delincuentes, o sea que hubo conflictos.... Hoy día también a veces te dicen, "Ah, ese es balsero, ese debe ser un vago porque es balsero...." Ves que entre los propios cubanos están poniendo carteles por grupos migratorios: si viniste antes del 80, si viniste después del 80, si viniste en los 90. Esas cosas están pasando.

Clearly, the tension regarding 'culture' from pre-Mariel/post-Mariel vantagepoints is reminiscent of the 'Wessi'/'Ossi' divide leading up to the reunification of Germany. The divisions that the Marielitos introduced in the original enclave also served to place Miami Cuban identity vis-à-vis Cuban identity in much sharper relief, as the ideological divide between South Florida and the island became socially evident within Miami itself for the first time since Castro's takeover, and 'exiles' began to be thought of more as 'immigrants' (Grenier 2015). The crisis spurred the creation of the Cuban American National Foundation (CANF) in 1981, officializing a hyphenated identity (cf. Pérez Firmat 1994) as well as a cultural agenda with humanitarian aims.

Time of arrival from Cuba hence emerged as a central aspect of one's identity as a Miami Cuban during the early 1980s, a variable that remains important to the present day. As we saw in Chapter 3, in high school settings in lower-income areas, meaningful social divisions are drawn between recent-arrival immigrants and US-based Miami Latinx students, which appear to shape the latter's attitudes toward English and Spanish. Beyond school settings, among the adult population, individual and group identity is conveyed not just through the choice to speak either Spanish or English, but in the ways that Spanish is spoken. Among Cubans, who constitute roughly half of Miami's majority Hispanic population, sociolect is a vital feature of one's identity. Generally, among earlier arrivals and their offspring, a pre-Castro/post-Castro ideological line is drawn, based upon the idea that the quality or correctness of Spanish on the island deteriorated under communism (Alfaraz 2014, 2018). Although the impression that someone is a 'good' or 'bad' speaker of any language tends to be a holistic one (Moreno Fernández 2017, 195), particular features of the speech of later-arrival Cubans that are perceptually salient are sometimes stigmatized by more long-standing Cubans in Miami: "Established Cubans point to the variety spoken by new arrivals..., with its abundance of unfamiliar lexical items, and perhaps with phonetic and grammatical changes that advanced over the course of forty-some years, and note it a corrupt form of the language they knew" (Alfaraz 2014, 85). At the same time, English language ability assumes an important indexical value, according fluent bilinguals a high degree of social prestige and, as we will see in Chapter 5, a heightened perception of Spanish language variability in

The Miami/Havana divide   167

relation to English. In these regards, Cuban Spanish appears multiply divided, foremost by the Florida Straits, and again within Miami.

In this chapter, I explore two key elements of Miami Cuban identity vis-à-vis the island: power and solidarity. These concepts constitute the basis of contemporary sociolinguistic inquiry in a general theoretical sense, but in situations of intense political conflict or abrupt social change, they assume fundamental importance (Tetel Andresen and Carter, 2016). In the context of postwar capitalism, Brown and Gilman (1960) published a seminal article in which they proposed that the evolving semantic distinction between *T* and *V* forms of address in Western Europe (e.g. *tu* and *vous* in French, *du* and *Sie* in German) was ideologically propelled, affirming that "a man's consistent pronoun style gives away his class status and his political views" (253). They argued that pronominal address serves to convey societal sameness or difference, as the choice of *T* or *V* projects ideological values of power and solidarity among individuals or groups in everyday interaction. At the micro-discursive level, the linguistic encoding of social relationships in pronouns of address may be symmetrical or asymmetrical. Interlocutors may address each other using different pronouns to reflect that one speaker holds—or seeks to hold—some sort of power over the other, i.e. 'deferential address,' or they may employ the same pronoun to signal that there is solidarity or equality between them. Brown and Gilman's notion of a semantics of solidarity is based upon the principle of like-mindedness, or similar ways of thinking about and experiencing the world, e.g. political orientation, religious views, or occupation. At the macro-discursive level, they attributed the expansion of *T* forms of address documented in their survey study of contemporary French, German, and Italian to a collective "will to extend the solidarity ethic to everyone" within the ideological framework of postwar Western Europe (1960, 276). Indeed, usage of *du* and *Sie* took on charged ideological connotations in East and West Germany.

Because of the highly meaningful, readily apparent messages that the choice of *T* or *V* forms of address convey about social status and interpersonal relationship in Spanish (Moyna 2016), I focus this chapter on the preferential patterns of *tú* and *usted* among Cubans in Miami. The choice of personal pronoun is of particular interest in our case for several reasons. *Tuteo* is highly favored on both sides of the Florida Straits by a solidarity ethic that stemmed from two historically different ideological milieus: in Miami, *tú* reflected the confidence and intimacy of the early exiles who established a successful enclave economy in the setting of US-based capitalism; and in Cuba, *tú* was symbolic of the egalitarian philosophy of comradeship in the context of Soviet-backed communism (Bestard Revilla 2012a). Both of these milieus favor the expansion of *tuteo*—albeit for rather different motives—but which one appears to propel *tú* farther? In one possible scenario, one could hypothesize that the expansion of *tuteo* would be arrested in Miami by a highly class-conscious societal structure that necessitates *usted* for the expression of differential status in some situations. In Cuba, theoretically, *usted*

168 *The Miami/Havana divide*

would be disfavored in the discursive 'compañero/a' repertoire and, at least in part, by the ideological abolishment of socioeconomic classes. In this scenario, there should be generally greater preference for *tú* on the island than in South Florida. In another possible scenario, however, one could suppose that *tuteo* would be favored in the discourse of US-based consumerism, as I will explain below, and, as an ongoing change in Spanish in most areas of the Spanish-speaking world (Moyna 2016), potentially be accelerated by contact with English (Silva-Corvalán 1994). In this scenario, there should be overall greater preference for *tú* in Miami than in Cuba.

In what follows, I present the results of a survey study in Miami that sought response to this question. I discuss the findings in terms of power and solidarity, following Brown and Gilman's (1960) proposal, and highlight other sociolinguistic and discourse variables in Miami Cuban Spanish that reflect this conceptual binary. I wish to emphasize that those sociolinguistic variables and discursive processes that acquire particular ideological value in the US context are not 'new' in terms of substance, i.e. there is nothing radical or innovative in the formal structures of Miami Cuban Spanish (cf. Silva-Corvalán 1994). Rather, linguistic structures take on novel meanings or innovative discursive uses, which in turn drive processes of language variation and change (a matter that I take up in Chapter 5). The evolution of particular variants is never the result of any singular factor, i.e. change does not correspond exclusively to language internal or external motivations, but rather to multiple factors working in conjunction at both levels, and thus must be viewed through multiple lenses (Malkiel 1967).

The ideological dimensions of expanding *tuteo*

According to Brown and Gilman (1960), *T* forms in Western European languages have been diachronically favored by ideologies of solidarity. In English, usage of the more formal *ye* was forbidden by the Quakers in the seventeenth century as an act of disavowing elitism; solidary *thou* or *thee* was prescribed by founder George Fox in all social circumstances and for all interlocutors. In French, *vous* was condemned as a feudal remnant by the Committee of Public Safety at the time of the French Revolution, and mutual *tu* was prescribed in the spirit of egalitarianism in the new Republic (Brown and Gilman 1960, 264–65). In Spanish, the use of *tú* during the turbulent years of the early twentieth century in Spain, which led to the Spanish Civil War of 1936, reflected the desire of particular political and social factions to establish group solidarity by breaking with the traditional linguistic convention of *usted,* thus defining themselves by oppositional differentiation. Tamarón (2005) described these events in the following terms:

> ¿Qué tuvieron en común Alfonso XIII, los comunistas, los Grandes de España, los socialistas y los falangistas? Que les gustaba el tuteo más que a un tonto un látigo. Entre todos ellos desencadenaron durante

The Miami/Havana divide 169

el primer tercio de este siglo un proceso que ahora está llegando a su consecuencia natural: la desaparición del *usted* en España. Es casi seguro que no era ése el resultado que buscaban los aficionados al tuteo. Lo que buscaban era diferenciarse.... El socialista lo que pretendía al tutear a los *compañeros*—de partido más aún que de clase obrera—era marcar las diferencias frente a los demás.

(2005, 87, italics in the original)

With Francisco Franco's victory in 1939, the *tuteo* of group solidarity waned. Following Franco's death in 1975, *usted* took on retrograde connotations of right-wing conservatism among the younger generations during the transition to democracy. With the rise of Spain's socialist government during the 1980s, *tú* expanded rapidly in all spheres of public and private life. Critical commentary in the country's principal newspaper *El País* in 1985 reflected this sociolinguistic phenomenon in relation to democratization: "El tuteo a lo salvaje es la definición más canalla de la libertad democrática" (Feliciano Fidalgo cited in Tamarón 2005, 87).

Similarly, in the context of the Sandinista Revolution in Nicaragua during the 1980s, *usted* appeared to be displaced by the more colloquial *vos* as a result of populist ideology (López Alonzo 2016, 199). Nicaraguans, like Argentines, always use the second-person singular pronoun *vos* rather than *tú* to address one another in social informality or intimacy. Prescriptive *tuteo* in written modes in Nicaragua has met with a backlash from some sectors, as in a 2013 commentary published in the Sandinista-leaning national newspaper *El Nuevo Diario*: "Si el *vos* se usa en Nicaragua del Pacífico al Caribe, ¿por qué tenemos que emplear el *tú* en la escritura si es una forma ajena al español hablado en Nicaragua? Entonces, tutear es una manera de renunciar a nuestra identidad" (*El Nuevo Diario* 2013). The relationship that the author of that commentary drew between *tuteo* and Americanized, consumerist culture in Nicaragua was quite explicit, comparing the choice of *tú* over *vos* to the preference for a hamburger rather than traditional Nicaraguan cuisine: "En Nicaragua, o en cualquier país voseante, utilizar el *tú* es como despreciar una sopa de gallina con albóndigas a favor de una hamburguesa." There have been similar complaints regarding the expansion of *tú* in advertising and commerce in neighboring Costa Rica. Rodríguez Solórzano (1999) expressed concern that *tuteo* was confusing the children about the meanings of affectionate *vos* and polite *usted*. He challenged the national newspaper *La Nación* to halt its use: "¿Por qué *La Nación* no hace un esfuerzo por desterrar el tuteo en su publicidad?"

In 2014, the Ministerio de Educación Pública of Costa Rica announced a campaign to promote the use of *vos* in advertising, commerce, and public education, describing the effort as "una de las formas para hacer un llamado al sentido de identidad que tiene que ser tan fuerte como la apertura a la mundialización"—the latter tendency alluding to *tuteo* (Barquero 2014). Asked about the 'confusion' of forms in Costa Rica, well-known author and

170 *The Miami/Havana divide*

singer-songwriter Dionisio Cabal replied: "La gente se confunde entre tanta televisión que tutea, entre tantos anuncios comerciales que tutean pasándole por encima a la realidad y al decoro y al derecho de los ticos de que se les trate y hable como son" (Barquero 2014). Despite its use in mass media and commerce, *tú* does not appear to be preferred among young Costa Ricans in interpersonal communication, but rather *usted* (Michnowicz, Despain, and Gorham 2016). It is noteworthy that throughout Central America and in Highland Colombia, *usted* may be used to convey solidarity, intimacy or endearment, reflecting a sort of tripartite continuum with *usted* at both ends, i.e. extreme deference and formality as well as extreme intimacy and informality may be conveyed by *usted*, with *tú* or *vos* falling semantically in the middle (Fernández 2003). In Cuba, as in the rest of the Caribbean, Mexico, and Spain, *voseo* does not occur, leaving *tú* in binary competition with *usted* for the expression of values of deference vs. confidence, distance vs. intimacy, formality vs. informality, power vs. solidarity.[1]

The rapid advance of *tú* among younger generations in post-Franco Spain—arguably now the most *tuteísta* speakers in the Hispanic world (Carricaburo 1997)—seems to be good evidence that egalitarian ideology, urbanization, and a capitalistic free enterprise economy propel the expansion of this pronoun. Callahan's (2000) comparative study of forms of address in the popular press of Spain, Mexico, and the US (Spanish-language print media) revealed several tendencies that support this suggestion. Callahan analyzed advertisements for eleven categories of products or services aimed at adults appearing in 38 different newspapers and magazines from those three countries. Not surprisingly, Spain was by far the country where *T* forms of address were most frequent in all types of advertisements, 65% *tú* versus 35% *usted*, while 55% of Mexican advertisements employed *T* and only 35% of US advertisements reflected this form of address. Callahan ventured that this latter finding might be explained by the preponderance of immigrants from rural and lower socioeconomic-class backgrounds in the US, both factors that have been correlated with higher rates of *V* usage in previous studies from various parts of the Spanish-speaking world (2000, 59). In diachronic terms, a comparison of magazine advertisements from the late 1970s and the time of Callahan's study (2000) confirmed that *T* had increased dramatically in Spain: *tú* forms appeared only 6% of the time in advertisements published in the late 1970s, compared to 65% of the time in 2000. Mexican and US advertising reflected the same trend, though the increase of *T* was less substantial than in the case of Spain. At any rate, it is noteworthy that in all three countries *tú* had become much more commonplace in print advertising over the two-decade period under study.[2]

Interesting associations between product type and form of address from the three countries were also observed in Callahan's (2000) study. *T* was used 75% of the time in advertisements for food, alcohol, or tobacco, and 66% of the time when clothing or personal accessories were advertised (60). On the other hand, *V* forms occurred more than 80% of the time in advertisements for business,

The Miami/Havana divide 171

legal or financial services, perhaps reflecting that *usted* is preferred where questions of power (economic or legal in this case) are at stake. *V* forms also predominated in advertisements related to travel (67%) and personal services (63%). In this latter category—including advertisements for psychic hotlines, relationship services, and products to improve luck or sexual prowess—*usted* might likely be preferred because of the delicate nature of the items involved and the need for anonymity or confidentiality. As Callahan explained:

> Consumers literally maintain a certain distance from the suppliers, as these are typically telephone or mail-order products. The desire for an item in this category is an admission of the need for help, which for many equates to weakness... in a highly personal aspect of life. In addition, the type of assistance offered in these ads does not enjoy the acceptance of mainstream society. Therefore, consumers may be especially sensitive to cues signaling respect or the lack thereof. Advertisers, realizing this, address potential clients in a formal way to emphasize their dignity and thus gain their confidence.
>
> (2000, 61)

These findings regarding product type reflect the general characterization of *usted* as the pronoun of power, distance, or deference, and *tú* as the pronoun of solidarity, intimacy, or informality. Importantly, the expansion of *tú* in all types of print advertising analyzed by Callahan has been concomitant with the exponential growth of consumer markets in the three countries in question (the Spanish-language market in the case of the US).

As previously noted, and as I will again highlight in Chapter 5, globalization has been concomitant with the expansion of US-style models of consumerism, mass media, and popular culture, which in turn condition widespread borrowings and discourse patterns calqued on English in languages the world over and motivate 'Americanized' or 'Anglicized' ways of speaking. Valdés and Pino (1981) suggested that, because American English speakers tend to conform to Lakoff's (1973) 'be friendly' politeness rule, their interactions "reflect the use of strategies that seek to create an impression of camaraderie with most interlocutors, rather than one of social distance" (Valdés and Pino 1981, 58). Based upon the results of a comparative speech act analysis of compliment responses in spontaneous conversation, they found that bilinguals in the US state of New Mexico appeared much less concerned about marking social distance than did their monolingual Mexican counterparts just across the border in Ciudad Juárez. They affirmed that in the choice of pronominal address, US bilinguals "carry out a fiction that involves treating others as if they were close friends" (62), a phenomenon they attributed to the effects of English language knowledge and use. According to Valdés and Pino, this discourse tendency among Mexican Americans stood in contrast to that of Mexicans across the border, whose strategies reflected a "more highly stratified" society (58).[3] For Mexican monolinguals in Ciudad Juárez, what Lakoff

172 *The Miami/Havana divide*

(1973) characterized as 'negative politeness' appeared to be the norm, i.e. 'don't impose' (58). Hardin (2001) reached a similar conclusion in a comparative analysis of the discourse strategies of persuasion observed in Spanish-language television advertising in the US, Spain, and Chile: "US and Spanish advertisers consider egalitarianism to be highly valued by their viewers. In contrast, the higher degree of negative politeness, power, and distancing strategies in Chile may reveal a society seen by advertisers as being stratified and class conscious" (180).

It is noteworthy that a 2012 Pew Research Center survey of Hispanics in the US (Taylor et al. 2012) revealed a highly significant relationship between language dominance and respondents' general attitudes regarding personal trust, presumably with unfamiliar people. Of 1,220 respondents, 93% of Spanish-dominant Hispanics indicated that "you can't be too careful when it comes to dealing with people," while 78% of those who were English-dominant said the same. For bilingual respondents, the rate of distrust was 84%. For the general American public as a whole, 61% indicated being distrustful (Taylor et al. 2012, 19–20). Even though the question posed was highly vague and evokes a myriad of political, economic, and historical factors, it is striking that English-language dominance would be such a significant determinant of people's responses. This finding perhaps lends further credence to Valdés and Pino's (1981) argument regarding the 'fiction of a friendship' that US English-speakers discursively enact with unfamiliar interlocutors. In the same survey, 63% of Hispanics of the second generation in the US and 69% of the third generation affirmed that they thought of themselves as "a typical American"; only 34% of foreign-born respondents indicated the same (Taylor et al. 2012, 16). It is also worth noting that socioeconomic class could also be a factor at play: among Hispanics who earned $75,000+ per year, 70% identified as "a typical American"; among those who earned $30,000–$75,000, only 55% stated the same; and the figure dropped to only 45% among those with annual incomes lower than $30,000 (Taylor et al. 2012).

In sum, knowledge and use of English, class consciousness, the perception of power and solidarity, and the discursive practices of US-style consumerism all appear to condition patterns of pronominal address among speakers of Spanish in the US. It stands to reason that, in many situations, bilingual US Hispanics would prefer the pronoun of confidence and solidarity, *tú*, more than first-generation Spanish-dominant speakers. *Tú* unequivocally appears as the pronoun of feigned friendship or marketplace solidarity within the postmodern culture of consumerism, and it also appears to be favored by US Spanish-English bilinguals. However, one might venture that social class consciousness in Miami would condition particular uses of *usted*—the pronoun of power and deference—that would be uncommon in Cuba. If that were the case, we might expect to find generally higher rates of *tuteo* among more recent arrivals from Cuba in comparison with those who left Cuba sooner,

The Miami/Havana divide   173

particularly during the 1960s and 1970s. I turn now to the results of a study that sought to address that question.

The study and its participants

The selection of pronouns of address in Spanish is not a categorical affair in social interaction. Because face-to-face interactions are dynamic, ongoing negotiations that respond to individual and group personalities and cultures, as well as shifting situational and conversational cues at the micro-discursive level, variable uses of pronominal forms of address are readily observable in all varieties of Spanish. Some Spanish speakers may even use both pronominal forms (*T* as well as *V*) at different moments in the same conversation with the same interlocutor in relation to the same topic. For this reason, in the survey instrument used to collect the data for the present analysis, participants were asked to indicate their preference along a Likert-scale continuum, as described below. Brown and Gilman adhered to this same Likert-scale method in their classic study (1960) on which they based their arguments regarding power and solidarity. Using this scale, participants were able to reflect in their responses the social, situational, and interpersonal variables inherent in the interactions that they were being asked to imagine.

The present survey was divided into two parts. All items appeared in bilingual format. The first part contained 24 items concerning sociolinguistic background: age, self-ascribed gender, birthplace, arrival age and year of exit from Cuba (or parents' or grandparents' arrival age and year of exit from Cuba in the case of US-born participants), family origins in Cuba (i.e. urban, rural, or mixed), duration and place of residence in Miami, highest level of formal education attained by the participant as well as the participant's mother and father, the participant's current occupation, estimated ability to speak and understand (separately) Spanish and English (separately), and estimated use of Spanish and English with family, with friends, on the street, in movies and television programs, and in music choices (separately). For these last nine items concerning language ability and use, a Likert scale with values from 1 to 5 was presented, as in Examples 4.1 and 4.2.

Example 4.1

¿Cómo describiría su propia habilidad para **entender inglés** cuando otros lo hablan? / How would you describe your own ability to **understand English** when other people speak it?

1	2	3	4	5
Poca habilidad / Little ability	Alguna habilidad / Some ability	Buena habilidad / Good ability	Muy buena habilidad / Very good ability	Excelente habilidad / Excellent ability

174   *The Miami/Havana divide*

Example 4.2

¿Con qué frecuencia habla usted las dos lenguas (español e inglés) **con su familia**? / How much do you speak Spanish and English **with your family**?

1	2	3	4	5
Español casi siempre / Spanish almost always	Principalmente español / Mostly Spanish	Las dos lenguas igualmente / Equally	Principalmente inglés / Mostly English	Inglés casi siempre / English almost always

The second part of the survey contained 28 items for which respondents were asked to indicate their likelihood of addressing an imagined interlocutor as *tú* or *usted* according to a Likert scale, as in Example 4.3.

Example 4.3

Una vendedora mayor en Macy's / An older saleswoman in Macy's

1	2	3	4	5
Tú de seguro / *Tú* for sure	*Tú* probablemente / *Tú* probably	*Tú o usted* según el caso / *Tú or usted* accordingly	*Usted* probablemente / *Usted* probably	*Usted* de seguro / *Usted* for sure

Since *vos* is not used in Cuba, our analysis is limited to *tú* vs. *usted*. Variables of age, gender, power, and affect were manipulated in these 28 items, all of which appear in the following section. Most of the items invoked unfamiliar addressees. Four of the items concerned parents and grandparents. Siblings and cousins were not included because the vast majority of Cubans would never address those interlocutors as *usted*, unlike speakers of some Central and South American varieties of Spanish.

The analysis is based on responses of 207 individuals who self-identified as Cuban or Cuban American, all of whom completed the survey voluntarily. A snowball convenience sample was used, originating with adult members of my own family and social networks, and then extending to their adult social networks and beyond. The respondents came from all proverbial walks of life and represent highly diverse origins in Cuba, different socioeconomic backgrounds and occupations in Miami, levels of formal education, and neighborhoods of the city. Women's greater willingness to respond to the survey meant that they comprised 59% of the sample; men constituted 41%. Respondents ranged from 18 to 78 years of age. Older adults (age 50+) comprised 28% of the sample, while young adults (age 18–29) comprised nearly half (47%).

The preponderance of young adults can be attributed to the need to include third-generation speakers in the study, i.e. individuals who were born and raised in Miami and whose parents were also born in Miami or arrived during early childhood. Because substantial numbers of Cubans did not begin to arrive in Miami until after 1960, most third-generation speakers were under the age of 30 at the time of this study; concomitantly, fourth-generation Cuban Americans were children or adolescents. The demographic of recent-arrival Cubans also contributed to a higher percentage of young adults in the sample. Among Cubans who had arrived in Miami within the previous five to ten years, most were under the age of 30. In sum, the inclusion of a representative sample of both US-born third-generation Miami Cubans and recent-arrival Cubans for purposes of comparison meant that the percentage of respondents under the age of 30 was greater in proportion to the other two groups (30–49 and 50+). At any rate, because sociolinguistic theory postulates that the patterns of young adults provide a glimpse into the likely future of language use (Labov 1972), I considered it desirable to include a good number of young people from all backgrounds and immigrant groups.

It is important to point out that, as in most all other studies of Spanish in the US, 'generation' is not based on the criterion of biological age, but rather one's age at the time of immigration to the US. For the present purposes, I defined first-generation respondents (of any age) as those who indicated having left Cuba sometime after the age of 16 ($n = 94$, or 45% of the sample, henceforth G1). Those who indicated having been born in Miami to G1 immigrant parents or who arrived in Miami before the age of eight were considered second generation ($n = 60$, or 29% of the sample, hence-forth G2). All third-generation respondents ($n = 53$, or 26% of the sample, henceforth G3) were born in Miami and indicated having G2 parents, i.e. it was their grandparents who had chosen to emigrate from Cuba. As explained above, all G3 respondents necessarily had grandparents who chose to leave Cuba as adults in the 1960s. For this reason, they—along with their G1 grandparents and G2 parents—form part of the first major ideological group (or exit group) of Miami Cuban immigrants (1959–1979), whom we will call 'pre-Mariel' or 'early exile' immigrants in keeping with the terms employed in numerous previously cited sociological studies. Because this group is the demographic majority in Cuban Miami and because all G3 and most G2 Miami Cubans correspond to this group, they comprise half ($n = 103$) of the sample analyzed. The remaining half ($n = 104$) represent the other major contingent discussed by sociologists who consider 1980 to be the crucial turning point in the cultural evolution of Cuban Miami. We will call these respondents 'post-Mariel immigrants.' I opted for a more fine-grained analysis by dividing this group further: those who arrived during the 1980s (17% of the present sample), the 1990s (14%), and 2000–2015 (19%). The distinction of these four exit groups (1: 1959–1979; 2: 1980–1989; 3: 1990–1999; 4: 2000–2015) is key to interpreting differential *tuteo*.

176 *The Miami/Havana divide*

Because I was concerned with ideological dimensions of language and political stance, it seemed important to include data from respondents with diverse opinions concerning US-Cuba relations. A separate item was thus included in which participants were asked to indicate their level of support for the US economic embargo against Cuba (1 = strongly in favor; 2 = in favor; 3 = no clear opinion; 4 = against; 5 = strongly against). Responses reflected a good diversity of opinions: 10% of the sample was 'strongly in favor' of the embargo; another 18% 'in favor' of it; 29% indicated having 'no clear opinion' regarding the embargo; another 29% indicated that they were 'against' the embargo; and the remaining 13% were 'strongly against' it. Only two people (1% of the sample) did not respond to the question. Furthermore, opinions appeared not to cluster according to particular exit groups. As Table 4.1 reflects, mean responses for all four groups were close to 3 (the middle value of the 5-point scale), and there were relatively high standard deviations in each case (>1).

As one might expect, the lowest mean response (3.01)—showing more support for the embargo—was found among Exit Group 1 immigrants (the early exiles and their offspring), and the highest mean response (3.51)—indicating slightly less support for the embargo—was observed among immigrants who had arrived in Miami since the year 2000. Importantly, though, all of the values were within the range of 3.0–3.51, suggesting that the sample was not skewed in this regard.

All of the data were entered into SPSS (Statistical Program for the Social Sciences) for statistical analysis. For each of the items constituting the second part of the survey (for which respondents were asked to indicate preference for *tú* or *usted*), internal consistency was tested via Cronbach's alpha. All exceeded acceptable reliability thresholds ($\alpha > .70$). Items were then submitted to factor analysis with varimax rotation in order to identify unifying semantic themes in responses. Based on the pattern of loadings, a three-factor solution was retained, which explained 70.3% of the total variance. For each of the three principal factors, composite scores were then calculated. To determine

Table 4.1 Results of the item "Please indicate your opinion regarding the US economic embargo against Cuba" according to Exit Group (1 = strongly in favor; 3 = no clear opinion; 5 = strongly against)

Exit group	M	n	SD
1 (1959–1979)	3.01	101	1.12
2 (1980–1989)	3.28	36	1.11
3 (1990–1999)	3.07	29	1.33
4 (2000–2015)	3.51	39	1.21
Total	3.16	205	1.17

Note: Two people (1% of the sample) did not respond to the question.

The Miami/Havana divide 177

sociolinguistic variables significantly related to the resulting factors, linear multiple regression was conducted on each. The following were included as predictors: age, gender, origin in Cuba (urban, rural, or mixed), exit group from Cuba (1: 1959–1979; 2: 1980–1989; 3: 1990–1999; 4: 2000–2015), generation in the US, area of residence in Miami, level of formal education, mother's level of formal education, father's level of formal education, ability to speak Spanish, ability to understand Spanish, ability to speak English, ability to understand English, language use with family, language use with friends, language use with people on the street, language use in movies and television programs, language use in music choices. Linear models as well as individual predictors were evaluated for statistical significance at a conventional alpha level ($\alpha = .05$). Predictor collinearity was evaluated for each model and did not reach concerning thresholds (e.g., VIF > 5). Significant categorical predictors were examined via estimated marginal means, as is typical in analysis of variance (ANOVA). Lastly, theoretically justifiable interactions between predictors were probed: statistically significant interactions were maintained while nonsignificant interactions were removed to maintain model parsimony. Because of the nature of the data, I first present the results of the statistical analyses, and then turn to a more thematically organized discussion of the findings in following sections.

Principal factors

In the first two principal factors that emerged, age and power differentials were clearly apparent. Indeed, age appears as a crucial social variable conditioning pronominal address throughout the Spanish-speaking world (Blas Arroyo 2003; Fernández 2003). The consensus of empirical research to date is that *usted* occurs with greater frequency among the older population and in communication directed to older interlocutors; *T* forms of address are more frequent among young people and in communication addressed to same-age or younger interlocutors. This age-related pattern can be interpreted in two different ways. On one hand, it might reflect a case of stable variation, in which older age is and will continue to be positively correlated with *V* usage and with deferential address on the part of younger speakers. On the other hand, it could suggest a language change in progress, just as Brown and Gilman argued in the context of Europe six decades ago (cf. Blas Arroyo 2003).

In the present study, all fifteen items that loaded onto the first factor involved addressing people who were unfamiliar and older [+age] or who held social power or authority [+power]. For several of those items, respondents appeared to confer authority upon the addressee even though age was not indicated: a physician, a professor, a priest, a lawyer who is going to represent your case. Another item in which age was not indicated—and in which authority would likely not be attributed to the addressee—involved an important power differential nonetheless: a plumber whom you call for an emergency at 3:00 a.m.

178 *The Miami/Havana divide*

The items comprising Factor 1, along with their respective loadings, appear in Table 4.2.

Linear regression analysis for Factor 1 yielded a significant model (p = .000; R^2 = .372) in which the following five independent variables were significant: generation in the US (p = .014); education level (p = .020); father's education level (p = .020); language use on the street (p = .020); and exit group from Cuba (p = .022). As displayed in Table 4.3, G1 respondents showed a significantly greater preference for *usted* forms of address than G2 and G3 respondents on items comprising this factor.

Lower levels of formal education correlated with significantly stronger preference for *usted* on items comprising this first factor. Fathers' level of education had a similar effect, i.e. respondents whose fathers had lower levels of education showed significantly stronger preference for *usted*. Although the general trend was the same with respect to mother's level of education, that variable did not prove to be significant. Respondents who reported using more Spanish with people 'on the street' were more likely to prefer *usted* on items comprising this factor (Table 4.4).

Table 4.2 Factor 1: Items reflecting [+age, +power]

Item	Loading
An older woman you do not know	.808
An older male waiter in a nice restaurant	.824
An older man you do not know	.834
A physician (male or female)	.820
Your professor (male or female)	.789
An older saleswoman in Macy's	.752
An older man who works in McDonald's	.778
A priest	.802
A lawyer who is going to represent your case	.750
An older male coworker whom you do not know well	.612
A plumber whom you call for an emergency at 3:00 a.m.	.603
An older man you want to sell your car to	.817
An older man who is selling you a new car	.728
An older police officer who stops you for speeding	.789
An older man who works at the driver's license office where you go to get your license	.744

Table 4.3 Factor 1 [+age, +power]: Pronominal preference according to generation in the US (1 = *tú* for sure; 5 = *usted* for sure)

Generation in US	M	SD
G1	4.73	0.39
G2	4.33	0.51
G3	4.09	0.52

The Miami/Havana divide 179

Table 4.4 Factor 1 [+age, +power]: Pronominal preference according to language use with people on the street (1 = *tú* for sure; 5 = *usted* for sure)

Language use on the street	M	SD
Spanish almost always	4.74	0.40
Mostly Spanish	4.70	0.41
Both languages equally	4.45	0.50
Mostly English	4.15	0.53
English almost always	3.91	0.62

Table 4.5 Factor 1 [+age, +power]: Pronominal preference according to exit group from Cuba (1 = *tú* for sure; 5 = *usted* for sure)

Exit group	M	SD
1 (1959–1979)	4.27	0.53
2 (1980–1989)	4.43	0.52
3 (1990–1999)	4.53	0.52
4 (2000–2015)	4.88	0.23

Exit group from Cuba also had a significant impact. As Table 4.5 shows, later exit from Cuba was correlated significantly with stronger preference for *usted*.

The second principal factor contained eight items that involved unfamiliar addressees who were of younger or similar age as the respondent [−age] and another item ("your gardener") in which age was not indicated but that reflected some familiarity and [−power]. It is interesting to note that even though [+power] would be evoked in the case of "a saleswoman or cashier of your same age in a store where you want to return an item without the receipt," age seemed to carry more weight in respondents' preference of pronominal address in this case. All of the items comprising this second factor, along with their respective loadings, appear in Table 4.6.

Linear regression analysis for Factor 2 yielded a significant model ($p = .000$; $R^2 = .401$) in which the following three independent variables were significant: exit group from Cuba ($p = .000$); age ($p = .015$); and language use with friends ($p = .039$). As in Factor 1, there was a linear relationship between exit group and preference for pronoun of address: later exit from Cuba was correlated significantly with stronger preference for *usted* (Table 4.7).

Older age and greater use of Spanish with friends also correlated significantly with stronger preference for *usted* (Tables 4.8 and 4.9, respectively).

Family was clearly the unifying theme of the third factor, which contained four items. Each of the items and their respective loadings appear in Table 4.10.

Linear regression analysis for this third factor yielded a significant model ($p = .001$; $R^2 = .206$). In this analysis, two independent variables were

180   *The Miami/Havana divide*

Table 4.6 Factor 2: Items reflecting [−age, −power]

Item	Loading
A young male waiter in a nice restaurant	.755
A young man you do not know	.835
A young saleswoman in Macy's	.857
A young woman who works at the driver's license office where	.760
you go to get your license	.780
A young woman you do not know	.628
Your gardener	.828
A young man who works at McDonald's	.725
A saleswoman or female cashier of your same age in a store	.587
where you want to return an item without the receipt	
Someone of your same age whom you just met at a party and	
with whom you begin to argue about politics	

Table 4.7 Factor 2 [−age, −power]: Pronominal preference according to exit group from Cuba (1 = *tú* for sure; 5 = *usted* for sure)

Exit group	M	SD
1 (1959–1979)	3.16	0.77
2 (1980–1989)	3.60	0.69
3 (1990–1999)	3.91	0.91
4 (2000–2015)	4.26	0.79

Table 4.8 Factor 2 [−age, −power]: Pronominal preference according to age (1 = *tú* for sure; 5 = *usted* for sure)

Age group	M	SD
18–29 years old	3.27	0.79
30–49 years old	3.70	0.87
50–78 years old	3.89	0.93

Table 4.9 Factor 2 [−age, −power]: Pronominal preference according to language use with friends (1 = *tú* for sure; 5 = *usted* for sure)

Language use with friends	M	SD
Spanish almost always	4.07	0.84
Mostly Spanish	3.98	0.83
Both languages equally	3.50	0.85
Mostly English	3.17	0.78
English almost always	3.20	0.79

The *Miami/Havana divide* 181

Table 4.10 Factor 3: Items reflecting family relationship

Item	Loading
Your mother	.885
Your grandmother	.903
Your grandfather	.840
Your father	.879

Table 4.11 Factor 3: Pronominal preference according to ability to understand English (1 = *tú* for sure; 5 = *usted* for sure)

Ability to understand English	M	SD
Little	2.42	1.56
Some	2.55	1.64
Good	1.85	1.13
Very good	1.63	1.08
Excellent	2.02	1.15

Table 4.12 Factor 3: Pronominal preference according to origins in Cuba (1 = *tú* for sure; 5 = *usted* for sure)

Origins in Cuba	M	SD
Urban	1.89	1.19
Mixed	2.19	1.37
Rural	2.30	1.33

significant: ability to understand English (p = .033) and origins in Cuba (p = .054). Greater ability to understand English correlated with a stronger preference for *tú* with parents and grandparents, although the great majority of respondents reported using *tú* in the family domain anyway (Table 4.11); and respondents with urban origins in Cuba were significantly more likely to use *tú* with parents and grandparents than those from rural areas (Table 4.12).

English language ability did not emerge as a significant variable for either Factor 1 [+age, +power] or Factor 2 [−age, −power]. One could hypothesize that *usted* goes unfavored as bilingualism develops among the population because *tú* is conceivably the unmarked form in Cuban Spanish and *you* is the only singular pronoun of address that exists in English. In this respect, the expansion of *tuteo* among Miami Cubans would be the product of linguistic simplification, driven indirectly by English language dominance, by which the use of an already less frequent variant is diminished in favor of a competing variant that is more widely used in everyday discourse (Silva-Corvalán 1994).

182 *The Miami/Havana divide*

Table 4.13 Factors 1 and 2: Pronominal preference according to exit group from Cuba among respondents with limited ability to speak English (1 = *tú* de seguro; 5 = *usted* de seguro)

Exit group	Factor 1 [+age, +power] (p = .001)		Factor 2 [−age, −power] (p = .006)	
	M	SD	M	SD
1 (1959–1979)	4.52	0.44	3.50	0.76
2 (1980–1989)	4.53	0.54	3.81	0.68
3 (1990–1999)	4.51	0.53	4.05	0.93
4 (2000–2015)	4.91	0.15	4.41	0.69

Comparing the mean responses of only those participants who indicated having limited ability to speak English (n = 69), for whom this language would theoretically exert little structural influence, we can still observe significant differences according to exit group. As displayed in Table 4.13, in the case of Factor 1, mean responses for the first three groups were about the same (around 4.52) but significantly higher for Exit Group 4 (4.91). In the case of Factor 2, the same linear pattern was again revealed, with the mean response climbing from 3.50 for Exit Group 1, to 3.81 for Exit Group 2, up to 4.05 for Exit Group 3, and 4.41 for Exit Group 4.

In light of this consistent pattern among respondents with limited ability to speak English, we can assume that active bilingualism per se is not the principal cause of the rapid expansion of *tuteo* in this case. Rather, the crucial variable appears to be time in Miami.

As previously explained, all G3 respondents belonged to Exit Group 1 (1959–1979) and were necessarily under the age of 30. Thus, there may be some degree of collinearity between the variables of generation in the US, exit group, and age. If we control for age by limiting the analysis only to those respondents under the age of 30 (n = 98), however, we still observe highly significant differences for Factors 1 and 2 according to generation in the US and exit group (Tables 4.14 and 4.15, respectively).

Clearly, when the sample is limited only to those respondents under the age of 30 (n = 98), the significant results of the statistical analysis still hold for both factors, i.e. G3 Miami Cubans prefer *usted* less than their G1 counterparts, and later arrival Cubans prefer *usted* more than those corresponding to earlier immigration. With these results, we can now proceed to the discussion with some confidence that age is not confounding the impact of 'generation' and 'exit group' in the analysis.

I originally conjectured that the communist ideology of equality and solidarity in Cuba could produce a stronger preference for T among later arrival Cubans in Miami and a greater observance of V forms of address among those who left more immediately after the Cuban Revolution (pre-1980). I hypothesized that the situation of Cuban Spanish might be similar to that

The Miami/Havana divide   183

Table 4.14   Factors 1 and 2: Pronominal preference according to generation in the US among respondents under age 30 (1 = *tú* for sure; 5 = *usted* for sure)

Generation in US	Factor 1 [+age, +power] (p = .001)		Factor 2 [−age, −power] (p = .001)	
	M	SD	M	SD
G1	4.71	0.44	3.88	0.82
G2	4.23	0.51	3.36	0.74
G3	4.09	0.53	3.02	0.72

Table 4.15   Factors 1 and 2: Pronominal preference according to exit group from Cuba among respondents under age 30 (1 = *tú* for sure; 5 = *usted* for sure)

Exit group	Factor 1 [+age, +power] (p = .001)		Factor 2 [−age, −power] (p = .001)	
	M	SD	M	SD
1 (1959–1979)	4.12	0.53	3.02	0.70
2 (1980–1989)	4.25	0.51	3.50	0.71
3 (1990–1999)	4.28	0.62	3.69	0.98
4 (2000–2015)	4.75	0.37	3.82	0.73

of Berlin German, in that several decades of communism might condition the use of more informal and familiar modes of address. Evidently, however, the conditions of life in South Florida favor more rapid expansion of *tuteo* in Cuban Spanish than do the circumstances of communism on the island. In light of this finding, I argue that multiple sociolinguistic factors conspire to favor *tuteo* among Miami Cubans: 1) the historical need to build solidarity within Cuban Miami; 2) social class consciousness and the pervasive influence of capitalist ideology envisioning upward social mobility and invoking the cultural 'fiction of a friendship' (Valdés and Pino 1981); 3) the pragmatic-discursive influence of English, concomitant with 2) above; and 4) internal diachronic tendencies of the Spanish language to move in the direction of *tuteo*. One must bear in mind my earlier suggestion that all these factors work in unison (Malkiel 1967). In the remaining pages of this chapter, I relate the present findings to Brown and Gilman's (1960) concepts of power and solidarity. We begin with the latter, since the historical basis of *tuteo* among Miami Cubans was for purposes of solidarity among the early exiles.

Solidarity: The discursive construction of Cuban Miami

In light of our findings, it appears that the ideological value of solidarity outweighs perceived power or status differentials among Miami Cubans. It

184   *The Miami/Havana divide*

seems likely that *T* modes of address are preferred significantly more by Exit Group 1 speakers because *tuteo* established itself among Cubans in Miami during the 1960s and 1970s as a means of expressing solidarity. Portes and Stepick (1993) affirmed the social strength and psychological value of solidarity in the foundation of Cuban Miami at that time:

> Social networks were essential in effecting the rapid transformation of political militants into ethnic entrepreneurs.... Language and common culture provided Cubans with a basis for solidarity but by themselves were not enough to create a level of mutual support stronger than that typical of many other immigrant communities. Rather, the common circumstance of exile and the common experience of successive political defeats had cemented a strong sense of 'we-ness' among these refugees.
>
> (135)

This tendency was probably later reinforced among the early exiles within the context of the intense political and cultural pressures created by the Mariel crisis in 1980 and its concomitant backlash among Anglos and African Americans, a backlash that was mediatized through a prominent Miami 'battleground' metaphor in local and national mass media, as described in Chapter 2. Given the needs and interests of the early exiles and the highly charged atmosphere in which they found themselves—including an economic recession during the 1970s and the stigma of the cocaine trade during the 1980s—a particular linguistic and discursive code likely emerged among them. *Tuteo*, as an overt expression of intimacy and confidence, surely would have been a central aspect of that code. Laguna (2010) argued that early exile comedian "Alvarez Guedes' use of *choteo* forges a narrative of exile that harnesses the power of positive affect for consolidating an empowered group identity organized around a shared political vision and *cubanía*" (527). I suggest that *tuteo* served the same function and had a similar positive politeness or 'be friendly' discursive effect (Lakoff 1973) within that narrative.

Data from respondents of age group 50+ support this contention. Most Cubans corresponding to this age group at the time of this study were born before Castro's revolution and hence they lived through the sociolinguistic evolution of Cuban Spanish (in contrast to being a product of the consequences of that evolution, as in the case of younger respondents). They also all acquired Spanish first and did not begin to use English until they arrived in the US. If we isolate respondents in this particular age group (50+), significant differences according to exit group obtain for Factor 2 [−age, −power], but not for the other two factors. Mean responses of Exit Group 1 for Factor 2 reflect a significantly stronger preference for *tú* than those of Exit Group 4 ($p = .031$), as displayed in Table 4.16.

It is noteworthy that significant differences among respondents age 50+ were observed according to exit group only for Factor 2, since all of the items

The Miami/Havana divide   185

Table 4.16 Factor 2 [−age, −power]: Pronominal preference according to exit group from Cuba among respondents of age group 50+ (1 = *tú* for sure; 5 = *usted* for sure)

Exit group	M	SD
1 (1959–1979)	3.58	0.90
2 (1980–1989)	3.94	0.70
3 (1990–1999)	4.25	1.02
4 (2000–2015)	4.57	0.48

in this factor involved younger or same-age interlocutors (except for 'your gardener,' in which age was not indicated). It makes good sense that the societal expansion of *tuteo* would be most favored among early exile Miami Cubans of same or younger age. A shift toward greater *tuteo* with older interlocutors (Factor 1) or with parents and grandparents (Factor 3) would have been much less likely, as this would have been an encroachment upon the social norms of respect or deference observed by the previous generation in pre-Castro Cuba. This tendency among this particular age group in [−age] items concurs with the widely accepted sociolinguistic premise that change is propelled by and among younger speakers (Labov 1972). During the 1960s and 1970s, as Cubans in Miami began to prefer *T* forms with unfamiliar same-age and younger interlocutors for solidarity purposes, their same-age counterparts back on the island, who were also born in pre-Castro Cuba, likely maintained a preference for *V* forms.

Of course, this latter hypothesis does not imply that Cubans on the island maintained the same frequency of *usted* usage as might have been observed prior to the revolution. As in most other parts of the Spanish-speaking world, *tuteo* has arguably expanded in Cuba over the past six decades, probably accelerated somewhat by the ideological values of Castro's regime. Indeed, if we limit the analysis only to those respondents who arrived in Miami from 2000 to 2015 (Exit Group 4), a significant difference ($p = .042$) can be observed between younger people (age 18–29) and older people (age 50+) for Factor 2 [−age, −power]. Once again, as noted above, it is in the items of Factor 2 in which one would expect to see the beginnings of an accelerated societal linguistic change favoring *tuteo*, i.e. in discourse addressed to same-age or younger interlocutors. Table 4.17 displays these significant age-related differences among Cubans of Exit Group 4 for Factor 2. For the other two factors, older respondents again indicated stronger preference for *usted* than younger ones, although the differences did not prove to be significant in either case.

One wonders why the communist ideology of solidarity has not served to accelerate *tuteo* at a greater rate in Cuba. Brown and Gilman noted in 1960 that in Yugoslavia a universal mutual *T* of solidarity emerged following the

186 The Miami/Havana divide

Table 4.17 Factor 2: Pronominal preference according to age among Exit Group 4 respondents (1 = *tú* for sure; 5 = *usted* for sure)

Age group	M	SD
18–29 years old	3.82	0.73
30–49 years old	4.30	0.89
50–78 years old	4.65	0.43

establishment of a communist regime there, but its use was apparently short-lived, a fact they attributed to the decline of revolutionary esprit de corps and the power asymmetry inherent in Yugoslavia's 'socialist manners,' i.e. "a soldier says *V* and *Comrade General*, but the general addresses the soldier with *T* and surname" (1960, 266). There is similar and explicit evidence from Cuba that the Castro regime has upheld the usage of *usted* as a means of signaling power and deference. In 1985, the Cuban Ministry of Education published the following statement as part of their proclamation concerning formal education in the Havana newspaper *Juventud Rebelde*: "Trataremos de *usted* a las personas que por sus méritos revolucionarios, laborales, culturales, etcétera, gocen de un elevado prestigio social. Ellos son merecedores del respeto y la consideración de todos" (cited in Tamarón 2005, 88–89). As Tamarón commented, "Precisamente donde se hubiera podido pensar que la revolución acabaría con el *usted* está intentando conservarlo" (2005, 97). Why would Cubans on the island continue to use a deferential pronominal form of address that implies social distance—seemingly antithetical to the ideology of egalitarianism—more than their South Florida counterparts, who live immersed in capitalist consumerism and socioeconomic class consciousness?[4]

One possible answer to this question lies precisely in the ideology of postmodern capitalism and consumerism, i.e. a fluid concept of social class in the potential for upward social mobility; social prestige and the accumulation of wealth or material power as the reward for hard work; purchasing power and the freedom of choice; and the incessant desire to continue purchasing (Baudrillard 1988). In this regard, Brown and Gilman (1960) argued that societal fluidity provides prime ground for expansion of *T* forms by casting *V* forms as markers of a static order of things, thus making formality psychologically and socially "onerous":

> In a fluid society crises of address will occur more frequently than in a static society, and so the pronominal coding of power differences is more likely to be felt as onerous…. Where status is fixed by birth and does not change each man has enduring rights and obligations of address. A strong equalitarian ideology of the sort dominant in America works to suppress every conventional expression of power asymmetry.

(268)

Although the latter statement is undoubtedly loaded on Brown and Gilman's part, it is unquestionable that prevailing political and economic ideologies exert an important influence on the linguistic conventions for expression of power. It is also noteworthy that, in international perspective, US discourse styles are often popularly perceived as being informal or friendly (*The Economist* 2009), i.e. the cultural 'fiction of a friendship' noted by Valdés and Pino (1981).

The political and affective solidarity that characterized early exile discourse in Cuban Miami had an important economic dimension. In the enclave economy that emerged during the 1960s and 1970s, financial and social networks depended upon interpersonal confidence, which was linguistically encoded by *tuteo*. In a cross-generational study of the speech acts of making requests and asking for favors among Miami Cubans, Gutiérrez-Rivas (2007) remarked upon the comfort and ease with which older, G1 men formulated role-play requests to borrow money from a male friend. While their female counterparts tended to make explicit promises to return the money, many of the men made jokes about the situation or commented that they had actually been in that situation before and that "entre amigos cubanos, es bien fácil" (158). Gutiérrez-Rivas observed: "Al parecer, entre los hombres de esta generación no implica una amenaza a la imagen pedirles dinero a los amigos o compadres" (2007, 158). As will be noted in the following section, however, the author observed a dramatic shift in attitude regarding money among the second generation of Miami Cuban men. Gutiérrez-Rivas concluded that older, early exile Miami Cubans "se valen de un código propio entendible por los otros miembros de su comunidad de habla para obtener lo que necesitan" (2007, 158). She also suggested: "Una de las razones por las que estos hablantes no muestran preocupación de perder la imagen frente a los demás es quizá porque para la primera generación de inmigrantes cubanos en los Estados Unidos las conexiones con la gente de su comunidad al inicio del exilio fueron fundamentales para la supervivencia económica y social" (158).

Political accord, or unified resistance to Castro's regime, was also a key element of group solidarity for the early exiles, as Grenier and Pérez (2003) affirmed: "Anti-Castroism might well be considered to be the master status of the community, establishing the limits and potentials for all group activity" (87). In interviews with early exiles and their offspring in Miami, I have observed the linguistic features of this clearly delineated 'opinion community' (Lynch 2009a). Members of an opinion community, as defined by Strauss (2004), must reflect through discourse conventions the 'cultural standing' of their opinions; propositions that have been the topic of prior discourse or agreement within a community attain such standing. Political postures, like other types of opinions in general, form part of a community linguistic repertoire that speakers must be able to manage in order to fit in with others. Strauss maintained: "Opinion norms are like behavioral norms. Members of a community do not automatically follow them, but they are expected to know them, and if they deviate, to acknowledge that somehow. Not to do so is to

188 *The Miami/Havana divide*

signal that one does not know or care about the group's opinion" (2004, 172). Common opinions are marked linguistically by: 1) short sentences with no qualification or support; 2) clichés, maxims, and semi-formulaic expressions; 3) no hesitations; 4) use of rhetorical questions; 5) use of the discourse marker *you know*; and 6) taboo words or emphatic language (Strauss 2004, 181–84). When expressing an opinion that speakers believe might be controversial, they attempt to mitigate their statements in various possible ways: 1) self-censoring or using euphemisms or indirect language; 2) denial; 3) hedging; 4) attribution to others or use of the second or third person; 5) lamination; 6) apologies, requests for permission, preemptive concession, or other verbal acknowledgments of uneasiness; 7) self-initiated repairs; and 8) pauses, disfluency, and hesitation (Strauss 2004, 174–78). These discourse elements are suggestive of what Strauss characterized as a 'controversial opinion.' An opinion considered controversial within the community has lower cultural standing than an opinion more commonly shared by community members.

One common opinion among Miami's early exiles is that no one should travel to Cuba. Exchange with Cuba is perceived not only as a breach of ideological solidarity with Miami's exile community but also as a form of economic aid to the island that unjustly facilitates the continuation of Castro's regime. This belief, stated repeatedly in Miami Cuban discourse for six decades and politically manifested in the long-standing US economic embargo against Cuba, is so commonly accepted as general truth among the early exiles that it is often expressed in syntactic fragments, with no sort of qualification or supportive explanation needed. This phenomenon is evident in the discourse of Onelia (age 76) and her husband Armando (age 73). Both had immigrated to Miami from Cuba as adults in the early 1960s. In the following excerpt of a conversation with me, recorded in 1998 (cited in Lynch 2009a, 29–30), there is good evidence that they regarded my question of sending aid to Cuba as highly controversial:

Onelia ¿Cuántos millones le producen los cubanos a Fidel cuando van allá-cuando están yendo allá y cuando están mandando dinero para allá? Millones. Millones.
Armando –Y el dinero que mandan de aquí. –Aquí se mandan dinero, se mandan ropa, se mandan zapatos, medicina, de los exiliados cubanos.
Onelia –De los exiliados cubanos. –
Armando Aparte de lo que mandan las- las- eso- las instituciones católicas y protestantes y-
Onelia Yo no, porque yo tengo la satisfacción de que nunca, ni una medicina, ni un centavo, ni una ropa, nada. Para Cuba, nada.
A. L. ¿Pero piensa que si tuviera familia allá mandaría cosas?
Onelia Bueno-
Armando Medicina sí, yo creo que sí. No sé.
Onelia Tal vez la medicina, tal vez la medicina. Pero ropa y esas cosas- ir para Cuba a llevar cosas como están yendo la gente de aquí que van a Cuba y

The *Miami/Havana divide*   189

lo de menos que van a- a ver a la familia. Se van a los cabaret y se van a divertirse, y van de turista y a dejarle dinero, dólares a Fidel Castro, no chico.

Armando Bueno, eso no. Pero si yo tuviera a mi mamá o a mi papá enfermo allá y eso, yo iba a Cuba y les llevaba medicina.

Onelia Si yo tuviera a mi papá y a mi mamá allá la cosa sería distinta, ¿no?

Armando Como hermanos, ¿verdad? Pero yo no tengo familia ninguna en Cuba.

Onelia Yo tampoco.

Numerous discourse features indicate that Onelia viewed the possibility of sending aid to Cuba as highly controversial: 1) her hesitation after beginning with the discourse marker *bueno*; 2) her repetition of the hedge *tal vez* in relation to sending medicines; and 3) her rather lengthy third-person reaffirmation of the common opinion about not going to Cuba, which ends with the emphatic tag *no chico*. One noteworthy feature is Armando's usage of the verbs *iba* and *llevaba* in the imperfect indicative form, giving them a higher degree of assertion than if he had chosen conditional (*iría* and *llevaría*) or imperfect subjunctive (*fuera* and *llevara*) verb forms, both of which are commonly heard in the apodosis of conditional sentences in Caribbean varieties of Spanish. Onelia then employed the conditional ("la cosa sería distinta") followed by the tag *no?* to echo her husband's sentiment, stating that if her mother or father were in Cuba the situation would be different. This usage of the conditional form allowed Onelia to convey a more tenuous argument than the one being asserted by her husband, and through the tag she appeared to seek confirmation for being a bit out of line with common opinion. As Armando continued his response in reaction to his wife's remark, he seemingly conveyed that perhaps what he had just stated was a bit too controversial—both in the eyes of his spouse and the community—by then offering an emphatic denial of having any family members back in Cuba ("Yo no tengo familia ninguna en Cuba"), a denial that seemed unnecessary since all of us were already aware that his entire family was in the US. His wife then confidently affirmed the same ("Yo tampoco").

In the following excerpt, Lázaro, who left Cuba in 1964, related to me that his sister had chosen to stay in Cuba and that he had refused to send her money when she called him for the first time in nearly four decades. He baldly asserted that he would not return to visit Cuba under Castro. Apparently, the purpose of Lázaro's recounting the telephone conversation with his sister was to provide support for his position that his money "no va para ese país en cuanto existe ese gobierno," stated in the highly assertive present indicative form. Also, in an assertive style, he ended his thought with an implicit command ("que espere hasta el fin") in reference to his sister's situation, emphasizing the inflexibility of his stance. Such emphatic language is characterized by Strauss (2004) as a discourse feature of a common opinion. Two other salient markers of common opinion described by Strauss are found

190 *The Miami/Havana divide*

in Lázaro's discourse: the cliché expression "abrí los ojos" to convey the unacceptability of Castro's regime; and his reference to Castro throughout the interview as "él," without saying his name—a frequent discursive strategy among older early exile Miami Cubans.

A. L. Si tuvieras la oportunidad ahora para ir a Cuba a visitar, ¿irías?
Lázaro No. Mi hermana vive en Cuba. Ella fue de él, yo fui de él, nosotros éramos fidelistas. Yo abrí los ojos y dije 'esto no sirve,' y me fui. Mi hermana se quedó. Y por primera vez en cuarenta años yo hablé con ella hace dos meses atrás. Ella me llamó para pedir dinero, y mi respuesta para ella fue que el dinero mío, si yo lo tuviera, no va para ese país. No va para ese país en cuanto existe ese gobierno. Y que si ella esperó y vivió durante cuarenta años con él, que espere hasta el fin.

(Lynch 2009a, 32)

Perhaps Castro brings such grief to early exile immigrants that they often avoid saying his name, thus avoiding others' having to hear it said—an act of negative politeness (Brown and Levinson 1987). But it seems more likely that older Miami Cubans generally refer to Castro simply as "él," and sometimes as "ese hombre" or "el señorito"—both of which can have derogatory connotations in Spanish—because Castro is the obvious referent of the conversation and, by not using his name, they establish solidarity with the interlocutor, i.e. 'you know who I'm talking about.'

This same strategy may be used by younger US-born G3 speakers, as in the following interaction with Ana, who referred to Castro[5] pejoratively as "el señorito" (Lynch 2009a, 32):

Ana Yo nací aquí pero yo tengo una cultura cubana y yo quiero a ese país como si yo hubiera nacido allí, porque mi- eso es de donde mis padres vinieron, donde se criaron, vaya, todo eso. Y como ellos hablan siempre de Cuba, Cuba, yo quisiera ver a Cuba. Ahora no, porque está el señorito allí, pero sí, tú sabes, quisiera conocer ese sitio.

Ana's parents emigrated from Cuba as young adults in the 1960s. Her desire to visit Cuba, fronted by "tú sabes," is common sentiment among speakers of the younger generation whose only personal experience with the island has been through discourse. Nonetheless, they oftentimes qualify the statement that they would visit Cuba by affirming that they would not do so as long as communism persists. It appears that they do so partly out of respect for the older generation who, in some cases, lost property or were imprisoned for political reasons when Castro took control.

Some G3 speakers, whose grandparents arrived in Miami in the early 1960s, tend to qualify their expression of willingness to visit Cuba, as José did in the following excerpt. He used the future indicative form ("no daré") to assert that he will not spend his own money for travel to Cuba because it would go to Castro's communist cause. In this way, he realigns himself with the common opinion (Lynch 2009a, 33):

A. L. Si tú tuvieras la oportunidad de ir a Cuba a visitar ahora, ¿irías?
José Bueno, creo que sí, si me dieran el chance. Yo no daré mi propio dinero porque yo sé que todo ese dinero va a Castro y el comunismo. Si fuera un viaje de gratis que alguien me regalaba, sí voy, pero de mi propio dinero no pienso comprar ticket de avión ni hotel ni nada porque no creo que mi dinero debe ir a Castro y su comunismo.

Although José assertively employed the present indicative form to convey his strong desire to visit Cuba ("sí voy"), he countered this assertion by conceding his view to the common opinion ("yo sé que todo ese dinero va a Castro") and by reaffirming his belief that no one should channel money into the island under Castro's regime ("no creo que mi dinero debe ir a Castro").

Ramón, another G3 Miami Cuban of early exile grandparents, stated to me that he would go to Cuba and even move there to help people in his capacity as a doctor if the island were liberated. When I then asked him why he would not visit at the present moment, his bald, negative response to my question was syntactically fragmented and stylistically highly assertive. His concluding remark ("Todo eso va pa' Castro, y yo de eso nada. Ni un kilo, ni un kilo pa' Castro.") is, both in syntactic and semantic terms, strikingly similar to that of Onelia above:

Ramón Me mudaría de Miami si Cuba se liberara. Y nunca he ido pero- pero quisiera ir. Y esa es una de mis cosas, que si el día que- yo creo que en mi vida se va a liberar Cuba y este, ya con haber sido médico hay veinte mil cosas que yo pudiera ir a hacer a mi patria.
A. L. ¿Irías a hacerlo?
Ramón Yo iría a hacerlo. Iría a hacerlo, sí.
A. L. Si tuvieras la oportunidad de visitar a Cuba ahora, ¿irías?
Ramón No. No, yo no iría a Cuba.
A. L. ¿Por qué?
Ramón Por- por- por la política, del dinero que yo gaste allí, inclusive el pasaje de avión. Todo eso va pa' Castro, y yo de eso nada. Ni un kilo, ni un kilo pa' Castro.

(Lynch 2009a, 31)

But not all children and grandchildren of the early exiles reflect this solidary anti-Castro discourse, nor do most post-Mariel immigrants (Lynch 2009a; Grenier 2015). Jennifer, a G3 Cuban American, explained to me that her parents, who were also born in Miami, were unconcerned with politics and rarely discussed the situation of Cuba. In the following excerpt of a conversation with her, she reasoned that Batista's regime had also been highly

192 *The Miami/Havana divide*

problematic, and felt that Cuba would still have faced a precarious future even if Castro had not come to power:

Jennifer Si estuviera Batista, si estuviera Castro, todavía hubiera problema si no estuviera ninguno de los dos. Entonces la isla esa ahora sería como un Miami, más o menos. Tanta riqueza pero allí- eso era un lugar donde la gente iban a jugar, so sería un lugar turístico pero no le veo, you know, no le veo mucho lanzamiento. Aunque muchos de los cubanos que llegaron de Cuba aquí a los Estados Unidos dicen que no- que Cuba era esto y Cuba era lo otro. Todos te hablan de la Cuba que era, pero nadie ve la Cuba que iba a ser. So, I don't know.

Although the wealthiest and politically most powerful segment of the Cuban population in Miami still maintains an outspoken, hardline stance against Cuba, some suggest that the stark polarization that once characterized South Florida vis-à-vis the island is gradually fading. Grenier (2015) noted that from 1995 to 2015, more than 300,000 Cubans left the island for Miami, constituting roughly one-third of the city's Cuban-origin population. He explained the potential impact of their political views in years to come:

Their opinions toward Cuba are dramatically different than those of the early exiles. They really do have a Cuban life. They have reasons to maintain contact. They have reasons to want to normalize relations above and beyond the political reasons. They have family there…. The demographic changes are pushing towards the inevitability of having a transnational community of Cubans…. More recent arrivals have a reason to want change and those are the folks who are more likely to be going back and forth.

(Grenier 2015)

Nonetheless, the streets of Calle Ocho and Hialeah filled with young Cuban Americans who celebrated the announcement of Fidel Castro's death on the night of November 25, 2016. A bilingual poll of Cuban Americans in Florida conducted by Bendixen & Amandi International (2021) in early March of 2021 found that 66% (54% of those polled in English and 75% of those polled in Spanish) were in favor of continuing the US economic embargo against Cuba. This reflected a 30-point increase in support for the embargo since the previous poll by the same agency in 2015. Of the 2021 sample, 56% opposed easing US State Department restrictions on travel to Cuba, a 21-point increase since 2015 (Bendixen & Amandi International 2021). Only 28% of those polled in 2021 indicated that the Biden administration should revert to Obama's prior policy of normalization of relations with Cuba, a 26-point increase in support of the unified stance against Cuba since 2015. Fernand Amandi, president of the highly prestigious agency, which has been tracking the Cuban community for five decades now, affirmed: "What we're seeing

The Miami/Havana divide 193

is a new back-to-the-future, retro-style to some of these issues, when it was believed that the Cuban community was going through a shift in perceptions during the Obama years. These results suggest that if there's any change, it's toward the hardline" (cited in Padró Ocasio and Gámez Torres 2021). On a personal note, like many of my friends, I still observe quite fervent anti-Castro discourse among some post-2000 Cuban immigrants in Miami. One would be mistaken to assume that the political 'hardline' is fading, especially given the vitality of Venezuelan voices of dissent aligned with those of Cubans.[6]

As I have argued in this section, solidary discourse was key to identity construction for early exile Cubans in Miami and to the ongoing maintenance of the Miami/Havana or capitalist/communist ideological divide. For six decades now, *tuteo* has been a vital feature of that discourse. Although the ideological value that *tú* usage had for the early exile immigrants probably goes unperceived by their G3 English-dominant grandchildren (who are nonetheless mostly aware of the formal connotations of *usted* in Spanish), the social expansion of *tuteo* in Miami appears unabated. In this respect, Miami Cuban Spanish is yet another instantiation of the proliferation of *tú* throughout the Spanish-speaking world. In the next section, I link this tendency to socioeconomic factors and the perception of upward social mobility in Miami and beyond.

Power: Class consciousness and upward social mobility

Throughout the Spanish-speaking world, the general consensus of studies related to pronominal address is that younger age, urbanization, and higher levels of formal education all appear to favor *tuteo*. The latter two factors are indices of upward social mobility, or what Brown and Gilman (1960) characterize as societal fluidity. Even in the case of age, one could argue that younger people envision greater upward social mobility for themselves than do middle-aged or older people, who often perceive themselves as being more entrenched in the life choices and occupational paths they have already taken. In the present study, several indices of upward social mobility correlated with stronger preference for *tú* forms of address among Cubans in Miami: higher education levels, semi-professional or professional occupations, and neighborhoods with higher median household incomes. This general pattern was evident across the board.

As previously noted, for Factor 1 [+age, +power], respondents' education level and their fathers' education level emerged as significant variables in the linear regression analysis. This factor contained many items in which one would expect education to play an important role, as many involved addressing an interlocutor who holds some sort of authority, e.g. a physician, a professor, a lawyer, a police officer. For respondents' level of education, a U-shaped pattern was observed, in which those with the lowest levels and the highest levels of education demonstrated the strongest preference for *usted*, and those in the middle ranges (some college study or bachelor's degree) appeared significantly less likely to use *usted* (Table 4.18).

194 The Miami/Havana divide

Table 4.18 Factor 1 [+age, +power]: Pronominal preference according to respondents' level of education (1 = *tú* for sure; 5 = *usted* for sure)

Level of education	M	SD
High school degree	4.61	0.49
Some college study	4.30	0.54
Bachelor's degree	4.49	0.53
Graduate or professional study	4.73	0.38

This pattern suggests that at both extremes of the educational spectrum, respondents are most conscious of social power boundaries and the nuances of deferential address. Brown and Gilman (1960) briefly alluded to the potential for this phenomenon: "If the worker becomes conscious of his unreciprocated polite address to the boss, he may feel that his human dignity requires him to change. However, we do not feel the full power of the ideology until we are in a situation that gives us some claim to receive deferential address" (268). In other words, those with graduate or professional studies—and hence more authoritative positions in the workplace—perhaps perceive themselves as having greater claim to deferential address than those with lower-level university studies or semi-professional occupations, making them most sensitive to the subtleties of pronominal address. Those with some college study, mostly in semi-professional occupations, would perceive—as Brown and Gilman put it—a greater need to obviate "unreciprocated polite address to the boss" for the sake of "human dignity." While those at the lower and upper ends of the socioeconomic class spectrum appear more disposed to mark social boundaries with the use of *usted*, those in between may attempt to obfuscate those boundaries with rather more use of *tú*.

Parents appear to play an important role in conditioning this process: increasing levels of education among parents correlated with diminishing preference for *usted*, especially in the case of fathers (Table 4.19).

Here it is important to note that the U-shaped pattern observed for respondents' level of education (Table 4.18) no longer holds in the case of fathers' level of education (Table 4.19). Although individuals with superior level studies or professional degrees preferred more deferential forms of address than those with only some college education (as noted in Table 4.18), parents with superior level studies or professional degrees appeared most likely to transmit a preference for less deferential forms of address to their children (in the case of both parents but significantly so for fathers, as reflected in Table 4.19).

Although these questionnaire data for Factor 1 [+age, +power] cannot account for the reasons behind greater *tuteo* among those whose fathers had higher levels of formal education, one could possibly venture that middle- and upper-class Cuban men in Miami were somewhat more likely than women to

The Miami/Havana divide   195

Table 4.19 Factor 1 [+age, +power]: Pronominal preference according to fathers' level of education (1 = *tú* for sure; 5 = *usted* for sure)

Fathers' level of education	M	SD
Primary schooling	4.72	0.38
High school degree	4.52	0.49
Some college study	4.36	0.56
Bachelor's degree	4.34	0.63
Graduate or professional study	4.24	0.50

instill in their children a sense of challenging class boundaries and social power structures. This quantitative trend could also perhaps mean that men were somewhat more conscious of the *tuteo* of solidarity within the Miami Cuban context, described in the previous section. Such hypotheses would merit more extensive sociolinguistic and ethnographic research. It is noteworthy that the pattern regarding fathers' education level emerged even among women respondents. Taking only the data from women (n = 122), one-way ANOVA tests revealed that fathers' level of education had a significant effect for all three main factors (Factor 1: p = .015; Factor 2: p = .044; Factor 3: p = .023). The educational attainment of mothers of women respondents, on the other hand, did not produce overall significant effects (Factor 1: p = .108; Factor 2: p = .060; Factor 3: p = .141).

Interestingly, the gender of the respondents themselves did not prove to be a significant variable in the linear regression analysis for any of the three factors. Although lacking general statistical significance, women's mean responses tended to be lower than those of men for the majority of items comprising the survey, suggesting that women prefer *tú* slightly more than men do. In one-way ANOVA tests for each individual item of the survey, gender emerged as a significant variable only in a few cases in which unfamiliar women interlocutors were indicated, e.g. an older saleswoman in Macy's; a young woman who works at the driver's license office; a young woman you do not know; a saleswoman or female cashier of your same age in a store where you want to return an item without the receipt. For all these particular items, tested independently, women were significantly more likely to prefer *tú* than men. In sum, the data as a whole reflect a broader tendency for women to use *tú*, especially when addressing other women, a finding that concurs with a general trend documented throughout the Spanish-speaking world (Fernández 2003; Moyna 2016).

Meaningful gender differences among Miami Cubans have been observed in phonological studies as well. Alfaraz (2012) observed that, in the speech of recent-arrival immigrants in Miami from central Cuba, nonstandard realizations of syllable- and word-final /r/ reflected differential patterns for men and women according to their previous roles in the island's economy. She

196 *The Miami/Havana divide*

noted that phonological assimilation, e.g. *parte* pronounced as [pátte] or *forma* as [fómma], which was largely associated with informal speech principally in Havana and other western areas of the island pre-Castro, had increased significantly among young people in central Cuba, particularly among men (2012, 304). She reasoned that the covert prestige of assimilated variants, characteristic of the nonstandard speech of the capital, would have appealed largely to men from the provinces who "wished to align themselves with, and project to others, the positive qualities associated with Havana, and highlight the social privileges granted to men" (Alfaraz 2012, 305). Lateralization, e.g. *carne* pronounced as [kálne] or *cantar* as [kantál], reflected a similar trend. A low-frequency variant in pre-Castro Cuba, the lateral appears to have increased in recent decades. Alfaraz found that this was especially true among younger, nonprofessional men who had been involved in secondary economic activities in Cuba, e.g. making and trading shoes or soap, or raising pigs and chickens to sell on the 'black market' (2012, 308).

Prior to the Cuban Revolution, lateralization was correlated with lower levels of formal education (Varela 1992). It was principally associated with the working class and with rurality, especially the speech of agricultural laborers. Probably for this reason, it has taken on special meaning in the context of Cuba's underground economy: "The lateral, in effect, represents the manual physical activities of blue-collar or working-class occupations, and here it takes on an additional layer of covert prestige because these activities are illegal" (Alfaraz 2012, 313–14). The relative decoupling of education level and occupation from social class perception in the case of final /r/, noted by Alfaraz (2012), appears strikingly similar to the expansion of colloquial or working-class phonological variants of *Berlinerisch* in East Berlin following the city's divide, as observed by Dittmar, Schlobinski, and Wachs (1988) in the 1980s: "In East Berlin, white-collar workers use the Berlin variety, too; it is not associated with a negative value system. For one, social prestige is not linked with the professions and is thus decoupled from the world of production. For another, there are only a few areas (broadcasting and the university) in which use of the standard can be turned into cultural—though not economic—capital" (41–42). In the context of Cuban Miami, however, where capitalism prevails, nonstandard phonological variants are often perceived negatively, just as they were in West Berlin at the time. As Alfaraz affirmed in the case of final /r/, "the covert prestige the lateral variant had for individuals on the island may be rejected by Cuban immigrants living in Miami" (2012, 314).

Nonstandard deletion of syllable- and word-final /s/, e.g. *costas* pronounced as [kóøtaø], also appears to have expanded substantially in Cuba in recent decades. Among recently arrived Cuban immigrants in Miami in 2000, Alfaraz observed that final /s/ deletion was least common among upper status speakers, older speakers, and females. She noted, however, that upper status speakers of rural origin presented the highest rates of deletion, suggesting that for them, within the context of the Cuban Revolution, there is a valuable

The Miami/Havana divide   197

ideological relationship of social status with rural ways of speaking. This relationship, according to Alfaraz, reflects "the positive effects of rural ties on
an individual's quality of life in Cuba, which make rural origins prestigious
within the local culture, and rural sociolinguistic variants an expression of that
prestige" (2000, 52). In concluding, Alfaraz affirmed that the "strong motivation for young college-educated males to use more nonstandard variants [e.g.
deletion] is an expression of locality and solidarity" in post-Castro Cuba (72).

In the context of Miami, the realization of final /s/ remains a meaningful
indicator of gender and social status vis-à-vis Cuba. In an earlier study,
I documented a significantly higher rate of sibilant realization among the
young Miami-born grandchildren of upper-middle class early exile speakers
than among same-age Marielito immigrants (Lynch 2009b). Moreover, the
frequency of the sibilant [s] among young Miami-born speakers was more
than double that observed among immigrant speakers of their grandparents'
generation, suggestive of a cross-generational language change favoring [s]
in the context of Miami. Among speakers of this latter group, the sibilant
occurred in only 12% of possible contexts, while the Miami-born speakers
produced it 25% of the time (Table 4.20), a difference that was statistically
significant.

The study also revealed that upper-middle-class G3 men produced
the standard sibilant [s] significantly more than their lower-middle-class
counterparts, 33% vs. 6%, respectively (Lynch 2009b). This finding suggested
that upper-middle-class Miami Cuban men were more concerned with overt linguistic prestige, i.e. sibilant usage, than lower-middle-class men, who presented
the highest rate of deletion (41%). Nonetheless, young Miami-born men
appeared to continue to observe the sociophonetic norms of deletion found
in the speech of their early exile grandfathers' generation (Table 4.20), perhaps
because of the covert 'masculine' prestige sometimes associated with this nonstandard variant in Caribbean Spanish. This trend was confirmed in a recent
and more extensive study comparing the speech of young middle-class Cuban
Americans who corresponded to pre-Mariel vs. post-Mariel immigration
(Lynch and Fernández Parera 2021). Among Miami-born pre-Mariel men in

Table 4.20 Realization of final /s/ among Miami Cubans according to generation
($n = 16$)

Speaker generation	[s]	[h]	[ø]
Immigrants	12% (106/888)	54% (478/888)	34% (304/888)
Miami-born	25% (391/1566)	44% (686/1566)	31% (489/1566)

$X^2 = 61.10$, df = 2, $p = .000$, Cramer's V = .158 (no cells with count less than 5)
(Lynch 2009b, 780)

198   *The Miami/Havana divide*

that study, the sibilant [s] occurred in semi-formal conversation 50% of the time, but only 20% of the time among their same-age post-Mariel counterparts in the same interview setting. Deletion, however, occurred at similar rates: 33% among young pre-Mariel men vs. 37% among post-Mariel speakers. This latter trend perhaps reflects the indexical value that deletion has in terms of masculinity. Maybe for this reason, deletion was highly disfavored among women of both groups (pre- and post-Mariel speakers), but similar to men, sibilance was extremely important as a social differentiator. Final [s] occurred 90% of the time in the semi-formal speech of Miami-born pre-Mariel women, but only 15% of the time in the speech of their post-Mariel counterparts. Among the latter, the most common variant by far (64%) was the aspirate [h], which has previously been characterized as the socially 'neutral' variant in studies of Caribbean Spanish (Lynch and Fernández Parera 2021).

The findings of both these studies (Lynch 2009b; Lynch and Fernández Parera 2021) suggest that longtime Miami Cubans, especially those corresponding to 1960s–1970s immigration, rely upon the sibilant [s] to differentiate themselves from more recent arrivals from the island, where deletion has increased in frequency over the past several decades (Alfaraz 2000). For Cuban-origin men in Miami, however, the value of the elided variant [ø] remains important, since it has historically been associated with masculinity across all varieties of Caribbean Spanish. When it comes to the speech of descendants of pre- and post-Mariel immigrants, men show similar rates of deletion, whereas women tend to disfavor deletion across the board. The variable realization of final /r/ and /s/, as described in these studies, offers convincing evidence of the sociolinguistic impact of the cultural and ideological divide between South Florida and Cuba, with variants historically characterized as nonstandard, rural, or working class becoming more generalized or acquiring a particular covert prestige in Cuba following the revolution, similar to the East/West scenario in Berlin (Dittmar, Schlobinski, and Wachs 1988).

In both the German and Cuban cases, the influence of the capitalist mode of production—and in our day the ideology of marketplace commodification—on language perception and use cannot be underestimated. Prevailing economic structures and social roles, e.g. gender and occupation, condition not only pronominal address and phonological variability, but also pragmatic-discursive patterns. As already mentioned above, Gutiérrez-Rivas (2007) observed in her study of the realization of requests among Miami Cubans that G1 men seemed particularly at ease when placed in the situation of asking a male friend to borrow money, a disposition that she attributed to the strong sense of solidarity among older, early exile immigrants. This attitude changed greatly among speakers of their sons' and grandsons' generations, however. Comparing G1 and G2 men, Gutiérrez-Rivas wrote: "Los primeros se sintieron relajados, gastaron bromas al respecto y manifestaron que entre ellos, con sus amigos cubanos, era algo fácil pedir dinero. Por otro lado,… para los últimos resultó un acto amenazador, que los hizo sentirse incómodos

The Miami/Havana divide   199

de tan sólo pensarlo. Fue esta la causa de que usaran más estrategias de tipo negativo" (2007, 176). One G2 man in Gutiérrez-Rivas' study even refused to attempt uttering the request because it caused him such discomfort (175).

The difference of attitude between G1 and G2 Miami Cuban men was especially curious when the situation of asking a male friend to borrow money was compared with another situation that Gutiérrez-Rivas posed to participants: having to ask a female neighbor for a ride to the airport because the car would not start. The author noted that masculine pride made this latter situation quite difficult for the same G1 men who had all seemed so relaxed with requesting a loan from a male friend. For G2 men, the reverse appeared to be true. Gutiérrez-Rivas explained:

> A los hombres de primera generación les pareció más amenazante pedirle el auto a una mujer que pedirle dinero a un compadre, quizá por el orgullo de no verse indefensos ante una mujer. En este caso, el género de la oyente sí representó una amenaza muy fuerte a la imagen…. A los hombres de segunda generación, les pareció más amenazante pedir dinero a un compadre o mejor amigo que pedirle a una mujer que los llevara al aeropuerto, debido quizá al gran valor que se le adjudica al dinero en una sociedad como la estadounidense.
>
> (2007, 221–22)

Gutiérrez-Rivas' interpretations are not meant to imply that older Cuban men are all sexist or that younger Cuban American men in Miami are more concerned with money or economic success than women. Rather, she observes an interesting evolution of cultural and ideological values with regard to money between G1 and G2 Cubans in the context of Miami, and of the ways in which 'face' or personal pride relates to economic success. This evolution could perhaps reflect a heightened desire among middle- and upper-class Cuban American men—who for the most part remain at the helm of banking, business, and politics in South Florida—to appear more educated or formal in their speech, and to differentiate themselves from other Miami Cubans of lower social status when speaking Spanish, which, as we saw in Chapter 1, is vital for business and commerce in South Florida. This disposition may also make men rather more inclined to prefer *usted*—as a marker of status and formality—than women, in a general sense. This should be especially true for those who are professionals with high levels of education, just as the present data confirm (Table 4.18).

Here it is worth noting that G3 men in Gutiérrez-Rivas' (2007) study used slightly more supportive moves and hedges than G3 women when asking for favors or formulating requests, particularly in situations in which the interlocutor was attributed [+power] (145). When elaborating such face-threatening requests (as defined by Brown and Levinson 1987), G3 men conveyed considerable indirectness, posing questions and providing "excessive justification" for having to ask a favor of the interlocutor (Gutiérrez-Rivas 2007, 222–23).

200   *The Miami/Havana divide*

Among G1 speakers, on the other hand, both men and women tended to be direct and resorted equally to positive politeness strategies in the same role-play situations (163–64), reflecting the same general discourse patterns that Ruzickova (2007) documented among monolinguals in Cuba. Unlike G3 speakers, G1 men and women produced roughly the same number of supportive moves (143). Gutiérrez-Rivas affirmed, however, that the similar linguistic behavior of G1 Cuban men and women was likely owed to quite different underlying motives: "Las mujeres de primera generación usaron las estrategias de cortesía positiva para marcar igualdad con el interlocutor, mientras que los hombres las usaron para mitigar el impacto a la imagen tanto del interlocutor como de sí mismo" (2007, 225). She observed that in a situation in which the speaker was asked to reprimand a work subordinate for not meeting a project deadline, G2 men used *usted* to address the interlocutor much more than women, a tendency that she explained as follows: "Mientras que las mujeres buscaban acortar la distancia con el interlocutor e identificarse con sus problemas por medio del uso del 'tú', los hombres usaban 'Ud.' para lograr el efecto contrario" (182). Following Gutiérrez-Rivas' reasoning, Miami Cuban women's efforts to "mark equality" through linguistic convention could be the cause of higher rates of *tuteo* among women in general in comparison to men. Her findings, like those of the present study, suggest that G2 and G3 Miami Cuban men appear to prefer *usted* somewhat more than women in an effort to 'save face,' especially in situations where a meaningful power differential is at play.

In the data of the present survey study, two seemingly contradictory gender-based patterns and two other seemingly contradictory class-based patterns of pronominal preference can be observed in Miami Cuban Spanish. Concerning gender, we noted that: 1) women tend to favor *tú* somewhat more than men; and 2) fathers' level of educational attainment conditions preference for *tú* more significantly than mothers' level of education. With regard to respondents' own level of education, we noted that among both men and women alike: 1) educational attainment—and the occupational and economic possibilities it brings—produces a consciousness that disfavors deferential address; yet at the same time, 2) formal education and concomitant social status foster a sense of entitlement regarding deferential address, just as Brown and Gilman suggested (1960, cited above). The claim to *usted* among professionals goes hand in hand with a greater likelihood to give deferential address to other interlocutors perceived as also having claim to it and, by corollary, not give it to those perceived as not having claim to it, as the present survey data suggest. A brief comparison of neighborhoods lends further credence to this class-based hypothesis. As Table 4.21 shows for Factor 2, people who lived in Coral Gables—the most affluent residential area of Miami included in this study—clearly preferred *tú* more than those who lived in Kendall, a solidly middle-class neighborhood, when addressing interlocutors perceived as [−age, −power]. Residents of Kendall, in turn, reflected greater *tuteo* than respondents who lived in Hialeah or in the area of Little Havana,

The Miami/Havana divide 201

Table 4.21 Factor 2 [−age, −power]: Pronominal preference according to area of residence in Miami (1 = *tú* for sure; 5 = *usted* for sure)

Neighborhood	M	SD
Coral Gables (upper and upper-middle class)	3.05	0.82
Kendall (middle class)	3.37	0.89
Hialeah (lower class)	3.61	0.87
Little Havana (lower class)	3.64	0.85

both of which reflect lower socioeconomic status. These neighborhood-based differences proved statistically significant in one-way ANOVA tests ($p = .027$). It is noteworthy that such differences emerged for this factor [−age, −power] but not for the other two factors.

The impact of class consciousness among Miami Cubans is all the more apparent in responses to four particular items included in the present survey regarding men working in restaurants, in which age and price were variables: an older waiter in a nice restaurant; an older man who works at McDonald's; a young waiter in a nice restaurant; and a young man who works at McDonald's. Given these situations, one might expect a pattern of behavior similar to that observed by Labov (1972) in his classic department store study in New York City, i.e. consciousness of higher price range conditioned use of variants associated with higher social class standing and more formal speech style. It is quite revealing that Cuban immigrants who arrived in 2000–2015 were not only significantly more likely to address an older waiter in a nice restaurant as *usted* ($p = .000$) than earlier arrivals, but also did not make a distinction between an older waiter in a nice restaurant and an older man working at McDonald's (4.97 and 4.92, respectively, Table 4.22). Both men would assuredly be addressed as *usted*. On the other hand, respondents of the other three exit groups did make a clear distinction, indicating a significantly lower likelihood of addressing the older man who works at McDonald's as *usted* (Table 4.22). Furthermore, it is remarkable that respondents corresponding to Exit Group 4 (2000–2015) were much more uniform in their certainty that an older server should be called *usted* irrespective of his workplace: the standard deviation of their mean responses to these two items (0.16 and 0.27) was extremely low in comparison to that of the other three exit groups (Table 4.22).

Perhaps more revealing still are the data for Exit Group 1 respondents only, according to generation in the US. If we limit the analysis to respondents who correspond to immigration from Cuba between 1959–1979, we observe a clear gradational pattern of age and price discrimination. As reflected below in Tables 4.23 and 4.24, an older waiter in a nice restaurant was most likely to be addressed as *usted*, followed by an older man who works at McDonald's. Still less likely to be called *usted* was a young waiter in a nice restaurant, and a young man who works at McDonald's was least likely of all to receive deferential address (Table 4.24). It is striking that G1 respondents of Exit Group 1

202   *The Miami/Havana divide*

Table 4.22 Items 4 and 15: Pronominal preference according to exit group from Cuba (1 = *tú* for sure; 5 = *usted* for sure)

Exit group	Item 4: "An older male waiter in a nice restaurant" (p = .000)		Item 15: "An older man who works at McDonald's" (p = .000)	
	M	*SD*	*M*	*SD*
1 (1959–1979)	4.43	0.77	4.00	0.94
2 (1980–1989)	4.61	0.60	4.28	0.81
3 (1990–1999)	4.66	0.55	4.31	0.93
4 (2000–2015)	4.97	0.16	4.92	0.27

Table 4.23 Items 4 and 15: Pronominal preference among Exit Group 1 respondents according to generation (1 = *tú* for sure; 5 = *usted* for sure)

Generation	Item 4: "An older male waiter in a nice restaurant" (p = .001)		Item 15: "An older man who works at McDonald's" (p = .000)	
	M	*SD*	*M*	*SD*
G1	4.80	0.41	4.65	0.49
G2	4.62	0.70	4.21	0.81
G3	4.14	0.84	3.59	0.98

Table 4.24 Items 12 and 35: Pronominal preference among Exit Group 1 respondents according to generation (1 = *tú* for sure; 5 = *usted* for sure)

Generation	Item 12: "A young male waiter in a nice restaurant" (p = .294)		Item 35: "A young man who works at McDonald's" (p = .927)	
	M	*SD*	*M*	*SD*
G1	3.63	1.01	2.85	1.23
G2	3.56	1.13	2.94	1.32
G3	3.27	0.97	2.84	1.05

were significantly more likely to address older men as *usted* than respondents of their grandchildren's generation (Table 4.23), especially since the latter would be much younger in age than their imagined interlocutors. However, this differential preference was not true when addressing young men, most obviously in the case of a young man who works at McDonald's: G1 = 2.85; G3 = 2.84 (Table 4.24).

The Miami/Havana divide   203

Table 4.25 Items 4, 15, 12 and 35: Pronominal preference among Exit Group 4 respondents (1 = *tú* for sure; 5 = *usted* for sure)

Item	M	SD
Item 4: "An older male waiter in a nice restaurant"	4.97	0.16
Item 15: "An older man who works at McDonald's"	4.92	0.27
Item 12: "A young male waiter in a nice restaurant"	4.38	0.96
Item 35: "A young man who works at McDonald's"	4.26	1.24

The pattern of apparent social class discrimination in relation to age is quite pronounced in these situations. Where older male servers were concerned (items 4 and 15), for G1 speakers there was a difference of 0.15 in the mean responses (4.80 in a nice restaurant versus 4.65 at McDonald's). This difference was nearly four times greater among G3 respondents (4.14 in a nice restaurant versus 3.59 at McDonald's). On the other hand, where younger servers were concerned (items 12 and 35), G1 respondents appeared to discriminate more in the case of a nice restaurant (3.63 in that context versus 2.85 at McDonald's) than did G3 respondents (3.27 in a nice restaurant versus 2.84 at McDonald's). The relatively high standard deviations for mean responses to these latter two items (Table 4.24) are quite meaningful, as they suggest that variability is higher in relation to younger addressees, and that older respondents appear collectively less certain about how younger interlocutors should be addressed where social class differentials intervene. All of these patterns again point to an accelerated language change favoring *tuteo* that finds it roots among early exile Cubans in Miami in address to younger interlocutors, and especially those perceived as having diminished social status or class position.

The impact of class consciousness among Exit Group 1 respondents is made all the more obvious by the data from Exit Group 4 respondents (i.e. immigrants 2000–2015), who did appear to discriminate based on age but not according to the type of restaurant. As previously noted, among Exit Group 4 participants, the mean responses for an older waiter in a nice restaurant and an older man who works at McDonald's were nearly the same: 4.97 and 4.92, respectively (Table 4.22). For a young waiter in a nice restaurant and a young man who works at McDonald's, the respective mean responses for Exit Group 4 participants were 4.38 and 4.26, reflecting once again on their part an apparent lack of discrimination based on the price range of the restaurant, as displayed in Table 4.25. Just as among Exit Group 1 respondents, standard deviations in relation to younger male addressees (items 12 and 35) for Exit Group 4 were relatively high, again reflecting greater variability at the locus of language change, as sociolinguistic theory would suggest (Labov 1972; Silva-Corvalán 1994).

As I previously affirmed, heightened preference for *tú* appears to be an aspect of the common discursive code that emerged among early exile immigrants in

204   *The Miami/Havana divide*

Miami during the 1960s and 1970s for purposes of solidarity. It is in that time and place that the already existent diachronic trend in favor of this pronoun of address was accelerated, to then be transmitted to successive generations of Cubans who were born and raised bilingually in Miami, and also adopted by successive groups of immigrants from the island. In light of the significant relationship between exit group and *tuteo* in Miami, it seems that the cultural and ideological milieu of US-style capitalism gives impetus to the expansion of *tú*, which is then transmitted to Cuban Spanish speakers who grew up in South Florida. Another factor likely contributing to this pattern is the pragmatic-discursive influence of English, whereby the lack of *T/V* distinction in that language would further serve to accelerate the inherent ongoing expansion of *tú* in Spanish. I again emphasize that all of these factors surely conspire to condition this process of language variation; no single factor or cause can be taken, in and of itself, as a satisfactory explanation for language change in the overall scheme of things (Malkiel 1967; Klee and Lynch 2009).

In Cuba, Castro's regime created its own sort of economic and social structures motivating *ustedeo*. The expediency of the services sector has had the effect of maintaining *usted* forms in Cuban society. In the only contemporary sociolinguistic study of pronominal address in Cuba of which I am aware, Bestard Revilla (2012a, 2012b, 2014) observed increasing use of *tú* forms in address to older people and strangers in public places in the city of Santiago. However, *usted* was common when addressing strangers—even those younger in age—who were hotel managers, employees of Cubana de Aviación offices, or workers in stores where products were sold in dollars (tiendas recaudadoras de divisas), based upon the perceived power differential. The author observed:

> El hablante le atribuye importancia (poder) a la ocupación del oyente a través del trato de respeto que le dispensa. El poder ha sido un elemento que ha sufrido variación en el contexto santiaguero pues se ha observado que sujetos con profesiones poco prestigiosas como choferes, porteros, dependientes, recepcionistas de hoteles han elevado su estatus socioeconómico debido a los puestos de trabajo que poseen (vinculados en su mayoría con la posibilidad del manejo y posesión de divisas) y que los ubica por encima del ciudadano común, por encima incluso de los profesionales universitarios.
>
> (Bestard Revilla 2014)

This observation is similar to that of Alfaraz (2012) regarding the significant influence of involvement in the black-market economy on phonological variation in Cuba, a sector in which traditional blue- vs. white-collar occupational distinctions apparently dissolved. In other words, economically motivated social power differentials appear to be still very much alive and well after six decades of communism in Cuba, but the settings and roles that favor *ustedeo* are rather different than in pre-Castro society or in present-day capitalistic Miami Cuban society. Additionally, as already noted in the previous section, the notion of hierarchy inherent in the communist regime continues to demand *ustedeo* (Tamarón 2005), as does the ideology of *caballerosidad proletaria* promoted by Castro, who affirmed in 1974: "Sería muy triste que con la Revolución no quedaran ni siquiera las reminiscencias de lo que en las sociedades burguesas algunos hombres hacían por razones de caballerosidad burguesa o feudal. ¡Y frente a la caballerosidad burguesa y feudal, debe existir la caballerosidad proletaria, la cortesía proletaria...!" (Castro 1974).

Conclusion

The fall of the Berlin Wall and the subsequent collapse of the Communist Bloc precipitated an unprecedented economic crisis in Cuba, which had been dependent upon Soviet aid. As the island entered its infamous Special Period of the 1990s, Cubans in Miami anticipated the demise of Castro's regime and a postnostalgic phase of Miami Cuban identity emerged, as I explained in Chapter 2. The dire circumstances on the island at the time led to the further proliferation of Cuba's underground economy as people sought the means to *resolver*, or make ends meet. Bestard Revilla (2012b) affirmed that, within that context during the 1990s, "se interrumpió bruscamente la sistematicidad habitual del cubano, ya que no era posible encontrar respuestas en la realidad presente pues el nexo se rompió en aspectos tan significativos como el traslado al centro laboral (dado el descenso total de combustible en el país), la desocupación laboral fue también un elemento de impacto que provocó la aparición de puestos laborales alternativos y de conductas indecorosas, desaparecidas desde el triunfo revolucionario de 1959" (36). At that time, the US dollar was legalized in Cuba and the Cuban convertible peso or CUC was introduced, pegged 1:1 to the value of the dollar. The island opened to tourism and foreign investment. Capitalism encroached.

In this chapter, we have considered evidence that the communist ideology of egalitarianism in Cuba over the past six decades has not accelerated *tuteo*—which appears to be in ongoing social expansion throughout the Spanish-speaking world—to the same degree as the circumstances of consumerist US society, where Spanish is in intimate contact with English, the code of global capitalism par excellence. There was a significant linear correlation between time in Miami and preference for *tú* when addressing people in positions of power (e.g. bosses and lawyers), those who work in stores and restaurants ('nice' ones as well as McDonald's), and in seeking possible favor (e.g. returning an item without the receipt, seeking a plumber's help in an emergency at 3:00 a.m., being stopped for speeding). This was true even among older, Spanish-dominant early exiles who arrived in the 1960s and 1970s. Clearly, English language knowledge and use condition greater frequency of *tú*, and the more socially restricted use of Spanish among G3

206 *The Miami/Havana divide*

speakers (beyond their friends and family) means that they do not have frequent occasion to address anyone as *usted*. But there is more at play than cross-linguistic structural influence and intergenerational language shift in the case of this particular pragmatic-discursive variable. I believe that cultural or ideological code constitutes another important factor in the reduction of *usted*, a form at odds with the solidarity dynamic of US-style capitalism and the 'fiction of a friendship' prevalent in mainstream US society (Valdés and Pino 1981). I would hypothesize that this is also likely true in other parts of the US, among Mexicans, who are generally more *ustedeístas* than Cubans, and among Colombians and Central Americans, for whom *usted* may signal intimacy, confidence, and solidarity. In this respect, Miami appears once again as an initial microcosm of a sociolinguistic change in Spanish that would later manifest across the US and beyond, concomitant with the global expansion of US-based neoliberal economic marketplace ideology. *Tuteo* is likely accelerated by postmodern consumerism and US-style mass media all across the Spanish-speaking world.

Back in a reunified Germany, a 2009 article in *The Economist* commented on the complex contemporary code of *T* and *V*, alluding to ideological dimensions of power and solidarity within consumerist culture:

> The rules are now confusing, so that instead of guarding the borders between friendship and acquaintance, *Sie* and *du* often now smuggle coded messages across them.... Bouncers at Berlin's clubs are gesiezt [addressed as *Sie*] but bartenders are geduzt [addressed as *du*]. Shoppers at upmarket KaDeWe are *Sie* but in shops packed with young Germans even those not so youthful may be called *du*.... Banks, law firms and ministries remain bastions of *Sie*, though egalitarian companies like Sweden's IKEA have converted to *du*.
>
> (*The Economist* 2009)

Recalling Blommaert's (2010) affirmation that sociolinguistic globalization is "an epiphenomenon of larger processes that are of a far more fundamental nature and have a far greater historical depth" (59), we recognize that an already inherent diachronic tendency toward *T* forms of address, and specifically *tuteo* across Latin America, is propelled by ideological forces driving a common discursive code of ostensible solidarity: "Consumption is a collective and active behavior, a constraint, a morality, and an institution." (Baudrillard 1988, 49). In the postmodern context of the globalizing culture of consumerism, it thus behooves us to consider the growing influence of Anglophone or 'Americanized' ways of speaking in varieties of Spanish around the world. I take up this matter in the next chapter, which brings into focus the social diffusion of English-based borrowings and calques among Spanish speakers in Miami.

Notes

1 Vestigial *voseo* has been previously documented in Cuba among older people in some rural areas of Granma and Camagüey (see Bjelland Aune 2019). López Morales (2018 [1971]) asserted that *vos* is not found in Cuba. Personally, I have never encountered a Cuban in Miami who used *vos* forms.

2 I note the prevalence of *usted* forms in advertising in prerevolutionary Cuba in television archives (e.g. www.youtube.com/watch?v=4teD0HdoZb4) and in examples documented by Varela (1992, 172–78).

3 Readers should bear in mind that: 1) patterns of *ustedeo* in Ciudad Juárez may have changed since the time of Valdés and Pino's (1981) study, conducted forty years ago; and 2) patterns in the north of Mexico are perhaps different than in other parts of the country.

4 Recently arrived Cubans in Miami have all emphasized to me the great importance of *ustedeo* in relation to age on the island, to convey respect. They have also affirmed that use of *usted* is nearly categorical in educational settings in Cuba (e.g. students addressing teachers).

5 This interview was conducted before Castro's death in 2016.

6 Fidel Castro and Hugo Chávez maintained a strong alliance between the two countries prior to their deaths, and the latter explicitly regarded the former as his role model.

5   The boundaries of Anglicisms

> Transparency no longer seems like the bottom of the mirror in which Western humanity reflected the world in its own image. There is opacity now at the bottom of the mirror, a whole alluvium deposited by populations… with an insistent presence that we are incapable of not experiencing.
>
> —Édouard Glissant, *Poetics of Relation* (1997)

In 2016, the Real Academia Española (RAE) and Academia de la Publicidad launched fictitious sales campaigns in Spain for two products whose television advertisements featured English prominently: one for 'Swine' perfume ("New fragrance, new woman") and another for 'Sunset Style with Blind Effect' sunglasses ("Abre tus ojos al *look fashion*"), both of which could be obtained free by ordering online. Upon receiving the products by mail, consumers learned of their true nature, which was hidden behind the use of English: 'Swine' perfume was actually "el perfume cuyo nombre en inglés te dice que huele a cerdo"; and 'Sunset Style' sunglasses were "las únicas gafas que no te dejan ver nada, oscuras como todas esas palabras en inglés" (Anglicismos 2016). The didactic parody exposing the mediatic allure of English was also subsequently revealed in follow-up television spots for each product. This national ad campaign gave preface to a public debate sponsored by the RAE, titled *¿Se habla español en la publicidad?*, in which the growing ubiquity of English was empirically noted: in 2003, fewer than 30 product brands used English in their advertisements; by 2016, that number had increased to 322 (RAE 2016). A formal study attributed this trend to the "isolation" and "autocracy of Spain" that is evoked by the exclusive use of Spanish in advertising, and the concomitant view among younger people that English—not Spanish—is the language of global import: "The already culturally legitimized tendency to associate English with the international, the global, the transnational… and even with communicative responsibility" (Santamarina 2016, 6–8).

The relationship of English to its tenable counterparts in globalization (e.g. Spanish, Mandarin, French, Portuguese, German, Arabic or Russian) has been important in the ideological reconfiguration of the postmodern order of things. Concerns regarding the Anglicization or Americanization

DOI: 10.4324/9780429438363-5

The boundaries of Anglicisms   209

of popular culture, mass media, sales and advertising, science and technology, among other domains of public and private life, have been emphatic at times. A Pew Research Center study (Gramlich and Devlin 2019) revealed that in 18 of 22 countries surveyed, from 2013 to 2018 there was a significant increase in the share of people who view American power and influence as a "major threat"; this sentiment increased by more than 25 percentage points in Spain, France, Germany, Mexico, and Brazil. The encroachment of English is viewed with trepidation. Germany's Verein Deutsche Sprache (VDS) has maintained an index of Anglicisms (Anglizismen-Index) since 1997 to counter the barrage of words and phrases from English. A spokesman noted: "German has been losing its importance for 100 years. Particularly in the areas of technology, medicine, the internet and the economy, English is becoming ever more important" (cited in Pidd 2011). Under continuous pressure from the VDS, Europe's largest industrial manufacturing conglomerate Siemens AG announced it would curb the use of Anglicisms, replacing terms like 'renewable energy' with 'erneuerbare Energie' and 'healthcare' with 'Medizintechnik' (Pidd 2011). Troubled by the increasing frequency of English loanwords in everyday French usage already by the late 1960s, President Charles de Gaulle decried *franglais*, and in 1966 the High Committee for the Defense and Expansion of the French Language (Haut Comité pour la défense et l'expansion de la langue française), predecessor of the contemporary Délégation générale à la langue française et aux langues de France, was created. From 1973 to 2004, France saw the enactment of 143 laws and decrees regarding the French language (Adamson 2007, 13). In Brazil, there was also official legislation by the end of the twentieth century to guard the Portuguese language against English-origin 'estrangeirismos' (Diniz de Figueiredo 2014). In Russia, the objective of the book *Russian Language on the Verge of a Nervous Breakdown* was to assuage what the author characterized as undue fear and panic regarding incursions of English (Krongauz 2007). And in China, migratory, media, and commercial flows now increasingly place Putonghua, the variant of common Mandarin legitimized during Mao's revolution, in an uncomfortable vis-à-vis not only with English but also with the nation's other dialects and minoritized languages commonly spoken as heritage languages in the Anglophone diasporic public sphere—a situation poignantly portrayed in the award-winning film *The Farewell* (2019).

Perhaps nowhere is the intimacy between English and another global or so-called exoteric language felt more than in the US, where Spanish speakers number more than 50 million. Although English clearly prevails in political and cross-generational terms, as we have seen in previous chapters, the importance of Spanish in retail, commerce, and mass media is undeniable. These vital sectors of US public life—made all the more vital by postmodern consumerism—constitute quasi-institutional spaces in which Spanish increasingly manifests as an object through the lens of language commodification, which leads to heightened perceptions and sensitivities regarding language correctness

210   *The boundaries of Anglicisms*

and pleasantness (Preston 2013) as well as authenticity and anonymity (Woolard 2008). This is especially the case in Miami. A 2011 front-page article in the *Miami Herald* noted: "In South Florida, where Spanish is a vital language in home life, business, culture and politics, one might expect a good report card when it comes to the quality of the Spanish being spoken. But the reality... is quite different" (Santiago 2011, H1). The author noted that the US is now the second most populous Spanish-speaking country in the world after Mexico, but with the widespread use of Spanish in public life and mass media, "the opportunities to mangle it are spreading like a virus"—an ill that she attributed to Anglicisms: "People will tell you they're *facebuqueando* (facebooking) and *tuiteando* (tweeting), words that don't exist in Spanish" (Santiago 2011, 21A). The story reported on the local visit of Gerardo Piña-Rosales, then director of the Academia Norteamericana de la Lengua Española, to promote his book *Hablando bien se entiende la gente* (Piña-Rosales et al. 2010), aimed at bringing awareness to the common problem of Anglicisms in US varieties of Spanish (cf. Lynch and Potowski 2014).[1] Piña-Rosales affirmed: "Our children are abandoning their mother tongue when they learn English. We want them to learn English, but we don't want them to abandon Spanish.... To be monolingual in an era of globalization is suicidal" (Santiago 2011, 21A).

This story reflected various facets of a recurrent topic in US mass media over the past three decades regarding the influence of English on Spanish: Anglicisms are a bad thing; their use not only leads to the deterioration of Spanish—like a "virus"—but ultimately to "abandonment" of the language in successive generations; conscious and careful speakers of Spanish must be vigilant of cross-linguistic phenomena (highlighted in a section titled "Many offenders"). Perhaps the most striking feature of the story was the unqualified affirmation that words such as *facebuquear* and *tuitear* "do not exist." The following year in Madrid, José Manuel Blecua, then director of the RAE, announced that 'tuitear' and its related variants 'tuit, tuiteo, tuitero' would appear in the 23rd edition of the *Diccionario de la Real Academia Española* (2014), officially recognizing "una actividad que ejercen millones de personas, a título particular o como representantes de instituciones." Blecua pointed out: "Es nuestro propio caso, el de la RAE, que tiene su propio canal en Twitter" (González 2012). On the occasion of the announcement, Blecua asserted: "La lengua pertenece a quienes la hablan.... Nos preguntan con frecuencia a los académicos si esta proliferación de textos, unida a sus códigos y estilos particulares, estropea o deteriora la lengua.... Solemos contestar que no, o, al menos, que no necesariamente" (González 2012). Blecua's affirmation stood in seeming contradiction to what Piña-Rosales had asserted only months before in Miami, and in contrast with the general tone of *Hablando bien se entiende la gente* (Piña-Rosales et al. 2010). The example of 'tuitear'—one of many Anglicisms that have attained official status in the RAE in recent years—prompts various questions: What is implicated in bringing a word into 'existence'? How does a bilingual speaker in the US know which Anglicisms are 'acceptable,' short of consulting the

The boundaries of Anglicisms 211

official dictionary of the RAE on an ongoing basis? Do words really belong to speakers, as Blecua affirmed? Do words belong to particular languages, or to some languages more than others?

The answers to such questions are of a more ideological than linguistic nature. They are perceptual. In his proposal for *A Framework for Cognitive Sociolinguistics*, Moreno Fernández (2017) posited that "speakers' perceptions and awareness directly and indirectly impact their attitudes and linguistic behaviors" (192); and that "the perception of variation and of linguistic varieties responds to a process of categorization based on discriminatory learning" (194). He explained that the perceived correctness or relative prestige of a particular variant may be attributed either to conservatism, i.e. historical continuity, or to innovation (193). 'Tuitear' is an example of the latter. As a structurally integrated loanword from the English-origin 'tweet,' 'tuitear' seemingly blurs the boundary between Spanish and English, as do integrated loanwords in all the world's languages—unless they go unperceived as such, either diachronically or synchronically (Thomason 2001). The more than 4,000 Arabic-origin words in contemporary Spanish, which date from the time of Al-Andalus, are a good example (Klee and Lynch 2009). Words such as 'almohada,' 'zanahoria,' and 'algodón' have been used for so many centuries that they are no longer perceived as extraneous or nonnormative, by any account. Synchronically, speakers may not attribute loaned or calqued forms to other languages because they have not somehow learned to identify them as such, or because such forms simply go unnoticed due to a high degree of parallelism or similarity between the two languages, a structural phenomenon that facilitates contact-induced language change (Thomason and Kaufman 1988; Silva-Corvalán 1994).

The bigger issue is perhaps related to perceptual saliency, and the consideration of whether what is indeed noticeable ends up in everyday usage and within the range of social acceptability. More than two decades of observation and personal inquiry in Miami have led me to a conclusion similar to that of Iglesias Illa (2010): "La convivencia del inglés y el español es un tema apasionante para quienes escribimos sobre Miami, pero con el tiempo me fui dando cuenta de que no lo es tanto para los miamenses, quienes ven la superposición de idiomas como algo tan normal y práctico que ni siquiera vale la pena prestarle demasiada importancia" (194). As I have affirmed in previous chapters, both languages are highly commonplace in practically all sectors and settings across the city; bilingualism is the social norm, to such extent that, beyond educational settings, my expressions of curiosity about bilingual practices have oftentimes been met with puzzlement. In light of the ubiquity of bilingualism in Miami, one wonders how perceptible the structural boundaries of Spanish and English are, and how acceptable incursions across those boundaries might be, understanding boundary not as something that separates one thing from another, but rather "as something that constitutes that which is bounded" (Cilliers 2016, 90). I believe that this enabling—rather than confining—role played by the perceptual 'boundary'

212 *The boundaries of Anglicisms*

is important to our understanding of the postmodern situation of Spanish in the US.

Various sorts of sociolinguistic boundaries in Spanish-speaking Miami come to mind. We might hypothesize that Anglicisms in Spanish are more characteristic of the discourse of second- and third-generation speakers in the US, especially among those with lower levels of Spanish language ability. We might additionally speculate that lower socioeconomic status and lower levels of formal education are more highly correlated with use and acceptability of Anglicisms, reflecting the popular conviction that middle- and upper-class speakers are more conscientious about language use. Additionally, we might suppose that the dynamic bilingual context of Miami serves to amplify an already widespread tendency to use Anglicisms among the city's majority of speakers from the Caribbean, where the influence of English has been historically extensive. As we will see in this chapter, based upon the results of a lexical survey and personal interviews, such intuitive hypotheses do not align easily with sociolinguistic reality in some regards. The matter is rather more complex. The effects of variables such as linguistic ability in Spanish and English, socioeconomic status, and formal education level depend upon the sort of so-called Anglicism in question. I will demonstrate in the following pages that loanwords are of a quite different sociolinguistic nature than calques; the former are more 'obvious' in their structural relationship to English, while the latter are less so—and in some cases, much less so. Such would be the difference in bilingual Spanish between the loanword 'laptop' and the calque 'introducir' (in reference to making someone's acquaintance for the first time). Furthermore, we will see that different sorts of calques manifest in quite different ways, i.e. one-word calques such as 'introducir' often take on decidedly different sociolinguistic profiles than syntactic calques such as 'Te llamo *pa(ra) atrás*' [I'll call you back] or '*¿Cómo* te gustó la película?' [How did you like the movie?].

To complicate things further, I will suggest that awareness, use, and acceptability are rather different matters as well. To state that any form—whether a loanword or a calque—is "characteristic" of Spanish in Miami, we might pose three related questions: To what extent are speakers aware of a particular form's use by others? Are they aware of using the form themselves when speaking? Do they regard the form as acceptable or 'correct,' whether or not they use it? We can think of these three variables—awareness, use, and acceptability—as different dimensions of the broader phenomenon of social diffusion, as I will explain in the first part of this chapter. In the second part, I place the analysis in theoretical perspective, arguing that ideological transparency and opacity, as proposed by Édouard Glissant (1997), drive the social diffusion of Anglicisms in Spanish-speaking Miami, in accordance with structural similarities with English.

As preface to the chapter, a caveat of sorts might be in order. One might not expect to find an analysis of cross-structural influence in a book about the

The boundaries of Anglicisms 213

postmodern circumstance of Spanish. Poststructuralism is not synonymous with postmodernity, however (Carter 2013). One could carry out poststructuralist analyses of language in any time period, i.e. from a historical perspective (Warren 2003), and many linguists still conduct structuralist research in contexts that are arguably postmodern. I have not intended to pose a poststructuralist argument about language in this book, nor do I engage with translanguaging (which one could consider poststructuralist) in this chapter because my analysis is explicitly concerned with the perception of particular linguistic variants on social and ideological grounds. Otheguy, García, and Reid (2015) clarify that the concept of translanguaging, which eschews 'named languages,' applies to considerations of mental grammars as evident in idiolectal repertoires (293). In my understanding, their argument principally seeks to expose the inequities that are created and perpetuated in institutional—and in particular, educational—spheres in which strict adherence to monolithic constructs of language obscures the complexity and richness of multilingual repertoires, thus jeopardizing individual success as gauged through formal instruction and assessment (cf. Bourdieu 1991). They affirm that sociolinguistic inquiries that make use of named languages are "perfectly acceptable so long as we remain aware that the named language categories have been ultimately constructed throughout history for social purposes that bear a well-known and well-documented connection to the imposition of political power" (Otheguy, García, and Reid 2015, 298). The latter was unequivocally Glissant's (1997) central concern.

As I will suggest in Chapter 6, from a sociolinguistic perspective, the reification and concomitant perception of languages as bounded entities have become all the more relevant—not to say ideologically pressing—within the postmodern framework of language commodification and the culture of consumerism. The great popularity of language learning apps like Duolingo, Babbel, or Rosetta Stone offers good evidence that people view languages as consumable goods, or objects for metaphorical purchase. Undoubtedly, people continue to think about language constructs as "something perfectly real, an extracognitive reality, external to the individual, Platonic, yet authentic" according to popular language theory (Moreno Fernández 2017, 195). In this regard, I agree with Varra (2018) that linguists cannot dispense with questions such as which word 'belongs' to which language "since speakers themselves orient to them in constructing the semiotic value of their linguistic behaviors... [and] understand their linguistic behavior in such terms" (7–8). Because the notion of 'possessing' a language is not static but dynamic, and since speaker orientations and attitudes toward the concept of 'my language' vary across the lifespan, perceptual studies are of the essence in language contact settings (Kabatek 2011). Our scrutiny of the evolution of boundaries in postmodernity must emphasize the social contours of language contact, which are characterized by the dynamic interplay and overlay of cross-linguistic differences and similarities, as we will see in this chapter.

214 *The boundaries of Anglicisms*

The social diffusion of Anglicisms

Upon the release of the 23rd edition of the *Diccionario de la Real Academia Española* in 2014, Darío Villanueva, who would be named director of the RAE later that same year, affirmed that decisions regarding the inclusion of new words in what is undoubtedly the foremost authority on the Spanish lexicon "nunca son caprichosas, sino objetivas" (Villarreal 2014). He explained that, every year, the RAE's Instituto de Lexicografía and the digital Corpus del Español del Siglo XXI capture some 25 million word uses in various text types—literature, journalism, science, politics, economics—published throughout the Spanish-speaking world (70% outside Spain). This "acopio de información," according to Villanueva, provides the basis for discussions about changes to the dictionary. He also pointed out that words of foreign origin, 'extranjerismos,' are generally subject to a five-year 'quarantine' to ensure that their use does not reflect a passing fad. Regarding what some characterize as an 'avalancha de anglicismos' in contemporary Spanish, the RAE's would-be director asserted that in the new millennium "se han ido incorporando palabras procedentes del inglés que tienen mucha presencia. El inglés ganó la Segunda Guerra Mundial y sustituyó a otras lenguas de referencia como el alemán en la ciencia o el francés en la diplomacia" (Villarreal 2014). This has been especially true in the postmodern advent of communication technologies and pervasive mass media flows. Villanueva clarified, however, that the RAE does not proceed with amendments made to the *Diccionario* in a purely mechanistic fashion "porque entonces no sería necesaria la academia.... En la última valoración que se hace por parte de la academia intervienen factores de contextualización cultural o pragmática: es la parte más creativa de nuestro trabajo" (Villarreal 2014). The RAE's director thus seemed to suggest that there are two—perhaps equally important—facets of bringing Anglicisms into official existence: the empirical lexicographic one, which is textually based, and the cultural institutional one, which he referred to as the "creative" aspect.

Beyond institutional confines or the textual world of mass media, there is the matter of language on the ground. With this phrase, I do not allude necessarily to language as it is used in everyday interaction, in the anthropological sense, but rather to language as it is perceived and ideologically constructed by nonspecialists in sociolinguistic terms. By the time a lexical item arrives at the doorstep of the RAE for consideration, it must already reflect a considerable degree of social diffusion. In his classic sociological proposal *Diffusion of Innovations*, Everett Rogers (2003 [1962]) defined the process simply as one "in which an innovation is communicated through certain channels over time among the members of a social system" (5). For Rogers, the adoptability of an innovation (e.g. a novel idea, practice, concept, object, technological device) depends upon five basic characteristics: 1) relative advantage, i.e. the extent to which individuals perceive an innovation as beneficial; 2) compatibility, i.e. the degree to which they perceive an innovation as consistent with

The boundaries of Anglicisms 215

past experiences and present values and practices; 3) complexity, i.e. how difficult they perceive the innovation to be in terms of understanding and use; 4) trialability, i.e. whether they have opportunity to experiment with or 'try out' an innovation before committing to it; and 5) observability, i.e. the degree to which they 'see' or notice an innovation (15–16).[2]

Rogers (2003) observed the importance of 'clusters' in the social diffusion of innovations, defined as distinguishable elements that are perceived as closely interrelated, e.g. the household practice of recycling paper in conjunction with recycling cans and bottles (14). In this respect, he emphasized the interdependence of innovations in a social system: individuals' experiences with one innovation condition their perception of the next related one (15). We will see this principle reflected in the diffusion of various types of calques, all of which appear interrelated in the varieties of Spanish spoken in Miami. We will also see that loanwords are, in many respects, a perceptually distinct phenomenon than calques, which follow rather different sociolinguistic trajectories than loanwords as a result of time and of communication channels. In defining the role of communication channels, Rogers (2003) emphasized the importance of 'heterophily,' or the degree of difference between two individuals with regard to particular attributes. Although communication is most effective and efficient among individuals who are 'homophilous,' i.e. those who "share common meanings and a mutual subcultural language, and are alike in personal and social characteristics" (19), diffusion of innovation is actually the product of 'heterophilous' interactions: "When two individuals are identical regarding their technical grasp of an innovation, diffusion cannot occur as there is no new information to exchange. The nature of diffusion demands that at least some degree of heterophily be present between the two participants in the communication process" (2003, 19).

For our present purposes, heterophily resides in the differences not only between Spanish and English, but also between varieties of Spanish. As I pointed out in Chapter 3, generalized Spanish-English bilingualism in Miami ideologically conditions the perception of varieties (regional or national) and variants (lexical, phonological, etc.) of Spanish through fractal recursivity (Irvine and Gal 2000). Diverse varieties of Spanish are contested and reworked through the fractal projection of the differentiation of Spanish and English. This ideological process conditions the perception and evaluation of particular variants or forms within and across Spanish varieties themselves. I explain this phenomenon in theoretical terms in the second part of this chapter, after describing the present study and its results. As we will see, variety of Spanish proved to be a significant variable in the diffusion of Anglicisms in Miami in two regards: supradialectal (principally Caribbean vis-à-vis others) and generational (principally first-generation adult immigrants vis-à-vis others). Generational varieties of Spanish in Miami—as in the rest of the US—reflect a complex array of sociolinguistic phenomena. First and foremost, they reflect the shift to English-language dominance through bilingual repertoires. These repertoires are principally a manifestation of time in

216 *The boundaries of Anglicisms*

the US—not age of the speaker, as in traditional sociolinguistic studies of variation and change in monolingual settings (Labov 1972). In other words, there are first-generation monolingual and bilingual speakers of Spanish of all ages in Miami. Among second- and third-generation speakers of all ages, however, all are English-dominant bilinguals. Due to the hegemonic status of English in formal education and peer socialization, which I described in Chapter 3, third-generation speakers typically have perceivably lower levels of communicative proficiency in Spanish than those of the second generation (Silva-Corvalán 1994; Lynch 2013; Escobar and Potowski 2015; Montrul 2016; among many others).

The 'innovation-decision' process, according to Rogers (2003), is a function of time. Stages of the process are: 1) becoming aware and gaining an understanding of an innovation; 2) forming an attitude toward it, which he characterized as 'persuasion'; 3) having sufficient exposure to or engagement with an innovation to be able to make a choice about adopting or rejecting it; 4) in the former case, 'implementing' it, i.e. putting it into practice or use; and 5) seeking 'confirmation,' during which time the choice to implement an innovation is reinforced by others (20). In the confirmation stage, individuals may fully adopt the innovation or discontinue its use, either because it is eventually perceived as unsatisfactory or gradually replaced by another innovation (21). The survey study presented in this section sought to capture three stages of social diffusion of English-based lexical innovations in diverse varieties of Spanish spoken in Miami: *awareness* (roughly corresponding to the first and third stages proposed by Rogers), *use* (reflecting stage 4, or 'implementation'), and *acceptability* (encompassing aspects of stages 2 and 5). Because language use is a matter of ongoing speaker reflexivity (Caravedo 2014; Moreno Fernández 2017), attitudinal or evaluative phenomena (stage 2) are inherently bound up with 'confirmation' (stage 5) regarding what is socially (un)acceptable or institutionally (in)correct. For the present purposes, I regard all three dimensions of social diffusion (awareness, use, acceptability) as perceptual phenomena. Each reflects a particular dimension of what is termed 'perception' in a broader sociolinguistic sense, given the methodological orientation of the study, which I now describe.

The study and its participants

The analysis presented in this chapter is based on the findings of a bilingual survey that initially sought to replicate a study conducted by Otheguy and García in Miami in 1983 (Otheguy and García 1988), with a few modifications.[3] The first section of the written survey ascertained information about respondents' social background: age, gender, country of origin, birthplace and age of immigration, parents' birthplace and age of immigration (in order to determine generation in the US), years of residence in Miami, current area of residence (for purposes of gauging spatial and socioeconomic

The boundaries of Anglicisms 217

variables), level of formal education attained by respondents as well as by their mother and father respectively, ability to speak and understand Spanish and English respectively, and extent of use of both languages with family members, friends, people 'on the street,' and in television, movie, and music choices. There was also a question regarding the importance of being able to speak Spanish in the context of the US. Participants responded to language use questions via a Likert scale that ranged from 1 ('Spanish almost always') to 5 ('English almost always'), as in Example 5.1.

Example 5.1

¿Con qué frecuencia habla Ud. las dos lenguas (español e inglés) **con gente 'en la calle'**? / How much do you speak Spanish and English **with people 'on the street'**?

1	2	3	4	5
Español casi siempre / Spanish almost always	Principalmente español / Mostly Spanish	Las dos lenguas igualmente	Principalmente inglés / Mostly English	Inglés casi siempre / English almost always

A similar scale was provided for items concerning self-reported abilities in Spanish and English, ranging from 'little ability' at one extreme to 'excellent ability' at the other, as in Example 5.2.

Example 5.2

¿Cómo describiría las habilidades que Ud. tiene para **hablar español**? / How would you describe your own ability to **speak Spanish**?

1	2	3	4	5
Poca habilidad / Little ability	Alguna habilidad / Some ability	Buena habilidad / Good ability	Muy buena habilidad / Very good ability	Excelente habilidad / Excellent ability

In the second part of the questionnaire, participants were presented a series of 43 sentences written in Spanish. As in Otheguy and García's (1988) original questionnaire, each sentence contained a bolded and underlined word or phrase to which participants must respond 'yes' or 'no' for each of the following three questions aimed at interpreting the degree of diffusion in local speech: 1) "¿Ha oído Ud. la frase o palabra subrayada?" [Have you heard the underlined phrase or word?]; 2) "¿Usa Ud. esta frase o palabra al hablar?" [Do you use this phrase or word when speaking?]; 3) "¿Considera correcto su

218   *The boundaries of Anglicisms*

uso al hablar?" [Do you consider its use correct when speaking?]. Example 5.3 illustrates the format of each item as it was posed to respondents.

Example 5.3

Oración	¿Ha oído Ud. la frase o palabra subrayada?		¿Usa Ud. esta frase o palabra al hablar?		¿Considera correcto su uso al hablar?	
Puedes llevar ropa **casual** para la fiesta el sábado.	Sí	No	Sí	No	Sí	No

Of the 40 lexical items appearing on Otheguy and García's (1988) survey, 32 were retained in their original form. Eleven new items were added to reflect the contemporary usage of Anglicisms in relation to technology (e.g. 'laptop,' 'chatear,' 'ATM') and to investigate the diffusion of several now common loanwords (e.g. 'mall') and calques (e.g. 'ropa casual,' 'llamar para atrás'). The selection of retained items and new items was made with the goal of maintaining Otheguy and García's (1988) distinction between loanwords, phonologically merged word calques (which I will henceforth refer to as *phonological calques*), phonologically independent word calques (which I will simply call *semantic calques* if only to avoid potential confusion with the former category on the reader's part), and phrasal calques (which I will term *syntactic calques*).[4] I define each of these categories and display the items that pertained to them in the following respective sections. Ten distractor items, all of which reflected normative monolingual Spanish usage, also appeared in the second part of the questionnaire.

Responses of 385 individuals comprised the data set. A snowball convenience sample was used, originating with adult members of my own family and social networks, and then extending to their adult social networks and beyond, to all areas of the city. The respondents came from all proverbial walks of life and represent highly diverse origins, different socioeconomic backgrounds and occupations in Miami, levels of formal education, and areas of residence. I should note that none of the respondents of the *tú/usted* study presented in the previous chapter responded to the present lexical survey; a completely different sample population constitutes the data analyzed in this chapter.

As in the case of the *tú/usted* survey, there was a preponderance of women among the respondents: 63% identified as women ($n = 244$) and 37% as men ($n = 140$); one respondent did not indicate their gender. In order to ensure that the relationship of speakers' gender identity to the linguistic phenomena under scrutiny was not confounded by the effects of formal education, an even distribution of respondents was sought in terms of those two independent variables. Education levels were classified as follows: 1) primary schooling;

The boundaries of Anglicisms   219

Table 5.1 Distribution of respondents according to gender and level of formal education (*n* = 384)

Gender	Level of formal education			
	Low (≤2)	*Mid (3)*	*High (≥4)*	*Total*
Women	22 within 'ed level' = 61%	121 within 'ed level' = 64%	101 within 'ed level' = 64%	244
Men	14 within 'ed level' = 39%	68 within 'ed level' = 36%	58 within 'ed level' = 36%	140
Total	36 (9%)	189 (49%)	159 (41%)	384 (100%)

Note: One respondent did not indicate gender.

2) secondary/high school education; 3) some postsecondary/college studies; 4) college degree or *licenciatura*; 5) graduate or professional studies. The same proportion of respondents (41%) from both groups had high levels of formal education (i.e. 101/244 women and 58/140 men had at least an undergraduate degree), and half of women and men equally had completed some postsecondary studies; only one in ten respondents of either gender indicated having only primary or secondary schooling (Table 5.1). I note that the American Community Survey estimated in 2014 that only 17% of Miami's Hispanic population held an undergraduate degree or higher (vs. 41% in our study); the same data indicated that 14% of the population had not graduated high school (Pew Research Center 2016). In this regard, the present sample is overeducated vis-à-vis Miami's sociodemographic reality.

Respondents ranged from 18 to 92 years of age, with the following group distribution: 18–25 years old = 47% of the sample (*n* = 181); 26–39 years old = 18% (*n* = 68); 40–59 years old = 22% (*n* = 85); 60+ years old = 13% (*n* = 51). There was a preponderance of young adults (again, as in the case of the *tú/usted* survey data) due to the need to include second- and third-generation speakers of diverse backgrounds. Most third-generation adult speakers in Miami are under age 30, because of the relative recency of immigration flows: Cubans began to arrive in the 1960s, but substantial immigration from Nicaragua and Colombia did not begin until the early 1980s; other important contingents such as Venezuelans, Puerto Ricans, Dominicans, Peruvians, and Argentines have mostly arrived in the past two to three decades. At any rate, linear regression analysis revealed that age was not a significant variable, yet generation in the US indeed was. In this respect, the given distribution of age groups seemed justified in the interest of scrutinizing the effects of language contact. Table 5.2 reflects the distribution of immigrant generations according to age group. As to be expected, there were few third-generation bilingual respondents in the 40–59 age group (*n* = 5)—by virtue of their being

Table 5.2 Distribution of respondents according to age and immigrant generation (*N* = 385)

Age	Immigrant generation in the US				
	G1 *(age 17+ upon arrival)*	*G1.5* *(age 11–16 upon arrival)*	*G2* *(age < 11 upon arrival or US-born)*	*G3* *(US-born)*	*Total*
18–25 years	30 within 'gen' = 22%	24 within 'gen' = 44%	90 within 'gen' = 64%	37 within 'gen' = 71%	181 (47%)
26–39 years	31 within 'gen' = 23%	10 within 'gen' = 18%	17 within 'gen' = 12%	10 within 'gen' = 19%	68 (18%)
40–59 years	47 within 'gen' = 34%	7 within 'gen' = 13%	26 within 'gen' = 18%	5 within 'gen' = 10%	85 (22%)
60+ years	29 within 'gen' = 21%	14 within 'gen' = 25%	8 within 'gen' = 6%	0 within 'gen' = 0%	51 (13%)
Total	137 (36%)	55 (14%)	141 (37%)	52 (13%)	385 (100%)

The boundaries of Anglicisms 221

hard to find—and none 60+, as this segment of the population does not exist in Miami, in sociological terms.

There is an important north/south divide in Miami, with the Atlantic Ocean to the immediate east and the Everglades farther to the west. As I pointed out in Chapter 3, areas to the north and northwest of downtown (including Hialeah, henceforth referred to as NW) can be characterized as lower to lower-middle socioeconomic class, while the south and southwest (including Kendall, henceforth referred to as SW) reflect generally middle and upper-middle class areas. Coral Gables, an independent city located a few miles to the southwest of downtown, is one of the most affluent areas of Miami-Dade County. For this reason, it was analyzed separately. Areas around downtown Miami, including the historic bastion of Cuban exile popularly referred to as Calle Ocho, as well as other neighborhoods located roughly within the central area that divides north and south (e.g. West Miami, Flagler, the Miami International Airport area), were categorized as 'Center' for the present purposes. Homes found in these zip codes are largely Spanish-speaking, and mostly lower to lower-middle in terms of socioeconomic status. The city of Miami proper, a geographically small area that includes only downtown and its immediate vicinity, is greatly mixed in terms of socioeconomic status, with high-rise luxury apartment buildings located only blocks away from the city's most impoverished neighborhoods. It bears repeating that, unlike in other major urban areas of the US (e.g. Los Angeles, Chicago or Houston), home Spanish use is no less prevalent in most middle- and upper-income neighborhoods than in most lower-income areas (Carter and Lynch 2015). Table 5.3 displays the distribution of respondents according to these four general areas of the city (NW, Center, SW, Coral Gables). As Table 5.3 reflects, a careful attempt was made to include respondents from each of these four areas who had differential degrees of ability in English (a composite measure of abilities to understand and speak the language) in roughly equal proportions, since English-based innovations could perhaps be differentially distributed in geographic space and according to socioeconomic status.

According to 2014 American Community Survey data, which gauges only speaking ability along a 4-point scale, some 44% of Miami's Hispanic population overall was estimated to speak English 'very well,' while another 40% was estimated to speak it 'less than very well' (Pew Research Center 2016). In the present study, a slight majority (58%) reported having 'excellent' ability to speak English (5 on the present Likert scale; not to be confused with the composite English language ability data in Table 5.3), a percentage that reflects the large number of second- and third-generation bilinguals in our sample, all of whom were English-dominant. Another 24% of the present sample indicated having less than 'very good' ability to speak English (<4.0 on the given Likert scale). In this respect, our sample reflects stronger oral ability in English than the city's general Hispanic population (according to American Community Survey estimates), but this difference seems justified in light of our interest in the effects of language contact.

Table 5.3 Distribution of respondents according to area of residence and English language ability (composite) (*n* = 382)

Area of residence in Miami	English language ability			
	Less than 'Good' *(<2.5)*	*'Good'* *(2.5–3.9)*	*'Very good' to 'Excellent'* *(4–5)*	*Total*
NW	17 within 'ability' = 31%	28 within 'ability' = 24%	46 within 'ability' = 22%	91 (24%)
Center	11 within 'ability' = 20%	29 within 'ability' = 24%	47 within 'ability' = 23%	87 (23%)
SW	16 within 'ability' = 30%	35 within 'ability' = 29%	67 within 'ability' = 32%	118 (31%)
Coral Gables	10 within 'ability' = 19%	27 within 'ability' = 23%	49 within 'ability' = 23%	86 (22%)
Total	54 (14%)	119 (31%)	209 (55%)	382 (100%)

Note: Three respondents did not answer the questions regarding English language ability.

The boundaries of Anglicisms   223

Correlations between responses to items regarding abilities in English and Spanish revealed that active bilingualism was pervasive among the sample population. While there were strong positive correlations between abilities to understand and speak Spanish and English respectively (.69 for Spanish and .90 for English), abilities to understand or speak one language were not negatively correlated with either of those abilities in the other language. In other words, strong abilities to understand and speak English did not appear to jeopardize those abilities in Spanish. The negative correlation between self-reported ability to understand English and Spanish respectively was −.03; the negative correlation between ability to speak English and Spanish respectively was −.20. This is a clear indication that, among the great majority sampled in this study, use of both languages was the norm, as we also observed among high school students in Chapter 3.

Given Miami's preponderance of Spanish speakers from the Caribbean, and in light of Mallet and Pinto-Coelho's (2018) observation that an important social division exists in Miami between Latino immigrants from the Caribbean and those from Continental Latin America, a separate variable was created to gauge potential distinctions (i.e. Caribbean- vs. non-Caribbean-origin speakers).[5] The former group included speakers who had migrated—or whose families had migrated—to Miami from Cuba, Puerto Rico, or the Dominican Republic. Although the Caribbean is a highly diverse, and in some ways fragmented, geographic region that is far from being a sociocultural monolith (Benítez-Rojo 1996), the varieties of Spanish spoken there bear important perceptual commonalities (cf. Ortiz López and Martínez Pedraza 2020, 264). I would emphasize that the intimate and complicated political, cultural, and economic relationship of these Caribbean nations to the US since the early twentieth century (as described in Chapter 1) has brought a more profound and pervasive influence of English in those respective varieties of Spanish than in others throughout Latin America (for Cuba, see Sánchez Fajardo 2017; for Puerto Rico, see González-Rivera and Ortiz López 2018; for Dominican Republic, see Alba 2004). In the interest of exploring this possible influence on Caribbean Spanish vis-à-vis other varieties of Spanish spoken in Miami, I sought fairly equal proportions of speakers from the two major groups (Caribbean vs. non-Caribbean) in terms of English language use. The same proportion of speakers (44%) from both groups indicated using principally English (as a composite of the five questionnaire items regarding language use). Only about one in five respondents indicated using principally Spanish in both groups.

As Table 5.4 reflects, Caribbean-origin speakers constituted 56% ($n = 215$) of the present sample population, a percentage that is fairly representative of Miami-Dade's demographic reality: 52% Cuban, 5% Puerto Rican, and 4% Dominican, according to American Community Survey (2019) Hispanic population estimates. Non-Caribbean speakers comprised the remaining 44% ($n = 170$) of the present sample population, including respondents from throughout Latin America, roughly in proportion to Miami-Dade's present

224 *The boundaries of Anglicisms*

Table 5.4 Distribution of respondents according to (non-)Caribbean origin and composite language use (*N* = 385)

Origin	Language use (composite)			
	Principally Spanish (*<2.5*)	Both languages equally (*2.5–3.5*)	Principally English (*>3.5*)	Total
Caribbean	47 within 'use' = 62%	74 within 'use' = 52%	94 within 'use' = 56%	215 (56%)
Non-Caribbean	29 within 'use' = 38%	67 within 'use' = 48%	74 within 'use' = 44%	170 (44%)
Total	76 (20%)	141 (37%)	168 (43%)	385 (100%)

Hispanic demographic reality: Colombians, Nicaraguans, and Venezuelans each comprised around 10% of the present sample population, and the remaining 15% included Peruvians, Argentines, Mexicans, Ecuadorians, Chileans, Bolivians, Paraguayans, Uruguayans, and speakers from every country of Central America except Belize. Eight respondents indicated that their families were from Spain. Speakers of mixed origins (e.g. Dominican-Peruvian, Cuban-Colombian, etc.) were excluded from the present analysis.

All of the quantitative survey data for the social and linguistic variables were entered into SPSS (Statistical Program for the Social Sciences) for statistical analysis. For the binary questions on the dependent variables (awareness, use, acceptability) for each lexical item, 'yes' was assigned a value of 1 and 'no' was assigned a value of 0. Before calculating composite scores for each item, the internal consistency of each was tested via Cronbach's alpha. All exceeded acceptable reliability thresholds ($\alpha > .70$). Consequently, composite scores were calculated as the mean of all items within each linguistic category of interest (loanwords, phonological calques, semantic calques, syntactic calques). To determine sociolinguistic variables significantly related to the awareness, use, and acceptability of each category, linear multiple regression was conducted on each. Generation, gender, area of residence, Spanish ability (composite), English ability (composite), language use (composite), origin (Caribbean vs. non-Caribbean), level of education, parents' level of education (composite), and perceived importance of being able to speak Spanish in the US were included as predictors. Linear models as well as individual predictors were evaluated for statistical significance at a conventional alpha level ($\alpha = .05$). Predictor collinearity was evaluated for each model and did not reach concerning thresholds (e.g. VIF > 5). Significant categorical predictors were examined via estimated marginal means, as is typical in analysis of variance (ANOVA). Lastly, theoretically justifiable interactions between predictors were probed: statistically significant interactions were maintained while nonsignificant interactions were removed to maintain model parsimony. From a qualitative perspective, about 50 participants responded to the written survey in a casual interview format, commenting on particular items aloud. Several other respondents afforded me the opportunity to ask them specific questions regarding their responses after they had completed the survey. Their comments and observations provided insights into why particular items elicited particular reactions and responses. Some of these are mentioned below.

In the following four sections, I present results separately for each of the four types of linguistic variables under analysis: loanwords, phonological calques, semantic calques, and syntactic calques. I do not discuss the distractor items; as expected, they reflected by far the highest rates of awareness, use, and acceptability (.92, .76, and .74, respectively). In the second part of this chapter, I highlight particular items of the survey in the interest of theoretical discussion. I wish to remind readers that, in everything that follows, the terms 'awareness,' 'use,' and 'acceptability' refer to perceptual activity. My objective in this study was not to observe and document actual language *production*, i.e. the occurrence of Anglicisms in 'real speech' or authentic texts. Rather, I sought an understanding of the *perception* of Anglicisms in Miami, taking into account numerous sociolinguistic variables. In this regard, the use of Otheguy and García's (1988) survey format allows us to garner the perspectives of a greater number of people regarding a wider array of linguistic variants. In both studies, speakers were asked to reflect on their awareness, use, and acceptance of specific variants, written on the page, posed to them as a questionnaire from someone interested in ways of speaking Spanish in Miami. Thus, I do not make any claims about the extent to which respondents may or may not use any of the variants in actual spoken interactions with people. Rather, my observations and arguments are based upon how they indicated perceiving a series of variants, within a broader concept of social diffusion of so-called Anglicisms among Miami's highly diverse Spanish-speaking majority. We turn now to the findings.

Loanwords

Otheguy and García (1988) defined *loanword* as a linguistic sign that "is imported whole from a source language [English], with greater or lesser phonological adaptation to the recipient language [Spanish]" (212–13). The following ten survey items were regarded as such:

* Necesito hacer un ***part-time*** para ganar dinero.
* Ese ***vacuum cleaner*** hace muchísimo ruido.
* ¿Tienes un ***quarter*** que me prestes?
* Tengo que ir al ***dealer*** a reparar el automóvil.
* Mi hijo estudió ***Real Estate***.
* La tienda se encuentra en el ***mall*** más grande de Miami.

226 *The boundaries of Anglicisms*

Table 5.5 Results for the social diffusion of loanwords [0 = 'no'; 1 = 'yes'] ($N = 385$)

	Awareness Have you heard it?	**Use** Do you use it?	**Acceptability** Do you consider it correct?	*Diffusion index*
M	.90	.63	.28	.60
Significant variables $p < .05$	origin	origin	generation gender parents' education neighborhood value of Spanish	

- Mi **laptop** fue más caro que el de mi hermano.
- Pusieron los **previews** de esa película.
- Los jóvenes pasan muchas horas **chateando** en Internet.
- Pasamos por el banco para sacar dinero del **ATM**.

Table 5.5 displays the mean response, according to a 0 ['no'] to 1 ['yes'] interval, for each of the three perceptual dimensions (awareness, use, acceptability) of this cluster of items. The social variables that were significantly correlated ($p < .05$) with each perceptual dimension in the linear regression analysis also appear. The final column of Table 5.5 displays a composite diffusion variable, calculated by taking the mean of all of the responses for the dependent variables (awareness, use, acceptability). While Otheguy and García (1988) derived their diffusion index from the average of percentages of 'yes' answers on the dependent variables (218), the present diffusion index was based upon the mean of responses on all three dependent variables. In mathematical terms, the same principle was followed in both studies, i.e. the diffusion index reflects an 'average of percentages' (Otheguy and García 1988) or a 'mean of means' (the present inquiry).

Bearing in mind that for the questions regarding awareness, use, and acceptability, a 'no' response was assigned a value of 0 and 'yes' a value of 1, we can affirm that our sample population was highly aware of loanwords (mean response of .90) and considered them mostly unacceptable (.28). They indicated using them frequently (.63), i.e. respondents mostly used them yet overwhelmingly deemed them incorrect.

For **awareness of loanwords**, the linear regression model was significant ($F(14, 361) = 1.77$, $p = .042$, $R^2 = .06$), with origin emerging as the only significant social variable ($p = .004$): Caribbean-origin speakers indicated hearing loanwords more than speakers of other varieties of Spanish (mean response of .92 for the former and .88 for the latter). Given Puerto Rico's history of intense contact with English for more than a century, it seems unsurprising that Puerto Rican respondents indicated the highest degree of awareness of loanwords (.93), followed by Cubans (.92), who have been in Miami the

The boundaries of Anglicisms 227

longest. The lowest degrees of awareness—still high nonetheless—were observed among Colombians (.86) and Central Americans (.85).

A similar pattern emerged in the regression analysis for **use of loanwords** ($F(14, 361) = 1.81$, $p = .035$, $R^2 = .07$): origin was the only significant social variable ($p = .000$). Caribbean-origin speakers indicated using loanwords more than speakers of other varieties of Spanish (mean responses of .68 and .57, respectively). Puerto Ricans indicated using loanwords the most (mean response of .70), followed by Cubans (.68); the lowest reported rates of use were among Colombians (.52) and Central Americans (.54).

Acceptability of loanwords was significantly correlated with speakers' generation in the US ($p = .050$) and their gender identity ($p = .008$) in the regression analysis ($F(14, 362) = 5.62$, $p = .000$, $R^2 = .18$). First-generation (henceforth G1) respondents were significantly more likely to deem loanwords correct (mean of .39) than second- or third-generation (henceforth G2 and G3) speakers, who yielded mean responses of .23 and .24, respectively. Speakers who immigrated to Miami during adolescence, i.e. the so-called '1.5' generation (henceforth G1.5), manifested by far the lowest degree of acceptability of loanwords (.17). These findings might come as a surprise to those who would assume that G1 speakers, by virtue of being the most Spanish-dominant group, would be the most emphatic about the unacceptability of English-origin words in an otherwise fully Spanish sentence. As I will explain in the second part of this chapter, however, this result is actually expected in terms of language contact theory and it corroborates the findings of other previous research on Spanish in the US, including Otheguy and García's (1988) study. The findings regarding gender were also predictable based upon previous sociolinguistic research: women were significantly more emphatic about the unacceptability of loanwords than men (.23 versus .36, respectively). Parents' education was also significantly correlated ($p = .018$): respondents whose parents had higher levels of education were more likely to accept loanwords. A parallel finding, linked to the notion of socioeconomic status, was that neighborhood emerged as a significant predictor in this case ($p = .037$), with higher degrees of acceptability of loanwords among respondents who lived in Coral Gables—the most affluent area of the city included in the survey. I will take up the matter of social status and loanwords in the second part of this chapter. A fifth and final variable that proved significant ($p = .000$) was participants' response to the following question: "¿Qué opinión tiene Ud. respecto a la importancia de poder hablar español en Estados Unidos? / What is your opinion regarding the importance of being able to speak Spanish in the United States?" Respondents who indicated that the ability to speak Spanish was 'very important' were significantly more likely to deem loanwords incorrect than those who were less emphatic about its importance. Among those who indicated 5 on the given Likert scale ['very important'], the mean response regarding loanword acceptability was .22; among those who indicated 4 ['important'], the mean response was .38. I would note that, of all 385 respondents, only ten attributed 'little' or 'no' importance to the ability

228   *The boundaries of Anglicisms*

to speak Spanish [values of '2' and '1' on the given scale, respectively], again suggestive of the explicitly positive attitudes toward Spanish among Miami's Latinx majority population (Chapter 3).

Phonological calques

In the case of phonological calques, Otheguy and García (1988) explained that use of a Spanish single-word item is modeled on the use of an English item that has a similar pronunciation: "The signal of the English model has merged with that of the Spanish word into which one of its senses has migrated" (214). The following eight survey items reflected this phenomenon:

- En la fiesta te voy a *introducir* a una señora muy agradable. [calqued on Eng. 'introduce'; Sp. 'presentar']
- El martes me *registré* en la universidad. [Eng. 'registered'; Sp. 'matriculé' or 'inscribí']
- Puso la *alarma* para despertarse a las 7:00. [Eng. 'alarm'; Sp. 'despertador']
- Puedes llevar ropa *casual* para la fiesta el sábado. [Eng. 'casual'; Sp. 'informal']
- El profesor les pidió que escribieran un *papel*. [Eng. 'paper'; Sp. 'ensayo']
- No quiero *envolverme* en los problemas de ella. [Eng. 'get involved'; Sp. 'involucrarme']
- Llené una *aplicación* para un trabajo en California. [Eng. 'application'; Sp. 'solicitud']
- Hay que llenar una *forma* para abrir la cuenta. [Eng. 'form'; Sp. 'formulario']

Table 5.6 displays the mean responses for awareness, use, and acceptability of this cluster of items and the social variables that were significantly correlated ($p < .05$) with each one in the linear regression analysis. The final column displays the composite social diffusion index, calculated by taking the mean of all responses for the dependent variables (awareness, use, acceptability).

Table 5.6 Results for the social diffusion of phonological calques [0 = 'no'; 1 = 'yes'] ($N = 385$)

	Awareness *Have you heard it?*	Use *Do you use it?*	Acceptability *Do you consider it correct?*	*Diffusion index*
M	.89	.63	.53	.68
Significant variables $p < .05$	origin gender English ability	generation education	generation gender education English ability	

The boundaries of Anglicisms 229

Based on these results, we can affirm that our sample population was highly aware of phonological calques (mean response of .89) and reported using them to the same extent as loanwords (.63). It is noteworthy that they deemed phonological calques far more acceptable than loanwords, however (.53 for the former versus .28 for the latter, Table 5.5).

Awareness of phonological calques was significantly correlated with origin ($p = .023$), gender ($p = .008$), and English language ability ($p = .045$) in the regression analysis ($F(14, 361) = 2.48$, $p = .002$, $R^2 = .09$). As in the case of loanwords, Caribbean-origin speakers indicated hearing phonological calques more than speakers of other varieties of Spanish (mean response of .91 for the former and .88 for the latter). Again, Puerto Rican respondents indicated the highest degree of awareness of phonological calques (.91), but in this tendency they were joined by Colombian-origin speakers (.91), closely followed by Cubans (.90) and Venezuelans (.89). The mean response for speakers of all other South American varieties was .84; among Central Americans it was .88. Women indicated being significantly more aware of phonological calques than men (.91 versus .86), a tendency that would again be expected in general sociolinguistic principle. Also perhaps predictably, higher levels of English language ability were significantly correlated with greater awareness of phonological calques, owing to the principle of similitude that I will explore in the second part of this chapter. Respondents who indicated having 'very good' or 'excellent' abilities in English presented a mean of .91; the mean response of those with only 'some' or 'little' ability in English was .80.

Use of phonological calques was significantly conditioned by immigrant generation ($p = .001$) and respondents' level of education ($p = .022$) in the regression analysis ($F(14, 361) = 3.43$, $p = .000$, $R^2 = .12$). There was a clear divide between G1 and G1.5 speakers on one hand, and G2 and G3 speakers on the other. For the former two, mean responses were .53 and .56, respectively; for the latter two, mean responses were .71 and .74, respectively. Thus, there appear to be two significantly distinct generational groups in Miami with respect to use of phonological calques. Formal education exerted a significant influence for everyone: higher levels of education conditioned lower rates of use. This is a compelling finding in light of the fact that although G1 speakers were schooled in Spanish in their respective countries of origin, and G1.5 speakers completed at least primary school in Spanish, formal education for G2 and G3 speakers was in English. This means that irrespective of language dominance or the language of education, schooling apparently made respondents more reluctant to use phonological calques when speaking Spanish (at least in terms of self-perception). The pattern was clear: G1.5 speakers with professional or graduate-level studies were the least likely of all to indicate using phonological calques (mean response of .44), a rate that was even lower than their highly educated G1 counterparts (.51), probably because of G1.5's characteristically more 'balanced' bilingualism; at the other extreme, G3 speakers with only high school education were the most likely of all to indicate using phonological calques (mean response of .79).

230 *The boundaries of Anglicisms*

Table 5.7 Acceptability of phonological calques [0 = 'no'; 1 = 'yes'] among G2 and G3 speakers according to formal education level ($n = 193$)

Formal education level	Acceptability of phonological calques (M)
High school diploma	.63
Some college studies	.63
College or university degree	.56
Graduate or professional studies	.45
Overall *M*	.59

For **acceptability of phonological calques**, generation ($p = .001$) and respondents' level of education ($p = .003$) had the same significant effect in the regression model ($F(14, 362) = 4.18$, $p = .000$, $R^2 = .14$). Generally, G1 and G1.5 speakers eschewed phonological calques significantly more than G2 and G3 speakers. Education had an important effect, however. G1.5 speakers with professional or graduate-level studies were the least likely of all to deem phonological calques correct (mean response of .21), a rate that was much lower than their highly educated G1 counterparts (.52). The effect of formal education on perceived correctness was particularly striking among G2 and G3 speakers, in that the most highly educated among them manifested rates of acceptability that were even lower than those of highly educated G1 speakers: mean response of .45 for both G2 and G3 speakers versus .52 for G1 speakers. Table 5.7 displays the linear relationship between formal education and perceived correctness of phonological calques among G2 and G3 speakers.

I reiterate the compelling nature of this finding since all G2 and G3 respondents were English-dominant and the majority had only taken high school Spanish language courses; some had never studied Spanish formally.

English language ability exerted a clear influence on the acceptability of phonological calques. Among G1 speakers, all of whom were Spanish-dominant, there was a significantly greater tendency to accept phonological calques among those with lower levels of English ability than among those with higher levels of ability ($p = .043$). As in the case of awareness (described above), this pattern can be attributed to greater familiarity with the forms and structures of English, which enables recognition of similarities between the two languages. That recognition in turn heightens subjectivity or sensibility regarding the imperative of difference or separation. Finally, a significant difference emerged with respect to gender ($p = .009$): women were less likely to deem phonological calques correct than men (.50 versus .58, respectively), a pattern that paralleled the differential awareness of these same forms (noted above). We will now observe a rather different pattern in the cases of semantic and syntactic calques. The perception of these types of calques appears to be conditioned more by familiarity with Spanish—rather than familiarity with English.

The boundaries of Anglicisms 231

Semantic calques

Semantic calques reflect the same process of extension of meaning as phonological calques but without the surface similarity of form, i.e. "the connection between [the two forms] is being established only on semantic grounds," independent of phonological parallelism (Otheguy and García, 1988, 214–15). The following seven survey items comprised this category:

- *Corrió* para gobernador en las últimas elecciones, pero no ganó. [Eng. 'ran'; Sp. 'se postuló']
- El maestro les *dio un examen* muy difícil. [Eng. 'gave them an exam'; Sp. 'les puso un examen']
- Los trenes no están *corriendo*. [Eng. 'running'; Sp. 'funcionando' o 'circulando']
- Antes de *darle el piso* a mi colega, el Senador Rodríguez, quisiera decirles otra cosa. [Eng. 'give the floor'; Sp. 'darle la palabra']
- Quiero que *camines al niño* hasta la escuela. [Eng. 'walk the child'; Sp. 'acompañes al niño']
- Esta máquina no está *trabajando* en este momento. [Eng. 'working'; Sp. 'funcionando']
- Los niños *hacen mejor* en las escuelas privadas. [Eng. 'do better'; Sp. 'salen mejor' or '(A los niños) les va mejor']

Table 5.8 displays the mean responses for awareness, use, and acceptability of this cluster of items and the social variables that were significantly correlated ($p < .05$) with each one in the linear regression analysis. The final column displays the composite social diffusion index.

As with loanwords and phonological calques, respondents appeared highly aware of semantic calques (mean response of .81) but reported using them less than the former two (.53). Although they regarded semantic calques as much more correct than loanwords (.46 versus .28, respectively), they did not consider them as acceptable as phonological calques overall (.53 for the latter).

Table 5.8 Results for the social diffusion of semantic calques [0 = 'no'; 1 = 'yes'] (*N* = 385)

	Awareness *Have you heard it?*	Use *Do you use it?*	Acceptability *Do you consider it correct?*	*Diffusion index*
M	.81	.53	.46	.60
Significant variables *p* < .05	parents' education	generation parents' education	generation gender education Spanish ability	

232 The boundaries of Anglicisms

Table 5.9 Awareness, use, and acceptability of semantic calques [0 = 'no'; 1 = 'yes'] according to generation in the US ($N = 385$)

Generation	Awareness *Have you heard it?*	Use *Do you use it?*	Acceptability *Do you consider it correct?*
G1	.74	.39	.39
G1.5	.87	.45	.39
G2	.85	.62	.50
G3	.84	.71	.63

For **awareness of semantic calques**, parents' level of education was the only significant predictor ($p = .000$) that emerged in the regression analysis ($F(14, 361) = 3.32$, $p = .000$, $R^2 = .11$). The pattern of the effect is rather thought-provoking: respondents whose parents had lower levels of education reported hearing semantic calques significantly more than those whose parents had high levels of education (.84 versus .78, respectively). This tendency was most notable among G1.5, G2, and G3 speakers, whose mean responses (combined) were .92 among respondents with less educated parents versus .81 among those whose parents had college degrees or graduate/professional studies. Although generation did not emerge as significant in the regression model ($p = .065$), there were noteworthy cross-generational differences, displayed in Table 5.9. G1 speakers appeared less aware of semantic calques (mean response of .74) than did successive generations in Miami (G1.5 = .87; G2 = .85; G3 = .84). This finding aligns with the general tendency we have observed thus far.

For **use of semantic calques**, immigrant generation ($p = .000$) and parents' level of education ($p = .004$) emerged once again as the only two significant predictors in the regression analysis ($F(14, 360) = 6.23$, $p = .000$, $R^2 = .20$). The clear linear relationship between generation and extent of reported use of semantic calques (Table 5.9) once again suggested a seeming divide between G1 and G1.5 speakers on one hand (mean responses of .39 and .45, respectively), and G2 and G3 speakers on the other hand (mean responses of .62 and .71, respectively). As with awareness, respondents whose parents had lower levels of education reported using semantic calques significantly more than those whose parents had high levels of education (.55 versus .48, respectively). Again, the tendency was most notable among G1.5, G2, and G3 speakers, whose mean responses (combined) were .68 among respondents with less educated parents versus .53 among those whose parents had college degrees or graduate/professional studies. I will entertain a hypothesis regarding the effect of parents' education on awareness and use of semantic calques in the second part of this chapter.

For **acceptability of semantic calques**, the regression analysis yielded a significant model ($F(14, 362) = 4.19$, $p = .000$, $R^2 = .14$) with the following

The boundaries of Anglicisms 233

four predictors: generation (p = .000), gender (p = .044), respondents' level of education (p = .043), and Spanish language ability (p = .021). There was a clear linear relationship between generation and acceptability of semantic calques: the lowest rate of acceptability was among G1 and G1.5 speakers (both .39), and the highest rate was among G3 speakers (.63), as displayed in Table 5.9. The effect of gender was the same as in the cases we have already seen thus far: women were significantly more likely to deem semantic calques incorrect than men (mean responses of .44 and .51, respectively). In terms of the effects of formal education, acceptability of semantic calques appeared to depend much more on the respondents' own level rather than that of their parents, as we just observed for awareness and use. Higher levels of education were correlated with lower rates of acceptability of semantic calques, as in the case of phonological calques. The reader will recall that, in the case of loanwords, it was parents' level of education that significantly conditioned acceptability, in an apparently inverse fashion: respondents whose parents had higher levels of education were more likely to accept loanwords than those whose parents had lower levels of education. Although this might seem a contradiction to what we have just observed regarding the effect of parents' education on the awareness and use of semantic calques (i.e. more educa-tion among parents correlates with less awareness and use on the part of respondents), this finding is actually expected given the quite different nature of loanwords versus calques. I will explain the difference in the theoretical discussion that follows. The fourth significant predictor also reveals much about what makes semantic calques different than loanwords or phonological calques, to wit: their perceived correctness depends on Spanish language ability, rather than English language ability.

Here, two fundamental distinctions begin to become more evident: 1) loanwords and phonological calques (which bear obvious surface similarities between Spanish and English) are different in nature than semantic calques and syntactic calques (neither of which bear any surface similarities between the two languages); 2) G1 speakers' perceptions are different than those of successive generations of Spanish speakers in Miami, in that variability is conditioned more by English ability among the former and more by Spanish ability among the latter. As we will now see, the findings for syntactic calques provide further evidence of this broad sociolinguistic pattern.

Syntactic calques

Syntactic calques, which Otheguy and García (1988) termed 'phrasal calques,' resemble the previous two types of calques "in that elements that belong to the borrowing language [Spanish] in their own right are being used in the manner of the lending language [English]," but in this case, there is no readily detectable modification of the Spanish forms (215). Syntactic calques convey an English-speaking sort of message without altering Spanish language form or meaning at all, i.e. this sort of calquing "leaves the linguistic system

234 *The boundaries of Anglicisms*

untouched" according to Otheguy and García (1988, 216). The following eight survey items were classified as such:

- Pregúntale si **sabe cómo hacerlo**. [calqued on Eng. 'knows how to do it'; Sp. 'sabe hacerlo']
- Su presencia **hará la diferencia**. [Eng. 'will make the difference'; Sp. 'será importante']
- Ella **está supuesta a llegar** hoy a las 5:00 de la tarde. [Eng. 'is supposed to arrive'; Sp. 'debe llegar']
- Se le olvidó **tomar asistencia** en la clase. [Eng. 'take attendance'; Sp. 'pasar lista']
- **Déjame saber** si puedes ayudarme mañana. [Eng. 'let me know'; Sp. 'dime' or 'avísame']
- **¿Cómo te gustó la película** que vimos anoche? [Eng. 'how did you like the movie?'; Sp. '¿te gustó la película?']
- Si le dejas un mensaje, seguro que te **llama para atrás**. [Eng. 'call you back'; Sp. 'te vuelve a llamar' or 'te devuelve la llamada']
- Con todos los problemas que tengo, **lo último que necesito** es un dolor de garganta. [Eng. 'the last thing I need'; Sp. 'lo único que me faltaba']

Table 5.10 displays the mean responses for awareness, use, and acceptability of this cluster of items and the social variables that were significantly correlated ($p < .05$) with each one in the linear regression analysis. The final column displays the composite social diffusion index.

Overall, syntactic calques reflected higher rates of acceptability (.55) than semantic calques (.46) and were reportedly used somewhat more (.58 versus .53, respectively). For this reason, they had a higher rate of social diffusion than semantic calques (.65 versus .60, respectively) but lower than phonological calques (.68, Table 5.6).

Awareness of syntactic calques was significantly predicted by parents' level of education ($p = .022$) in the regression analysis ($F(14, 361) = 2.15$, $p = .009$, $R^2 = .08$), just as in the case of awareness of semantic calques. Respondents

Table 5.10 Results for the social diffusion of syntactic calques [0 = 'no'; 1 = 'yes'] ($N = 385$)

	Awareness *Have you heard it?*	**Use** *Do you use it?*	**Acceptability** *Do you consider it correct?*	*Diffusion* *index*
M	.82	.58	.55	.65
Significant variables $p < .05$	origin parents' education	origin generation parents' education	generation English ability Spanish ability	

whose parents had lower levels of education reported hearing syntactic calques significantly more than those whose parents had high levels of education (.84 versus .80, respectively). This tendency was most notable among G1.5, G2, and G3 speakers, whose mean responses (combined) were .87 among respondents with less educated parents versus .82 among those whose parents had college degrees or graduate/professional studies. Origin ($p = .035$) also had a significant effect on awareness of syntactic calques: Caribbean-origin speakers reported hearing them significantly more than speakers of other varieties (.84 versus .80, respectively). This finding paralleled that for awareness of loanwords, i.e. Puerto Ricans reported hearing syntactic calques the most (.85), followed by Cubans (.84); Colombians and speakers of other South American varieties (excluding Venezuela) indicated hearing them least (.78 and .76, respectively).

For **use of syntactic calques**, origin was again a significant predictor ($p = .008$) in the regression analysis ($F(14, 361) = 5.05$, $p = .000$, $R^2 = .16$). As in the case of awareness, Caribbean-origin speakers reported using syntactic calques significantly more than speakers of other varieties (.62 versus .53, respectively), with the highest mean response among Puerto Ricans (.64), followed by Cubans (.61); the lowest rates were again reported by Colombians (.50) and speakers of other South American varieties (.46), excluding Venezuela (.56). Also, parents' level of education once again emerged as a significant predictor ($p = .050$), with respondents whose parents had lower levels of education indicating that they used syntactic calques more than those whose parents had high levels of education (.61 versus .54, respectively). Speaker generation was a third significant predictor of use. As in the cases of both phonological and semantic calques, there was a linear relationship between generation and use of syntactic calques: the rates were lowest among G1 and G1.5 speakers (both .50) and highest among G3 speakers (.68).

For **acceptability of syntactic calques**, generation reappeared as a significant predictor ($p = .000$) in the regression analysis ($F(14, 362) = 6.13$, $p = .000$, $R^2 = .19$). There again appeared to be two significantly distinct Spanish-speaking groups in Miami with respect to acceptability of syntactic calques, as in the cases of phonological and semantic calques: G1 and G1.5 speakers on one hand (mean responses of .49 and .44, respectively), and G2 and G3 speakers on the other (mean responses of .61 and .68, respectively). The significant effects of English ability ($p = .030$) and Spanish ability ($p = .045$) were dependent upon generation. Since all G1 speakers were Spanish-dominant, for them English ability conditioned the perceived correctness of syntactic calques: those with limited ability to speak and understand English deemed syntactic calques correct significantly more than those with strong English ability (.60 versus .45, respectively). Conversely, because all G2 and G3 speakers indicated having excellent ability in English, for them Spanish ability conditioned the perceived correctness of syntactic calques: those with less than 'excellent' abilities in Spanish (<4.5 on the given Likert scale) deemed syntactic calques correct significantly more than those with 'excellent' Spanish ability

236 *The boundaries of Anglicisms*

(.65 versus .61, respectively). These findings suggest that greater familiarity with the structures of both languages inhibits the acceptability of syntactic calques. Ratings provided by G1.5 speakers, the majority of whom indicated having 'excellent' abilities in both languages, provide further support for this suggestion. Of all four generational groups, they manifested the lowest mean response not only for acceptability of syntactic calques (.44) but for the other three types of Anglicisms as well. This finding contributes to the theoretical argument that I will make in what follows, regarding the perception of language boundaries along lines of ideological transparency and opacity.

Ideological transparency and opacity in the perception of language boundaries

In the study of language contact situations, there is consensus that lexicon is borrowed before structure, understanding borrowing as "the incorporation of foreign features into a group's native language by speakers of that language" (Thomason and Kaufman 1988, 37). Structural or grammatical borrowing never occurs without lexical borrowing and is observed only in situations of intensive language contact, in which there is widespread bilingualism over an extensive period (Thomason and Kaufman 1988, 47–48). Overall, the situation of Spanish in the US lends itself to lexical borrowing but not structural borrowing because the latter criterion (persistence of bilingualism over several generations) is not met, i.e. by the fourth generation in the US, would-be bilinguals are Anglophone monolinguals in their majority.

For this reason, Otheguy (2003) affirmed: "El que no haya una variedad reconocible que pudiera llamarse *Spanglish* no debe… regocijar en exceso a los que amamos el español, pues la causa primordial de la ausencia de un *Spanglish* la constituye, no sin un punto de triste ironía…, la casi desaparición del español en la tercera generación" (17). Otheguy reasoned that, despite extensive lexical borrowing in the varieties of Spanish spoken in New York City (NYC), structural borrowing does not occur because bilingualism is not sustained long enough: "Los hablantes que empiezan a dejar entrever en su español rasgos mixtos… no han llegado nunca a formar comunidad ni a cuajar en un habla estable…. Esos hablantes en cuyas hablas hay áreas de interpenetración estructural casi siempre usan poco el idioma ellos mismos y son, en todo caso, la última generación del español en EE.UU. Los hijos de estas personas ya no hablarán español, ni mezclado ni sin mezclar" (2003, 17). Following Otheguy's argument, then, one could conclude that the concerns expressed in *Hablando bien se entiende la gente* (Piña-Rosales et al. 2010) are unsubstantiated in terms of potential hybridization of Spanish in contact with English. From a structural perspective, the bilingual varieties of Spanish spoken in the US do not bear the traces of any sort of creolization, nor do the varieties of lower-proficiency heritage speakers. As McWhorter (2020) argued, heritage language phenomena are fundamentally different than processes of linguistic creolization.[6]

The boundaries of Anglicisms   237

Within the context of the Francophone Caribbean, where creole varieties have indeed flourished historically, Glissant (1997) formulated his widely cited argument regarding the 'right to opacity.' The Martinican writer, cultural critic, and philosopher characterized the flawed fate of French in the post-colonial era as being tied to the ideology of transparency, noting "its literary dedication to clarity, a mission that has led to its reputation for a pleasing rationality, which is, in fact, the guarantee of a legitimate pleasure to be had in the manipulation of a unity composed of consecutive, noncontradictory, concise statements" (Glissant 1997, 113). A fundamental aspect of this dedi-cation—or mission—he affirmed, is conciseness and correctness in language learning and use—notions that, in his opinion, belie the relational poetics of languages in contact (hence the title of his book) and ultimately prove detri-mental to the linguistic nuance and aesthetic quality of more 'opaque' varieties of French spoken throughout multilingual Francophonie (115). Opacity, for Glissant, is the metaphorical "alluvium deposited by populations, silt that is fertile but, in actual fact, indistinct and unexplored even today" (1997, 111). In opacity, we sense the traces, influences, incursions, and crossings of other languages, varieties, and voices.

Glissant (1997) argued that the ideological imposition of transparency has become anachronistic in the contemporary era: "Languages combine, vary, clash so rapidly that the lengthy training of earlier times is no longer worth much" (101); "The share of opacity allotted to each language, whether vehicular or vernacular, dominating or dominated, is vastly increased by this new multiplicity [of languages]" (119). Although his proposals were mainly directed to the situation of the Francophone Caribbean, Glissant decried the expansion of other exoteric vehicular languages, including the 'Anglo-American sabir' code of postcolonial imperialism, to which I will return later. He also explicitly mentioned the situation of Spanish in the US:

> Normative decrees have ceased to be the authoritative rule as far as vehicular languages are concerned. English and Spanish, the most massive of these, and seemingly the best entrenched in a sort of continental nature, met on the territory of the United States (Puerto Ricans, Chicanos, the immigrants in Florida). It may well be that their massiveness has become fissured, that alongside the variances proliferating Anglo-American, lucky contaminations from Spanish will occur, and vice-versa. This pro-cess will no doubt move more quickly than any analysis one will be able to make of it.
>
> (Glissant 1997, 98–99)

Given the findings of our present inquiry, we could agree with Glissant regarding the celerity of the proliferation of variances of English and Spanish in South Florida. However, the directionality of what he characterized as "lucky contaminations" is overwhelmingly from English into Spanish, though some Spanish-origin calques can be observed in Miami English, e.g.

238 *The boundaries of Anglicisms*

'get down from the car' [Sp. bajarse del carro]; 'throw a photo' [Sp. tirar una foto]; 'put the light' [Sp. poner la luz] (Mullen 2015). Although the language contact situation of the US in no way reflects linguistic creolization—nor do I think Glissant was supposing such in the passage of his text cited above—his proposals regarding ideological transparency and opacity can be fruitfully exploited in a sociolinguistic interpretation of the perceived boundaries of Anglicisms in Miami, where active bilingualism is socially widespread.

I urge readers to bear in mind that Glissant (1997) was not using the terms 'transparency' and 'opacity' in the cognitive linguistic sense of form-meaning mapping, prevalent in semantic theory (see Field 2002, 89–94), but rather in the language ideological sense of correctness and variability in sociopolitical context: "The only merit to correctness of language lies in what this language says in the world: even correctness is variable" (101). The variability of correctness—in the differential degrees of ideological transparency and opacity conceptualized as a sort of spectrum—is here our main theoretical concern. Of course, form-meaning mapping is inherent in the phenomena of structural similarity of interest to us, but our main focus is the social and ideological lens through which language forms are perceived—not the cognitive linguistic mechanisms by which meanings attach to them. Forms that are semantically transparent in terms of linguistic structure could be ideologically opaque in terms of sociopolitical context; forms that are semantically opaque could be ideologically transparent. Indeed, for any linguistic contact variant, both ideological tendencies are typically reflected at the same time, similar to the 'centripetal' and 'centrifugal' forces described by Bakhtin: "Every concrete utterance of a speaking subject serves as a point where centrifugal as well as centripetal forces are brought to bear" (2000 [1934], 271).

Ideologically speaking, correctness characterizes '*the* language' (Glissant 1997, 119, italics in the original), a sociopolitical construct, atavistic in nature, made explicit in formal learning, decrees, and dictates that "attempt to form a dam against what makes languages fragile" and thus keep it 'transparent' (101). Social status stems from the position that one takes regarding the meaning of correctness, i.e. correctness "has repercussions not just on the idea that one has of the language but on the idea one forms of its relationship with other languages" (1997, 115). I wish to emphasize this latter concern (i.e. one's idea about the language's relationship with other languages), as it is central to the argument that I pursue in the remainder of this chapter.

Loanwords appear the most obvious site in this respect. Because they are structurally quite conspicuous, the idea one has about the relationship of Spanish with English (in our case) can be readily mapped onto them. For that reason, they easily accrue social indexical value. Stated another way, because they stand out so much, loanwords get a lot of attention in terms of the ideas people have about the sociopolitical relationships between languages. Although their actual frequency is rare within the typical discourse flow of Spanish speakers in the US (Silva-Corvalán 1994; Otheguy 2003; Moreno Fernández 2007; Varra 2018; among others), loanwords are the object of

The boundaries of Anglicisms 239

most societal or political discussions about language contact. Sánchez's (1994) historically rooted interpretation of the semiotic value of loanwords in the US Southwest reflects the contradictory tendencies of transparency and opacity: "The presence of loans in Chicano Spanish... is contradictorily both a sign of acculturation and a sign of resistance, for it is the subjugation of the English language to Spanish grammar as much as it is the penetration of American culture into Chicano Spanish" (127). In this respect, loanwords are obvious incursions (within an ideology of transparency) that may take on highly symbolic value (within a claim to the 'right to opacity' in Glissant's terms). In the present study, the perceived acceptability of loanwords was significantly tied to variables of social status.

Calques, on the other hand, are structurally less conspicuous, and thus not as readily implicated in the representation of social status or the contestation of signs, i.e. of acculturation or resistance in Sánchez's 1994 terms. The perceived acceptability of calques in the present study depended significantly more upon language ability than upon variables of social status. This was especially the case of syntactic calques, for which both English ability and Spanish ability emerged as significant predictors of acceptability in the regression analysis (Table 5.10). Syntactic calques are by far the most structurally ensconced manifestation of cross-linguistic influence (Otheguy 2011). Curiously, in reference to the Francophone Caribbean context, Glissant remarked that "faults of syntax are... less decisive than faults of relation (though they may be symptoms among others of the latter)" (1997, 101). This also appears to be true of Spanish in Miami: although syntactic calques are—like loanwords and other types of calques—symptomatic of 'faults of relation' between Spanish and English, they are ideologically less consequential because they generally go unnoticed by those who do not have high degrees of ability in both languages. In this respect, quite different than loanwords, syntactic calques perhaps deserve more attention than they actually get in the overall ideological scheme of things.

Formal education appeared to condition language perception in the present study in two distinct ways, which are certainly not unrelated. In the statistical regression analyses reported in the previous sections (Tables 5.5–5.10), the effects of formal education proved significant on two different social fronts—respondents' own education level and that of their parents—and were experienced differently according to the perceptual dimension in question—awareness and use on one hand versus acceptability on the other. Parents' education was positively correlated with acceptability of loanwords but had no effect on awareness or use. For semantic and syntactic calques, on the other hand, parents' education was negatively correlated with both awareness and use, but had no effect on acceptability. Respondents' own education level had no significant effect on any of the perceptual dimensions of loanwords, but it did prove significantly influential in the perceived correctness of phonological and semantic calques. Two distinct though related facets of education thus become evident: social status on one hand, and metalinguistic

240 *The boundaries of Anglicisms*

consciousness on the other. As I will suggest in what follows, parents' formal education seemed principally tied to social status, while respondents' own formal education appeared to condition the metalinguistic consciousness. Respondents then placed this consciousness at the service of discerning structural boundaries within the latticework of language similitude, in adherence to an ideology of transparency in their evaluations of correctness and irrespective of language dominance. The effects of respondents' formal education indeed proved statistically true whether the dominant language was Spanish (in the case of G1 speakers) or English (in the case of G2 and G3 speakers). Simply stated, heightened consciousness of form—fostered by the institutional construct of education in either language—prompted greater vigilance of linguistic boundaries. In the case of loanwords, which are easily discernible regardless of one's bilingual ability, the perception of correctness appeared to depend less upon metalinguistic consciousness (which is conditioned by respondents' own education level) and more upon social status (of which parents' education level appears to be an influential aspect). I take up each of these matters in the following two sections.

Social status and linguistic (in)security

Let us recall that all four types of Anglicisms defined for purposes of the present study had relatively high rates of social diffusion among Spanish speakers in Miami (between .60 and .68). The great majority of speakers reported hearing all of them (i.e. mean responses for awareness ranged from .81 to .90). Rates of reported use were lower, however (between .53 and .63), and varied significantly according to generation in the US. Everyone reported using loanwords at similar rates (G1 speakers used them the most), but G2 and G3 speakers reported using all types of calques significantly more than G1 and G1.5 speakers (Figure 5.1). G1 speakers overall perceived loanwords as correct significantly more than G2 and G3 speakers, while the latter accepted all types of calques significantly more than the former (Figure 5.2).

The fact that G1 speakers deemed loanwords correct significantly more than G1.5, G2 or G3 speakers (Figure 5.2) may, at first blush, seem counter-intuitive. However, this same finding presented itself in Otheguy and García's (1988) original study. At the time, they reasoned that G1 speakers "are more willing to adopt [lexical innovations] and to accept them as correct because... they simply see the innovations as the Spanish of [Miami-]Dade County, as the way, that is, that this language is spoken in the new—and to them Spanish monolingual—community that, as all new communities, can be expected to have its linguistic quirks" (1988, 226). Otheguy and García also affirmed: "Loans do not violate the integrity of any signs. And they are, in fact, the only way to be completely true to the English message while speaking in Spanish. Speakers appear to be aware of these qualities of loans and are willing to adopt them even when they recognize them as not Spanish" (1988, 222).

The boundaries of Anglicisms 241

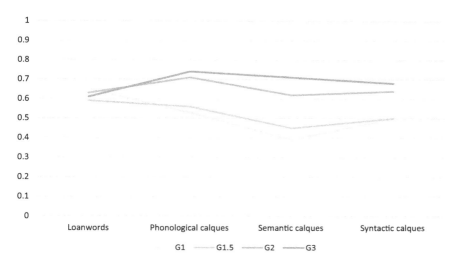

Figure 5.1 Use of Anglicisms according to generation in Miami

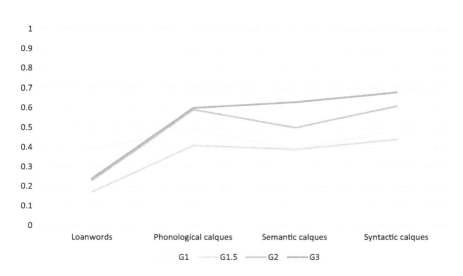

Figure 5.2 Acceptability of Anglicisms according to generation in Miami

As I just suggested above, the structural salience of loanwords, i.e. their obvious quality of being borrowed from English, lends them a symbolic value that calques do not typically acquire. Indeed, in the Spanish-speaking world beyond the US, English loanwords are convenient accessories of trendiness or cosmopolitanism, as in the case of marketing in the fashion and

242   *The boundaries of Anglicisms*

cosmetics industries targeted by the RAE in their faux advertising campaign. They commonly characterize the stylized speech of youth and the educated middle and upper socioeconomic classes of urban Latin America and Spain (Luján García 2013; Villalobos Graillet 2015). The prestige of English-origin loanwords in urban speech and Spanish-language consumerism is compelling evidence that sociolinguistic identity construction does not proceed according to perceptions of language 'purity' but rather in accordance with the social connotations of discourse patterns: "La subjetividad implica un yo situado, y una situación con respecto a una lengua o a diferentes lenguas que se expresa en una relación de posesión" (Kabatek 2011, 8), i.e. what Glissant termed a 'poetics of relation.' Varra's (2018) extensive study of Spanish speakers in NYC revealed that lexical borrowing, which in her analysis included loanwords as well as multi-word units from English, was more frequent among those of higher socioeconomic status. Occupation was in fact the strongest predictor of lexical borrowing among G1 speakers in her study, who also appeared not to manifest important ethnonational or dialectal differences, i.e. first-generation Puerto Ricans did not reflect substantially different patterns than Mexicans, on the whole. While lexical borrowing was more frequent among middle-class speakers than those of working-class backgrounds, Varra noted that this may have to do with the prestige status of Spanish in NYC. She suggested that in other settings where the recipient language (i.e. Spanish) has a higher instrumental marketplace value than in NYC, lexical borrowing could theoretically be higher among speakers of lower socioeconomic status (2018, 128–29).

Assuredly, one could think of no other place in the US where Spanish has a higher instrumental marketplace value than Miami, for reasons I have explained in the previous chapters. It is noteworthy that, in the regression analysis, loanwords were the only category for which stance regarding the importance of the ability to speak Spanish in the US (unequivocally alluding to the language's instrumental value) emerged as a significant predictor. As already noted, respondents who attributed high importance to the ability to speak Spanish were significantly more likely to deem loanwords incorrect than those who were less emphatic about the language's importance (.22 versus .39, respectively). The former also indicated being a bit less likely to use loanwords than the latter (.62 versus .66, respectively), a difference that was not statistically significant. For G2 and G3 speakers alone, however, the difference in rate of use was indeed significant in one-way ANOVA (p = .016): G2 and G3 speakers who indicated that the ability to speak Spanish was 'very important' were significantly less likely to use loanwords than those who indicated 'important' (.59 versus .68, respectively). G1 speakers did not manifest significant differences of reported use of loanwords (p = .363 in one-way ANOVA) in correlation with their stance regarding the importance of being able to speak Spanish in the US. Interestingly, however, for them, there was a highly significant difference in terms of awareness (p = .002 in one-way ANOVA): G1 speakers who indicated that the ability to speak Spanish was 'very important' appeared significantly more aware of loanwords than those

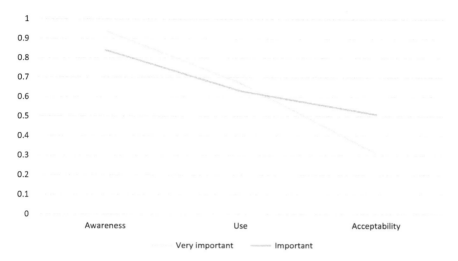

Figure 5.3 Social diffusion of loanwords among G1 speakers according to perceived importance of Spanish in the US

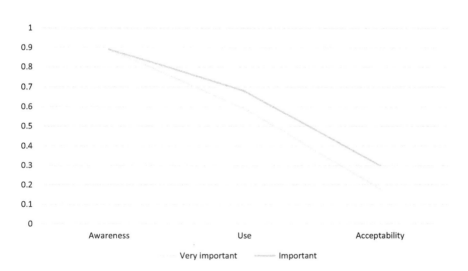

Figure 5.4 Social diffusion of loanwords among G2 and G3 speakers according to perceived importance of Spanish in the US

who indicated 'important' (.94 versus .84, respectively). Figures 5.3 and 5.4 capture these differences in both groups (G1 versus G2 and G3, respectively).

Such differences (Figures 5.3 and 5.4) suggest that the more emphatic Miami Latinxs are about the importance of being able to speak Spanish in the

244   *The boundaries of Anglicisms*

US, the more likely they are to shun English-origin loanwords, irrespective of generation. Nonetheless, they all indicated using them at relatively high rates.

Here the proverbial plot thickens. Pearson correlations between responses to the question about the importance of Spanish in the US and any of the variables of social status were extremely low (below .05), indicating that respondents' stance regarding the importance of Spanish was in no way conditioned by the area of the city in which they resided, nor by their education level, nor that of their parents.[7] The more importance they attributed to Spanish, the less likely they were to accept loanwords, irrespective of social status. However, those who had highly educated parents (i.e. with university degrees or graduate/professional studies) were significantly more likely to accept loanwords than those whose parents were less educated. Additionally, respondents who lived in Coral Gables, the highest income area of the city included in the survey, were significantly more likely to accept loanwords than those who lived in any of the other three areas (of middle- or lower-income status). As previously noted, parents' education level and neighborhood both proved to be significant predictors in the regression analysis for acceptability of loanwords (Table 5.5). This suggests that higher social status correlates with greater symbolic value—or perceived correctness—of loanwords in Miami.

In this regard, the present inquiry in Miami cannot lend support for Varra's (2018) hypothesis about potentially higher rates of lexical borrowing among speakers of lower socioeconomic status in areas where Spanish has high instrumental marketplace value. It bears recalling, however, that Varra's study was based on oral production, while the present one was based on a written survey about perception. Were one to analyze actual speech production, Varra's hypothesis may well find support in Miami. In fact, in the present data, reported use of loanwords was substantially though not significantly higher ($p = .07$ in one-way ANOVA) in NW than in Coral Gables (mean responses of .68 versus .57, respectively), despite significantly higher rates of acceptability in Coral Gables. In sum, these findings suggest that social status was a vital facet of linguistic (in)security in our sample population. Respondents of lower social status were significantly less willing to assert the acceptability of loanwords than those of higher status, despite using them more. The former thus appeared to adhere to an ideology of transparency more than the latter in the case of loanwords.

Linguistic (in)security also clearly manifested along the boundary lines of dialect origins. As I pointed out in Chapter 1, previous studies have unequivocally concluded that, despite being the predominant variety spoken in Miami in demographic, political, and historical terms, Cuban Spanish tends to be regarded as less correct than Peninsular Spanish in particular and South American varieties in general, especially those of Colombia and Argentina (Alfaraz 2014; Fernández Parera 2017; Carter and Callesano 2018). These local findings are reflective of a broader tendency throughout the Spanish-speaking world to regard Caribbean varieties of Spanish as less correct

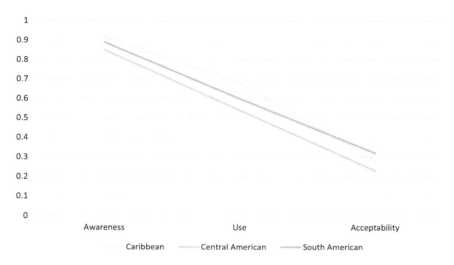

Figure 5.5 Social diffusion of loanwords according to speaker origin

(Sobrino Triana 2018). Because of the long history of US intervention in the Caribbean—especially Puerto Rico—speakers of Caribbean origin in Miami appeared more sensitized to English-origin borrowings. As previously noted, Caribbean-origin speakers indicated hearing and using loanwords significantly more than those of non-Caribbean backgrounds (Table 5.5 and related discussion). However, as Figure 5.5 displays, Caribbean-origin speakers were overall less likely to consider loanwords correct than speakers of South American varieties (.27 versus .32, respectively), a difference that, although not significant, was nonetheless interesting in that it reversed the trend manifested in the other two perceptual dimensions.

Not just in the sociolinguistic data that I explore in this book but also in interviews that I have conducted and interactions with heritage language students whom I have taught over the past twenty years in Miami, many Caribbean-origin speakers have declared to me that their variety of Spanish is inferior. Cubans and Puerto Ricans in particular have sometimes qualified their metalinguistic commentary with me by stating—occasionally with a laugh or a look of concern—such things as: "Bueno, yo hablo el español cubano"; "Los cubanos no hablamos bien"; "Recuerda que yo soy boricua"; "En Puerto Rico hablamos espanglish"; or even "No sé cómo lo dirían los españoles. Ellos hablan mejor que nosotros." With regards to the latter, Carter and Callesano's (2018) implicit perception study yielded compelling results.

A closer look at three particular items proves thought-provoking in terms of dialectal boundaries. Of the ten loanwords included in the survey, 'chatear' ("Los jóvenes pasan muchas horas ***chateando*** en Internet") was the only one

246 *The boundaries of Anglicisms*

for which Caribbean-origin speakers indicated significantly lower rates of awareness, use, and acceptability (p = .006, .002, .043 in one-way ANOVA, respectively) than their non-Caribbean counterparts. All those rates were highest among speakers of South American varieties of Spanish (including Colombians and Venezuelans), suggesting that this form has a significantly higher index of social diffusion among South American–origin speakers. 'Laptop' ("Mi *laptop* fue más caro que el de mi hermano") also presented a particularity within the loanwords category, in that its social diffusion appeared substantially lower among Cubans than among Puerto Ricans and speakers of all South American varieties. Commentary during interviews with Cubans revealed the source of this dialectal difference: assigned gender of the loanword rather than the word itself. Several Cubans commented to me that the given sentence sounded strange or unacceptable to them because it should read "Mi *laptop* fue más cara que la de mi hermano," taking feminine rather than masculine form. A search of websites originating in Cuba confirmed that 'laptop,' which is of common usage on the island, typically takes feminine gender. Among G2 and G3 Miami Cubans, however, 'el laptop' is commonly heard, reflecting a general trend I have observed among Spanish speakers in Miami to assign masculine gender to English-origin loanwords. Otheguy (2011, 507) documented the same tendency in NYC, and it appears to manifest throughout the Spanish-speaking world (Núñez Nogueroles 2017). Among Cubans, the cross-generational effect of English dominance on the perception of the word 'clóset' ("El *clóset* es muy pequeño para toda la ropa que tiene") was also noteworthy, in that G1 speakers mostly considered it correct (mean response of .73) while most Cubans of successive generations in Miami did not (G1.5 = .40, G2 = .34, G3 = .27), a difference that was highly significant (p = .000). The normativity of 'clóset' on the island is seemingly undone among successive generations of Cubans in Miami, who readily attribute it to English. In interviews, when I told some G2 and G3 Cubans that both 'clóset' and 'cake' (pronounced as [kéi] in Cuban Spanish, not included in the present survey) were examples of historically integrated Anglicisms in normative Cuban Spanish, they seemed surprised and stated that they had always assumed both were used only in Miami. In reality, 'clóset' is common in many varieties of Spanish across Latin America, and the majority of G1 speakers of all backgrounds in the present inquiry indicated using and accepting it (.86 and .63, respectively), while most G1.5, G2, and G3 speakers indicated they used it yet considered it incorrect. Venezuelans presented the highest rates of use and acceptability of 'clóset,' followed by Central Americans. Different than speakers of these latter two groups, Puerto Ricans indicated a very high rate of use (.88) but a remarkably low rate of acceptability (.35).

For purposes of statistical testing, I categorized 'laptop,' which was added in my modification to Otheguy and García's (1988) original survey, as a loanword. I categorized 'clóset,' which was also included in their survey, as a distractor. The criteria for characterizing 'laptop' as a loanword and 'clóset' as

The boundaries of Anglicisms 247

a distractor are debatable. Both reflected extremely high rates of awareness (.94 and .98, respectively) and use (.75 and .82, respectively), suggesting that they are very widespread in Spanish-speaking Miami. In terms of awareness and use, they indisputably 'exist.' 'Clóset' appears in the official dictionary of the RAE; 'laptop' does not, although it is the second term that appears in WordReference.com as a translation of the English laptop, following 'portátil.' Rates of acceptability of both 'clóset' and 'laptop' were high among G1 speakers, but quite low among G2 and G3 speakers. For these reasons, these two items illustrate the murky environment of language normativization and the linguistic insecurity that it entails within an ideology of transparency (Glissant 1997). These items also illustrate Moreno Fernández's (2017) observation regarding the relationship between established rules—or what Glissant calls 'dictates'—and patterns of practice: "Sociolinguistic usage itself also contributes to the development of the normative metalanguage and the ideology that sustains the normative metalanguage, thus allowing for categorization and relationships between different types of speakers to be established with respect to the norm" (69). Such is clearly the case of 'tuitear,' which I highlighted in the introduction.

The social skepticism about English-origin loanwords—which in some sectors becomes politicized—sometimes leads to metalinguistic commentary or institutional debate in the Spanish-dominant countries of Latin America and in Spain, reshaping normative metalanguage. In the US, however, where Spanish is a minoritized and, in some settings, racialized language (Rosa 2019), that same skepticism generally creates linguistic insecurity among English-dominant bilinguals, a pattern that is unequivocally manifest in the significantly lower acceptability ratings of G2 and G3 speakers in the present inquiry (Figure 5.2). As Figure 5.6 displays, even among G1 speakers (all of whom were Spanish-dominant), those with 'very good' or 'excellent' abilities to speak and understand English were significantly more likely to consider loanwords incorrect than those with 'little' or 'some' ability in English (mean acceptability ratings of .30 and .54, respectively; $p = .002$ in one-way ANOVA). This finding aligns with Varra's (2018) observation that lower levels of English proficiency among G1 Spanish speakers in NYC led to higher rates of reproductive borrowing in language production, i.e. the tendency to use borrowings already in widespread circulation (96–97). Poplack, Sankoff, and Miller (1988) reached a similar conclusion in Francophone Canada.

In sum, among G1 Spanish speakers in Miami, higher levels of bilingual ability conditioned significantly lower rates of acceptability for all four categories of Anglicisms (Figure 5.6), including loanwords and calques. Let us recall, however, that among speakers of all generations, bilingual ability emerged as a significant predictor of acceptability only in the regression analyses for calques. I now turn to a potential explanation for that finding, appealing to the notion of metalinguistic consciousness.

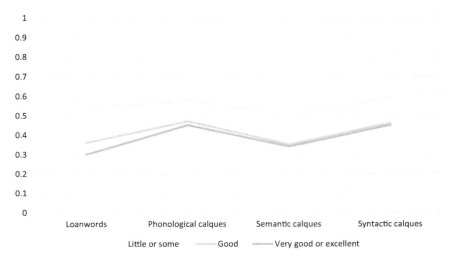

Figure 5.6 Acceptability of Anglicisms among G1 speakers according to English language ability

Bilingual ability and metalinguistic consciousness

Calquing is what Thomason (2001) characterized as a 'quasi-invisible' consequence of language contact: "All the building blocks are native…, so the foreign origin of the words might not even be suspected, and certainly could not be proved, without the speakers' explicit statements about their foreignness" (81). If viewed from the perspective that "all differences between languages are ultimately lexical in nature" (Muysken 2000, 37), calques offer unique insights into bilingual repertoires, in that they are lexical borrowings that may have syntactic implications. Among Mexicans in Los Angeles, Silva-Corvalán (1994) attributed the influence of English in productive bilingual repertoires to incipient transfer of discourse-pragmatic functions, by which speakers exploit structural parallelisms, i.e. similarities, between the two languages: "Transfer arises when a bilingual identifies a lexical or syntactic structure of the secondary system with one in the primary system and, in reproducing it, subjects it to the semantic-pragmatic rules of the primary language" (217).

Combinational restrictions or semantic constraints may be altered in multiple-word units such as bound collocations, e.g. 'eso está bien conmigo' [that's fine with me], or lexico-syntactic calques, e.g. 'llamar para atrás' [to call back] or 'tener un buen tiempo' [to have a good time] (Silva-Corvalán 1994, 217). Preposition stranding is a related phenomenon that also has important syntactic implications, e.g. '¿Qué es esto para?' [what's this for?] (Pascual y Cabo and Gómez Soler 2015). Otheguy (2011) explained that interpretation of the grammatical consequences of forms such as 'enamorarse con' [to fall in love with] in bilingual Spanish, in which the structure [__PP] appears altered, depends upon the analyst's perspective: in a micro-subcategorization account, a different syntax in the contact lect emerges (i.e. specific prepositions are governed by specific verbs); but in a broader approach to subcategorization, the same grammar underlies both 'enamorarse con' and 'enamorarse de' (i.e. all preposition-taking verbs have a singular entry specifying [__PP]) (520–21). As in the latter account, a meaning coherence approach would interpret that there is merely a reconceptualization of [__PP] that does not invoke a separate grammar in the contact variety (521). In short, linguistic debate regarding the grammatical implications of semantic and syntactic calquing is suggestive of the great nuance of such structures and the difficulty of attributing their properties to one or another language.

We should thus expect the same dilemma or enigma, so to speak, in bilingual perception. Recognition of the semantic overlay of English onto Spanish lexical and syntactic form depends upon the degree of familiarity one has with the structures of each language independently. As we have seen, among G1 Spanish speakers in Miami, there is a significant linear relationship between English language ability and the perception of loanwords and calques of all types (Figure 5.6). Different than in the case of loanwords, G2 and G3 speakers consistently considered calques more acceptable than G1 speakers (Figure 5.2). But like their G1 counterparts, successive generations of Spanish speakers in Miami with stronger bilingual abilities were less likely to deem calques acceptable. As reflected in Figure 5.7, G2 and G3 speakers (all of whom were English-dominant) with 'excellent' abilities to speak and understand Spanish tended to regard all types of calques as less correct than those with 'some' or 'good' abilities in Spanish, although the differences were not statistically significant.

The negative correlation between bilingual ability and acceptability of calques for speakers of all generations (Figures 5.6 and 5.7) points to the role of metalinguistic consciousness. The more familiar respondents were with the structures of each language independently, the more apt they were to perceive the overlay of an English-based meaning onto a Spanish-based form. Although in theory the recognition of that linguistic overlay need not be concomitant with social unacceptability, such is in fact the case in Miami.

Education appeared to play a crucial role in this regard. As Figure 5.8 displays, there was a significant negative correlation between respondents' own level of education and acceptability ratings for all types of calques, across all generations. Differences were most salient between those with graduate or professional studies and those with only college-level studies or secondary schooling. On the other hand, in the case of loanwords, there was a substantial difference between those with secondary studies and those with postsecondary studies (.41 versus .27, respectively), but education did not emerge as a significant predictor of acceptability in the regression analysis (Table 5.5).

250 *The boundaries of Anglicisms*

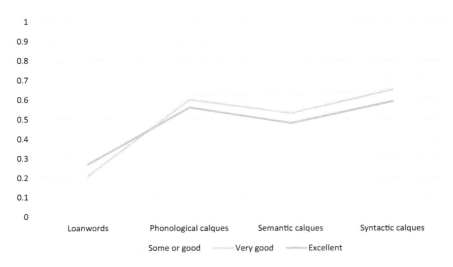

Figure 5.7 Acceptability of Anglicisms among G2 and G3 speakers according to Spanish language ability

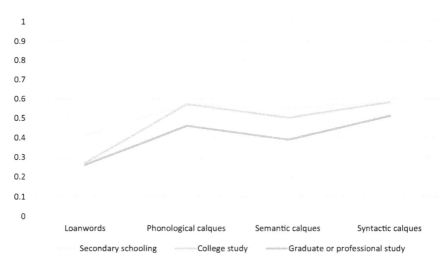

Figure 5.8 Acceptability of Anglicisms according to level of formal education

Among speakers of all generations, syntactic calques garnered the highest ratings of acceptability overall (Figure 5.2). Indeed, of all 43 variants posed in the survey, the one with the highest acceptability rating (.88)—even higher than any of the distractor items—was "Pregúntale si **sabe cómo hacerlo**,"

The boundaries of Anglicisms 251

arguably a syntactic calque. Besides distractors, the only other item of the survey that garnered an acceptability rating above .80 was "*Déjame saber* si puedes ayudarme mañana," arguably a syntactic calque as well. I state that both of these variants are "arguably" calqued on English syntax because they undeniably reflect the normative syntactic structures of any noncontact variety of Spanish. What distinguishes the former as a possible contact-preferred variant is the semantic modification of the manner-specific meaning of the interrogative adverb 'cómo' in Spanish. In the construction 'Pregúntale si sabe cómo hacerlo,' the semantically less restricted meaning of English 'how' is extended to Spanish (Silva-Corvalán 1994, 177). The latter variant, 'déjame saber,' reproduces a multiple-word unit in English, in this case the bound collocation 'let me know.' However, this instance does not reflect syntactic transfer from English, since the construction 'déjame + Verb' is normative in noncontact Spanish with other verb types, e.g. 'déjame leer esto.' Both of these variants thus reflect an English lexical and semantic overlay that is extremely subtle in terms of form.

While there were no differences in the acceptability ratings for "Pregúntale si *sabe cómo hacerlo*" according to respondents' level of education (.89 among those with secondary schooling, .88 among those with college-level study, and .87 among those with graduate or professional studies), a differential pattern was detected for "*Déjame saber* si puedes ayudarme mañana" (.89, .80, and .78, respectively), although it was not significant in one-way ANOVA. However, Spanish language ability did indeed emerge as a significant predictor of acceptability of 'déjame saber': those who reported 'excellent' ability in Spanish were more likely to deem it incorrect than those who indicated having lower levels of ability (.76 versus .92, respectively; $p = .022$). No other social variables emerged as significant in one-way ANOVAs for either of these two variants, however. I would point out that 'déjame saber' is heard throughout the Caribbean, although 'avísame' and 'dime' are much more frequent. Its use and diffusion are sociolinguistically accelerated within the context of bilingualism in South Florida, at the expense of other variants more frequently used among monolinguals in Puerto Rico, Cuba, and the Dominican Republic (cf. Silva-Corvalán 1994). Indeed, Caribbean-origin speakers indicated using it significantly more than non-Caribbean speakers (.86 versus .77, respectively; $p = .021$ in one-way ANOVA). Puerto Ricans reported the highest rate of use and acceptability overall (.96 in both cases). In its expansion, 'déjame saber' likely draws little social attention from anyone in Miami precisely because it occurs in monolingual Caribbean speech and, for speakers of non-Caribbean varieties, it conforms quite imperceptibly to the structural pattern of normative Spanish.

Use of this phrase has become nearly formulaic in customer service encounters in Miami, e.g. "Déjame [Déjeme] saber si te [le] puedo ayudar en algo" in stores, calqued on the formulaic English "Let me know if I can help you with anything"; and "Déjame [Déjeme] saber si te [le] puedo traer algo más/... si desea[s] algo más" in restaurant settings, calqued on the English "Let

252   *The boundaries of Anglicisms*

me know if there's anything else I can bring you/… if you'd like anything else." In this regard, this particular calque is a fitting example of the influence of the discourse of US consumerism in Spanish, by which formulaic English-origin phrases or collocations are integrated into specific registers of Spanish that many would perceive as formal, or at least semi-formal, because they manifest deferential voices heard in somewhat formal social settings. Other possible examples—highly common in Miami—are "¿Cómo puedo ayudarlo[la][le]?", calqued on English "How can I help you?", and "Que tenga[s] un buen día," heard at all hours of the day in customer service encounters. My impression is that the latter is a fixed phrase or collocation calqued on English "Have a good/nice day," much less common—though not unheard—in customer service interactions beyond the US. Over the years, some monolingual visitors or recently arrived (im)migrants from Latin America have commented to me that "Que tenga[s] un buen día" sounds odd to them in this particular context. Asked why, they have said that 'pasar' rather than 'tener' would be preferable (i.e. "Que pase[s] un buen día"). Others have noted the syntactic construction itself, suggesting that "Que lo pase[s] bien" or "Que le [te] vaya bien" might be a bit more suitable (with *usted* and not *tú* form, cf. Chapter 4). Still others have remarked that no salesperson or restaurant server in their respective countries of origin would likely say any such thing in the given context, but rather 'gracias' followed by an appropriate farewell ('hasta luego,' 'adiós,' etc.). In any case, what seems to capture their attention is the social context and frequency of the form, i.e. not the fact that *someone* says "Que tenga[s] un buen día" to them but rather that *so many* people say it in customer service encounters.

In the interviews that I conducted for the present inquiry, I was equally struck by a comment that a few G1 speakers made regarding the syntactic calque 'estar supesta[o] a' ("Ella *está supuesta a llegar* hoy a las 5:00 de la tarde"), to wit: it seemed 'more formal' to them than possible equivalents in the varieties of their respective countries of origin (e.g. 'debe llegar'). What those particular G1 speakers had in common were low levels of English language ability and lower levels of formal education. Indeed, in one-way ANOVAs, G1 respondents who reported having less than 'good' abilities in English indicated using this variant significantly more than those with 'very good' to 'excellent' abilities in English (.73 versus .45, respectively; $p = .001$); the former also considered it correct significantly more than the latter (.76 versus .39, respectively; $p = .001$). Among those with low-level English abilities, the fact that the mean response for acceptability (.76) was higher than that of use (.73)—a pattern that was quite opposite across the survey in general (i.e. speakers indicated using Anglicisms of all types at rates much higher than they accepted them as correct)—is suggestive of the appearance of formality in the case of 'estar supuesto a.' Education yielded a similar result: G1 respondents who had only completed secondary studies indicated using this variant significantly more than those who had postsecondary studies (.68 versus .38, respectively; $p = .051$); the former also tended to accept it more than the latter (.68 versus .44, respectively, although this difference was not

The boundaries of Anglicisms 253

statistically significant). Again, however, one is struck by the fact that college-educated G1 speakers considered this variant correct at a rate higher than they indicated actually using it (mean response of .38 for use and .44 for acceptability), confirming the perception of formality that some individuals remarked upon during interviews with me.

'Estar supuesto a' presented a much higher social diffusion among Caribbean-origin G1 speakers than those of other varieties of Spanish. In all three perceptual dimensions (awareness, use, acceptability) their mean responses were significantly higher than those of their non-Caribbean G1 counterparts in one-way ANOVAs (p = .000, .002, .041, respectively). Interestingly, G2 and G3 speakers did not manifest such differences, suggesting that 'estar supuesto a' is of perhaps more generalized use in the bilingual repertoires of successive generations in the US. G3 speakers of both Caribbean and non-Caribbean origins indicated using 'estar supuesto a' significantly more than G1 speakers (.71 versus .50, respectively; p = .036), and they accepted it at substantially (though not significantly) higher rates (.65 versus .52, respectively; p = .062). Overall, as previously noted, Caribbean origin proved to be a significant predictor of awareness and use of all types of syntactic calques in the regression analysis (Table 5.10), as it did in the case of loanwords (Table 5.5). Yet also as in the case of loanwords, Caribbean-origin speakers were not more likely than others to deem calques correct, probably because of a sense of historically conditioned linguistic insecurity—according to an ideology of transparency (Glissant 1997)—as I suggested above.

Different than loanwords, calques of all types manifested significantly higher rates of use and acceptability among G2 and G3 speakers than among G1 and G1.5 speakers (Figures 5.1 and 5.2) and appeared more equally diffused across all areas of the city, suggesting that they were not as strongly linked to socioeconomic status as loanwords were. In these regards, the characteristic notion of correctness aligned with '*the* language' in an ideology of transparency, according to Glissant, is not evident in the case of calques in Miami, for the most part. Rather, the perceived correctness of calques corresponds more to the individual metalinguistic consciousness, i.e. one's ability to recognize particular forms and nuanced meanings that characterize each language and thus differentiate between them on linguistic (rather than social) grounds.

This suggestion seems to find confirmation in the statistical significance of parents' level of education. As reported above, parents' education was a significant predictor of ratings of awareness and use for semantic and syntactic calques, principally among G2 and G3 speakers. As Figures 5.9 and 5.10 display, G2 and G3 respondents whose parents had lower levels of formal education indicated hearing and using semantic and syntactic calques significantly more than those whose parents had higher levels of formal education.

As previously noted, in the dimension of acceptability, the significant effects of parents' level of education were manifest not for semantic and syntactic calques, but rather for loanwords, and in an inverse fashion, i.e. G2 and G3 respondents whose parents had lower levels of formal education indicated

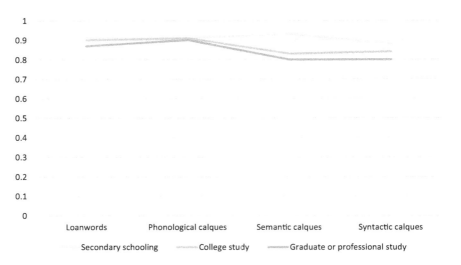

Figure 5.9 Awareness of Anglicisms among G2 and G3 speakers according to parents' level of formal education

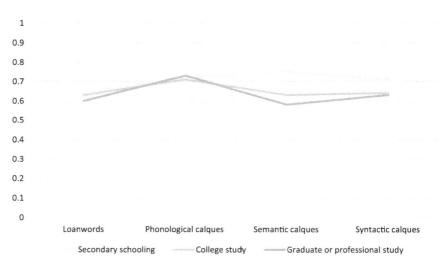

Figure 5.10 Use of Anglicisms among G2 and G3 speakers according to parents' level of formal education

accepting loanwords significantly less than those whose parents had higher levels of formal education (as previously explained). Figure 5.11 displays this significant differential pattern of acceptability ratings among G2 and G3 speakers.

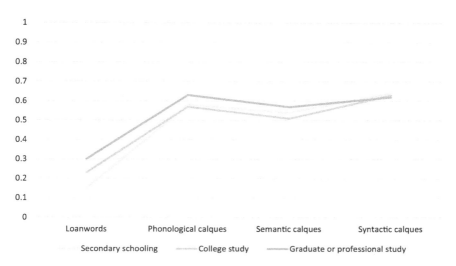

Figure 5.11 Acceptability of Anglicisms among G2 and G3 speakers according to parents' level of formal education

These findings suggest that Miami Latinx bilinguals who are the children of G1 or G2 parents with high levels of education hear and consequentially use calques less than their counterparts whose parents are less educated, likely in part because less educated G1 and G2 parents are using them significantly more in discourse with their G2 and G3 children.

This parental pattern does not affect G2 and G3 speakers' own perception of the acceptability of calques, however. As we saw in the previous section (Figure 5.8), one's own level of education had significant effects in the dimension of perceived correctness of phonological and semantic calques. Again, I would suggest this is likely because the perception of correctness of calques depends upon metalinguistic consciousness, which is developed and heightened through formal education. Making a value judgment concerning the acceptability of a particular form is a quite different matter than hearing or even using that same form (Labov 1972). Syntactic calques, however, apparently evaded the effects of formal education on perceived correctness, i.e. neither respondents' nor parents' level of education had a significant effect on the acceptability ratings of syntactic calques in the regression analysis. A plausible explanation is that they are more difficult to detect, seemingly ensconced in normative Spanish lexical and syntactic structures. Thus, only 'excellent' language abilities in both languages make syntactic calques sufficiently conspicuous to acquire a perception of potential incorrectness. This might explain why—besides generation—language ability in both Spanish and English were the only significant predictors of acceptability for syntactic calques (Table 5.10).

256   *The boundaries of Anglicisms*

There was one exception to this general profile: "Si le dejas un mensaje, seguro que te *llama para atrás.*" Despite being a structurally ensconced variant (i.e. it reflects the syntactic structure V + *para* + adverb heard in noncontact Spanish), it appears to have taken on a salient social profile in Miami. Its use and acceptability are significantly correlated with variables of language ability, metalinguistic consciousness, origin, and social status. Perhaps first and foremost, it is a characteristically Caribbean variant in Miami ($p = .000$ in one-way ANOVAs for awareness, use, and acceptability, comparing Caribbean vs. non-Caribbean-origin speakers), although its use is widely documented in diverse Spanish-speaking communities across the US (Sánchez 1994; Silva-Corvalán 1994; Otheguy 2011), including Isleño Spanish in Louisiana, as well as in Trinidad and Gibraltar (Lipski 1987). In the present study, Puerto Ricans reported by far the highest rates of use and acceptability of 'llamar para atrás' (.64 and .42, respectively), followed by Cubans (.55 and .28, respectively); the lowest rates of use and acceptability were observed among Colombians (.08 and .05, respectively) and among speakers of other South American varieties of Spanish (.12 and .06, respectively). The great majority of respondents reported hearing it, with the lowest rates of awareness among Colombians (.68). During the 1980s, Lipski (1987) noted that "in Puerto Rico itself, the constructions with *pa tras*, unheard of only a few years ago, are becoming increasingly common, presumably as greater social mobility gives Puerto Ricans a chance to travel to the United States... and as more 'Nuyoricans' emigrate to live in Puerto Rico" (89). He also observed that use of 'pa tras' was increasing among young Cuban Americans "despite the small amount of active linguistic contact between Cubans and either Puerto Rican or Chicano Spanish speakers" (89).

The present evidence suggests that this was indeed the case, and that 'llamar para atrás' has rapidly expanded in the dynamic bilingual majority context of Miami, not only across the city's superdiverse dialectal spectrum but also cross-generationally. The highest rates of use and acceptability were reported by G3 speakers (.54 and .41, respectively; $p = .043$ and $.000$ cross-generationally), while speakers of all generations reported hearing this variant at similarly high rates (mean awareness responses between .81 and .91; no significant differences). Further evidence of the expansion of 'llamar para atrás' is that, among G2 and G3 speakers, its use and acceptability was not significantly correlated with Spanish language ability, although rates were somewhat higher among those who indicated having lower levels of ability in Spanish. Among G1 speakers, however, use and acceptability were indeed significantly correlated with English language ability: .69 and .36, respectively, among those with low-level abilities to speak and understand English versus .25 and .12, respectively, among those who reported having 'very good' to 'excellent' abilities in English ($p = .000$ for use; $p = .008$ for acceptability). This finding demonstrates that what begins as a common variant for G1 speakers, principally of Caribbean origin, is 'deborrowed' as Spanish-dominant immigrants become more familiar with English (see Varra 2018). In successive generations,

The boundaries of Anglicisms 257

however, it acquires more generalized use and acceptability, irrespective of bilingual ability. Further evidence of this general expansion is that, among G2 and G3 speakers, there was no significant effect of education level—neither that of respondents nor of their parents—on awareness, use, or acceptability of 'llamar para atrás.' For G1 speakers, on the other hand, both the education level of respondents and that of their parents were significantly correlated with all three perceptual dimensions ($p <$ .05 in all cases): higher levels of education conditioned lower rates of awareness, use, and acceptability. In sum, bilingual ability and metalinguistic consciousness had overall significant effects on the perception of 'llamar para atrás' for G1 speakers but not for G2 and G3 speakers, suggesting that, among the latter, its perception corresponds more generally to an ideology of opacity.

However, in its cross-generational expansion, 'llamar para atrás' appears to have assumed a social status profile for speakers of all generations. Its use and acceptability were significantly differentiated according to area of the city. The highest rates of use were observed in NW (.50) and the lowest in Coral Gables (.28), which represent the two extremes of the socioeconomic spectrum ($p =$ .014 in one-way ANOVA). The highest rates of acceptability were in NW (.30), but in this case the lowest rates were in the more firmly middle-class areas of SW and Miami Center (.16 for both), with the mean response in Coral Gables somewhat higher than the latter (.21) ($p =$ .051 in one-way ANOVA). This pattern could suggest hypercorrection of the middle class, which is indicative of social stigmatization of the variant in question, as commonly cited in sociolinguistic research (Labov 1972). Comments made by several respondents in reflective interviews provide further evidence for this hypothesis. Repeatedly, the appearance of 'llamar para atrás' on the page prompted laughter (something that did not generally happen with other variants), and numerous respondents affirmed that it was "español malhablado" and sounded "uneducated." Several remarked that it was Cuban or Puerto Rican Spanish, and still others confidently declared that it was a perfect example of Spanglish. Cuban interviewees sometimes used an affected intonation as they read the sentence aloud on the page, emphasizing the truncation of *para atrás* and exaggerating the deletion of the final /s/, as in [pa-tráø] (Lynch 2017). Others also exaggerated the tendency to assimilate or lateralize the final /r/ in *llamar*, as in [ya-máp-pa-tráø] or [ya-mál-pa-tráø]. As I pointed out in Chapter 4, all of these phonological variants characterized the speech of the lower socioeconomic strata in Cuba prior to the revolution and appear to have expanded on the island in recent decades (Alfaraz 2000, 2012, 2014). These specific perceptual aspects of 'llamar para atrás' align clearly with an ideology of transparency, by which "it takes no time to reach the conclusion that there is a 'right' way to use the language" (Glissant 1997, 114). According to Glissant, the "natural result" of this ideological trajectory of transparency is "scales of value to appraise usage" according to which language reveals the hierarchical organization of culture and society (1997, 114). In sum, 'llamar para atrás' provides a fitting example of the seemingly contradictory ways

258 *The boundaries of Anglicisms*

in which Anglicisms simultaneously reflect ideologies of both transparency and opacity, or 'centripetal' and 'centrifugal' forces in Bakhtin's terms (2000 [1934]).

Conclusion

Probably best characterized as a case of conceptual convergence between Spanish and English (Otheguy 2011), 'llamar para atrás' offers us a window into the ideological workings of fractal recursivity in bilingual Miami (Irvine and Gal 2000). As I previously mentioned, through this process, diverse varieties of Spanish are contested and reworked through the fractal projection of the differentiation of Spanish and English. What began as a Caribbean variant in South Florida, most frequent among Puerto Ricans and already attested in Puerto Rico in the 1980s (Lipski 1987), has acquired unique and highly significant differential values according to speaker origin and social status in Miami as a result of the broad societal and cultural distinction between Spanish and English. In terms of Glissant's (1997) *Poetics of Relation*, it clearly reflects the transparency/opacity dialectic in the ideological configuration of two globally hegemonic languages in what is arguably the most postmodern sociolinguistic setting of the Spanish-speaking world, as I have suggested in previous chapters. It is also a vivid illustration of the complexity of the indexical value of all sorts of Anglicisms throughout the Spanish-speaking world.

As we have seen in this chapter, loanwords in Miami have significant value in terms of social status and appear more highly diffused among speakers of Caribbean origin. Because of their obvious 'otherness' in terms of language structure (Caravedo 2014), loanwords readily acquire indexical value, just as they do in noncontact varieties throughout the Spanish-speaking world (Luján García 2013; Villarreal 2014). They are easy targets for debate around language correctness and, as such, readily lend themselves as markers of social status and speakers' proverbial place in the hierarchical order of things. To no surprise, they were the only type of Anglicism in our study for which respondents' area of residence and their view on the importance of Spanish in the US emerged as significant predictors in statistical regression analyses. They manifest linguistic insecurity among Caribbean-origin speakers in Miami, who indicated using them at significantly higher rates than speakers of other varieties yet generally deemed them unacceptable more than their non-Caribbean counterparts, reflecting an ideology of transparency at work in the norms of correctness in the Caribbean (Glissant 1997). This is likely due to the long history of US political and economic intervention in Puerto Rico, Cuba, and the Dominican Republic. Likewise, loanwords appeared to manifest linguistic security for speakers of upper socioeconomic status: respondents from Coral Gables, the most affluent neighborhood surveyed in this inquiry, accepted loanwords at significantly higher rates than anyone else, despite using them at lower rates.

The boundaries of Anglicisms   259

With the exception of the seemingly iconic form 'llamar para atrás,' the perception of calques appeared linked much less to variables of social status. The perceived acceptability of phonological and semantic calques depended significantly upon respondents' familiarity with English or Spanish (respectively) and with their metalinguistic consciousness, the product of their own level of formal education. This was equally true across generations. The perception of syntactic calques—the most structurally ensconced English-influenced forms—was conditioned by ability in both languages together and, in terms of awareness and use, origin and parents' level of education (i.e. not their own level of education). As in the case of loanwords, there was significantly greater diffusion of syntactic calques among Caribbean-origin respondents, and the children of less formally educated G1 and G2 speakers reported hearing and using them significantly more. The latter tendency stood in inverse relationship to the acceptability dimension of loanwords. In that case, as we saw, the children of highly educated people accepted loanwords at significantly higher rates, a finding that corroborates Varra's (2018) conclusion regarding the prevalence of borrowing among Spanish speakers of higher socioeconomic status in NYC.

I also highlighted my impression that the use of "Déjame [Déjeme] saber si te [le] puedo ayudar en algo" and "Que tenga[s] un buen día" has become widespread and seemingly formulaic in service encounters in Miami. I believe the pervasiveness of these variants across diverse sectors of the city (e.g. retail, hospitality, health care, customer service) evidences the mapping of formulaic English-origin phrases or collocations onto Spanish language structures, calquing the discourse of US consumerism in specific registers of Spanish that are perceived as (semi)formal. There were four other phonological calques included in the survey that arguably reflected this same tendency: "El martes me *registré* en la universidad"; "Llené una *aplicación* para un trabajo en California"; "Puso la *alarma* para despertarse a las 7:00"; and "Puedes llevar ropa *casual* para la fiesta el sábado." The former two, which are not only common in formal workplace and educational settings but also in the discourse of internet and technology, did not differ according to generation. The latter two did, however: G1 speakers accepted both at significantly higher rates than G2 and G3 speakers ($p = .008$ for 'alarma' and $p = .000$ for 'ropa casual'). Given the considerable subtlety of English influence in the cases of 'alarma' and 'ropa casual,' one might hypothesize that these calques would go mostly undetected by English-dominant Miami-born Latinx bilinguals, especially G3 speakers, but that was in fact not the case. I suppose the widespread use of both these calques in noncontact varieties of Spanish beyond the US conditions the higher rates of acceptability observed among G1 speakers. The use of both is likely driven by global consumerism. The calquing of 'alarma' at the expense of 'despertador' is arguably the result of the large-scale purchase and use of digital clocks and cellphones, mostly manufactured in China and sold throughout Latin America and Spain, bearing the English

260 *The boundaries of Anglicisms*

term 'alarm.' The linguistic calquing of 'ropa casual' [Eng. 'casual clothing'] is probably the result of the cultural calquing of US-based (concomitantly globalized) models of consumer marketing and sales. I have heard the term 'ropa casual' on multiple occasions and in various retail settings in Spain, and I have encountered it on numerous retail websites for clothing based in Spain, Colombia, and Venezuela, among other countries. One can think of countless examples of this sort of consumer-driven tendency throughout the contemporary Spanish-speaking world (see Núñez Nogueroles' 2017 bibliography).

Undoubtedly, the RAE's fictitious campaign for 'Swine' perfume and 'Sunset Style with Blind Effect' sunglasses lies along the fault lines of ideological transparency and opacity. The struggle regarding these opposing ideological forces is entirely evident in the words chosen by the RAE for its big reveal of the latter product: "Las únicas gafas que no te dejan ver nada, oscuras como todas esas palabras en inglés" (Anglicismos 2016). Both of these faux products represent only the tip of the proverbial iceberg of Anglophone influence in Spanish, far beyond Miami and the US context, "un transformador proceso de cambio de costumbres cotidianas, tan íntimas, unas, como colectivas y generalizadas, otras; transformaciones en nuestro vivir, en nuestro hacer, en nuestro pensar... y hasta en nuestro sentir" (Riquelme 1998, 18). The discourse of global consumerism is but one aspect of this process of 'transculturation' in Riquelme's (1998) terms, which Glissant (1997) referred to as the "leveling effect" of the 'Anglo-American sabir,' a "technical salesman's Esperanto, a perfunctory containerization of expression" (112). As I will suggest in the next chapter, "containerization of expression" seems the linguistic *modus operandi* of neoliberal economic ideology, the prevailing current in postmodernity. Within this current, languages—particularly global ones such as English and Spanish—become increasingly bounded off from each other, parceled and contained, 'Taylorized' (Heller and Duchêne 2012), and given a 'neutral' voice for marketing, mass media, assessment, and a whole host of other purposes. With good reason Iglesias Illa (2010) commented: "Lo que hay en Miami son dos idiomas que conviven paralelos, bastante más puros de lo que uno creería desde fuera. La gente de la ciudad... habla mucho *Spanish* y mucho *English*, intercalando y saltando con comodidad de uno a otro, pero bastante poco *Spanglish*, aquel híbrido intermedio que no es ni una cosa ni la otra y que, por lo menos en Miami, parece estar perdiendo parte de su popularidad" (196).

Notes

1 I refer interested readers to Moreno Fernández's *Diccionario de anglicismos del español estadounidense* (2018) for a general definition of 'Anglicism' in the context of the Spanish-speaking US. In the present chapter, 'Anglicism' refers to a lexical or lexico-syntactic variant that may be attributed to English, in terms of form or function.

The boundaries of Anglicisms 261

2 Rogers did not address linguistic innovation or language change specifically in his work.

3 Otheguy and García's original study (1988) was focused solely on Cubans. The findings of my replication of that study, encompassing only Cuban-origin speakers in Miami, are reported in Lynch (2017).

4 The distinction between semantic and syntactic calques is not easy to make in some cases, and there are theoretically various types of syntactic calques (Silva-Corvalán 1994, 174–84). I thus recognize the limitations of the categorical groupings in the present study, which was based on Otheguy and García (1988). Had I been attempting an analysis of grammatical variability in Spanish, I would have been more concerned about such fine-grained distinctions. However, I was more interested in how people *perceive* the given forms in a social sense, and less in the ways they might actually *use* those forms productively (i.e. in terms of discursive frequency and linguistic constraints). Exploratory factor analysis confirmed that, statistically, the dependent variables generally patterned according to the *a priori* categories established. Important discussions could nonetheless be had, beyond the scope of the present study.

5 Mallet and Pinto-Coelho (2018) affirmed that, in Miami, "Overall, Continental respondents appear to stereotype Caribbean Latinos as belonging to less stable and more fragmented families. They clearly separate 'them' and 'us' to show that the commonalities between them are reduced to a minimum (e.g., Spanish language)" (107).

6 One could argue that the sociolinguistic situation of Spanish in Miami is not characteristic of that of a typical 'heritage language,' just as one might suggest that Haitian Creole in Miami manifests processes of creolization (both diachronically and synchronically) as well as heritage language acquisition (synchronically). Within the field of creolistics, Haitian is not a typical creole language, as McWhorter (2020) observed: "Haitian is the kind of creole that developed in a close, diglossic relationship with its lexifier, and thus has incorporated a good deal of the lexicon and grammar of French" (269). McWhorter even argued that "Haitian Creole is a significantly less grammatically complex rendition of French" (267). These debates, however compelling, are beyond the scope of the present study.

7 Occupation was not included for three main reasons: 1) it was difficult to distinguish between various sorts of semi-skilled or semi-professional jobs in Miami's immense service sector, which demand bilingual abilities yet do not require high levels of education nor provide high salaries, e.g. retail managers and low-level health care workers; 2) there were many G1 respondents involved in occupations that did not correspond to their levels of formal education or training in their countries of origin, e.g. an Uber driver who was previously an executive in Venezuela and a hotel front desk agent who had been a teacher in Cuba; and 3) many G3 speakers were too young (only in their 20s to early 30s) to have established professions, although they were either studying to complete or had already completed college or professional degrees. Thus, I considered that level of education and parents' level of education would be more reliable predictors of language perception.

6 Beyond Miami

> The Caribbean flows outward past the limits of its own sea with a vengeance.
> —Antonio Benítez-Rojo, *The Repeating Island* (1996)

In February of 2021, trap artist Mariah Angeliq, of "Perreito" fame, released the song "Reggaeton de antes." Popularly referred to as 'La princesa de Miami,' she was born in Miami and raised bilingually by a Puerto Rican mother and Cuban father. Reflecting on the creation and 'flow' of the song, her collaborator Ecko, born and raised in Buenos Aires, explained that the idea to pay homage to 'old school' reggaeton came to him at his studio in Argentina (Pulso Pop 2021). Originating in Puerto Rico with Jamaican influences in the 1990s, the flow of reggaeton spread into South Florida by the late 1990s, and across the US and Latin America in the 2000s, when Mariah Angeliq and Ecko were small children. By 2020, when Mariah Angeliq's agent contacted her on Ecko's behalf with a proposal for a nostalgic song about the genre, she had been nominated for the award for female breakthrough artist in Premios Lo Nuestro. Ecko came to Miami to film the music video for the song with her.

The story of "Reggaeton de antes" seems a fitting example of the sort of cross-Caribbean flows described by Antonio Benítez-Rojo (1996) in his widely cited postmodern account *The Repeating Island*: "Within the sociocultural fluidity that the Caribbean archipelago presents, within its historiographic turbulence and its ethnological and linguistic clamor… one can sense the features of an island that 'repeats' itself, unfolding and bifurcating until it reaches all the seas and lands of the earth" (3). Benítez-Rojo conceptualized the Caribbean, historically and culturally, as an island bridge that connects North and South America "in another way" (1996, 2), a sort of meta-archipelago, in which he included Miami. Engaging with the notion of natural chaos (in relation to complexity theory), he maintained that the Caribbean has neither a boundary nor a center, instead constantly emanating outward in "a continual flow of paradoxes" that are nonlinear, fractal, and iterative: "I have emphasized the word *repeats* because I want to give the term the almost paradoxical sense with which it appears in the discourse of Chaos,

DOI: 10.4324/9780429438363-6

Beyond Miami 263

where every repetition is a practice that necessarily entails a difference and a step toward nothingness.... Which one, then, would be the repeating island, Jamaica, Aruba, Puerto Rico, Miami, Haiti, Recife? Certainly none of the ones that we know" (3). 'Chaos' does not imply the absence of regularities or patterns; on the contrary, it refers to a condition or state within which iterative patterns and feedback loops emerge to reveal complex systems that are characterized by instability and flux. In complex systems, the boundary is unclear even after it has emerged. In his influential work on complexity theory in philosophy and science, Cilliers (2016) affirmed that the boundary is "neither purely a function of our description, nor is it a purely natural thing. We can never be sure that we have 'found' or 'defined' it clearly, and therefore the closure of the system is not something that can be described objectively. An overemphasis on closure will also lead to an understanding of the system that may underplay the role of the environment" (90).

Environment seems the most crucial element of any account of Spanish in the US, I believe. To date, our understanding has generally relied upon static, linear models of language that emphasize the cross-generational dimension of acquisition and use. Within those models, processes of incomplete acquisition and grammatical simplification result from reduced input and use of Spanish among the US-born (Montrul 2016). The intergenerational portrait of a seemingly 'futureless' or ephemeral language thus emerges. In retrospect, studies of language shift published during the 1970s and 1980s could have in no way anticipated the demographic, economic, and cultural boom of Spanish that would occur in the 1990s. From a societal perspective, Spanish has become more present than ever, despite cross-generational discontinuity, and it has garnered a remarkable degree of public legitimacy in mass media, commerce, political debate, and the discourse of consumerism. What the remarkable expansion of Spanish in the US since the 1980s demonstrates is that the language's future in this country is nonlinear, i.e. "a product of emergence" (Byrne and Callaghan 2014, 6). The heyday of US Hispanophilia during the 1910s and 1920s followed by its dramatic contraction during the Great Depression and the advent of WWII, which I briefly described in Chapter 1, illustrates this sort of tendency. Complex systems evidence non-equilibrium, with astounding phases of growth and dissipation that, from a linear modeling perspective, are unforeseeable (Miller and Page 2007; Byrne and Callaghan 2014; Cilliers 2016).

As complexity theorists argue, in the generation of knowledge, models of social reality necessarily involve a reduction in complexity, meaning that multiple intervening factors must be cast aside for sake of the model. This reflects the inevitable disconnect between our descriptions of the world and the world itself (Byrne and Callaghan 2014, 99), as in the successful modeling yet ultimate failure of political polls, sophisticated economic systems, and technological ventures (Appadurai and Alexander 2020). From the cultural perspective of the Caribbean, Benítez-Rojo (1996) observed: "What happens is that postindustrial society... navigates the Caribbean with judgments and

264   *Beyond Miami*

intentions that are like those of Columbus; that is, it lands scientists, investors, and technologists—the new (dis)coverers—who come to apply the dogmas and methods that had served them well where they came from, and who can't see that these refer to the realities back home" (1–2). Complexity theorists argue, however, that linear models pose significant limitations anywhere, especially in relation to complex systems, which I believe is surely the case of Spanish not just in Miami but in the US more broadly.[1]

Hurricanes, complex systems all too familiar in the Caribbean, illustrate but one of many sorts of unforeseeable factors that may shape the situation of Spanish in the US. The sociolinguistic impact of the estimated 280,000 displaced Puerto Ricans who arrived in Florida following Hurricane Maria in 2017 is case in point (Dixon 2018). What model of sociolinguistic (dis) continuity could have possibly anticipated the storm and its consequences? Similarly, who in 1959, upon Castro's rise to power, could have possibly imagined the numbers of Cubans arriving in Miami still to the present day? Who in 1979 could have predicted the sociolinguistic effects of the Sandinistas' overthrow of Somoza's regime in Nicaragua? Or the profound societal instability caused by the FARC in Colombia and Shining Path in Peru? Or the fall of the Berlin Wall, which would have ripple effects in Cuba, subsequently driving massive numbers of 'balseros' to Miami during the mid-1990s? Or the support that Hugo Chávez would garner in Venezuela by the late 1990s? Or the collapse of the Argentine banking system in 2001? All of these events—like so many others on a smaller scale—have sent hundreds of thousands of migrants to Miami, constantly renewing the vitality of Spanish and reshaping the sociolinguistic landscape in tandem with neoliberal economic practices, global investment, the city's rise as a crucial center for Latin American banking and mass media, for contemporary debates around language and ethnicity, racial identity, presidential election outcomes—all sorts of postmodern phenomena sketched by Appadurai (1996) in his series of 'scapes' that I described in Chapter 1. Such phenomena, events, factors, and contingencies have wielded far more profound consequences for the use and continuity of Spanish in South Florida than any sociological or variationist model of cross-generational language use could have ever anticipated. Surely no one in 1970s Miami could have imagined Mariah Angeliq's collaboration with Ecko in 2021, nor the musical genre that they now perform to global popularity.

Miami is not so unique in these regards. Recent history has offered us irrefutable evidence of the unforeseeable nature of the main factors that sustain the Spanish-speaking presence in the US setting: "Processes, dynamics, and rhythms that show themselves within the marginal, the regional, the incoherent, the heterogeneous, or, if you like, the unpredictable that coexists with us in our everyday world" (Benítez-Rojo 1996, 3). In a sea of unknowns and seemingly unpredictable undercurrents, we can nonetheless be quite certain of three things: neoliberal economic practices (and concomitant global consumerism) reflect the new world order and are with us for the foreseeable future; technology and mass media will become ever more pervasive in the everyday; and nationalism remains part and parcel of political postmodernity, as recent political voices have unequivocally manifested. These facts—facets or factors—have profound consequences for the situation of Spanish in the US, of which Miami is a brilliant microcosm. In what follows, by brief way of conclusion, I highlight five language ideological phenomena that I believe will continue to characterize the postmodern Spanish-speaking US, based upon my research and observations in Miami.

Commodification and asset valuation

As I explained in Chapter 1, neoliberal economic practices and the forging of the so-called Hispanic or Latinx market in the US situated Spanish in the realm of public (marketplace) discourse approaching the new millennium. In this respect, the language acquired a novel sense of legitimacy in the US, however consumerist, i.e. Hispanics have the power of a dollar and the power of a vote. In Miami, the commercial value of Spanish dates to the mid-twentieth century; by the 1970s, it was clear that the city's economic future would be highly intertwined with that of Latin America. Today, Miami indisputably constitutes the center for flows between Latin America, the Caribbean, and the US (Nijman 2011). Marketing and sales in Spanish brought written and spoken forms of the language into clear visibility, divesting the language in some ways of its previous value as ethnic identity marker. As the language acquired economic viability and cultural gravitas, its perceived 'asset value' (in the sense of Brown 2015) increased throughout the 1980s and 1990s, driving rapid growth of Spanish language enrollments at all educational levels and heightening public perception of the need for bilingual education. As I explained in Chapter 2, Miami was seemingly at the forefront of both sides of the English-only / value of bilingualism polemic that would sweep the nation during the 1980s.

In the broader US context, the presence of Spanish in consumerism has had a similar ideological effect of legitimation as in Miami, albeit less intense. Although I am unaware of any comparative diachronic studies of national-level attitudes toward Spanish spanning the past several decades, I have the impression that the young adults of today share overall more positive and receptive views of Spanish in public life than their grandparents—a generation that bore witness to corporal punishment for speaking Spanish in schools across the Southwest. The cultural significance of this evolutive tendency in US society cannot be understated, and it bodes well for Spanish language vitality in the immediate future. Undeniably, however, backlash toward Spanish remains very much part of the US social fabric. Political and societal discourse in recent years clearly manifests the profound reluctance on the part of some sectors of US society to 'accept' Spanish in public spaces (Torres 2019). As always, such sentiments are linked to nationalist, anti-immigrant postures that have gained renewed prevalence in recent years.

266 *Beyond Miami*

The influence of consumerism in patterns of Spanish language use, which sometimes calque English-language forms, seems undeniable. As I suggested in Chapter 4, among Cubans in Miami, the influence of the Anglophone discourse of consumerism appears to have driven the inherent expansion of *tú*—the pronoun of solidarity in Spanish—at a faster rate than the ideology of communism in Cuba. Accelerated *tuteo* is but one feature of what I would characterize as 'English-informed' varieties of Spanish, particularly in Spain and among the urban youth of Latin America (Villalobos Graillet 2015; Lynch 2018b). Indeed, in the Real Academia Española's official inquiry into the incursion of English in Spanish marketing and sales—and its related advertising campaign to counter Anglophone effects, mentioned in Chapter 5—it was concluded that "the importance of Spanish [versus English] as a base for the cultural industries of Spain and Latin America" was seemingly ignored in public opinion as well as in professional spheres in Spain (Santamarina 2016, 7). Emergent 'English-informed' varieties reflect pragmatic-discursive patterns inspired by Anglophone ways of saying and 'doing things with words,' as well as English loanwords—particularly related to popular culture, television and film, fashion, science, and technology—and English-influenced lexical and phrasal calques, the dynamics of which I explored in Miami in Chapter 5.

Media(tiza)tion

I argued in Chapter 2 that the ideological commodification of Spanish in Miami was already evident in the bilingual local television sitcom *¿Qué Pasa, USA?* (1977–1980) and in the US mainstream network hit series *The Golden Girls* (1985–1992). In that chapter, I considered the mediatization of Spanish in Miami through metaphors of battleground during the 1980s and marketplace in the 1990s. These mediatic discursive phenomena extended throughout the US and, to some extent, still remain quite prevalent. Over the years, I have asked many people of all walks of life in Miami if they think that a bilingual show like *¿Qué Pasa, USA?* could be as successful today as it was forty years ago. Their answer is usually a resounding 'no'—without hesitation.

Indeed, attempts to produce bilingual television formats in US markets have met with quite limited success and with cynicism. SíTV was the first cable channel with English-language programming for US Latinos. Launched in 2004, it was characterized as "a 'bicultural' alternative to networks such as Univision or Telemundo, and marketed toward audiences who enjoy a Spanish flavor without all the actual Spanish" (O'Neal 2011). The target audience was 18–34-year-old Latinxs who "have long since assimilated into American convention, and who don't necessarily have any particular fealty to the sort of programming that goes to great lengths to remind them of their heritage—unlike their first-generation parents or grandparents" (O'Neal 2011). In 2011, SíTV partnered with Jennifer Lopez and changed its name to NUVO TV. The CEO at the time explained the reasoning for the name change as follows: "SíTV was confusing. People would ask if that was 'sea' like the ocean or 'see' like you can see television. You can imagine what it's been like dealing with that sort of confusion. We also... realized that it conveyed a sense of exclusivity. The bicultural Latino audience is much broader than that... They don't see themselves watching a television network that has a Spanish-language name" (cited in Steinberg 2011). Founder Jeff Valdez explained the difficulties of launching the channel with general market agencies in the early 2000s: "They told us that SíTV was either not big enough or that they could not help us because 'You are Hispanic. You have to go to the Hispanic agencies.' Hispanic agencies would say that 'This is great. But your programming is in English. We could only put commercials in Spanish on your channel. That's all we do! We are not allowed to do English-language commercials'" (Puente 2014, 66).

Fusion TV, a news and satire channel that Univision launched in 2013, featuring *America with Jorge Ramos*, the iconic anchor, transmitted programming entirely in English. Westgate (2014) observed: "Fusion contributes to the segregation of Spanish-language from English-language stories by relegating the former to the Noticias Univision news site; as was the case with NBC Latino, the Fusion news site does not contain any Spanish-language stories. Disney, its ABC subsidiary, and Univision subjugate any potential public interest in multilingual news to their private interests in monolingual content" (89). Universo, the Telemundo enterprise that began as Mun2, has met with some success. Universo offers programs in English and Spanish, but not in shows that combine the two languages in an unbounded fashion. Perhaps nowhere is the bounded nature of bilingualism more evident than in The CW's mainstream hit series *Jane the Virgin* (2014–2019). Depicting three generations of Venezuelan-origin women who live in Miami, the show's script parcels off Spanish and English in highly unusual—not to say artificial—asymmetrical dialogues, in which the grandmother (Alba, played by Ivonne Coll) rarely ever speaks English and her second-generation daughter (Xiomara, played by Andrea Navedo) and third-generation granddaughter (Jane, played by Gina Rodriguez) never say anything to her in Spanish. The presence of Spanish is relegated categorically to Alba and to the scripted confines of the Miami-made telenovelas in which Jane's father stars.

What happened between the time of the great success of *¿Qué Pasa, USA?* and the flop of SíTV? I would say that, with the commodification of language in marketing and mass media, Spanish constitutes somewhat less of a talking point regarding ethnic identity. When a language becomes a commodity, it is more monitored, more regulated, and made more uniform. Da Silva, McLaughlin, and Richards (2007) affirmed the same: "If language... is at the heart of the language industry, then one could expect that code-switching, language mixing, 'foreign' borrowings and neologisms (all characteristics of vernacular bilingualism) would be accepted because they are authentic means of communication. But they are not. In fact, these forms of communication pose problems for those in the language industry, because they work with languages as separate systems" (189). In sum, unbounded language practices

268 *Beyond Miami*

appear irreconcilable with postmodern ideologies of the marketplace value of Spanish within the discourse of globalization.

Boundedness

I imagine that the unbounded language patterns found in *¿Qué Pasa, USA?* discomfit the present-day discursive practices of the US cultural industries because of the ideological tendency toward the commodification of language. This tendency is highly standardizing and leads to a preference for more bounded language practices, especially with regard to exoteric, global languages such as Spanish and English. The marketplace value that has bestowed Spanish a certain sense of legitimacy in US public life entails an ideological imperative of standardization and uniformity, concomitant with parceling and packaging. Univision and Telemundo's television products can certainly be characterized as industry efforts of social engineering to establish a 'neutral' Spanish in the context of the US (Valencia and Lynch 2016, 2020), as I noted in Chapter 1.

The bounding-off and neutralizing of Spanish (re)presented in contemporary US mass media provide good evidence of what Mikhail Bakhtin characterized over a century ago as the 'centripetal' force of society, which leads to 'unitary language.' Bakhtin wrote in the context of revolutionary Russia that language naturally displays the push-and-pull tendencies of human nature (2000 [1934]). According to him, it is in our nature to gravitate toward a center in our constant quest for social consensus and in-group acceptance. This is what he called the 'centripetal' force of language. He also affirmed that it is in our human nature to pull away from a center in the constant effort to question the status quo and establish difference within and between the social groups that constitute our everyday lives. This was, for him, the 'centrifugal' force of language. These two forces reflect the 'heteroglossic' essence of language in society, in his view. Where there is standardization, another form of differentiation will inherently arise, in turn leading to yet another effort toward uniformity.

The contemporary cases of normativization of Quechua, Guaraní, Galician, and Basque are illustrative. For all these minoritized languages, the effort to institutionally standardize and socially normalize them has given rise to rather unfamiliar or uncanny second-language sorts of codes in those respective societies (Lynch 2018b). What results is a kind of 'high' variety in the sense identified by Ferguson (1959) in his classic argument about diglossia, which appears artificial to non-Spanish-dominant speakers, especially those from rural areas, who are oftentimes viewed as the 'authentic' speakers of the language. In relation to Basque specifically, the phenomenon has even given rise to two rather politicized terms: on one hand, *euskaldunberri* to refer to someone who has learned *euskara* as a second language, principally in an academic setting, and on the other hand, *euskaldunzahar* to refer to someone who acquired the language naturalistically, more in line with the ideological

Beyond Miami 269

concept of a 'native speaker.' In this respect, historicity and social authenticity come into play for so-called 'new speakers' (Smith-Christmas et al., 2018), for heritage language speakers, and for second-language users across the globe.

Although the language-bounded models of television and mass media probably lack social authenticity for US-born Latinxs, they nonetheless appear to favor such practices in the media that they consume and even in literary texts written by Latinx bilingual authors (Aguiló Mora and Lynch 2022). For the situation of Spanish in Miami, and the US more broadly, previously quasi-diglossic configurations of the twentieth century are ceding to what I might term consumerist enregisterment (Agha 2007), in which the voice of Spanish in public life (i.e. no longer confined to private, domestic or local neighborhood spheres) takes on a seemingly monochromatic quality that is somehow anonymous (Woolard 2008) though decidedly Mexican-sounding in many respects, especially from a Caribbean perspective (Valencia and Lynch 2020).[2] This seemingly self-organizing quality, which appears an adaptive process in terms of complexity theory, is related to language commodification. Heller and Duchêne (2012) characterize this phenomenon as 'Taylorizing' talk, which "moves language away from being understood as the natural possession of the 'native' (natural-born) speaker to being understood as a skill that we don't even need a human to be able to produce. It allows us to think of language as something measurable.... We slide around somewhere between the prototypical poles of the organic native speaker arising from the earth, and the robot able to automatically not only produce any utterance imaginable, but also to translate it into any language of the world" (13).

As I demonstrated in Chapter 5, insinuations of 'Spanglish' are socioeconomically stratified and oftentimes censured. Intuitively, I concur with Iglesias Illa (2010) that the social cachet of code-switching so prevalent in the 1970s and 1980s is generally lost upon today's young Miami Latinx bilinguals (196, cited at the end of Chapter 5). Although I am unaware of any systematic inquiries into this possibility, I would rather confidently hypothesize that active code-switching is most frequent among second-generation Cubans whose families immigrated to Miami during the 1960s, 1970s, and 1980s. The Spanish language practices of this particular generation correspond to the 1970s zeitgeist of diversity and ethnic identity affirmation represented in *¿Qué Pasa, USA?*. Code-switching strikes me as less prevalent in the everyday interactions of younger Miami Latinx bilinguals, irrespective of their family's national origins or their generation in the US. I conjecture that this sociolinguistic tendency may also be true to some extent in other urban areas of the US; in San Diego, Zentella (2013) documented it among young Mexican American 'transfronteriz@' adults; and in Chicago, Rosa (2019) noted that "Spanglish [codemixing] practices are often characterized as ghetto" among Latinx teens (165), who appeared to value Spanish language skills "only if they did not interfere with one's ability to produce perceived unmarked English" (153). From the Caribbean perspective, I recall Glissant's (1997) affirmation: "One can imagine language diasporas that would change

270   *Beyond Miami*

so rapidly within themselves… that their fixity would lie in that change. Their ability to endure would not be accessible through deepening but through the shimmer of variety. It would be a fluid equilibrium. This linguistic sparkle, so far removed from the mechanics of sabirs and codes, is still inconceivable for us, but only because we are paralyzed to this day by monolingual prejudice" (98).

Paradoxical stance and parodic reflexivity

Bilingualism is very positively valued in Miami, as we saw in Chapter 3. But even though Miami Latinx youth explicitly attribute great importance to Spanish, there is an unequivocal pattern of cross-generational shift to English dominance. Implicit perception techniques may reveal negative bias toward Spanish among Miami Latinx college students, as Phillip Carter and I found in a matched guise study (Carter and Lynch 2018b). Spanish use is pervasive in Miami, across all socioeconomic sectors and all in spheres of public life, but in school contexts, children and adolescents are met with *de facto* restrictive policies and practices that altogether disfavor Spanish. Schooling is not the only phenomenon that inhibits Spanish use, however. My personal sense is that, even if more proactively bilingual pedagogical practices were implemented in public schools, Miami Latinx youth would still largely prefer to speak English among themselves. Time and again, I have observed children of only three or four years of age speaking almost exclusively in English to each other despite only ever speaking Spanish with their parents and caregivers, living in a city where they constantly hear Spanish. I would attribute this to the hegemony of English in popular culture and mass media, not only at the local and national levels, but also globally. Moreover, small children are fully aware that older children and adolescents speak principally in English with each other, and so they follow suit. Several of the Miami Latinx interviewees in Lanier's (2014) study remarked upon the influence of English—and their being encouraged to speak it with same-age peers—even when they visited their family's countries of origin.

As I argued in Chapter 3, the positive valuation of Spanish at the local level and in the higher-order discourse of economic globalization and consumerism does not neatly correlate with actual use of Spanish among those born in Miami. I explained that a paradox thus emerges: Spanish is everywhere yet the Miami-born tend not to speak it among themselves. The ideological emphasis on English is even greater in the lower and lower-middle socioeconomic strata. In the middle and upper socioeconomic strata, bilingualism (i.e. use of both English and Spanish taken together) attracts greater ideological attention, likely the result of the discourse of the neoliberal economic marketplace that became mainstream during the 1990s, as we saw in Chapter 2. I attributed this class-driven paradox to Hutcheon's (2002) concept of parody in postmodernity, i.e. politically ironic acknowledgment of the limits and the powers of representation "in any medium," historically situated and contextually grounded (94).

Not just in Miami, but across the US and Latin America generally, the indexical values of Spanish and English (as prominent languages of globalization) are contested or disrupted on local, translocal, and global scales in a vertical sense. This is especially true in major cities and in media spaces, which constitute a fundamental dimension of social complexity in the contemporary era (Appadurai 1996; Agha 2011; Androutsopoulos 2014). Two illustrative cases of the contestation of language indexical values are the use of 'inverted Spanglish' observed by Rosa (2019) among Latinx youth in Chicago and the controversy that emerged in Phoenix in 2015 when local television news anchor Vanessa Ruiz pronounced Arizona toponyms with Spanish-like phonology in English-language broadcasts (Santos and Hauser 2015). On a global level, Gabilondo (2006) argued that, on the internet, Spanish is a peripheral language in some respects: "The internet brings about a qualitative change in this marginalization [of Spanish], since even translation is no longer an option.... The reference to the periphery... requires a new imagination that nationalist understandings of culture have made unthinkable for most Spanish users: the Spanish speaker is a peripherally-situated web-user.... The interconnectedness of the web demands the acceptance of the *hybrid* nature of any Spanish use of the web" (123–24). Undeniably, the predominance of English on the internet, taken together with the hegemony of English in global popular culture and the Anglophone framework of global consumerist discourse, is gradually conditioning rather more 'English-informed' varieties of Spanish throughout the world, especially in major urban areas and the middle and upper socioeconomic strata (e.g. Villalobos Graillet 2015 in Mexico), as I already mentioned.

Nonlinearity

Nonlinearity is a defining feature of a complex system, the latter understood simply as a group of parts or elements that are interrelated, and in which some pattern of interaction is discernible. In a complex system, which is decentralized and highly adaptive, the whole is not 'equal' to the sum of its parts; it may be greater or less than the sum of its separate parts as a result of strong interconnectivity and synergy (Byrne and Callaghan 2014). Behind the concept of nonlinearity is the principle that relatively small changes to initial conditions can ultimately have large effects overall. A classic example is the nonlinear rate of reduction of drag on individual birds when they fly in a V formation; human interaction reflects similar dynamics (e.g. research on crowd dynamics). Another example is the pattern of growth and collapse of cyclonic storms, which reflect non-equilibrium in stages of sustenance and dissipation of energy; the so-called booms and crashes of economic systems pattern in this way, as do political systems in times of abrupt change, i.e. a

272 *Beyond Miami*

'tipping point' or 'phase transition' is reached, though for the most part no one could have predicted in linear fashion when that point would arrive. This is the productive boundary between stable order and unstable chaos (Miller and Page 2007). Growth or expansion in nonlinear systems happens through positive feedback loops, i.e. growth drives further growth in a compounded fashion (Cillers 2016). Such growth, at times explosive, is necessarily unsustainable by virtue of its chaotic nature, understanding 'chaos' as nonlinearity over time, e.g. the well-known 'butterfly effect' or the fractal patterns of flow across the Caribbean from Benítez-Rojo's (1996) cultural vantage point.

From a computational modeling perspective in the social sciences, Miller and Page (2007) affirmed that "agents in social systems typically interact in highly nonlinear ways," resulting in complexity (39). Like bees or robots, humans depend upon interactive connections, which they must navigate in highly adaptive ways. Some connections are relatively stable and, from a computational perspective, simple (e.g. family and close friends), but many others are unstable and complicated (e.g. traders in a marketplace). The instability of such connections and local interactions rapidly leads to complexity in the broader patterns (Miller and Page 2007, 24). In their groundbreaking work on complexity theory in the social sciences, Byrne and Callaghan (2014) asserted the same: "Whilst measurement and quantitative description are absolutely valid tools in the development of a social science of the complex, the development of systems of equations, however sophisticated, may well have very little to tell us about the social world" (5). I assume that the nonlinear, iterative, and fractal nature of Spanish in US society, both diachronically and synchronically, is best interpreted as a phenomenon of complexity. I do not insinuate that quantitative linear models are not an essential part of the sociolinguist's research toolkit. After all, I have made use of them in the studies presented in this book; they help us understand the language in its present moment. Rather, I am skeptical about what they can tell us about the future of Spanish in the US.

Models of cross-generational loss or incomplete acquisition represent the situation of a particular group in US society, not the situation of Spanish in US society. Such models are highly valuable from the perspective of heritage language studies (cf. Montrul 2016; Otheguy 2016), but perhaps less so from some societal, political-economic, mediatic, or cultural viewpoints. I do not necessarily intimate a 'micro' versus 'macro' level distinction, since one could contemplate micro-level dimensions of Spanish in commerce, consumerism, politics, and mass media in the US, as well as macro-level implications of patterns of generational discontinuity. Complexity theory underscores the importance of the uncertain and in some ways paradoxical relationship between 'micromotives' and 'macrobehaviors': "The link between the micro and macro is not as clear as we once thought. We must explore a new realm that both acknowledges the microfoundations of macrobehavior while simultaneously recognizing the potential for seemingly magical transformations that link one level to another" (Miller and Page 2007, 221).

In my time researching the situation of Spanish in Miami, I have become convinced of the nonlinear and (unforeseeably) iterative continuity of the language in the US. Benítez-Rojo's (1996) postmodern argument about chaos and complexity has resonated quite strongly; as has Hutcheon's (2002) characterization of postmodern reality as "resolutely contradictory and unavoidably political" (1); Blommaert's (2010) proposal regarding the dynamic push-and-pull vertical scalar orders of language, which confront the local and the global; Caravedo's (2014) notion of 'mental spaces' in contemporary urban zones of migration; Glissant's (1997) advocacy for the 'right to opacity' through the contestation of ideological transparency; Appadurai's (1996) sketch of the globalizing scapes of social, cultural, and spatial rupture; and Baudrillard's (1988) suggestion that, in the years that lie ahead, the sign will take increasing precedence over the social and political realities of human life.

Notes

1 Larsen-Freeman argued for a complexity theory framework in research on language acquisition (see Ortega and Han 2017).
2 Rosa (2019) posits that 'raciolinguistic enregisterment' occurs in institutional settings as well.

References

Aarsleff, Hans. 1982. *From Locke to Saussure: Essays on the Study of Language and Intellectual History*. Minneapolis: University of Minnesota Press.

ABC. 2013. "La marea verde invade Mallorca contra el trilingüismo en la mayor protesta de su historia." September 29, 2013.

Adams, Dale. 2007. "Saludos Amigos: Hollywood and FDR's Good Neighbor Policy." *Quarterly Review of Film and Video* 24: 289–95.

Adamson, Robin. 2007. *The Defence of French: A Language in Crisis?* Clevedon, UK: Multilingual Matters.

Agha, Asif. 2007. *Language and Social Relations*. Cambridge: Cambridge University Press.

Agha, Asif. 2011. "Meet Mediatization." *Language & Communication* 31: 163–70.

Aguiló Mora, Francisca. 2010. "Welcome to Miami/Bienvenidos a Miami." In *Dexter: ética y estética de un asesino en serie*, ed. Patricia Trapero, 183–202. Palma de Mallorca: Editorial Laertes—Edicions UIB.

Aguiló Mora, Francisca, and Andrew Lynch. 2017. "*¿Hablas castellano? Do you speak English?* o *Xerres mallorquí?*: Ideologías y actitudes lingüísticas en Mallorca en una era de crisis económica." *Studies in Hispanic and Lusophone Linguistics* 10: 189–223.

Aguiló Mora, Francisca, and Andrew Lynch. 2022. "Percepciones latinxs del cruce lingüístico en textos literarios: el reto de la (pos)modernidad en los Estados Unidos." *Revista Letral* 28: 167–93.

Aja, Alan. 2016. *Miami's Forgotten Cubans: Race, Racialization, and the Miami Afro-Cuban Experience*. New York: Palgrave Macmillan.

Alba, Orlando. 2004. *Cómo hablamos los dominicanos: un enfoque sociolingüístico*. Santo Domingo: Grupo León Jimenes.

Alberts, Heike. 2005. "Changes in Ethnic Solidarity in Cuban Miami." *The Geographical Review* 95: 231–48.

Alfaraz, Gabriela. 2000. "Sound Change in a Regional Variety of Cuban Spanish." Ph.D. diss., Michigan State University.

Alfaraz, Gabriela. 2002. "Miami Cuban Perceptions of Varieties of Spanish." In *Handbook of Perceptual Dialectology*, Vol. 2, eds. Daniel Long and Dennis Preston, 1–11. Amsterdam: Benjamins.

Alfaraz, Gabriela. 2012. "Cuban Spanish in the US Context: Linguistic and Social Constraints on the Variation of Syllable-Final (r) among Cuban Newcomers." *Sociolinguistic Studies* 5: 291–320.

Alfaraz, Gabriela. 2014. "Dialect Perceptions in Real Time: A Restudy of Miami Cuban Perceptions." *Journal of Linguistic Geography* 2: 74–86.

References   275

Alfaraz, Gabriela. 2018. "Framing the Diaspora and the Homeland: Language Ideologies in the Cuban Diaspora." *International Journal of the Sociology of Language* 254: 49–69.

Alim, Samy, John Rickford, and Arnetha Ball. 2016. *Raciolinguistics: How Language Shapes Our Ideas About Race.* New York: Oxford University Press.

Allman, T. D. 1987. *Miami: City of the Future.* New York: Atlantic Monthly Press.

Alvarez, Lizette. 2020. "Latinos Can Be Racist, Too. My Community Shows How." *The Washington Post*, July 28, 2020.

Alvord, Scott. 2010a. "Variation in Miami Cuban Spanish Interrogative Intonation." *Hispania* 93: 234–52.

Alvord, Scott. 2010b. "Miami Cuban Spanish Declarative Intonation." *Studies in Hispanic and Lusophone Linguistics* 3: 3–39.

Alvord, Scott, and Brandon Rogers. 2014. "Miami Cuban Spanish Vowels in Contact." *Sociolinguistic Studies* 8: 139–70.

American Association of Teachers of Spanish and Portuguese. n.d. "History of the AATSP." Accessed June 18, 2021. www.aatsp.org/?page=History

American Community Survey. 2019. Miami-Dade County, Florida. US Census Bureau.

Anderson, Benedict. 1983. *Imagined Communities: Reflections on the Origin and Spread of Nationalism.* London: Verso.

Anderson, Craig, and Brad Bushman. 2002. "The Effects of Media Violence on Society." *Science* 295: 2377–79.

Androutsopoulos, Jannis. 2014. "Mediatization and Sociolinguistic Change: Key Concepts, Research Traditions, Open Issues." In *Mediatization and Sociolinguistic Change*, ed. Jannis Androutsopoulos, 3–48. Berlin: De Gruyter.

Anglicismos. 2016. Creatividad en Blanco. Accessed June 7, 2020. www.youtube.com/watch?v=jvnOS6KWEhc

Anzaldúa, Gloria. 1987. *Borderlands/La Frontera: The New Mestiza.* San Francisco: Aunt Lute Books.

Aparicio, Frances. 2003. "Jennifer as Selena: Rethinking Latinidad in Media and Popular Culture." *Latino Studies* 1: 90–105.

Appadurai, Arjun. 1996. *Modernity at Large: Cultural Dimensions of Globalization.* Minneapolis: University of Minnesota Press.

Appadurai, Arjun. 2013. *The Future as Cultural Fact. Essays on the Global Condition.* London: Verso.

Appadurai, Arjun. 2015. "Mediants, Materiality, Normativity." *Public Culture* 27: 221–37.

Appadurai, Arjun, and Neta Alexander. 2020. *Failure.* Cambridge: Polity.

Aranda, Elizabeth, Sallie Hughes, and Elena Sabogal. 2014. *Making a Life in Multiethnic Miami: Immigration and the Rise of a Global City.* Boulder: Lynne Rienner.

Arnaz, Desi. 1977. *A Book.* New York: Warner.

Árvay, Erzsébet. 2016. "When Security Overrules Reason: McCarthyism in View of the Cases of Charles Chaplin and Lucille Ball." *Diacronie* 28: Article 14.

Asayesh, Gelareh. 1985. "Schools Speak Language of Pride." *Miami Herald*, January 6, 1985: NW10.

Associated Press. 2006. "South Beach: Life Imitates Art, Quite Vicely." *NBC News*, July 25, 2006. www.nbcnews.com/id/wbna14026631

Bakhtin, Mikhail. 1984 [original publication 1929]. *Problems of Dostoevsky's Poetics.* Ed. and trans. Caryl Emerson. Minneapolis: University of Minnesota Press.

276 References

Bakhtin, Mikhail. 2000 [original publication 1934]. "Unitary Language." In *The Routledge Language and Cultural Theory Reader*, eds. Lucy Burke, Tony Crowley, and Alan Girvin, 269–79. London: Routledge.

Barquero, Karla. 2014. "MEP saldrá al rescate del 'vos' para alejar a los ticos del 'tú', una costumbre ajena a Costa Rica." *Crhoy.com*, September 19, 2014. https://archivo.crhoy.com/mep-saldra-al-rescate-del-vos-para-alejar-a-los-ticos-del-tu-una-costumbre-ajena-a-costa-rica/nacionales/

Barrows, Susanna. 1981. *Distorting Mirrors: Visions of the Crowd in Late Nineteenth Century France*. New Haven: Yale University Press.

Battistella, Edwin. 2014. *Sorry about That: The Language of Public Apology*. Oxford: Oxford University Press.

Baudrillard, Jean. 1988. *Selected Writings*, ed. Mark Poster. Stanford: Stanford University Press.

Baudrillard, Jean. 1994. *Simulacra and Simulation*. Trans. Sheila Faria Glaser. Ann Arbor: University of Michigan Press.

Baudrillard, Jean. 2002. *The Spirit of Terrorism and Other Essays*. Trans. Chris Turner. London: Verso.

Bauman, Zygmunt. 2000. *Liquid Modernity*. Malden, MA: Blackwell.

Bell, Maya. 1987. "Voters Catch Language Hot Potato: Dade to Decide on Bilingualism Law." *The Orlando Sentinel*, July 22, 1987: D1.

Bendixen & Amandi International. 2021. "Survey of Florida Cuban-American Voters, March 2021." Accessed June 1, 2021. www.scribd.com/document/498988872/Full-Survey-Cuban-Americans-2021#download

Benítez-Rojo, Antonio. 1996. *The Repeating Island: The Caribbean and the Postmodern Perspective*, 2nd ed. Trans. James Maraniss. Durham, NC: Duke University Press.

Bestard Revilla, Alina. 2012a. *Estudio sociolingüístico de formas de tratamiento en áreas urbanas de Santiago de Cuba*. Editorial Académica Española.

Bestard Revilla, Alina. 2012b. "Estudio sociolingüístico de las formas de tratamiento del habla coloquial de Santiago de Cuba." *Boletín de Lingüística* 24: 28–55.

Bestard Revilla, Alina. 2014. "La dicotomía poder/solidaridad en el uso del sistema pronominal y nominal de tratamiento de hablantes santiagueros." *EFDeportes.com, Revista Digital* 18. www.efdeportes.com/efd188/la-dicotomia-poder-solidaridad-de-hablantes.htm

Beyer, Scott. 2015. "Welcome to Brickell, Miami's 'Wall Street South'." *Forbes*, May 7, 2015. www.forbes.com/sites/scottbeyer/2015/05/07/welcome-to-brickell-miamis-wall-street-south/#3d2e24431f31

Bills, Garland. 1997. "New Mexican Spanish: Demise of the Earliest European Variety in the United States." *American Speech* 72: 154–71.

Bjelland Aune, Karoline. 2019. "El voseo en Cuba: un estudio comparativo." Master's thesis, University of Bergen.

Blas Arroyo, José Luis. 2003. "Perspectivas (socio)lingüísticas en el estudio de la variación y el cambio lingüístico en español." *Estudios de Sociolingüística* 4: 654–93.

Blommaert, Jan. 2003. "Commentary: A Sociolinguistics of Globalization." *Journal of Sociolinguistics* 7: 607–23.

Blommaert, Jan. 2005. *Discourse*. Cambridge: Cambridge University Press.

Blommaert, Jan. 2010. *The Sociolinguistics of Globalization*. Cambridge: Cambridge University Press.

Blommaert, Jan, Elina Westinen, and Sirpa Leppänen. 2015. "Further Notes on Sociolinguistic Scales." *Intercultural Pragmatics* 12: 119–27.

Booth, Cathy. 1993. "Miami: The Capital of Latin America." *TIME Magazine*, November 18, 1993.

Boryga, Andrew. 2019. "How the Turmoil in Puerto Rico Affects Florida." *South Florida Sun Sentinel*, July 26, 2019.

Boswell, Thomas. 1994. *The Cubanization and Hispanicization of Metropolitan Miami*. Miami: Cuban American National Council.

Boswell, Thomas. 2000. "Demographic Changes in Florida and Their Importance for Effective Policies and Practices for Non-English Language Background Students." In *Research on Spanish in the United States: Linguistic Issues and Challenges*, ed. Ana Roca, 406–31. Somerville, MA: Cascadilla.

Bourdieu, Pierre. 1991. *Language and Symbolic Power*, ed. John Thompson. Cambridge: Polity.

Bracker, Milton. 1963. "Bitter, Frustrated, Divided: Cuba's Refugees." *New York Times Magazine*, April 21, 1963.

Brah, Avtar. 1996. *Cartographies of Diaspora: Contesting Identities*. London: Routledge.

Brandist, Craig. 2000. "Bakhtin, Marxism and Russian Populism." In *Materializing Bakhtin. The Bakhtin Circle and Social Theory*, eds. Craig Brandist and Galin Tihanov, 70–93. London: Palgrave MacMillan.

British Council Chile. 2014. "English for Prosperity Colombia Chile Panel Plenary IV." Accessed June 18, 2021. www.youtube.com/watch?v=8n7Ys5WRWBE

Brown, Penelope, and Stephen Levinson. 1987. *Politeness: Some Universals in Language Usage*. Cambridge: Cambridge University Press.

Brown, Roger, and Albert Gilman. 1960. "The Pronouns of Power and Solidarity." In *Style in Language*, ed. Thomas A. Sebeok, 253–76. Cambridge, MA: The MIT Press.

Brown, Wendy. 2015. *Undoing the Demos: Neoliberalism's Stealth Revolution*. Brooklyn: Zone Books.

Byrne, David, and Gill Callaghan. 2014. *Complexity Theory and the Social Sciences. The State of the Art*. London: Routledge.

Callahan, Laura. 2000. "Forms of Address in the Popular Press: A Comparison of Spain, Mexico and the United States." *Kansas Working Papers in Linguistics* 25: 53–72.

Callesano, Salvatore. 2020. "Perceptual Dialectology, Mediatization, and Idioms: Exploring Communities in Miami." Ph.D. diss., University of Texas at Austin.

Cámara, Madelín. 2003. "Words without Borders." In *By Heart / De Memoria: Cuban Women's Journeys in and out of Exile*, ed. María de los Ángeles Torres, 151–67. Philadelphia: Temple University Press.

Campbell, Janie. 2013. "Julia Tuttle, the 'Mother of Miami', Was One Awesome Lady." *HuffPost*, May 12, 2013.

Caravedo, Rocío. 2014. *Percepción y variación lingüística. Enfoque sociocognitivo*. Madrid/Frankfurt: Iberoamericana/Vervuert.

Carricaburo, Norma. 1997. *Las fórmulas de tratamiento en el español actual*. Madrid: Arco/Libros.

Carter, Phillip. 2013. "Poststructuralist Theory and Sociolinguistics: Mapping the Linguistic Turn in Social Theory." *Language and Linguistics Compass* 7: 580–96.

Carter, Phillip, and Salvatore Callesano. 2018. "The Social Meaning of Spanish in Miami: Dialect Perceptions and Implications for Socioeconomic Class, Income, and Employment." *Latino Studies* 16: 65–90.

278   References

Carter, Phillip, Lydda López Valdez, and Nandi Sims. 2020. "New Dialect Formation through Language Contact: Vocalic and Prosodic Developments in Miami English." *American Speech* 95: 119–48.

Carter, Phillip, and Andrew Lynch. 2015. "Multilingual Miami: Current Trends in Sociolinguistic Research." *Language and Linguistics Compass* 9: 369–85.

Carter, Phillip, and Andrew Lynch. 2018a. "On the Status of Miami as a Southern City: Defining Language and Region through Demography and Social History." In *Language Variety in the New South*, eds. Jeffrey Reaser, Eric Wilbanks, Karissa Wojcik, and Walt Wolfram, 306–20. Chapel Hill: University of North Carolina Press.

Carter, Phillip, and Andrew Lynch. 2018b. "Variable Perceptions of Spanish and English in Miami: A Matched Guise Study on Campus and in the Community." Paper presented at the Ninth International Workshop on Spanish Sociolinguistics, Queens College, April 5, 2018.

Castells, Manuel. 2010. *The Information Age: Economy, Society and Culture*. Oxford: Blackwell.

Castro, Fidel. 1974. "Discurso pronunciado en el acto de clausura del II Congreso de la Federación de Mujeres Cubanas, efectuado en el teatro Lázaro Peña, el 29 de noviembre de 1974." Accessed June 18, 2021. www.cuba.cu/gobierno/discursos/1974/esp/f291174e.html

Castro, Max. 1992. "On the Curious Question of Language in Miami." In *Language Loyalties. A Sourcebook on the Official English Controversy*, ed. James Crawford, 178–86. Chicago: University of Chicago Press.

Chakrabarty, Dipesh. 2009. "The Climate of History: Four Theses." *Critical Inquiry* 35: 197–222.

Chavez, Leo. 2013. *The Latino Threat: Constructing Immigrants, Citizens, and the Nation*, 2nd ed. Stanford: Stanford University Press.

Chen, Liyan. 2015. "Forbes 2015 Global 2000: The World's Largest Banks." *Forbes*, May 6, 2015.

Chepesiuk, Ron. 2010. *Gangsters of Miami*. Fort Lee, NJ: Barricade Books.

Chomsky, Noam. 2015. *Turning the Tide: US Intervention in Central America and the Struggle for Peace*. London: Pluto.

Cline, Howard. 1966. "The Latin American Studies Association: A Summary Survey with Appendix." *Latin American Research Review* 2: 57–79.

Cilliers, Paul. 2016. *Critical Complexity: Collected Essays*, ed. Rika Preiser. Berlin: De Gruyter.

Corcoran, David. 1987. "Miami Vice: Monolingualism. To Get Ahead, Habla Español." *The Record* (New Jersey), August 27, 1987: B13.

Córdova, David, and Richard Cervantes. 2010. "Intergroup and Within-Group Perceived Discrimination among US-Born and Foreign-Born Latino Youth." *Hispanic Journal of Behavioral Sciences* 32: 259–74.

Coulmas, Florian. 1992. *Language and Economy*. Oxford: Blackwell.

Coupland, Nikolas. 2014. "Language Change, Social Change, Sociolinguistic Change: A Meta-Commentary." *Journal of Sociolinguistics* 18: 277–86.

Coupland, Nikolas, and Tore Kristiansen. 2011. "Critical Perspectives on Language (De)standardisation." In *Standard Languages and Language Standards in a Changing Europe*, eds. Tore Kristiansen and Nikolas Coupland, 11–35. Oslo: Novus.

Cros Sandoval, Mercedes. 2008. Interview by Julio Estorino. Luis J. Botifoll Oral History Project, University of Miami Cuban Heritage Collection, May 21, 2008. https://digitalcollections.library.miami.edu/digital/collection/chc5212/id/840

References 279

Criscenti, Joseph, ed. 1993. *Sarmiento and His Argentina*. Boulder, CO: Lynne Rienner.

Croucher, Sheila. 1997. *Imagining Miami. Ethnic Politics in a Postmodern World.* Charlottesville: University of Virginia Press.

Da Silva, Emanuel, Mireille McLaughlin, and Mary Richards. 2007. "Bilingualism and the Globalized New Economy: The Commodification of Language and Identity." In *Bilingualism: A Social Approach*, ed. Monica Heller, 183–206. London: Palgrave Macmillan.

Davidson, Ann. 1949. "Tourists' Schools: Florida Universities Give Courses for Visitors." *New York Times*, February 6, 1949: X17.

Dávila, Arlene. 2001. *Latinos, Inc.: The Marketing and Making of a People.* Berkeley: University of California Press.

Dávila, Arlene, and Yeidy Rivero, eds. 2014. *Contemporary Latina/o Media: Production, Circulation, Politics.* New York: NYU Press.

Dawson, Graham. 1994. *Soldier Heroes: British Adventure, Empire and the Imagining of Masculinities*. London: Routledge.

De la Torre, Miguel. 2003. *La Lucha for Cuba: Religion and Politics on the Streets of Miami*. Berkeley: University of California Press.

Del Valle, José, ed. 2007. *La lengua, ¿patria común? Ideas e ideologías del español.* Madrid/Frankfurt: Iberoamericana/Vervuert.

Del Valle, José. 2013. "Linguistic Emancipation and the Academies of the Spanish Language in the Twentieth Century: The 1951 Turning Point." In *A Political History of Spanish: The Making of a Language*, ed. José Del Valle, 229–45. Cambridge: Cambridge University Press.

Del Valle, José. 2014. "The Politics of Normativity and Globalization: Which Spanish in the Classroom?" *Modern Language Journal* 98: 358–72.

Del Valle, José, and Luis Gabriel-Stheeman. 2002. "Nationalism, Hispanismo and Monoglossic Culture." In *The Battle over Spanish between 1800 and 2000: Language Ideologies and Hispanic Intellectuals*, eds. José Del Valle and Gabriel-Stheeman, 1–13. London: Routledge.

Delgado, Humberto, and Lorna Veraldi. 2007. "¿Qué Pasa, USA?" *TV Quarterly* 37: 47–52.

Demographic Profile Miami-Dade County 1960–2000. 2003. Planning Research Section, Miami-Dade County Government.

DePalma, Anthony. 2006. *The Man Who Invented Fidel: Castro, Cuba, and Herbert L. Matthews of The New York Times*. New York: Public Affairs.

Derrida, Jacques. 1976 [original publication 1976]. *Of Grammatology*. Trans. G. C. Spivak. Baltimore: Johns Hopkins University Press.

Diamond, Jared. 1999. *Guns, Germs, and Steel*. New York: W.W. Norton & Co.

Didion, Joan. 1987. *Miami*. London: Weidenfeld & Nicolson.

Dijksterhuis, Eduard Jan. 1961. *The Mechanization of the World Picture.* Oxford: Clarendon.

Diniz de Figueiredo, Eduardo. 2014. "Portuguese Only: A Discourse Analysis of 'Projeto de Lei 1676/1999' from Brazil." *Critical Discourse Studies* 11: 342–59.

Dittmar, Norbert, Peter Schlobinski, and Inge Wachs. 1988. "Berlin Urban Vernacular Studies: Contributions to Sociolinguistics." In *The Sociolinguistics of Urban Vernaculars: Case Studies and their Evaluation*, eds. Norbert Dittmar and Peter Schlobinski, 1–144. Berlin: De Gruyter.

Dixon, Drew. 2018. "Florida Has Handled Nearly 300,000 Puerto Rican Refugees Since Hurricane Maria; Gov. Scott Says State Will Welcome More." *The Florida*

280 *References*

Times-Union, January 2, 2018. www.jacksonville.com/story/business/2018/01/02/florida-has-handled-nearly-300000-puerto-rican-refugees-hurricane-maria/15783418007/

Dodge, Charles. 1894. "Subtropical Florida". *Scribner's Magazine* 15: 345–62.

DuBord, Elise. 2013. "Language, Church and State in Territorial Arizona." In *A Political History of Spanish: The Making of a Language*, ed. José Del Valle, 260–77. Cambridge: Cambridge University Press.

Duchêne, Alexandre, and Monica Heller, eds. 2012. *Language in Late Capitalism: Pride and Profit*. London: Routledge.

Dudley, Steve. 2003. "Tell Us What You Think." *Miami New Times*, September 18, 2003.

Dugger, Celia. 1984. "Metro Oks Bilingualism Law Changes." *Miami Herald*, October 17, 1984: 1D.

Dulfano, Isabel. 2013. "Assessing the Economic Value of the Spanish Language." *Global Business Languages* 18: Article 2.

Dulfano, Isabel, and Fernando Rubio. 2014. "Reset or Forge ahead? Is There a Future and 'Value' in the Study of Spanish? Historical Trends and Calculations of the Merit or Dollar Worth of the Language." *Journal of Multilingual and Multicultural Development* 35: 139–50.

Eckert, Penelope. 1989. *Jocks and Burnouts: Social Categories and Identity in the High School*. New York: Teachers College.

Editorial. 1993. "Say Yes, *Sí, Oui* for Us All." *Miami Herald*, May 18, 1993: 10A.

Eilers, Rebecca, D. Kimbrough Oller, and Alan Cobo-Lewis. 2002. "Bilingualism and Cultural Assimilation in Miami Hispanic Children." In *Language and Literacy in Bilingual Children*, eds. D. Kimbrough Oller and Rebecca Eilers, 43–63. Clevedon, UK: Multilingual Matters.

El Nuevo Diario. 2013. "¿Vos o tú?, he ahí la cuestión." January 19, 2013. www.elnuevodiario.com.ni/opinion/274878-vos-o-tu-he-cuestion/

Elder, Rob. 1975. "Miami Is Changing, New Surveys Show." *Miami Herald*, June 22, 1975: 1A.

Elfrink, Tim. 2010. "Latin American Dictators Love South Florida." *Miami New Times*, September 16, 2010.

Escobar, Anna María, and Kim Potowski. 2015. *El español de los Estados Unidos*. Cambridge: Cambridge University Press.

Espinosa, Aurelio. 1917. "Hispania." *Hispania* 1: 19–23.

Ferguson, Charles. 1959. "Diglossia." *Word* 1: 325–40.

Fernández, Mauro. 2003. "Constitución del orden social y desasosiego: pronombres de segunda persona y fórmulas de tratamiento en español." Colloquium on Second Person Pronouns and Forms of Address in the European Languages. Paris: Instituto Cervantes.

Fernández Parera, Antoni. 2017. "Lexical Influences and Perceptions of Cuban Spanish in Miami." In *Cuban Spanish Dialectology: Variation, Contact and Change*, ed. Alejandro Cuza, 211–27. Washington, DC: Georgetown University Press.

Field, Fredric. 2002. *Linguistic Borrowing in Bilingual Context*. Amsterdam: Benjamins.

Finnegan, William. 2015. "The Man Who Wouldn't Sit Down." *The New Yorker*, October 5, 2015.

Fisher, Marc. 1983. "After Three Years, Bilingualism Law Foments Discontent." *Miami Herald*, October 2, 1983: 1B.

References 281

Fisher, Marc. 1984. "Valdes Seeks Bilingual Law Reform. Foreign Language Signs Urged." *Miami Herald*, September 6, 1984: 1B.

Fisher, Mark. 2009. *Capitalist Realism: Is There No Alternative?* Ropley, UK: John Hunt.

Fishman, Joshua. 1992. "The Displaced Anxieties of Anglo-Americans." In *Language Loyalties. A Sourcebook on the Official English Controversy,* ed. James Crawford, 165–71. Chicago: University of Chicago Press.

Fiske, John. 1996. *Media Matters: Everyday Culture and Political Change*. Minneapolis: University of Minnesota Press.

Florida Department of Education. 2018. "Results of Florida Standards Assessments: English Language Arts, 2018." Accessed June 19, 2021. www.fldoe. org/accountability/assessments/k-12-student-assessment/results/2018.stml

Foucault, Michel. 1994 [original publication 1966, English translation first published 1970]. *The Order of Things. An Archaeology of the Human Sciences.* New York: Vintage Books.

Fradd, Sandra. 1996. "The Economic Impact of Spanish Language Proficiency in Metropolitan Miami." Miami: Greater Miami Chamber of Commerce and the Cuban American National Council.

Franco-Rodríguez, José. 2007. "El español en el condado de Miami-Dade desde su paisaje lingüístico." *Lingüística en la Red* 5.

Frías, Carlos. 2017. "'¿Qué Pasa, USA?' Cashes In, but Cast Feels Left Out." *Miami Herald*, December 21, 2017.

Gabilondo, Joseba. 2006. "Spanish, Second Language of the Internet? The Hispanic Web, Subaltern-Hybrid Cultures, and the Neo-liberal Lettered City." *Revista Canadiense de Estudios Hispánicos* 31: 107–29.

Gándara, Patricia, and Kathy Escamilla. 2017. "Bilingual Education in the United States." In *Bilingual and Multilingual Education*, eds. Ofelia García, Angel Lin, and Stephen May, 439–52. Springer International.

García, María Cristina. 1996. *Havana, USA: Cuban Exiles and Cuban Americans in South Florida, 1959–1994*. Berkeley: University of California Press.

Gebhard, David. 1967. "The Spanish Colonial Revival in Southern California (1895–1930)." *Journal of the Society of Architectural Historians* 26: 131–47.

Giddens, Anthony. 1990. *The Consequences of Modernity*. Cambridge: Polity.

Geyer, Georgie Anne. 1993. "Speak English." *Miami Herald*, June 15, 1993: 19A.

Geyer, Michael, and Charles Bright. 1995. "World History in a Global Age." *The American Historical Review* 100: 1034–60.

Gillis, Justin, and Luis Feldstein Soto. 1987. "Valdes: No English-Only Referendum." *Miami Herald*, August 18, 1987: 1B.

Glissant, Édouard. 1997. *Poetics of Relation*. Trans. Betsy Wing. Ann Arbor: University of Michigan Press.

González, Héctor Alejandro, and Ania Liste. 2017. "El otro muro: el acento neutro en las series y telenovelas hispanas." *Diario de las Américas*, March 24, 2017.

González, Victoria. 2012. "La Real Academia Española aceptará las palabras tuitear, tuiteo, tuit y tuitero." *Muyinteresante.es*. www.muyinteresante.es/cultura/arte-cultura/articulo/la-real-academia-espanola-aceptara-las-palabras-tuitear-tuiteo-tuit-y-tuitero

González Pino, Bárbara, and Frank Pino. 2007. "An Exploration of Cross-Cultural Antagonism in Heritage Students of Spanish: *La Leyenda Negra* in a New Guise." *NAAAS Conference Proceedings*, 226–38. National Association of African-American Studies.

282 References

González-Rivera, Melvin, and Luis Ortiz López. 2018. "El español y el inglés en Puerto Rico: una polémica de más de un siglo." *Centro Journal* 30: 106–31.

Goodhue, Bertram. 1916. *The Architecture and the Gardens of the San Diego Exposition.* San Francisco: Paul Elder & Co.

Gramlich, John, and Kat Devlin. 2019. "More People around the World See U.S. Power and Influence as a 'Major Threat' to Their Country." Pew Research Center, February 14, 2019.

Greater Miami Convention and Visitors Bureau. 2019. "Record Tourism Industry Performance in 2018." April 30, 2019. www.miamiandbeaches.com/press-room/miami-press-releases/record-tourism-industry-performance-in-2018

Green, Duncan. 2003. *Silent Revolution: The Rise and Crisis of Market Economics in Latin America*, 2nd ed. New York: Monthly Review.

Grenier, Guillermo. 2015. "Interviews from Havana: Are Cuban American Attitudes Changing?" Interview by Cristina Escobedo, TeleSUR. www.youtube.com/watch?v=Mys5PsHogaI

Grenier, Guillermo, and Lisandro Pérez. 2003. *The Legacy of Exile: Cubans in the United States*. Boston: Allyn & Bacon.

Groppa, Carlos. 2004. *The Tango in the United States: A History*. Jefferson, NC: McFarland & Co.

Gutiérrez-Rivas, Carolina. 2007. "Variación pragmática del español de los cubanos y cubanoamericanos en Miami: el efecto de género y generación en el uso de estructuras discursivas." Ph.D. diss., University of Florida.

Gutiérrez-Rivas, Carolina. 2011a. "Variación y cambio pragmático en el español de los cubanos en Miami: el efecto de la generación en el discurso bilingüe." In *Estudios de variación pragmática en español*, eds. Carmen García and María Elena Placencia, 167–83. Buenos Aires: Dunken.

Gutiérrez-Rivas, Carolina. 2011b. "El efecto del género en el discurso bilingüe. Un estudio sobre peticiones." *Estudios de Lingüística Aplicada* 54: 37–59.

Hampton, Jim. 1993. "Bind Up Anti-Bilingual Wounds." *Miami Herald*, May 2, 1993: 2M.

Hardin, Karol. 2001. *Pragmatics in Persuasive Discourse in Spanish Television Advertising*. Dallas: SIL International/University of Texas at Arlington.

Harvard Youth Poll. Spring 2020. https://iop.harvard.edu/youth-poll/harvard-youth-poll

Harvey, David. 2005. *A Brief History of Neoliberalism*. Oxford: Oxford University Press.

Haslip-Viera, Gabriel. 2010. "The Evolution of the Latino Community in New York." In *Hispanic New York: A Sourcebook*, ed. Claudio Remeseira, 33–56. New York: Columbia University Press.

Hayek, Friedrich. 1944. *The Road to Serfdom*. London: Routledge.

Hayek, Friedrich. 1960. *The Constitution of Liberty*. Chicago: University of Chicago Press.

Heller, Monica, ed. 2007. *Bilingualism: A Social Approach*. London: Palgrave Macmillan.

Heller, Monica. 2011. *Paths to Post-Nationalism: A Critical Ethnology of Language and Identity*. Oxford: Oxford University Press.

Heller, Monica. 2013. "Repositioning the Multilingual Periphery: Class, Language and Transnational Markets in Francophone Canada." In *Multilingualism and the Periphery*, eds. Sari Pietikäinen and Helen Kelly-Holmes, 17–34. Oxford: Oxford University Press.

References   283

Heller, Monica, and Alexandre Duchêne. 2012. "Pride and Profit: Changing Discourses of Language, Capital and Nation-State." In *Language in Late Capitalism: Pride and Profit*, eds. Alexandre Duchêne and Monica Heller, 1–21. London: Routledge.

Hernández, Jillian. 2009. "'Miss, You Look Like a Bratz Doll': On Chonga Girls and Sexual-Aesthetic Excess." *National Women's Studies Association Journal* 21: 63–91.

Hiatt, Anna. 2012. "*Dexter* Returns Sunday: Designer Jessica Kender on Season Seven, Florida Weirdness, and Creating Miami on the West Coast." *Miami New Times*, September 28, 2012.

Hill, Jane. 1998. "Language, Race and White Public Space." *American Anthropologist* 100: 680–89.

Hobsbawm, Eric. 1996. *The Age of Revolution: 1789–1848*, 6th ed. New York: Vintage Books.

Holquist, Michael. 2002. *Dialogism: Bakhtin and His World*, 2nd ed. London: Routledge.

Hutcheon, Linda. 2002. *The Politics of Postmodernism*, 2nd ed. London: Routledge.

Hutcheon, Linda. 2006. "Postmodernism." In *The Routledge Companion to Critical Theory*, eds. Simon Malpas and Paul Wake, 115–26. London: Routledge.

Iglesias Illa, Hernán. 2010. *Miami. Turistas, colonos y aventureros en la última frontera de América Latina*. Buenos Aires: Editorial Planeta/Seix Barral.

Irvine, Judith, and Susan Gal. 2000. "Language Ideology and Linguistic Differentiation." In *Regimes of Language*, ed. Paul Kroskrity, 35–84. Santa Fe: School of American Research Press.

Jaffe, Alexandra. 2011. "Sociolinguistic Diversity in Mainstream Media." *Journal of Language and Politics* 10: 562–86.

Jameson, Fredric. 1991. *Postmodernism, or the Cultural Logic of Late Capitalism*. Durham, NC: Duke University Press.

Jiménez Ángel, Andrés. 2018. *Ciencia, lengua y cultura nacional: La transferencia de la ciencia del lenguaje en Colombia, 1867–1911*. Bogotá: Editorial Pontificia Universidad Javeriana.

Jones, Stuart. 1999. "Taine and the Nation-State." In *Writing National Histories: Western Europe since 1800*, eds. Stefan Berger, Mark Donovan, and Kevin Passmore, 85–96. London: Routledge.

Kabatek, Johannes. 2011. "Algunos apuntes acerca de la 'hibridez' y de la 'dignidad' de las lenguas iberorrománicas." In *Variación lingüística y contacto de lenguas en el mundo hispánico. In memoriam Manuel Alvar*, eds. Yolanda Congosto Martín and Elena Méndez García de Paredes, 271–90. Madrid/Frankfurt: Iberoamericana/Vervuert.

Katzberg, William. 1993. "You're in America." *Miami Herald*, June 15, 1993: 19A.

Kelly, James. 1981. "South Florida: Trouble in Paradise." *TIME Magazine*, November 23, 1981.

Kirkland, Ewan. 2011. "Dexter's Whiteness." In *Dexter and Philosophy*, eds. Richard Greene, George Reisch, and Rachel Robison-Greene, 199–208. Chicago: Open Court.

Klee, Carol, and Andrew Lynch. 2009. *El español en contacto con otras lenguas*. Washington, DC: Georgetown University Press.

Koch, Wendy. 2006. "U.S. Urged to Apologize for 1930s Deportations." *USA Today*, April 4, 2006.

Korzenny, Felipe, Sindy Chapa, and Betty Ann Korzenny. 2017. *Hispanic Marketing: The Power of the New Latino Consumer*, 3rd ed. London: Routledge.

284   *References*

Krongauz, Maxim. 2007. *Russkij jazyk na grani nervnogo sryva*. Moscow: Languages of Slavic Cultures.

Krotz, Friedrich. 2009. "Mediatization: A Concept with Which to Grasp Media and Societal Change." In *Mediatization: Concept, Changes, Consequences*, ed. Knut Lundby, 19–38. New York: Peter Lang.

Labov, William. 1972. *Sociolinguistic Patterns*. Philadelphia: University of Pennsylvania Press.

Laguna, Albert Sergio. 2010. "*Aquí Está Álvarez Guedes*: Cuban *Choteo* and the Politics of Play." *Latino Studies* 8: 509–31.

Laguna, Albert Sergio. 2017. *Diversión: Play and Popular Culture in Cuban America*. New York: NYU Press.

Lakoff, George, and Mark Johnson. 1980. *Metaphors We Live By*. Chicago: University of Chicago Press.

Lakoff, Robin. 1973. "The Logic of Politeness, or, Minding Your P's & Q's." In *Papers from the Ninth Regional Meeting Chicago Linguistic Society*, eds. Claudia Corum, T. Cedric Smith-Stark, and Annika Weiser, 292–305. Chicago: Chicago Linguistic Society.

Lambert, Wallace, and Donald M. Taylor. 1996. "Language in the Lives of Ethnic Minorities: Cuban American Families in Miami." *Applied Linguistics* 17: 477–500.

Lanier, Elizabeth G. 2014. "Identity and Language Perceptions among Second-Generation Spanish Speakers in Miami." Master's thesis, University of Miami.

Lavelle, Ciara. 2017. "*Shit Miami Girls Say*'s Halloween Special is a White Girl's Nightmare." *Miami New Times*, October 27, 2017.

Levi, Michael, and Peter Reuter. 2006. "Money Laundering." *Crime and Justice* 34: 289–375.

Limón, Renata. 2014. "The Science of Folklore: Aurelio Espinosa on Spain and the American Southwest." *Journal of American Folklore* 127: 448–66.

Lippi-Green, Rosina. 1997. *English with an Accent: Language, Ideology, and Discrimination in the United States*. London: Routledge.

Lipski, John. 1987. "The Construction *Para atrás* among Spanish-English Bilinguals: Parallel Structures and Universal Patterns." *IberoAmericana* 28/29: 87–96.

Looney, Dennis, and Natalia Lusin. 2019. "Enrollments in Languages other than English in United States Institutions of Higher Education, Summer 2016 and Fall 2016: Final Report." Modern Language Association. Accessed June 15, 2021. www.mla.org/content/download/110154/2406932/2016-Enrollments-Final-Report.pdf

Londoño, Ernesto, Daniel Politi, and Santi Carneri. 2021. "'Like a Dream': Latin Americans Head to U.S. for Covid Shots." *New York Times*, May 29, 2021.

López, Mark Hugo. 2013. "Hispanic Identity." Pew Research Center, October 22, 2013.

López Alonzo, Karen. 2016. "Use and Perception of the Pronominal Trio *Vos, Tú, Usted* in a Nicaraguan Community in Miami, Florida." In *Forms of Address in the Spanish of the Americas*, eds. María Irene Moyna and Susana Rivera-Mills, 197–232. Amsterdam: Benjamins.

López Morales, Humberto. 2003. *Los cubanos de Miami. Lengua y sociedad*. Miami: Ediciones Universal.

López Morales, Humberto. 2018 [original publication 1971]. *Estudios sobre el español de Cuba*. Madrid: Verbum.

Luján García, Carmen. 2013. *The English Language and Anglo-American Culture: Its Impact on Spanish Language and Society*. Newcastle upon Tyne: Cambridge Scholars.

References 285

Lummis, Charles. 1911 [original publication 1892]. *Some Strange Corners of Our Country*. New York: Century Co.

Lundby, Knut. 2009. "Introduction: 'Mediatization' as Key." In *Mediatization: Concept, Changes, Consequences*, ed. Knut Lundby, 1–18. New York: Peter Lang.

Lynch, Andrew. 1999. "The Subjunctive in Miami Cuban Spanish: Bilingualism, Contact, and Language Variability." Ph.D. diss., University of Minnesota.

Lynch, Andrew. 2000. "Spanish-Speaking Miami in Sociolinguistic Perspective: Bilingualism, Recontact, and Language Maintenance among the Cuban-Origin Population." In *Research on Spanish in the United States: Linguistic Issues and Challenges*, ed. Ana Roca, 271–83. Somerville, MA: Cascadilla.

Lynch, Andrew. 2009a. "Expression of Cultural Standing in Miami: Cuban Spanish Discourse about Fidel Castro and Cuba." *Revista Internacional de Lingüística Iberoamericana* 14: 21–48.

Lynch, Andrew. 2009b. "A Sociolinguistic Analysis of Final /s/ in Miami Cuban Spanish." *Language Sciences* 31: 767–90.

Lynch, Andrew. 2013. "Observaciones sobre comunidad y (dis)continuidad en el estudio sociolingüístico del español en Estados Unidos." In *El español en los Estados Unidos: E pluribus unum? Enfoques multidisciplinarios*, eds. Domnita Dumitrescu and Gerardo Piña-Rosales, 67–83. New York: Academia Norteamericana de la Lengua Española.

Lynch, Andrew. 2017. "The Social Diffusion of English-Based Lexical Innovations in Miami Cuban Spanish." In *Cuban Spanish Dialectology: Variation, Contact and Change*, ed. Alejandro Cuza, 165–87. Washington, DC: Georgetown University Press.

Lynch, Andrew. 2018a. "A Historical View of US Latinidad and Spanish as Heritage Language." In *The Routledge Handbook of Spanish as a Heritage Language*, ed. Kim Potowski, 17–35. London: Routledge.

Lynch, Andrew. 2018b. "Spatial Reconfigurations of Spanish in Postmodernity: The Relationship to English and Minoritized Languages." In *The Dynamics of Language Variation and Change: Varieties of Spanish across Space and Time*, eds. Jeremy King and Sandro Sessarego, 11–34. Amsterdam: Benjamins.

Lynch, Andrew. 2019. "Miami como encrucijada dialectal del mundo hispanohablante." *Archiletras Científica 2. El español, lengua migratoria*, ed. Francisco Moreno Fernández, 125–40. Madrid: Prensa y Servicios de la Lengua.

Lynch, Andrew, and Antoni Fernández Parera. 2021. "Variable Realization of Final /s/ in Miami Cuban Spanish: The Reversal of Diachronic Language Change." In *Sociolinguistic Approaches to Sibilant Variation in Spanish*, ed. Eva Núñez Méndez, 164–91. London: Routledge.

Lynch, Andrew, and Carol Klee. 2005. "Estudio comparativo de actitudes hacia el español en los Estados Unidos: educación, política y entorno social." *Lingüística Española Actual* 27: 273–300.

Lynch, Andrew, and Kim Potowski. 2014. "La valoración del habla bilingüe en Estados Unidos: fundamentos sociolingüísticos y pedagógicos en *Hablando bien se entiende la gente*." *Hispania* 97: 32–46.

Lynch, Kevin. 1960. *The Image of the City*. Cambridge, MA: The MIT Press.

Lyotard, Jean-François. 1984 [original publication 1979]. *The Postmodern Condition: A Report on Knowledge*. Trans. Geoff Bennington and Brian Massumi. Minneapolis: University of Minnesota Press.

286 *References*

MacCannell, Dean, and Juliet Flower MacCannell. 1993. "Social Class in Postmodernity: Simulacrum or Return of the Real?" In *Forget Baudrillard?*, eds. Chris Rojek and Bryan Turner, 124–45. London: Routledge.

Mahler, Sarah. 2018. "Monolith or Mosaic? Miami's Twenty-First-Century Latin@ Dynamics." *Latino Studies* 16: 2–20.

Mailander Farrell, Jodi. 1998. "Dade's Program Different." *Miami Herald*, June 4, 1998: 8A.

Malkiel, Yakov. 1967. "Multiple versus Simple Causation in Linguistic Change." In *To Honor Roman Jakobson*, 1228–46. The Hague: Mouton.

Mallet, Marie, and Joanna Pinto-Coelho. 2018. "Investigating Intra-Ethnic Divisions among Latino Immigrants in Miami, Florida." *Latino Studies* 16: 91–112.

Mandeville, Bernard. 1724. *The Fable of the Bees*. Oxford: Clarendon Press.

Martínez, Glenn. 2013. "Public Health and the Politics of Spanish in Early Twentieth-Century Texas." In *A Political History of Spanish: The Making of a Language*, ed. José Del Valle, 293–304. Cambridge: Cambridge University Press.

McCaroll, Thomas. 1993. "It's a Mass Market No More." *TIME Magazine*, November 18, 1993.

McGeary, Johanna, and Cathy Booth. 1993. "Cuba Alone." *TIME*, December 6, 1993.

McQuail, Denis. 2005. *McQuail's Mass Communication Theory*, 5th ed. London: Sage.

McWhorter, John. 2020. "Heritage Language, Creole Language: Incomplete Acquisition and Modern Language Contact Typology." *Heritage Language Journal* 17: 264–77.

McWilliams, Carey. 1990 [original publication 1948]. *North from Mexico. The Spanish-Speaking People of the United States*. New York: Greenwood.

Meltzer, Matt. 2007. "*Scarface*: Why the Iconic Miami film Was Not Even Shot in Miami." *Miami Beach 411*, October 2, 2007. www.miamibeach411.com/news/scarface

Meluza, Lourdes. 1986. "Critics: Show Fuels Ill Will. Donahue Touches Bilingual Nerve in Show's Finale." *Miami Herald*, February 8, 1986: 1B.

Merino, María-Eugenia, Andrew Webb, Sarah Radcliffe, Sandra Becerra, and Carmen Gloria Aillañir. 2020. "Laying Claims on the City: Young Mapuche Ethnic Identity and the Use of Urban Space in Santiago, Chile." *Latin American and Caribbean Ethnic Studies* 15: 1–22.

Meyrowitz, Joshua. 1985. *No Sense of Place: The Impact of Electronic Media on Social Behavior*. Oxford: Oxford University Press.

Miami Herald. 1988. "The Survey and Its Results." October 16, 1988: 20A.

Miami Herald. 1998. "A Wake-Up Call." March 18, 1998: 16A.

Miami-Dade County Public Schools. 2018a. "Department of Bilingual Education and World Languages Elementary/ K-8 Language Offerings, 2017–2018." Accessed March 10, 2020. http://mdcpsbilingual.net/pdf/WL/Program_Offerings.pdf

Miami-Dade County Public Schools. 2018b. "Statistical Highlights, 2017–2018." Accessed March 10, 2020. http://drs.dadeschools.net/StatisticalHighlights/SH1718.pdf

Michaud, Nicolas. 2011. "Can We Blame a Man with No Choice?" In *Dexter and Philosophy*, eds. Richard Greene, George Reisch, and Rachel Robison-Greene, 35–43. Chicago: Open Court.

Michnowicz, Jim, J. Scott Despain, and Rebecca Gorham. 2016. "The Changing System of Costa Rican Pronouns of Address: *Tuteo*, *Voseo*, and *Ustedeo*." In

Forms of Address in the Spanish of the Americas, eds. María Irene Moyna and Susana Rivera-Mills, 243–65. Amsterdam: Benjamins.

Miller, John, and Scott Page. 2007. *Complex Adaptive Systems. An Introduction to Computational Models of Social Life*. Princeton: Princeton University Press.

Molina, Natalia. 2006. *Fit to Be Citizens? Public Health and Race in Los Angeles, 1879–1939*. Berkeley: University of California Press.

Montalbán, Ricardo. 2002. "On His Ads for Chrysler's Cordoba." Interview by the Television Academy Foundation. https://interviews.televisionacademy.com/interviews/ricardo-montalban?clip=50458#interview-clips

Montrul, Silvina. 2016. *The Acquisition of Heritage Languages*. Cambridge: Cambridge University Press.

Mora, Cristina. 2014. *Making Hispanics: How Activists, Bureaucrats and Media Constructed a New American*. Chicago: University of Chicago Press.

Morales, Ed. 2018. *Latinx: The New Force in American Politics and Culture*. London: Verso.

Morales, Maria, and Dexter Filkins. 1993. "Battle Lines Drawn over English-Only at Metro." *Miami Herald*, April 29, 1993: 1B.

Moreno Fernández, Francisco. 2007. "Anglicismos en el léxico disponible de los adolescentes hispanos de Chicago." In *Spanish in Contact: Policy, Social and Linguistic Inquiries,* eds. Kim Potowski and Richard Cameron, 41–58. Amsterdam: Benjamins.

Moreno Fernández, Francisco. 2016. "La búsqueda de un español global." Paper presented at the Séptimo Congreso Internacional de la Lengua Española, San Juan, Puerto Rico.

Moreno Fernández, Francisco. 2017. *A Framework for Cognitive Sociolinguistics*. London: Routledge.

Moreno Fernández, Francisco. 2018. *Diccionario de anglicismos del español estadounidense*. Instituto Cervantes at Harvard University.

Morton, Luis. 1963. "National Security and Area Studies. The Intellectual Response to the Cold War." *Journal of Higher Education* 34: 142–47.

Moyna, María Irene. 2016. "Introduction: Addressing the Research Questions." In *Forms of Address in the Spanish of the Americas*, eds. María Irene Moyna and Susana Rivera-Mills, 1–12. Amsterdam: Benjamins.

Mullen, Kristen. 2015. "A Cross-Generational Analysis of Spanish-to-English Lexico-Semantic Phenomena in Emerging Miami English." Master's thesis, Florida International University.

Muschert, Glenn, and Johanna Sumiala. 2012. "Introduction: School Shootings as Mediatized Violence." In *School Shootings: Mediatized Violence in a Global Age*, eds. Glenn Muschert and Johanna Sumiala, xv–xxix. Bingley, UK: Emerald.

Muysken, Pieter. 2000. *Bilingual Speech: A Typology of Code-Mixing*. Cambridge: Cambridge University Press.

Negrón-Muntaner, Frances. 1997. *Puerto Rican Jam: Rethinking Colonialism and Nationalism*. Minneapolis: University of Minnesota Press.

New York Times. 1898. "Topics of the Times." August 24, 1898: E3.

New York Times. 1926. "Would Make Cuba a Tourists' Mecca." July 11, 1926: E3.

Nieto-Phillips, John. 2004. *The Language of Blood. The Making of Spanish-American Identity in New Mexico, 1880s-1930s*. Albuquerque: University of New Mexico Press.

288 References

Nijman, Jan. 2011. *Miami: Mistress of the Americas*. Philadelphia: University of Pennsylvania Press.

Nowotny, Helga. 1994. *Time: The Modern and the Postmodern Experience*. Oxford: Polity.

Núñez Nogueroles, Eugenia Esperanza. 2017. "An Up-to-Date Review of the Literature on Anglicisms in Spanish." *Diálogo de la Lengua* 9: 1–54.

O'Neal, Sean. 2011. "SíTV." *AV Club*, March 22, 2011. www.avclub.com/si-tv-1798224799

Ortega, Lourdes, and ZhaoHong Han, eds. 2017. *Complexity Theory and Language Development. In Celebration of Diane Larsen-Freeman*. Amsterdam: Benjamins.

Ortiz López, Luis, and Cristina Martínez Pedraza. 2020. "Real Perception or Perceptive Accommodation? The Dominirican Ethnic-Dialect Continuum and Sociolinguistic Context." In *Hispanic Contact Linguistics: Theoretical, Methodological and Empirical Perspectives*, eds. Luis Ortiz López, Rosa Guzzardo Tamargo, and Melvin González-Rivera, 264–82. Amsterdam: Benjamins.

Otheguy, Ricardo. 2003. "Las piedras nerudianas se tiran al norte: meditaciones lingüísticas sobre Nueva York." *Ínsula* 679–80: 13–19.

Otheguy, Ricardo. 2011. "Functional Adaptation and Conceptual Convergence in the Analysis of Language Contact in the Spanish of Bilingual Communities in New York." In *The Handbook of Hispanic Sociolinguistics*, ed. Manuel Díaz-Campos, 504–29. Malden, MA: Wiley-Blackwell.

Otheguy, Ricardo. 2016. "The Linguistic Competence of Second-Generation Bilinguals: A Critique of 'Incomplete Acquisition.'" In *Romance Linguistics 2013: Selected Papers from the 43rd Linguistic Symposium on Romance Languages*, eds. Christina Tortora, Marcel den Dikken, Ignacio Montoya, and Teresa O'Neill, 301–19. Amsterdam: Benjamins.

Otheguy, Ricardo, and Ofelia García. 1988. "Diffusion of Lexical Innovations in the Spanish of Cuban Americans." In *Research Issues and Problems in United States Spanish: Latin American and Southwestern Varieties*, eds. Jacob Ornstein-Galicia, George Green, and Dennis Bixler-Márquez, 203–43. Brownsville, TX: Pan American University.

Otheguy, Ricardo, Ofelia García, and Wallis Reid. 2015. "Clarifying Translanguaging and Deconstructing Named Languages: A Perspective from Linguistics." *Applied Linguistics Review* 6: 281–307.

Otheguy, Ricardo, Ofelia García, and Ana Roca. 2000. "Speaking in Cuban: The Language of Cuban Americans." In *New Immigrants in the United States*, eds. Sandra McKay, and Sau-ling Wong, 165–88. Cambridge: Cambridge University Press.

Padró Ocasio, Bianca, and Nora Gámez Torres. 2021. "Most Cuban Americans Do Not Support Normalizing Relations with the Island, New Poll Shows." *Miami Herald*, March 16, 2021.

Parks, Arva Moore. 1991. *Miami: The Magic City*. Miami: Centennial Press.

Parks, Arva Moore, and Gregory W. Bush. 1996. *Miami: The American Crossroad*. Coral Gables: University of Miami/Simon & Schuster.

Pascual y Cabo, Diego. 2015. "Language Attitudes and Linguistic Identities in Miami." In *New Perspectives on Hispanic Contact Linguistics in the Americas*, eds. Sandro Sessarego and Melvin González-Rivera, 373–404. Madrid/Frankfurt: Iberoamericana/Vervuert.

Pascual y Cabo, Diego, and Inmaculada Gómez Soler. 2015. "Preposition Stranding in Spanish as a Heritage Language." *Heritage Language Journal* 12: 186–209.

References   289

Pasols, Aaliyah. 2020. "Miami's Hispanic Community Has a Blind Spot in Recognizing Racism and Colorism." *Miami New Times*, July 17, 2020.

Pedalino Porter, Rosalie. 1998. "The Case Against Bilingual Education: Why Even Latino Parents Are Rejecting a Program Designed for Their Children's Benefit." *The Atlantic*, May 1998.

Pérez, Louis. 1999. *On Becoming Cuban: Identity, Nationality, and Culture.* Chapel Hill: University of North Carolina Press.

Pérez Firmat, Gustavo. 1994. *Life on the Hyphen: The Cuban-American Way.* Austin: University of Texas Press.

Pew Research Center. 2016. "Hispanic Population and Origin in Select U.S. Metropolitan Areas, 2014." September 6, 2016.

Phillips, R. Hart. 1948. "Cubans Enliven Miami Season." *New York Times*, September 5, 1948: X11.

Pidd, Helen. 2011. "Mind Your Language: German Linguists Oppose Influx of English Words." *The Guardian*, March 14, 2011.

Pietikäinen, Sari, Alexandra Jaffe, Helen Kelly-Holmes, and Nikolas Coupland, eds. 2016. *Sociolinguistics from the Periphery: Small Languages in New Circumstances.* Cambridge: Cambridge University Press.

Piña-Rosales, Gerardo, Jorge I. Covarrubias, Joaquín Segura, and Daniel Fernández, eds. 2010. *Hablando bien se entiende la gente.* New York: Academia Norteamericana de la Lengua Española.

Poniewozik, James. 2001. "What's Wrong with This Picture?" *TIME Magazine,* May 28, 2001: 80–82.

Poplack, Shana, David Sankoff, and Christopher Miller. 1988. "The Social Correlates and Linguistic Consequences of Lexical Borrowing and Assimilation." *Linguistics* 26: 47–104.

Porcel, Jorge. 2006. "The Paradox of Spanish among Miami Cubans." *Journal of Sociolinguistics* 10: 93–110.

Porras, Diana, Jongyean Ee, and Patricia Gándara. 2014. "Employer Preferences: Do Bilingual Applicants and Employees Experience an Advantage?" In *The Bilingual Advantage: Language, Literacy and the US Labor Market*, eds. Rebecca Callahan and Patricia Gándara, 234–57. Bristol: Multilingual Matters.

Porter, Bruce, and Marvin Dunn. 1984. *The Miami Riot of 1980: Crossing the Bounds.* Lexington, MA: D.C. Heath & Co.

Portes, Alejandro, and Aaron Puhrmann. 2015. "A Bifurcated Enclave: The Economic Evolution of the Cuban and Cuban American Population of Metropolitan Miami." *Cuban Studies* 43: 40–64.

Portes, Alejandro, and Rubén Rumbaut. 2014. *Immigrant America: A Portrait*, 4th ed. Berkeley: University of California Press.

Portes, Alejandro, and Richard Schauffler. 1994. "Language and the Second Generation: Bilingualism Yesterday and Today." *International Migration Review* 28: 640–61.

Portes, Alejandro, and Alex Stepick. 1993. *City on the Edge: The Transformation of Miami.* Berkeley: University of California Press.

Portes, Alejandro, Alex Stepick, and Juan Clark. 1985. "Three Years Later: The Adaptation of Mariel Cuban and Haitian Refugees in South Florida." *Occasional Papers Series of the Latin American and Caribbean Center*, Dialogue no. 60. Miami: Florida International University.

290 References

Powell, Philip Wayne. 1971. *Tree of Hate: Propaganda and Prejudices Affecting United States Relations with the Hispanic World*. Albuquerque: University of New Mexico Press.

Preston, Dennis. 2013. "Language with an Attitude." In *The Handbook of Language Variation and Change*, 2nd ed., eds. J. K. Chambers and Natalie Schilling, 157–82. Malden, MA: Wiley-Blackwell.

Puente, Henry. 2014. "Nuvo TV: Will It Withstand the Competition?" In *Contemporary Latina/o Media: Production, Circulation, Politics*, eds. Arlene Dávila and Yeidy Rivero, 62–81. New York: NYU Press.

Pujolar, Joan. 2007. "Bilingualism and the Nation-State in the Post-National Era." In *Bilingualism: A Social Approach*, ed. Monica Heller, 71–95. London: Palgrave Macmillan.

Pulso Pop. 2021. "Exclusiva con ECKO y Mariah Angeliq: Reggaeton de antes." February 10, 2021. www.youtube.com/watch?v=QGVA8zcNOSw

Quiroga, José. 2009. "Miami Remake." In *City/Art: The Urban Scene in Latin America*, ed. Rebecca Biron, 145–64. Durham, NC: Duke University Press.

Rama, Ángel. 1998 [original publication 1984]. *La ciudad letrada*. Montevideo: ARCA.

Ramírez Berg, Charles. 2002. *Latino Images in Film: Stereotypes, Subversion, and Resistance*. Austin: University of Texas Press.

Ramos, Ronnie. 1988. "Official English Now Draws New Battle Lines." *Miami Herald*, November 18, 1988: 2D.

Real Academia Española. 2016. "¿Se habla español en la publicidad? Conclusiones." Primer debate sobre el uso del español en la publicidad, Madrid, May 18, 2016. www.youtube.com/watch?v=hgST69HSo_M&index=7&list= PLAc67Zs0vjcKBcfK1Ezn-w5Ga3xxRz7rW

Redford, Polly. 1970. *Billion-Dollar Sandbar: A Biography of Miami Beach*. New York: E.P. Dutton.

Resnick, Melvyn. 1988. "Beyond the Ethnic Community: Spanish Language Roles and Maintenance in Miami." *International Journal of the Sociology of Language* 69: 89–104.

Rieff, David. 1987. *Going to Miami: Exiles, Tourists, and Refugees in the New America*. Boston: Little, Brown & Co.

Rieff, David. 1993. *The Exile: Cuba in the Heart of Miami*. New York: Simon & Schuster.

Riquelme, Jesucristo. 1998. *Los angli(ci)smos: anglismos y anglicismos, huéspedes de la lengua*. Alicante, Spain: Editorial Aguaclara.

Rivero, Yeidy. 2012. "Interpreting Cubanness, Americanness, and the Sitcom. *¿Qué Pasa USA?* (1975–1980)." In *Global Television Formats: Understanding Television across Borders*, eds. Tasha Oren and Sharon Shahaf, 90–107. London: Routledge.

Robertson, Roland. 1992. *Globalization: Social Theory and Global Culture*. London: Sage.

Roca, Ana. 1991. "Language Maintenance and Language Shift in the Cuban American Community of Miami: The 1990s and beyond." In *Language Planning*, ed. David Marshall, 245–57. Amsterdam: Benjamins.

Rodríguez, Clara. 2004. *Heroes, Lovers, and Others. The Story of Latinos in Hollywood*. Washington, DC: Smithsonian.

Rodríguez, Rene. 2016. "The Miami Sound Is Gone. But the Beat Goes On. Here is What Replaced It." *Miami Herald*, June 26, 2016.

References 291

Rodríguez, Rene. 2018. "Telemundo's New Headquarters Embraces the Future. It May Transform This Area, Too." *Miami Herald*, April 9, 2018.

Rodríguez, Richard. 2009. *Next of Kin: The Family in Chicano/a Cultural Politics*. Durham, NC: Duke University Press.

Rodríguez Solórzano, Adrián. 1999. "Mezcla de tuteo y voseo." *La Nación*, May 31, 1999.

Rogers, Everett. 2003 [original publication 1962]. *Diffusion of Innovations*, 5th ed. New York: Free Press.

Rosa, Jonathan. 2019. *Looking Like a Language, Sounding Like a Race: Raciolinguistic Ideologies and the Learning of Latinidad*. Oxford: Oxford University Press.

Ruzickova, Elena. 2007. "Customer Requests in Cuban Spanish: Realization Patterns and Politeness Strategies in Service Encounters." In *Research on Politeness in the Spanish-Speaking World*, eds. María Elena Placencia and Carmen García, 213–44. Mahwah, NJ: Lawrence Erlbaum.

Sadowsky, Scott, and María José Aninao. 2020. "Internal Migration and Ethnicity in Santiago." In *The Routledge Handbook of Spanish in the Global City*, ed. Andrew Lynch, 277–311. London: Routledge.

Sánchez, Rosaura. 1994 [original publication 1983]. *Chicano Discourse. Socio-Historic Perspectives*. Houston, TX: Arte Público.

Sánchez Fajardo, José Antonio. 2017. "The Anglicization of Cuban Spanish: A Historical Account." *Annals of the University of Craiova* 1–2/2017: 185–201.

Santamarina, Cristina. 2016. "El español en la publicidad. Investigación sociológica exploratoria." Primer debate sobre el uso del español en la publicidad, Madrid, May 18, 2016. www.rae.es/sites/default/files/Ponencia_Cristina_Santamarina.pdf

Santander. 2020. "Our History." Accessed June 10, 2020. www.santander.com/en/about-us/our-history#1856–1950

Santiago, Fabiola. 1996. "Is Dade's Bilingual Advantage at Risk?" *Miami Herald*, March 19, 1996: 1B.

Santiago, Fabiola. 2011. "It's Scholars vs. Spanglish." *Miami Herald*, February 20, 2011: H1, 21A.

Santos, Fernanda, and Christine Hauser. 2015. "Arizona News Anchor Is Drawn into Debate on Her Accent and the Use of Spanish." *New York Times*, September 4, 2015: A17.

Sassen, Saskia. 2005. "The Global City: Introducing a Concept." *Brown Journal of World Affairs* 11: 27–43.

Sassen, Saskia. 2007. "Introduction." In *Deciphering the Global: Its Scales, Spaces and Subjects*, ed. Saskia Sassen, 1–18. New York: Routledge.

Saussure, Ferdinand de. 2000a [original publication 1916]. "Linguistic Value." In *The Routledge Language and Cultural Theory Reader*, eds. Lucy Burke, Tony Crowley, and Alan Girvin, 105–13. London: Routledge.

Saussure, Ferdinand de. 2000b [original publication 1916]. "The Nature of the Linguistic Sign." In *The Routledge Language and Cultural Theory Reader*, eds. Lucy Burke, Tony Crowley, and Alan Girvin, 21–32. London: Routledge.

Scott Shenk, Petra. 2007. "'I'm Mexican, Remember?' Constructing Ethnic Identities via Authenticating Discourse." *Journal of Sociolinguistics* 11: 194–220.

Searle, John. 1995. *The Construction of Social Reality*. New York: Free Press.

Searle, John. 2007. *Freedom and Neurobiology: Reflections on Free Will, Language, and Political Power*. New York: Columbia University Press.

292 *References*

Sebba, Mark. 2015. "Iconisation, Attribution and Branding in Orthography." *Written Language & Literacy* 18: 208–27.

Seuren, Pieter. 2016. "Saussure and His Intellectual Environment." *History of European Ideas* 42: 819–47.

Sherrill, Robert. 1987. "Can Miami Save Itself? A City Beset by Drugs and Violence." *New York Times Magazine*, July 19, 1987.

Sicius, Francis. 1998. "The Miami-Havana Connection: The First Seventy-Five Years." *Tequesta* 58: 5–45.

Silva-Corvalán, Carmen. 1994. *Language Contact and Change: Spanish in Los Angeles.* Oxford: Clarendon.

Smith, Victoria. 2011. "Our Serial Killers, Our Superheroes, and Ourselves: Showtime's *Dexter.*" *Quarterly Review of Film and Video* 28: 390–400.

Smith-Christmas, Cassie, Noel P. Ó Murchadha, Michael Hornsby, and Máiréad Moriarty, eds. 2018. *New Speakers of Minority Languages: Linguistic Ideologies and Practices.* London: Palgrave Macmillan.

Sobrino Triana, Roxana. 2018. "Las variedades de español según los hispanohablantes: corrección, incorrección y agrado lingüísticos." *Cuadernos de Lingüística de El Colegio de México* 5: 89–119.

Solé, Carlos. 1979. "Selección idiomática entre la nueva generación de cubano-americanos." *The Bilingual Review / La Revista Bilingüe* 6: 1–10.

Solé, Carlos. 1982. "Language Loyalty and Language Attitudes among Cuban-Americans." In *Bilingual Education for Hispanic Students in the United States*, eds. Joshua Fishman and Gary Keller, 254–68. New York: Teachers College.

Sorenson, Travis. 2016. "¿De dónde sos? Differences between Argentine and Salvadoran *Voseo* to *Tuteo* Accommodation in the United States." In *Forms of Address in the Spanish of the Americas*, eds. María Irene Moyna and Susana Rivera-Mills, 171–96. Amsterdam: Benjamins.

Steinberg, Brian. 2011. "SíTV to change name as it aims for bicultural Latinos." AdAge, March 14, 2011. https://adage.com/article/media/si-tv-aims-english-speaking-latinos/149362

Stepick, Alex, Guillermo Grenier, Max Castro, and Marvin Dunn. 2003. *This Land Is Our Land: Immigrants and Power in Miami.* Berkeley: University of California Press.

Strauss, Claudia. 2004. "Cultural Standing in Expression of Opinion." *Language in Society* 33: 161–94.

Stuart-Smith, Jane. 2011. "The View from the Couch: Changing Perspectives on the Role of Television in Changing Language Ideologies and Use." In *Standard Languages and Language Standards in a Changing Europe*, eds. Tore Kristiansen and Nikolas Coupland, 223–39. Oslo: Novus.

Tamarón, Marqués de. 2005. *El guirigay nacional.* Barcelona: Áltera.

Tankersley, Jim. 2020. *The Riches of this Land: The Untold, True Story of America's Middle Class.* New York: Hachette.

Taylor, Paul, Mark Hugo López, Jessica Martínez, and Gabriel Velasco. 2012. "When Labels Don't Fit: Hispanics and Their Views of Identity." Pew Research Center, April 4, 2012.

Tetel Andresen, Julie, and Phillip Carter. 2016. *Languages in the World: How History, Culture, and Politics Shape Language.* Malden, MA: Wiley-Blackwell.

The Economist. 2009. "The Du und Du Waltz: The Complex Etiquette of Du and Sie in Germany." November 28, 2009.

References 293

Thomason, Sarah. 2001. *Language Contact*. Washington, DC: Georgetown University Press.

Thomason, Sarah, and Terrence Kaufman. 1988. *Language Contact, Creolization, and Genetic Linguistics*. Berkeley: University of California Press.

Thompson, John. 1984. *Studies in the Theory of Ideology*. Berkeley: University of California Press.

Thompson, John. 1990. *Ideology and Modern Culture*. Cambridge: Polity.

Tió, Salvador. 1948. "Teoría del espanglish." *Diario de Puerto Rico*, October 28, 1948.

Tölölyan, Khachig. 2012. "Diaspora Studies: Past, Present and Promise." Working Paper 55, International Migration Institute, Oxford University.

Torres, Lourdes. 2019. "Spanish is Not Spoken Here!" *Latino Studies* 17: 1–4.

Tucci, Terig. 1969. *Gardel en Nueva York*. New York: Webb.

Trainor, Brian. 1998. "The Origin and End of Modernity." *Journal of Applied Philosophy* 15: 133–44.

United Press International. 1987. "Non-Hispanic Whites Vacating Dade, Data Says." *The Orlando Sentinel*, May 4, 1987.

U.S. Citizenship and Immigration Services. n.d. "INS Records for 1930s Mexican Repatriations." Accessed December 5, 2020. www.uscis.gov/history-and-genealogy/our-history/historians-mailbox/ins-records-1930s-mexican-repatriations

U.S. Senate Historical Office. n.d. "Special Committee on Organized Crime in Interstate Commerce." Accessed December 10, 2020. www.senate.gov/about/powers-procedures/investigations/kefauver.htm

Valdés, Guadalupe, and Cecilia Pino. 1981. "Muy a tus órdenes: Compliment Responses among Mexican-American Bilinguals." *Language in Society* 10: 53–72.

Valdés, Juan Gabriel. 1995. *Pinochet's Economists. The Chicago School in Chile*. Cambridge: Cambridge University Press.

Valdez, Juan. 2013. "Language in the Dominican Republic: Between Hispanism and Panamericanism." In *A Political History of Spanish: The Making of a Language*, ed. José Del Valle, 182–96. Cambridge: Cambridge University Press.

Valencia, Marelys. 2017. "The Children of the Cuban Revolution in the Diaspora: From Internationalism to Transnational and Cosmopolitan Imaginaries." Ph.D. diss., University of Miami.

Valencia, Marelys. 2018. "Televisión de Miami y vínculos transnacionales de emigrados cubanos recientes." *Temas* 93–94: 109–16.

Valencia, Marelys, and Andrew Lynch. 2016. "Migraciones mediáticas: la translocación del español en televisoras hispanas de Estados Unidos." *Cuadernos AISPI. Revista de la Associazione Ispanisti Italiani* 8: 171–96.

Valencia, Marelys, and Andrew Lynch. 2020. "The Mass Mediation of Spanish in Miami." In *The Routledge Handbook of Spanish in the Global City*, ed. Andrew Lynch, 73–104. London: Routledge.

Valenzuela, Angela. 1999. *Subtractive Schooling: U.S.-Mexican Youth and the Politics of Caring*. Albany: State University of New York Press.

Varela, Beatriz. 1992. *El español cubano-americano*. New York: Senda Nueva.

Varra, Rachel. 2018. *Lexical Borrowing and Deborrowing in Spanish in New York City*. London: Routledge.

Veciana-Suarez, Ana. 1988. "In Our House, It's a Struggle to Speak in Spanish." *Miami Herald*, March 31, 1988: 1B.

294 References

Vélez, Jorge. 2000. "Understanding Spanish-Language Maintenance in Puerto Rico: Political Will Meets the Demographic Imperative." *International Journal of the Sociology of Language* 142: 5–24.

Vertovec, Steven. 2007. "Super-Diversity and Its Implications." *Ethnic and Racial Studies* 30: 1024–54.

Viglucci, Andres. 1988a. "'Official English' Debate Set to Simmer." *Miami Herald*, July 31, 1988: 1A.

Viglucci, Andres. 1988b. "In Hialeah, Speech Separates Neighbors." *Miami Herald*, July 31, 1988: 14A.

Viglucci, Andres. 1988c. "Top Latins Sitting Out Language Fray." *Miami Herald*, August 9, 1988: 1B.

Villalobos Graillet, José Eduardo. 2015. "La globalización lingüística: el conflicto entre el inglés y el español. Actualización del caso de México y los Estados Unidos." *Glosas* 8: 4–15.

Villarreal, Antonio. 2014. "Cuando el inglés usurpa la riqueza léxica del español." *ABC*, April 26, 2014.

Voloshinov, Valentin. 1973 [original publication 1929]. *Marxism and the Philosophy of Language*. Trans. Ladislav Matejka and I. R. Titunik. New York: Seminar Press.

Wallace, Richard. 1988. "Hispanic Groups to Monitor Official English." *Miami Herald*, December 28, 1988: 2B.

Warren, Michelle. 2003. "Post-Philology." In *Postcolonial Moves: Medieval through Modern*, eds. Patricia Clare Ingham and Michelle Warren, 19–45. New York: Palgrave Macmillan.

Weber, David. 2000. *La frontera española en América del Norte*. Trans. Jorge Ferreiro. Mexico City: Fondo de Cultura Económica.

Wells Fargo. 2020. "History of Wells Fargo." Accessed June 10, 2020. www.wellsfargo.com/about/corporate/history/

West, Patrick. 2009. "The City of Our Times: Space, Identity, and the Body in *CSI: Miami*." In *The CSI Effect: Television, Crime, and Governance*, eds. Michele Byers and Val Marie Johnson, 111–31. Lanham, MD: Lexington Books.

Westgate, Christopher. 2014. "One Language, One Nation, and One Vision: NBC Latino, Fusion, and Fox News Latino." In *Contemporary Latina/o Media: Production, Circulation, Politics*, eds. Arlene Dávila and Yeidy Rivero, 82–102. New York: NYU Press.

Wilson, Woodrow. 1915. "State of the Union Address." December 7, 1915. Infoplease.com. Accessed July 8, 2020. www.infoplease.com/primary-sources/government/presidential-speeches/state-union-address-woodrow-wilson-december-7-1915

Woolard, Kathryn. 2008. "Language and Identity Choice in Catalonia: The Interplay of Contrasting Ideologies of Linguistic Authority." In *Lengua, nación e identidad: La regulación del plurilingüismo en España y América Latina*, eds. Kirsten Süselbeck, Ulrike Mühlschlegel, and Peter Masson, 303–23. Madrid/Frankfurt: Iberoamericana/Vervuert.

Yúdice, George. 2004. *The Expediency of Culture. Uses of Culture in the Global Era*. Durham, NC: Duke University Press.

Zavala, Virginia. 2019. "Youth and the Repoliticization of Quechua." *Language, Culture and Society* 1: 59–82.

Zentella, Ana Celia. 1997. *Growing Up Bilingual*. Malden, MA: Blackwell.

References 295

Zentella, Ana Celia. 2013. "Bilinguals and Borders: California's Transfronteriz@s and Competing Constructions of Bilingualism." *International Journal of the Linguistic Association of the Southwest* 32: 17–50.

Zoglin, Richard, and Denise Worrell. 1985. "Cool Cops, Hot Show." *TIME Magazine*, September 16, 1985.

Zurer Pearson, Barbara. 2002. "Narrative Competence among Monolingual and Bilingual School Children in Miami." In *Language and Literacy in Bilingual Children*, eds. D. Kimbrough Oller and Rebecca Eilers, 135–74. Clevedon, UK: Multilingual Matters.

Index

Note: Page numbers with an 'n' denote Notes.

'1.5' generation, language of:
bilingual ability and metalinguistic
consciousness 253; and loanwords
227; and phonological calques 229,
230; and semantic calques 232, 233;
social status and linguistic (in)security
240, 246; and syntactic calques 235,
236

Academia de la Publicidad 208
Academia Norteamericana de la Lengua
Española 42, 210
accent 88, 103, 105–6; Cuban-accented
discourse 96, 99, 116; Hispanic-
accented English 17, 36, 95, 105;
neutral accent 56–57; Puerto Rican–
accented Spanish 92; significance of
106
acculturation, and English use 155
Acosta, Vivian 56–57
activism 57
advertisements 1, 3, 27, 38, 42, 48, 105,
169–72, 208–9, 242, 266
affective solidarity 187
African Americans 20, 26, 51, 52, 53, 93,
140, 184
Afro-Cubans 52–53
Age of Revolution 5
Agha, Asif 87, 98
agricultural industrialists, Western 20
Aja, Alan 52, 53
Alcázar Hotel (now Lightner Museum)
15
Alfaraz, Gabriela 53, 159, 195–97, 204
All in the Family 99
Allman, T. D. 66
allophone 23–24

Alvarado, Don 16
Alvarez, Lizette 51, 52
Amandi, Fernand 192
American Association of Teachers of
Spanish and Portuguese (AATSP) 17
Americanization 10, 11, 13, 28, 146, 169,
171, 206, 208–9
American Revolution of 1776 5
America with Jorge Ramos 267
Anderson, Benedict 5, 7, 41, 63
Andes (Peru) 147
Androutsopoulos, Jannis 72
Angeliq, Mariah 262, 264
Angel y Khriz 142
Anglicism(s) 55, 258–60, 260n1;
bilingual ability and metalinguistic
consciousness 248–58; cultural
institutional 214; empirical
lexicographic 214; impact on Spanish
210–11; perceptual saliency 211–12;
social status and linguistic (in)security
240–48
Anglicism(s), social diffusion of 214–16,
240; loanwords 225–28; phonological
calques 228–30; semantic calques
231–33; study and its participants
216–25; syntactic calques 233–36
Anglicization 11, 12, 18, 171, 208–9
'Anglo-American sabir' code 237, 260
Anglo modernity 14
Anglophone resistance 69–70
Anglo Republicans 12
Antarctica 5
Anthony, Marc 58
Appadurai, Arjun 1, 2, 31–32, 40–41, 46,
51, 57–58, 59, 63–64, 72, 149, 264, 273
Arabic 44, 211

Index 297

Arab Spring 41
Argentina 61–62, 244, 262; and economic instability 48, 61–62
Argentines 59, 115, 116, 159, 169, 219, 224; tango professionals 16
Arnaz, Desi 1, 66–67
Art Deco District 86
aspiration of /s/ 198
asset valuation 265–66
atomization, of Spanish-speaking identity 156, 160, 161–62
Aymara language 147, 148

Babbel app 213
Babel Proclamation (1918) 18
Bad Bunny 142
Bahamonde, José 99, 108
Bakhtin, Mikhail 21–22, 24–25, 144, 238, 268
Bakhtin Circle 21, 24, 25
Balboa Park 14, 15
Balearic Islands 147
Ball, Lucille 1, 66
'Balsero crisis' 109–10, 114, 264
Banco Santander 3
banks/banking sector 3, 39–40, 47, 78, 246; advertisements 1; Brickell Avenue banking district 48
Barcelona 53–54, 144, 147
Basque language 268
Batista, Fulgencio 62, 68, 75
battleground metaphor, Miami as 70–73; see also modern ethnolinguistic boundaries, defending
Baudrillard, Jean 29, 34, 36–39, 43, 86, 114, 155, 156, 161–62, 273
Bauzà, José Ramón 147
Bay of Pigs invasion 69, 103, 163
Belaval, Emilio 11
Bell, Maya 83
Bello, Andrés 8
Bendixen, Sergio 88
Bendixen & Amandi International 192
Benítez-Rojo, Antonio 262–64, 272, 273
Berzaín, Carlos Sánchez 62
Bestard Revilla, Alina 204, 205
Beyer, Scott 48
bilingual ability 110, 128, 240, 247, 248–58
bilingualism 44, 96–97, 123–25, 211, 212, 215, 270; identity and language use 137–43; pedagogical practices 270; roles and values of Spanish 126–32;

socioeconomic mobility and language commodification 132–37; study and participants of 125–26; subtractive bilingualism 135; television formats 266; television sitcom narratives of 97–107
Biltmore Hotel 15
Bjelland Aune, Karoline 207n1
Black Lives Matter movement 41, 51
'black market' economy in Cuba 196, 204
Blackness and Spanish language, link between 52–53
Blecua, José Manuel 210
Blommaert, Jan 119, 122, 143, 145, 150, 153, 157, 206, 273
Booth, Cathy 49
Boswell, Thomas 112, 113
bound collocations 248, 251
boundedness, to language 21, 268–70
Bourdieu, Pierre 23
Bracker, Milton 69–70, 87
Brah, Avtar 121, 145
Brazil 209; and Anglicisms 209; student demonstrations 30
Brazilian Portuguese 44
Bregman, Martin 85
Brickell 48, 59; banking district 48
Brown, Les 102
Brown, Roger 163, 167, 168, 173, 177, 185–86, 193, 194, 200
Brown, Wendy 33–34
Buenos Aires 16, 61, 157
Burn Notice 84, 88, 89
butterfly effect 272
Byrne, David 272

Cabal, Dionisio 170
Cabrera, Alain 56
Callaghan, Gill 272
Callahan, Laura 170, 171
Calle Ocho 100, 118, 119, 161, 192, 221
Callesano, Salvatore 53, 54, 245, 270
caló 26–27
calques/calquing 206, 211, 212, 215, 239, 248, 249, 259; phonological calques 218, 224, 225, 228–30; semantic calques 218, 231–33, 239, 261n4; syntactic calques 218, 233–36, 239, 261n4
Cámara, Madelín 60
capitalism 5, 35, 36–37; and nation-state 3; postwar 167; print capitalism 3, 5–7

298   *Index*

Capone, Al 75, 84
Caravedo, Rocío 121, 144, 145, 158, 273
Caribbean 2, 9, 35, 43, 223, 253, 262;
    cultural perspective of 263–64;
    Francophone 237, 239; and Hispanic
    129; and Miami 49, 92; -origin belief
    systems 92; -origin speakers 17, 51,
    227, 229, 235, 245, 246, 251, 256;
    varieties of English 53; varieties of
    Spanish 53, 92, 121, 189, 198, 245,
    256, 258
Caro, Miguel Antonio 9
Carter, Phillip 53, 54, 245, 270
Cartographies of Diaspora 145
Castilian Spanish 9
Castro, Fidel 27, 47, 49, 60, 61, 68, 70,
    81, 109, 110, 114, 158, 163, 166,
    188–92, 204, 205, 207n6, 264
Catalan language 147–48
Cayo Blanco del Sur (Cuba) 163
Central Americans 118, 126, 206, 227,
    229, 246
centrifugal force of language 22, 238,
    258, 268
centripetal force of language 22, 238,
    258, 268
Cervantes, Miguel de 9
Cervantes, Richard 141
chaos theory 262–63, 272, 273
Chávez, Hugo 61, 207n6
Chile/Chileans 27, 32, 102, 110, 147, 172,
    224
China 32; and Anglicisms 209; economic
    reform in 29
Chinese language 44, 112
Chirino, Willy 58
Chomsky, Noam 21
"chongas" 118, 119
choteo, use of 97, 116, 132, 149, 184
Cilliers, Paul 263
Ciudad Juárez (Mexico) 171–72, 207n3
class consciousness 193–205
CNN 111
Cobo, Leila 58
Cocaine Cowboys 76
Cocaine Cowboys: The Kings of Miami
    76
cocaine wars 47, 76, 78
code-switching 91, 118, 267, 269
Cohen, Hermann 24
Colombia 48, 120, 244; cocaine cartels
    78; and Miami 57
Colombian identity 157–58

Colombians 48, 61, 62, 78, 116, 119, 121,
    206, 219
Colombian voice 54
Committee on Latin American Studies
    25
common opinions 188–91
communication and commodification,
    link between 98
communication channels 215
communication technologies 2, 28, 214
communism 27–28, 29, 35–37, 49, 60, 66,
    164–67, 183, 190, 204, 266
Communist Bloc, collapse of 2, 27, 28,
    35, 36, 60, 114, 150, 205
complexity theory 87, 146, 263–64, 269,
    272, 273
"Conocí la paz" (song) 90
consumerism 37–40, 63, 168, 171, 172,
    205, 206; and postmodern capitalism
    186; and postmodern paradox 122,
    131, 147, 149, 152, 153, 155–57,
    161–62; and solidarity 156, 186
contact-induced language change *see*
    language contact
containerization of expression 260
Contra war 61
controversial opinion 188
Cookman, Tomas 59
Coral Gables 14, 15, 45, 69, 122, 200,
    221, 227, 243, 244, 257, 258
Coral Way Elementary School, bilingual
    program at 110, 112
Córdoba, Pedro de 16
Córdova, David 141
Corpus del Español del Siglo XXI 214
correctness 53, 116, 164, 166, 210, 211,
    237, 238, 239–40, 245, 253, 258
Cortez, Ricardo 16
Costa Rica: and expansion of *tú* 169; *vos*
    usage in 169–70
Costello, Frank 75
County Public Schools (Dade County)
    111
Cours de Linguistique Générale 20, 25
creole varieties 44, 53, 237, 261n6
critical self-reflexivity 146, 148, 149
Cros Sandoval, Mercedes 52
cross-generational loss of Spanish 46,
    120, 121–22, 232, 263, 272
cross-generational shift to English
    dominance 12, 101, 120, 121, 154, 232,
    246, 270
Croucher, Sheila 53

CSI: Miami 84, 87, 88, 89
Cuba 2, 27; cocaine cartels 78; English in 10; and racialized social class division 52; and US 9–10
Cuban American National Foundation (CANF) 166
Cubanisms 118, 119
Cuban Miami 60, 196; discursive construction of 183–93; media feature of 114; right-wing ideology 60
Cubans 1; arriving in Miami 264; cyclical migrations to the north 10; exile identity 97; habitus and worldview of 158
Cuban Spanish 10, 53
Cuban voice 54
Cuervo, Rufino José 8, 9, 12, 25
Cullom, William 85–86
cultural authenticity, language through 125, 126–32
cultural globalization 28–29
cultural imaginary 14–15, 40, 42, 47, 72, 119, 120; modern ethnolinguistic boundaries and 87, 95; postnostalgic identity and 115, 116; valuing of Spanish and 98, 102; *see also* ethnolinguistic dimension of Miami crime; *Golden Girls, The*; modern ethnolinguistic boundaries, defending; *¿Qué Pasa, USA?*
culturalists 57
cultural reflexivity 72
cultural standing 98, 187, 188
CW, The 107, 267

Daddy Yankee 142
Da Silva, Emanuel 4, 267
Dawson, Graham 42
Deering, James 15
deferential address 167, 177, 186, 194, 200
de Gaulle, Charles 209
deletion of /s/ 196–98, 257
Delgado, Humberto 102
del Río, Dolores 16, 36
DeMille, Cecil B. 16
democratic transition, of Spain 42
democratization of politics 18
de Molina, Tirso 9
Deng Xiaoping 32
De Palma, Brian 84, 85
Derrida, Jacques 4, 25, 31
Descartes, Rene 5
Dexter 84, 88, 89–96, 132

diasporic communities 2, 46, 51
Diccionario de anglicismos del español estadounidense 260n1
Diccionario de la Real Academia Española 210, 214
Didion, Joan 50, 87, 108, 113, 123
differential diaspora 59
diffusion of innovations 214–15
Diffusion of Innovations 214
diglossia 268–69
Dittmar, Norbert 164, 196
Dominican Republic 11, 18, 36, 53, 223, 251, 258
Donahue, Phil 110
Doral 45
Dreaming in Cuban 114, 132
Duchêne, Alexandre 269
Duolingo app 213

Ecko 262, 264
economic globalization and Spanish, in news 107–13
economic neoliberalism 28, 32–37, 46, 70, 73, 97, 147, 161
Economist, The 206
Edison, Thomas 15
Emergency School Aid Act (ESAA-TV) 98
English for Speakers of Other Languages (ESOL) 111, 133, 139–40
English language 3; and Anglicization of Puerto Rico 11; Caribbean varieties 53; in Cuba 10; dominance, cross-generational shift to 12, 101, 120, 121, 154, 232, 246, 270; in formal education 121, 124, 216; Hispanic-accented 17, 36, 95, 105; ideological orientation to 132–37; incursion in Spanish marketing and sales, RAE's inquiry into 266; indexical values of 271; influence on Spanish 9; language ability 19, 133, 141, 166, 173, 181, 221, 229, 230, 233, 249, 252, 255, 256; in peer socialization 216; personal affective dimensions of 137–43; use in acculturation 155; *see also* language(s)
English-only ordinance, of Dade County 77, 78–80, 82–83, 108, 110
Enlightenment 5, 30, 59
environment, and Spanish in US 263
environmentalism 31
Equal Educational Opportunities Act (1974) 110

300 *Index*

Espinosa, Aurelio 12, 13, 14, 25
Estefan, Emilio 58
Estefan, Gloria 58, 114
Estevez, Juan 58
ethnic enclave economy 49, 70, 187
ethnic identity 3, 4, 33, 107, 110, 155,
  265, 267, 269
ethnolinguistic dimension, of Miami
  crime 84; linguistic misrepresentation
  and mockery and 89–96; linguistic
  order defense and 84–89
ethnolinguistic identity 84, 146
ethnoscape 49–55, 59, 88, 144
excesses of democracy 23
exiles, 49–50
Exposé 58

Fable of the Bees 38
facebuquear 210
Fantasy Island 105
FARC 61, 264
Farewell, The 209
fascism 13, 26
Federal Bilingual Education Act (1968)
  110
Ferguson, Charles 268
Fernández Parera, Antoni 53
Ferré, Maurice 85, 108
financescape 46–49, 59, 151
Finns 20
first-generation, language of 20,
  114, 121, 135, 175, 178, 216;
  bilingual ability and metalinguistic
  consciousness 249, 252–53, 255, 256,
  257, 259; and loanwords 227, 240,
  242–43, 249, 253; occupation and
  lexical borrowing 242; parents 255;
  and phonological calques 229, 230,
  240, 249, 253; and semantic calques
  232, 233, 240, 249, 253; social status
  and linguistic (in)security 240, 242–43,
  246–47; and syntactic calques 235,
  240, 249, 252, 253; and upward social
  mobility 198–202
Fisher, Carl 67, 75
Fishman, Joshua 110
Fiske, John 123
Flagler, Henry 14–15, 74
Florida 14–15, 48–49, 59–60; *see also*
  South Florida
Florida State Constitution, Article II
  (Section 9) 82
Flower MacCannell, Juliet 156

folklore 12, 13
Ford 20
formal education 146, 173, 186, 217–19,
  229–30; and Anglicisms 212; English
  in 121, 124, 216; and exiles 70;
  and language perception 239; and
  lateralization 196; of parents 177, 178,
  194, 217, 239–40, 243, 253–55, 259; in
  Spanish, lack of 46, 160
Foucault, Michel 6–7, 25, 31
Fox, George 168
Fradd, Sandra 48
Framework for Cognitive Sociolinguistics,
  A 211
France 30, 209; and Anglicisms 209;
  dirigisme in 35
Franco, Francisco 42, 169
Francophone Canada 247
Francophone Caribbean 237, 239
Francophonie 237
Freedom Tower 15
free markets 32, 37, 63, 164
French Creole languages 44
French language 4, 44, 167, 168, 209, 237
French Revolution of 1789 5, 168
Fusion TV 267

Gabilondo, Joseba 271
Galician language 268
Galileo 5
García, María Cristina 132
García, Ofelia 216–18, 225, 226, 228,
  233, 240
García Menocal, Mario 67–68
Gardel, Carlos 16–17
"Gasolina" (song) 142
geographic space 144–45, 158, 221
German Americans 18
German language 12, 17, 18, 20, 24, 44,
  110, 167; Berlin dialect 164, 183, 206
Germany 32, 163–64, 167, 209; and
  Anglicisms 209; reunification of 166,
  206
Gilman, Albert 163, 167, 168, 173, 177,
  185–86, 193, 194, 200
Glades, The 88, 89
Glissant, Édouard 208, 212, 213, 237–38,
  242, 247, 257, 258, 260, 269–70, 273
global city 1, 119, 144, 151, 152, 154, 158
global consumerism 2, 63, 259–60, 264
globalization 2, 41, 149, 171; economic
  107–13; neoliberal economic
  discourse of 4; as a series of 'scapes'

Index 301

2; sociolinguistic 206; transnational processes of 4
glocalization 29
Golden Girls, The 98, 102–7, 150, 266
González Pino, Bárbara 13
Goodhue, Bertram 14, 15
Good Times 99
Gorbachev, Mikhail 28
Graham, Bob 85
Great Depression 26, 36, 46, 263
Greenberg, Murray 78–79
Grenier, Guillermo 164, 187, 192
Grimm, Jacob 8
Groppa, Carlos 16
group solidarity 150, 156, 168–69, 187
Guaraní 268
Guedes, Álvarez 97, 107, 184
Guevara, Ernesto "Che" 68
Gutenberg's printing press 6
Gutiérrez-Rivas, Carolina 187, 198–99, 200

Hablando bien se entiende la gente 210, 236
Haitian Americans 140–41
Haitian Creole language 44, 53, 261n6
Hampton, Jim 83
Handbook of Latin American Studies 25
Hardin, Karol 172
Harvey, David 32
Havana: and Miami 48, 67, 68 (*see also* power and solidarity; solidarity); tourism in 46
Hayakawa, S. I. 110
Hayek, Friedrich 32
Hayworth, Rita 17
Hebrew 24, 44
Heller, Monica 146, 149, 150, 269
herencia 11, 114–15
heterophily 215
Hialeah 45, 80–81, 118–19, 124–25, 139, 153, 157, 192
High Committee for the Defense and Expansion of the French Language 209
Hill, Jane 94
Hispanic market 3, 35, 37, 43, 57, 109, 151, 162, 265
Hispanic(s)/Latina/o/x(s) 44–45, 64–65n3; agencies 267; and bilingualism 112; in Chicago 271; cultural imaginary 116; in Florida

80–81, 83, 84; in Hollywood 35–36, 105; identity 51, 54, 128, 129–30, 160, 162; 'Latino threat' 3; in Los Angeles County 48; and mass media 57; in Miami 44–45, 48, 52, 62, 89, 92–93, 112, 166, 221, 223; in Miami-Dade County 53, 78, 112; Miami Latinx 52, 243, 255, 270; Miami Latinx youth 117–22, 123–25, 131–32, 142, 160, 269–70; in South Florida 115; television industry 56, 92–93, 103, 104; in United States 172; US Hispanophilia 14–18; *see also* postmodern paradox
Hispanism 11, 25
hispanismo 14
Hispanocentricism 9
Hispanophilia 14–18, 36, 263
Hispanophobia 13
Hobbes, Thomas 5
Hollywood: film stars, and Spanish identity 15–17; Hispanics/Latinas in 35–36, 105; Production Code Administration 26
homophilous individuals 215
Hoover, J. Edgar 75
human beings as market actors 33
hurricanes 62, 74, 76, 163, 264
Hurtado, Telmo Ricardo 62
Hutcheon, Linda 29, 118, 123, 131, 146, 149, 150, 162, 270, 273
hyperreality 39, 43, 86, 146

identity and language use 137–43
ideological transparency and opacity 212, 236–40, 260, 273
ideology, language, and social reality, link between 64
ideoscape 2, 55, 59–63, 144, 151
Iglesias, Enrique 35, 58
Iglesias Illa, Hernán 62–63, 70, 86, 115, 116, 123, 159, 211, 260, 269
Image of the City, The 86
Imagined Communities 5, 63
imagined community 6, 41
independence movements: of Americas 5, 7, 8; Cuban 9, 74
indexical values of Spanish and English 271
industrialization 5, 13, 19–20, 28
Industrial Revolution 38
information and communication technologies (ICTs) 28

302 *Index*

innovation: adoptability of 214–15; innovation-decision process 216
Instituto Cervantes 42
interactive connections 272
International Bank Act 47
internet, Spanish on 136, 271
intertextuality 24, 144, 157
inverted Spanglish 271
Isleño Spanish 256
Italian language 44, 112, 167

Jaffe, Alexandra 73
Jane the Virgin 107, 267
Japanese Americans 26
Jiménez Ángel, Andrés 9
Jones, Stuart 23
Jordán, Gilberto 62
Juventud Rebelde 186

Kagan, Matvaei Isaevich 24
Kelly, James 76, 77, 78, 82
Kendall 45, 200–201, 221
Key Biscayne 45, 78
Key West 10, 60, 67
Kirkland, Ewan 89, 93
Kirkpatrick, Clifford 12
Kitman, Marvin 102
knowledge-based economy 28, 30, 39
Kristeva, Julia 25

Labov, William 201
Laguna, Albert Sergio 97, 114, 115, 116, 132, 149, 184
Lakoff, Robin 171–72
Lambert, Wallace 135–37
language ability 239; English 133, 141, 166, 173, 181, 221, 229, 230, 233, 249, 252, 255, 256; Spanish 96, 136, 173, 212, 233, 251, 255, 256
language boundaries 5–8, 263
language-bounded models of television and mass media 269
language contact 59, 70, 122, 151, 168, 205, 211, 221, 251; and age 219; and lexical borrowing 236, 237, 238; perceptual studies 213; 'quasi-invisible' consequence of 248
language ideological phenomena: boundedness 268–70; commodification and asset valuation 265–66; mediatization 266–68; nonlinearity 271–73; paradoxical stance and parodic reflexivity 270–71

language(s) 7–8; apps for learning 213; as autonomous structural system 21; commodification of 3, 34, 98, 100–101, 114, 129, 132–37, 161, 209, 213, 265–66, 267, 268, 269; constructs 213; dynamic push-and-pull vertical scalar orders of 273; expropriation 144; as form rather than substance 21, 23; ideologies of 34; legitimate language 23; and liberalism 33; and modernity 6; normativization of 247, 268; ontology 7; 'order' in 22; in postmodernity 28–32; racialization, of 52–53; reproducible print languages 5–6; and sociolinguistic change 72; variation and change, debate regarding 8–9; varieties/variants of 144–45, 147, 148; *see also* English language; Spanish language
langue 21, 22, 23
Lanier, Elizabeth G. 124, 130, 154, 157, 158, 159, 162n2, 270
Lansky, Meyer 75
lateralization of /r/ 196
Latin America 2, 17, 42, 152–53, 154, 223, 266; banking and mass media 264; bilingual education policy 147; hispanismo 14; and Hollywood 26; imports from 75, 77; and left-wing ideologies 62–63; and Miami 49, 50, 61, 62, 78, 120, 122, 126, 264, 265; music industry 58–59; nation-states, autonomy of 8; and South Florida 77–78, 115, 262; tourists from 49; and United States 9, 13, 27, 47, 48, 109, 271
Latin American Spanish 9
Latina/o/x *see* Hispanic(s)/Latina/o/x(s)
Latin cultural 'boom' 35–36
'Latin fever' 35
Lau vs. Nichols 110
left-wing ideologies 20, 27, 63
Leppänen, Sirpa 153
lexical borrowing 236, 242, 244, 248; *see also* loanwords
leyenda negra 13
Liberty City and Overtown riots (1980) 77, 96
Lima, *'el habla de'* 144–45
Life (magazine) 75
linguistic creolization 236, 238
linguistic order: defense of 84–89; of modernity 5, 18–28, 37, 43

Index 303

linguistic (in)security 240–48, 249
Lippi-Green, Rosina 88, 106
Lipski, John 256
Little Havana 96, 108, 118, 200–201
'llamar para atrás' 248, 256–57, 258, 259
loanwords 209, 211, 212, 215, 225–28, 238–39, 240, 249; acceptability of 227–28; awareness of 226–27; as convenient accessories of trendiness or cosmopolitanism 241–42; structural salience of 241; in urban speech 242
local dialect features 12
locals 49
Locke, John 5
Lopez, Jennifer 35–36, 266
López Morales, Humberto 165, 207n1
Los Angeles Times 111
la lucha 60
Lucy and Ricky 1, 3
Lummis, Charles 13–14
Lynch, Kevin 86, 270
Lyotard, Jean-François 30, 39

MacCannell, Dean 156
Machado, Gerardo 62, 67–68
Madrid 42, 144, 210
Mahler, Sarah 57
Mallet, Marie 52, 160, 261n5
Mandeville, Bernard 38
Margo, Ana 99
Marielitos/Mariel crisis 36, 76, 78, 85, 96, 114, 115, 165–66, 184, 197
Marín, Luis Muñoz 11
marketplace metaphor 70, 71, 83; *see also* Spanish, valuing of
market saturation 36–37
Martí, José 10
Martin, Ricky 35
Marxism and the Philosophy of Language 24
mass media 28, 57, 63, 77–84, 136, 209, 210, 214, 264, 265, 268, 269; and branding and advertising 38; locally based Spanish-language mass media industry 110; and marketplace 72–73; in Mexico City 42; and migration 40–41; portrayal of city as battleground 72, 103, 165, 184; potential to shape popular perception and ideas about language 71; and representation of reality 43; representations 43; and simulation 39; and social agency 40; targeting of

the Mexican-origin population in Los Angeles 26
mass mediation 40–41
mass migrations 18, 40–41
Masvidal, Raul 81
Matos, Manuel Rivera 11
Maude 99
McLaughlin, Mireille 4, 267
McLuhan, Marshall 148
McWhorter, John 236, 261n6
McWilliams, Carey 26, 27
mechanization 6
mediascape 2, 55–57, 59, 71, 113, 144
mediation and materiality, relationship between 72
mediatization 72, 113–14, 147, 184, 266–68; communication and commodification link and 98; inside-outside dynamic of 87; modern ethnolinguistic boundaries and 76, 83, 86; postmodern society and 86–87
medievalism, and postmodernity 31
mega-solidarity 156–57
Mendoza, Manny 98–99, 108
mental spaces 121, 122, 144–45, 151, 158, 273
Merrick, George 15, 69
metalinguistic commentary 98, 157, 245, 247
metalinguistic consciousness 239–40, 247, 248–49, 253, 255, 256, 257, 259
metanarratives 30, 31
Mexican advertisements 170
Mexican Americans 26, 129, 171
Mexican immigrants 18, 39; and acculturation 155; as mass media target 26
Mexican Revolution 18, 20
Mexicans: in Chicago 141, 157; forcible deportation by federal government 26; political and economic positionalities 160; US-based 139
Mexico 12, 36, 147, 209; Association of Spanish Language Academies 42; communism in 27; English language education in 147; and Great Depression 26; and Miami 57; student demonstrations against authoritarianism 30
Mexico City 26, 42, 144
Miami 1–2; Anglicism (*see* Anglicism(s)); as battleground 70–73,

304 *Index*

75, 78–84; "bubble" phenomenon
51–52; and Caribbean 49, 92; and
Colombia 57; crime, ethnolinguistic
dimension of 84–96; Cubans
arriving in 264; exceptionalism of
50; and Havana (*see* power and
solidarity; solidarity); as marketplace
107–12; modernity (*see* modernity);
postmodernity (*see* postmodernism/
postmodernity); social crisis in
107; *see also* Miami-Dade County;
postmodern circumstance of Spanish
in Miami; sociolinguistic mobility and
Spanish paradox in Miami
Miami (Didion) 47, 50
Miami (Iglesias Illa) 116
Miami Beach 45, 47, 67, 74, 75, 85;
see also South Beach
Miami Chamber of Commerce 85, 86,
111
Miami-Dade County 44, 48, 53, 62, 70,
75–76, 107; anti-bilingual ordinance
of 77, 78–80, 82–83, 108, 110; Dade
County Metro Commission 83;
population of 51
Miami Federal Reserve Bank 47
Miami Herald 73, 136, 210; Miami as
battleground and 75, 78, 79, 80, 81,
82, 83, 84; Miami as marketplace and
107–12
Miami Latinx 52, 270; youth 117, 118,
119–21, 123, 142, 160
Miami New Times 62, 90, 161
Miami Sound Machine 58
Miami Vice 47, 71, 84–88, 103, 165
Michaud, Nicolas 90
Miller, Christopher 247
Miller, John 272
mobiles, population segment 50
mock Spanish 94, 95, 106
modern ethnolinguistic boundaries,
defending 73–76; ethnolinguistic
dimension of Miami crime and 84–96;
language about language in mass
media and 77–84
modernity 2, 5, 13, 71, 143, 147;
Anglo modernity 14; and language
boundaries 5–8; language in 5–28;
linguistic legacy of Spain in the
Americas 8–14; linguistic order of
5, 18–28, 37, 43; metanarratives
30–31; one nation–one language
ideology 2, 4; and solidarity 156;

US Hispanophilia 14–18; *see also*
postmodernism/postmodernity
modern medievalism 3
Money Laundering Control Act 47
Montalbán, Ricardo 105
Mora, Cristina 35
Morales, Ed 162n1
Moreno, Antonio 36
Moreno Fernández, Francisco 211, 247,
260n1
Movistar 148
Mujica, Mauro 110
multiaxiality, of social class 122–23
music 16, 42, 90, 114, 142; choice of 125,
128, 136, 173, 177, 217; music industry
49, 58–59

Nación, La 169
named languages 213
national identity 2, 8, 33, 156, 158
nationalism 4, 35; and language 18–19;
in nineteenth-century Europe 7; and
political postmodernity 265
nationness 3, 6
NationsBank 39
nation-state 2, 3, 5, 23, 28, 149; flow of
the universal into the particular 31;
and globalization 4; and modernity 5,
30, 41, 46, 133, 148
Naturalization Act of 1906 19
Nazism 13
negative politeness 172, 190
neighborhood 2, 100, 118, 174, 243
neoliberal economy 4, 264–65
neoliberalism 28, 31, 32–37, 40, 63, 70,
73, 97, 147, 161
'neutral' Spanish 42, 56, 268
'neutral' voice 42, 260
New Mexico 11–12, 13, 171
new speakers 269
Newton, Sir Isaac 5
New York Times 10–11, 61, 87, 107
Nicaragua/Nicaraguans 47, 61, 115–16,
139, 169, 219, 224, 264
niche markets 35
Nicholas II, Tsar 20
Nijman, Jan 49–50, 85, 116
non-Caribbean speakers 223–24, 245,
246, 251, 253, 258
noncontact varieties 251, 258, 259
non-English languages: and second great
immigration 19; view in American
society 17–18

non-Hispanic Blacks 51
non-Hispanic Whites 51, 83, 93, 107
nonlinearity 271–73
Novarro, Ramón 15–16, 36
Nuevo Diario, El 169
Nuevo Herald, El 79
nuevomexicanos 12
NUVO TV 266–67

occupation, and lexical borrowing 242
Occupy movement 41
Office of Coordinator of Inter-American
    Affairs (CIAA) 26
Of Grammatology 31
Oñate, Juan de 12, 14
One Day at A Time 99
one nation–one language ideology 2, 4,
    10–11, 36
opacity, right to *see* ideological
    transparency and opacity
Operation Condor 36
opinion community 187
opinion norms 187–88
Order of Things, The 31
organized resistance, among immigrant
    work force 20
Orlando Sentinel 82
Otheguy, Ricardo 213, 216–18, 225, 226,
    228, 233, 236, 240, 246, 248–49

pachuquismo 27
Page, Anita 16
Page, Scott 272
País, El 169
Panama-California Exposition 14
Pan-Germanism 18, 20
paradoxical stance 270–71
parallelism 7, 35, 211, 231, 248
parents' education level 177, 178, 194,
    217, 239–40, 243, 253–55, 259
parodic reflexivity 270–71
parody: Hutcheon on 146, 149, 152; in
    postmodernity 270–71
parole 21, 22
Pasols, Aaliyah 51–52
Pearl Harbor attack, impact on Japanese
    Americans 26
Penelas, Alex 83
Peninsular Spanish 25, 244
perceived correctness 211, 230, 233, 235,
    239, 243, 253, 255
perceptual saliency, of Anglicisms
    211–12

Pérez, Lisandro 10, 15, 187
"Perreito" (song) 262
personal affective dimensions, of
    Spanish and English 137–43
Peru/Peruvians 48, 62, 116, 144, 147,
    148, 219, 224, 264
phonemes 21, 23–24
phonological assimilation 196
phonological calques 218, 224, 225,
    228–30; acceptability of 230;
    awareness of 229; use of 229
phrasal calques *see* syntactic calques
Piña-Rosales, Gerardo 210
Pino, Cecilia 171, 172, 187, 207n3
Pino, Frank 13
Pinochet, Augusto 27, 32, 34–35
Pinto-Coelho, Joanna 52, 160, 261n5
Pitbull 58
Poetics of Relation 242, 258
political marketplace 4
political postures 4, 187
political solidarity 187
polycentricity 144, 157
Ponce de León, Juan 1, 69
Ponce de León, Nestor 10
Ponce de León Hotel (Flagler College)
    15
Poplack, Shana 247
population segments, of city 49–50
Portes, Alejandro 115, 122, 127, 151,
    164, 184
postmodern capitalism, and
    consumerism 186
postmodern circumstance of Spanish
    in Miami 43–46; ethnoscape 49–55;
    financescape 46–49; ideoscape 59–63;
    mediascape 55–57; scapes 63–64;
    technoscape 57–59
postmodernism/postmodernity 2, 63–64;
    and consumerism 37–40; language in
    28–32; mass media enterprise 4;
    and neoliberalism 32–37;
    postmodern imaginary 40–43;
    significance of 71
postmodern paradox 118–23; *see also*
    bilingualism; sociolinguistic mobility
    and Spanish paradox in Miami
postmodern reality 273
postmodern society and mediatization
    86–87
postnostalgic identity 113–17
poststructuralism 213
Powell, Philip Wayne 13

306   *Index*

power and solidarity 163–68; class consciousness and upward social mobility 193–205; discursive construction of Cuban Miami 183–93; *tuteo* expansion and ideological dimensions 168–83
preposition stranding 248
print capitalism 3, 5–7, 41
Prío Socarrás, Carlos 67–68
privatization, impact of 3
Problems of Dostoevsky's Poetics 24
Proposition 227 (California) 111
Pueblo Feliz 15
Puerto Ricans 62, 116, 159–60, 245; activism of 57; in Chicago 141, 157; immigration 17, 223; political and economic positionalities 160
Puerto Rico 10, 96, 258; Anglicization of 11; US intervention 14, 245, 258
Pujolar, Joan 147, 148

Quechua language 145, 147, 148, 268
¿Qué Pasa, USA? 96–102, 108, 115, 116, 150, 266, 268, 269
Quiroga, José 47, 85, 87

racialization, of language 52–53
racism, and accent 56; against Marielitos 165
radical liberalism 9, 25
Rama, Ángel 8, 9
Ramírez Berg, Charles 88
Ramos, Jorge 50, 267
Rapist in Your Path, A 41
reactivists 57
Reagan, Ronald 28, 32
Reagan administration 61
Real Academia Española (RAE) (Royal Spanish Academy) 3, 8, 9, 208, 210–11, 214, 242; fictitious ad campaigns 260; incursion of English in Spanish marketing and sales, inquiry into 266; Instituto de Lexicografía 214
Record, The 83
Redford, James 80, 82
Redford, Polly 74
'ref' (refugees) phenomenon 124, 136, 138–42, 159, 160
reggaeton 59, 142
"Reggaeton de antes" (song) 262
Reid, Wallis 213
religious practice 13
Repeating Island, The 262

Resnick, Melvyn 154
Richards, Mary 4, 267
Rieff, David 87, 164
right-wing ideologies 20, 23, 29, 60, 61, 62, 99, 169
Riquelme, Jesucristo 260
Rivero, Yeidy 99, 101
Riverón, Gerardo 56
Robbins, Terry 80
Rockefeller, John D. 14–15
Rodríguez, Rene 58–59
Rodríguez Solórzano, Adrián 169
Rogers, Everett 214, 215, 216
Romanticism 12, 13, 22
Roosevelt, Franklin D. 26
Roosevelt, Theodore 19
Rosa, Jonathan 113, 139, 141, 146, 157, 159–60, 269, 271
Rosetta Stone 213
Royal Palm Hotel 15, 74
Ruiz, Vanessa 271
Russia, and Anglicisms 209
Russian immigrants 20
Russian language 44
Ruvin, Harvey 80
Ruzickova, Elena 200

Sánchez, Rosaura 150, 151, 155, 156, 239
San Diego 14–15, 269
Sandinista Revolution (Nicaragua) 169
Sankoff, David 247
San Martín, Ramón Grau 67
Santa Teresa 9
Santeiro, Luis 99, 115
Sarmiento, Domingo Faustino 8
Sassen, Saskia 4, 119, 149
Saussure, Ferdinand de 20–21, 22, 23, 25
scale, notion of 143
scale jumping 152–61
scapes 63–64, 264, 273; definition of 46; ethnoscape 49–55, 59, 88, 144; financescape 46–49, 59, 151; and globalization 2; ideoscape 2, 55, 59–63, 144, 151; mediascape 2, 55–57, 59, 71, 113, 144
Scarboro, L. O. 68
Scarface 47, 84–85, 88, 99, 165
Schauffler, Richard 127, 151
Schlegel, Friedrich 8
Schlobinski, Peter 164, 196
School of the Americas in the Panama Canal Zone 28
scientific paradigm in linguistics 8–9

Scott Shenk, Petra 129
Secada, Jon 58
Secades, Eladio 68
second-generation, language of 20, 45–46, 53, 114, 128, 157, 172, 175, 178, 212, 216, 219, 221; bilingual ability and metalinguistic consciousness 249, 253–55, 256, 257, 259; bilingualism 81; code-switching 269; and loanwords 227; and phonological calques 229, 230; and semantic calques 232; social status and linguistic (in)security 240, 242, 246, 247; and syntactic calques 235; and upward social mobility 198–200
semantic calques 218, 231–33, 239; acceptability of 232–33; awareness of 232; and syntactic calques, distinction between 261n4; use of 232
September 11, 2001 attacks 29, 31
Shakira 35, 58
Sherrill, Robert 71, 106, 107
Shit Girls Say 118, 132
Shit Miami Girls Say 118, 119, 125, 161
Sicius, Francis 60
Siemens AG 209
sign 6–7, 21, 22, 38
silence 27
Silva-Corvalán, Carmen 248
Simulations 86
SíTV 266–67
Sleepy Lagoon Case 26
Smith, Adam 38
Smith, Victoria 90
social class, multiaxiality of 122–23
social formations 123
social imagination 40–41
social mobility, upward 193–205
social separatism, among immigrants in Miami 160
social status 141, 167, 199, 200, 239–40, 256; and calques 239, 259; and correctness of language 238; and linguistic (in)security 240–48; and loanwords 239, 258; and rural ways of speaking 197
social stigma, of speaking Spanish in school 124
social stigmatization and stereotyping, of Cuban immigrants 159
societal fluidity 186, 193
socioeconomic mobility, and language commodification 132–37

socioeconomic status 39, 48, 106, 140, 150, 160, 201, 221, 270; and Anglicisms 212; and language use 45, 122; and lexical borrowing 242, 244; of students 124, 127
sociolects 42, 120, 166
sociolinguistic boundaries 212
sociolinguistic globalization 206
sociolinguistic mobility and Spanish paradox in Miami 143–44; complex vertical scalar orders and 144–52; vertical movement across linguistic space and 152–61
Solé, Carlos 127
solidarity: affective solidarity 187; and consumerism 156, 186; group solidarity 150, 156, 168–69, 187; mega-solidarity 156–57; and modernity 156; political solidarity 187; and power (*see* power and solidarity); semantics of 167; and *T* forms of address, in Western Europe 184, 185–86, 193; and usage of *usted* 185
Somoza, Anastasio 62
Somoza government 61
Sorenson, Travis 116
Soto, Osvaldo 82
South Beach 71, 86; *see also* Miami Beach
Southern California 15
South Florida 1, 2, 62, 75, 77, 82, 122, 123; bilingualism as asset in television sitcom narratives 97–113; and modern ethnolinguistic boundaries 73–79, 81, 82, 84, 85, 87; and postmodern paradox 118, 119, 122, 123, 128, 136, 141, 145, 150, 151, 154, 160, 161; power and solidarity 163–66, 168, 183, 186, 192, 198, 199, 204; vitality of bilingualism in 63; *see also* Florida
Spain, linguistic legacy in the Americas 8–14
Spanglish 236, 245, 257, 260, 269; 'inverted' 271
Spanish American League Against Discrimination (SALAD) 82
Spanish and British empires, rivalry of 13
Spanish Colonial Revival style 15
Spanish language 3–4, 215; American variants of 9, 210; as asset 34; and Anglicism (*see* Anglicism(s)); and

308 *Index*

Blackness, link between 52–53; Caribbean varieties of 53, 92, 121, 189, 198, 245, 256, 258; in consumerism 242, 265–66; cross-generational loss of 46, 120, 121–22, 232, 263, 272; Cuban varieties of 10, 53, 56, 121; and cultural imaginary 98, 102; in formal education 46, 160; generational varieties 215–16; as ideological matter of consumerism 34; indexical values of 271; on internet 136, 271; Isleño Spanish 256; language ability 96, 136, 173, 212, 233, 251, 255, 256; Latin American Spanish 9; learning motivations 33–34; living around 102–7; in mass media (*see* mass media); missing out, notion of 131; 'neutral' Spanish 42, 268; in New Mexico's 1912 Constitution 12; in news 107–13; noncontact varieties 251, 258, 259; personal affective dimensions of 137–43; positive valuation at local level 270; Puerto Rican–accented 92; pure varieties 12; RAE (*see* Real Academia Española (RAE) (Royal Spanish Academy)); roles and values in bilingualism 126–32; sell-out, notion of 131, 157; sociolinguistic siege, notion of 69–70; South American varieties 174, 228, 235, 244, 245, 246, 256; Spanish-speaking identity, atomization of 156, 160, 161–62; speaking in school, social stigma 124; superdiversity of 120–21; supradialectal varieties 215; traditional grammar 9; valuing of 96–113; varieties and variants 116, 119, 120–21, 153, 161, 206, 215, 223, 235–38, 250–53; and Whiteness, link between 52–53, 89; *see also* language(s); postmodern circumstance of Spanish in Miami; sociolinguistic mobility and Spanish paradox in Miami

speaker's voice (national origin) 53–55
statism 145, 146
Stepick, Alex 53, 115, 140, 141, 164, 184
Strauss, Claudia 98, 187, 188, 189
structural borrowing 236
subtractive bilingualism 135
'Sunset Style with Blind Effect' sunglasses ("Abre tus ojos al *look fashion*") 208

superdiversity, of Spanish 120–21
'Swine' perfume ("New fragrance, new woman") 208
syntactic calques 218, 233–36, 239; acceptability of 235–36; awareness of 234–35; use of 235

Tagalog 44
Taine, Hippolyte 22–23
Tamarón, Marqués de 168–69, 186
Tampa 10, 67
Taylor, Donald M. 135–37
'Taylorized' language 260
'Taylorizing' talk 269
technoscape 2, 57–59
Telefónica 147–48
Telemundo 57, 58, 266, 267, 268
television industry 42–43, 56, 97–113, 266, 269
tertiary economy 39
T forms of address, in Western Europe 167, 206; ideological dimensions 168, 170, 173, 177, 182; and power 193–95; and solidarity 184, 185–86, 193
Thälmann, Ernst 163
Thatcher, Margaret 32
third-generation, language of 45–46, 114, 128, 172, 175, 182, 190, 212, 216, 219, 221; bilingual ability and metalinguistic consciousness 249, 253–55, 256, 257, 259; and loanwords 227; and phonological calques 229, 230; and semantic calques 232, 233; social status and linguistic (in)security 240, 242–43, 246, 247; and syntactic calques 235; and upward social mobility 193, 197, 199–200, 202, 206
Thomason, Sarah 248
TIME 76, 85, 109
time, universalization of 6
time and place 7
Tió, Salvador 11
Todorov, Tzvetan 25
Tölölyan, Khachig 149
Torres, Raquel 16
Trainor, Brian 3, 31
transculturation 260
transience 49
translanguaging 118, 213
transparency *see* ideological transparency and opacity
Treaty of Paris in 1898 10
Trotsky, Leon 20

"Trouble in Paradise" 76, 77–78, 82
Tucci, Terig 16
'tuitear' 210, 211, 247
tuteo, ideological dimensions of
  expansion of 168–73; principal factors
  in 177–83; study and participants of
  173–77
tuteo, usage of 184–85, 187, 193, 200,
  203, 206
Tuttle, Julia 2, 14

unitary language 21, 24, 268
United Press International 107
Universo 267
Univision 50, 56, 57, 58, 266, 267, 268
upjumping 152, 153
upward social mobility and class
  consciousness 193–205
Ureña, Pedro Henríquez 11, 12
US consumerism in Spanish 252
usted, usage of 167, 207n2–4; ideological
  dimensions of *tuteo* expansion 168,
  169, 170, 171, 174, 177, 181; and
  power 199–202, 204; and solidarity
  185

Valdes, George 79–80
Valdés, Guadalupe 171, 172, 187, 207n3
Valdez, Jeff 267
Valencia, Marelys 56
Valentino, Rudolph 16
Valera, Beatriz 9
Valera, Juan 8
Varela, Beatriz 207n2
Varra, Rachel 213, 242, 244, 247, 259
Veciana-Suarez, Ana 81
Vélez, Lupe 36
"Ven Báilalo" (song) 142
Venezuela/Venezuelans 48, 61, 219, 260
Venezuelan voices 193

Vennera, Chick 105
Veraldi, Lorna 102
Verein Deutsche Sprache (VDS) 209
vertical scalar orders, complex 144–52
V forms of address, in Western Europe
  167, 185, 186, 206; ideological
  dimensions and 170–71, 173, 177, 182
Viglucci, Andres 80
Villanueva, Darío 214
Villa Vizcaya 15
von Humboldt, Wilhelm 8
vos, usage of 169–70, 174, 207n1

Wachs, Inge 164, 196
Warner Music Latina 49
Weber, David 13
Weber, Jon 81
Wells Fargo 1, 3; "Iconic Conversations"
  campaign 1, 3
Wessi/Ossi divide, of Germans 164,
  166
West, Patrick 89
Westgate, Christopher 267
Westinen, Elina 153
Whiteness and Spanish language, link
  between 52–53, 89
Wilson, Woodrow 18
Wittgenstein, Ludwig 30
Woodlawn Cemetery 68
workers' movements 20
World War I 18, 19
World War II 20, 27, 263

xenophobia 35, 110

Yerkovich, Anthony 85
Yúdice, George 43, 115

Zentella, Ana Celia 269
Zoot Suit Riots 26–27

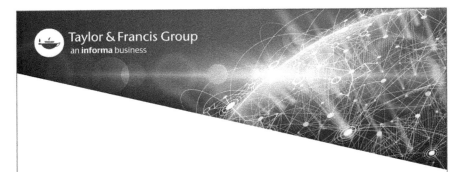

Milton Keynes UK
Ingram Content Group UK Ltd.
UKHW031500071224
451979UK00015B/165